For more than 150 years, HSBC Bank USA has served th[...] W9-BMS-063 in New York City. We offer the Hispanic and Chinese communities a full range of financial services. HSBC is proud to support *The New York Times Guide for Immigrants in New York City.*

With over 9,500 offices in 79 countries, HSBC is one of the world's largest financial services organizations. Founded in 1850 to finance trade on the Great Lakes, HSBC is the tenth largest bank holding company by assets in the United States. With over 400 branches in New York State, HSBC has the state's most extensive branch network, as well as offices in Florida, California, Pennsylvania. Washington, Oregon, and Panama. HSBC offers a full range of personal and commercial financial services including banking, investment, insurance, loans and mortgage products.

For more information on HSBC Bank USA, visit us at **us.hsbc.com** or call our toll free number **1-800-975-HSBC** (1-800-975-4722).

Durante más de 150 años, HSBC Bank USA ha atendido las necesidades financieras de los inmigrantes en la Ciudad de Nueva York. Nosotros ofrecemos a las comunidades Hispana y China una gama completa de servicios financieros. HSBC está orgulloso de apoyar *La Guía para Inmigrantes en la Ciudad de Nueva York del New York Times.* (*The New York Times Guide for Immigrants in New York City*).

Con más de 9,500 oficinas en 79 países, HSBC es una de las más grandes organizaciones mundiales de servicios financieros. Fundado en 1850 para financiar el comercio en los Grandes Lagos, HSBC es la décima corporación bancaria por activos en los Estados Unidos. Con más de 400 sucursales en el Estado de Nueva York, HSBC posee la más extensa red de sucursales en el estado, además de oficinas en Florida, California, Pensilvania, Washington, Oregón y Panamá. HSBC ofrece una gama completa de servicios financieros, personales y comerciales, que incluyen actividades bancarias, inversiones, seguros, créditos y productos hipotecarios.

Para más información sobre HSBC Bank USA, visítanos en **us.hsbc.com** o llama a nuestra línea gratuita al **1-888-433-HSBC** (1-888-433-4722).

美國匯豐銀行一直照顧紐約市移民的理財需要，150多年來，致力為西班牙裔和華裔社群提供全面的理財服務。我們全力支持《紐約時報紐約市移民指南》，為該指南的出版感到自豪。

匯豐在79個國家和地區設有9,500多家辦事處，是全球最大的金融機構之一。匯豐早於1850年創立，為大湖區提供貿易融資，現時是美國第十大銀行控股公司（以資產計）。我們在紐約州設有400多家分行，是該州最大的分行網；此外，在佛羅里達州、加利福尼亞州、賓夕凡尼亞州、華盛頓州、俄勒岡州、巴拿馬等地亦設有辦事處。我們提供全面的個人和商業理財服務，包括銀行、投資、保險、貸款和房貸產品。

想知道更多有關美國匯豐銀行的資料，請上網到**us.hsbc.com**，或打免費電話**1-800-711-8001**。

"This important resource is a valuable roadmap to help newcomers achieve their American dream."

— Mark Handelman, President and CEO,
New York Association for New Americans, Inc.
(NYANA)

"An essential survival guide for the new immigrant in New York. This excellent resource will undoubtedly change, if not save lives."

— Iris Chang, New York Times bestselling author of
The Rape of Nanking and *The Chinese in America:
A Narrative History*

"It's designed for immigrants but *The New York Times Guide for Immigrants in New York City* is a rich source of information even for the native, born and bred. This is a book I would place in every school in the city, perhaps on every desk in every school. It is a lesson in civics, practical and precise. The wonder is that such a book took so long in coming. I wish someone had placed something like this in my hands when I first landed in New York."

— Frank McCourt, Pulitzer Prize-winning author of
Angela's Ashes and *'Tis*

"*The New York Times Guide for Immigrants in New York City* is an amazing and invaluable compendium of useful information about almost everything that a newcomer to this city might need. I know from my parents' experience — they came to New York from Cuba in 1943 — that figuring out the ins and outs of life in this metropolis, and adjusting to a new language, can sometimes be a quite daunting and confusing experience; the fact that this guide is being published in English, Spanish and Chinese will be of immeasurable assistance to those who, in fact, will be a vital part of our future and the legacy of this city. A wonderful and welcome book."

— Oscar Hijuelos, Pulitzer Prize-winning author of
The Mambo Kings Play Songs of Love and *A Simple
Habana Melody*

THE NEW YORK TIMES GUIDE FOR IMMIGRANTS IN NEW YORK CITY

Joan P. Nassivera

*In Partnership with
the Lower East Side Tenement Museum*

THOMAS DUNNE BOOKS

ST. MARTIN'S GRIFFIN ❧ NEW YORK

THOMAS DUNNE BOOKS.
An imprint of St. Martin's Press.

THE NEW YORK TIMES GUIDE FOR IMMIGRANTS IN NEW YORK CITY.
Copyright © 2004 The New York Times Co. All rights reserved.

Printed in the United States of America. No part of this book may be
used or reproduced in any manner whatsoever without written permission
except in the case of brief quotations embodied in critical articles or
reviews. For information, address St. Martin's Press, 175 Fifth Avenue,
New York, N.Y. 10010.

Book design and production by Deborah Rust Design
Cover Design by Sandra DiPasqua
Illustrations by Sue Rose
Cover Photograph by Brad LaPayne

Customers other than bookstores or libraries may order 50 or more
copies of *The New York Times Guide for Immigrants in New York City*
at a specially reduced price. Call 212-556-7075.

www.stmartins.com

ISBN 0-312-28196-X

First Edition: March 2004

10 9 8 7 6 5 4 3 2 1

CONTENTS

INTRODUCTION AND ACKNOWLEDGMENTS

"Many people throughout the years have concerned themselves with our needs and problems and have tried to remedy many of them. Now we want to show you something real, based on our own experiences.

It is hard for most of the new immigrants to get information when they first come here. Everything about this place is strange to them. They don't know how they can go to schools, find jobs, where the hospitals are located, how to get health care with insurance, etc. We ourselves paid money for things we didn't know we could get for free, we have suffered exploitation from our bosses because we didn't know our rights.

We put our minds, our hearts, our souls and our bodies into helping new immigrants. We want to tell our stories so people arriving today will have the orientation we never had, and won't make the same mistakes we made."

These are the words of immigrants newly settled in New York City, men and women from China, from Mexico, from the Dominican Republic, Hong Kong, Ecuador, Madagascar and El Salvador.

They may be people like you, or like your mother a decade ago, or your grandfather a generation before that. They left their home countries to seek a better life in a city of infinite promise. Some had family or friends here; others arrived not knowing a soul.

Some, having grown up in towns and cities where the police and government officials were feared, refused to turn to agencies and officials in New York who might have pointed them in the right direction. Others reached out, only to be rebuffed or sent from wrong place to wrong person, finding nothing but discouragement. But they were determined that their life journey to New York would succeed despite the hardships they encountered. And that determination can be found on every page of this book.

These immigrants share your dreams, the dreams of every New Yorker: a job that pays a decent wage, a safe place to live, government officials who are not corrupt or abusive, the opportunity for a diverse education, medical care by trained doctors and nurses.

New York offers all that and more. But for most immigrants, realizing that better life means navigating a complex, bewildering city. Every day brings more questions: How can I find an affordable place to live? Is there anyone who will care for my child so I can work nights? Will a doctor see me if I am poor and sick? Where can I learn English? Can I get help in an emergency if I don't speak the language? How do I become an American citizen?

With this book, The New York Times and the Lower East Side Tenement Museum answer those questions and hundreds more that are asked by immigrants every day.

The Times has been a vibrant, vital part of New York's ever-changing immigrant landscape for more than 150 years. It is an essential and respected member of those communities where newcomers from Europe settled in the early 1900's and where those from Latin America, Asia and elsewhere are putting down roots today.

The museum, centered in a Lower East Side tenement building that was home to some 7,000 immigrants from more than 20 nations between 1863 and 1935, provides a rich historical perspective on the wide array of immigrant experiences in a neighborhood that continues to serve as a first home for thousands of newcomers to America. The museum also serves contemporary immigrants in many different ways, including offering free English classes that introduce new arrivals to the stories of those who came before.

Original, savvy, useful reporting is a hallmark of The Times. We listened carefully as immigrants at the museum's classes and others throughout New York described what they needed to build and better their lives in the city.

In one class, students learned how 19th-century immigrants arriving at Ellis Island were met by charity workers who spoke their native languages and helped them with basic needs. This bit of knowledge prompted one student to exclaim: "No one was there for us at Kennedy Airport. No one!" Now, The Times and the museum have joined forces to create the first comprehensive, user-friendly guide to be "there" for immigrants today.

Another resource that is there for newcomers to the city is the Mayor's Office of Immigrant Affairs, whose mission is to promote the participation of immigrant New Yorkers in all aspects of city life by fostering communication and connection between city agencies and immigrant communities. Visit the office's Web site at www.nyc.gov/immigrants.

Each chapter of the guide has been reviewed by immigrants from the Tenement Museum's classes as well as by experts from immigrant rights groups and service providers, including the New York Association for New Americans, the New York Immigration Coalition and University Settlement. Going far beyond fact-checking, they have worked to ensure that the guide fully and accurately responds to the needs of its audience: contemporary immigrants, their employers and the people who help them make their way in this, the greatest city in the world.

A work like this owes much to many. First and foremost are Alyse Myers of The Times and Ruth J. Abram of the Tenement Museum, whose vision and understanding of New York's immigrant communities were the catalysts for this project and its success.

Meighan Meeker and Tessa Rosario of The Times and Liz Ševčenko of the Tenement Museum were the project directors who oversaw each phase and whose most valuable, frustrating and nearly constant task was to remind me that the word deadline has meaning outside the newsroom.

The Tenement Museum's Alison Bowles, Lisa Chice and Michael Sant' Ambrogio supervised the research and review by immigrant experts, a herculean task done by Ms. Bowles, Ms. Chice, Geovanny Fernandez, Jana Hasprunova, Sushma Joshi, Stephen Morton, Marilyn Ordoñez, Elizabeth Rivera and Rosten Woo.

Immigrant service providers and their agencies who were generous with their time and suggestions were: John Albert, Safe Horizon; Asian Americans for Equality; Emily Blank, Cypress Hills Advocates for Education; Sister Mary Burns, The Maura Clarke–Ita Ford Center; Maria Contreras-Collier, Ethel Cordova and Idalia Garcia, Cypress Hills Family Day Care Program/Cypress Hills Child Care Network; Ellen Davidow, Administrative Services Unit, New York State Department of Labor, Division of Labor Standards; Sara Dunne, Hard Work Disabilities Project of St. Barbara's Church; Andrew Friedman, Make the Road by Walking; Roberta Herche, N.Y.A.N.A. (New York Association for New Americans); Steve Jenkins, Make the Road by Walking and Workplace Justice Project; Wasim Lone, G.O.L.E.S. (Good Old Lower East Side); Jacqueline Lugo, La Providencia; David Morales, Banco Popular; Melissa Mowery, C.A.M.B.A. (Church Avenue Merchants Block Association); and Jimmy Yan, Advocates for Children; Margie McHugh and Dan Smulian, the New York Immigration Coalition.

The New York Times Guide for Immigrants in New York City was made possible through the generous support of the Louis and Anne Abrons Foundation, Altman Foundation, Carnegie Corporation of New York, the Nathan Cummings Foundation, Furthermore: a program of the J.M. Kaplan Fund, and the Wolfensohn Family Foundation.

Special thanks to: Susan Chira, Deborah Hartnett, Nancy Lee, Diane McNulty, Jennifer Pauley, Lee Riffaterre, Susan Rose, Arlene Schneider, Katherine Snider, Gabrielle Stoller and Fran Straus.

Last but far from least are the immigrants whose enthusiasm, suggestions and persistence guided this project: *Argentina:* Julia Justo, Fernando Salamone; *Brazil:* Marli Silva; *China:* May Chen, Pak Ping Ng; *Dominican Republic:* Nayib Ega, Andrea Hernandez, Rosalba Jimenez, Paulenia Ortiz, Yleana Paulino, Esther Pestituyo, Rosalina Rodriguez, Victoria Rosario; *Ecuador:* Laura Pilozo, Judith Tagle; *El Salvador:* Ernesto Ibañez; *Guinea:* Aminato Conde Diallo; *Hong Kong:* Ling Leung; *Iran:* Doran Gowhari; *Lithuania:* Zoya Shterenberg; *Madagascar:* Sophie Herivelomalala; *Mexico:* Gilela Bello, Maricela Gonzalez, Alicia Julian, Enriqueta Ramirez, Anselmo Zanes; *Poland:* Karolina Gorak, Ilya Seldinas; *Puerto Rico:* Mercy Alves, Carmen Diaz, Judith Marinez, Placida Rodriguez; *Russia:* Inna Kaminskaya, Marina Lebedeva, Olga Seldina; and *Ukraine:* Marik Davydov.

These men and women offered the most eloquent description of their dreams for the guide: "We hope that this project will not be the end but instead a good beginning for new immigrants, with the help of other people who are interested in the well-being of those who come to New York in search of a better life."

Joan P. Nassivera
New York City, December 2003

HOW TO USE THE GUIDE

The most important goal of this guide is to be useful to you, the immigrant, to your employers and to the many government workers and social service providers whose job it is to help you as you make your way around your new home, New York City. Following are some tips to help you make the most of the guide.

Finding Topics
The guide is divided into chapters. Chapter titles and descriptions on the Contents page reflect broad topics you will deal with as you settle in. For example, Housing deals with, among other things, finding a place to live; Labor and Employment includes suggestions for finding a job and information about how much you must earn under the law. In Education, you can find out how to enroll your child in public school and where you can go to learn English.

Finding Answers
Each chapter consists of questions that our immigrant contributors/reviewers found were the most important — and often the hardest — to get answers to in their first weeks and months in the city. Each answer provides basic information and often includes the name of an agency and a phone number to call for more information. Many answers also include useful Web sites.

Getting More Help
Each chapter has gray boxes with the names of community groups and social service agencies that provide more information and help. When the name of a group or an agency is followed by a page number, it means that our immigrant contributors/reviewers found that group or agency to be so helpful and dependable that it merited a more extensive profile in the Resource Directory at the back of the guide.

In the directory, symbols appear above each profile and refer to the issues that the resource agency, group or service provider deals with, for example, housing or child care.

Wherever applicable, the name of each resource agency, group or service provider is followed by its most common abbreviation.

Each profile then details the location(s) of the resource agency, group or service provider, its telephone and fax numbers, e-mail and Web addresses, services offered, language(s) spoken, and documents or other requirements, if any.

Multilingual Format
The entire guide is printed first in English, then in Spanish and finally in Chinese.

Our reviewers — both immigrants and service providers — stressed to us that some information was so important that it should be referred to more than once in the guide. An example is the basic steps for getting a Permanent Resident Card, also known as an Alien Registration Card and commonly called a green card, a document that is critical to so many aspects of an immigrant's life, including housing and employment, to name just two. Therefore, you will find these steps described in the Lawful Status chapter and referenced in the Housing, Labor and Employment and Documents chapters.

And since each answer is intended to be comprehensive enough to stand on its own, especially significant information, like the two main divisions of the relatively new federal Department of Homeland Security — the Bureau of Immigration and Customs Enforcement (B.I.C.E.) and the United States Citizenship and Immigration Services (U.S.C.I.S.) — are introduced and explained several times in different contexts.

Every effort has been made to ensure that all of the information contained in the guide is accurate and up to date at the time of printing. But it is very important to remember that immigration law and policies affecting immigrants are revised often, especially since the attacks of Sept. 11, 2001. In addition, other government agencies, as well as social service groups and immigrant service providers, also change policies and programs. Therefore, it is always best to contact a group or agency listed in the Resource Directory at the end of this guide, or to consult a reputable immigration lawyer to find out the most current information about the issues addressed in the guide.

We hope that interest and funding will allow us to update the guide and to print it in other languages. You are invited to e-mail your comments, criticisms and suggestions for improvement and for additional languages to **immigrantguide@ny times.com**. We cannot answer your e-mail messages, but your comments will be considered when the next edition is compiled.

HOUSING

"The sunlight and fresh air of our mountain home were replaced by four walls and people over and under and on all sides of us. Silence and sunshine, things of the past, now replaced by a new urban montage. The cobbled streets. The endless, monotonous rows of tenements that shut out the sky. The traffic of wagons and carts and carriages, and the clopping of horses' hooves that struck sparks at night. The clanging of bells and the screeching of sirens as a fire broke out somewhere in the neighborhood. Dank hallways. Long flights of wooden stairs and the toilet in the hall."

— *Leonard Covello, Italian, 1910's* [1]

■

New York City has a shortage of housing, particularly housing that low- and moderate-income residents can afford. This means that for most immigrants, the search for housing is likely to be long and difficult, but certainly not impossible. While affordable housing has often been scarce, immigrants have always found a path to success in their search. They have been making their homes in New York for centuries, shaping and reshaping the city.

How do I find an apartment in New York?
- Contact a community group that helps immigrants find housing.
- Ask the clergy and people at your house of worship or at houses of worship in the neighborhood where you want to live.
- Look for signs posted in public places, like bodegas, laundries or houses of worship, that advertise a room or an apartment for rent.
- Post your own sign or notice ("Looking for a room. Can pay $500/month") in a public place.

■ Look in daily and community newspapers for ads placed by people who want to share a room or an apartment and for listings of apartments for rent. Look in free newspapers like The Village Voice and LOOT. Such ads may lead you to a broker or an agent. What these people do and how much they charge are explained below.

What should I do if I see an ad for an apartment that I think I can afford?
Act fast. Call the number given and make an appointment to see the apartment right away.

What fees can landlords, real estate brokers and rental agents legally charge?
The landlord can charge you a security deposit, which usually equals a month's rent. A real estate broker can charge you a commission, usually 12 to 15 percent of the first year's rent, for helping you find the apartment that you take. The commission should not be paid until you are offered a lease signed by the landlord. An apartment-referral agency can charge you a fee for a list of available apartments. But the agency must return all but $15 of the fee if you do not rent an apartment from the list.

Which fees are illegal for landlords, real estate brokers and rental agents to charge?
It is illegal for anyone to require you to pay a bonus on top of the legal rent and security deposit. This illegal bonus is often called key money.

What does "no fee" mean in a newspaper ad or on a sign for an apartment for rent?
It means that you do not have to pay extra money besides the security deposit.

What happens to the security deposit I give the landlord?
The landlord may keep the security deposit only if you move without paying your rent or if the apartment is so badly damaged the landlord has to make repairs after

need more help?

These groups offer advice about finding housing:

■ Asian Americans for Equality (A.A.F.E.) (Page 96)
■ Chinese-American Planning Council (Page 103)
■ Flatbush Development Corporation (Page 108)
■ Hellenic American Neighborhood Action Committee (H.A.N.A.C.) (Page 110)
■ People's Fire House (Page 125)

> ❝ Do not rely on anything that a landlord has promised you unless it is written into a lease that you both sign. Your landlord cannot change what is in the lease as long as it is in effect. ❞

you move. If you have paid all your rent and the apartment is not damaged, the landlord must give you back your security deposit when you move.

What is in a lease?
- How much rent you must pay each month.
- How long you may live in the apartment.
- Who pays for utilities, like electricity, gas, heat and phone service.

Do I have to have a lease?
No, it is not mandatory, but without a lease, you have very few rights, and they are hard to prove in court.

Do I have to pay for utilities?
Yes, the tenant is almost always responsible for setting up and paying for most utilities, like electricity and gas. This means that you have to call the utility companies and tell them that you are moving into the apartment on a certain date and that from that date on the utility bill should be sent to you. Most apartments are wired for telephone service, but the tenant usually has to provide the phone(s) and choose a local carrier, long-distance carrier and calling plan.

All long-distance calling plans seem too expensive. How can I afford to call home and other places?
Many immigrants buy phone cards to make calls. The type of card and its price determine where you can call and how long you can talk. Many people recommend phone cards for international calling because they are cheaper than having your own phone with an international calling plan.

Where can I buy a phone card?
Bodegas, newsstands, special phone-card stores and some check-cashing places.

Can a landlord refuse to rent me an apartment?
Yes. A landlord can decide whom to rent to, and you can be turned down if, for example, the landlord thinks you can't pay the rent. But a landlord may not refuse to rent to you on the basis of your age, race, religion, national origin, type of job, sexual orientation, marital status, pregnancy status or disability or the number of children you have.

My landlord wants to know how much I earn. Do I have to tell him?
Yes, and he also has the right to see a pay stub or other proof of your income, to make sure you earn enough money to pay the rent.

When can my landlord raise my rent and by how much?
Your landlord can raise your rent when your lease is up. The increase is based on the rules of the **Rent Guidelines Board.** For more information, call the board at **1-212-385-2934** (English only) or visit its Web site at **www.housingnyc.com.**

I think my landlord is charging me too much rent. What should I do?
Call the **Office of Rent Administration, 1-718-739-6400** (English and Spanish), and ask for a copy of your apartment's rent history. You can do this when you are negotiating your first lease or when you face your first rent increase.

I pay my rent in cash. How can I prove I've paid my rent each month?
It is very important for you to get a receipt from your landlord with the date, the amount you paid, your name and the apartment number and address. The person who took the rent must sign the receipt and state his title.

Who can live with me in my apartment, and does my landlord have a right to know who is living with me?
Members of your immediate family can live with you, as can one roommate and that roommate's minor children. But there are Health Department rules against overcrowding. You can find these at **www.housingnyc.com/index.html.** A landlord may ask if someone is living with you, but may not ask about that person's relationship to you.

Someone I live with signed the lease. May I still live in the apartment?
Yes, but only while the person who signed the lease still lives there. If no one who signed the lease is living in the apartment, the landlord may evict the occupants. Only an original tenant may renew a lease.

Something in my apartment is broken. What should I do?
If you did not break it, it is not your responsibility to fix it or to pay to have it fixed. Ask the landlord or building superintendent to fix it. If you did break something, it is your responsibility to fix it or to pay to have it fixed.

What does the law say a landlord must do for me?
- Provide hot water (at least 120 degrees Fahrenheit) at all times.
- Provide heat from Oct. 1 to May 31. If the temperature outside falls below 55 degrees Fahrenheit from 6 a.m. to 10 p.m., there must be enough heat so your apartment is at least 68 degrees Fahrenheit. From 10 p.m. to 6 a.m., if the temperature outside falls

below 40 degrees Fahrenheit, your apartment must be at least 55 degrees Fahrenheit.
- Put a smoke alarm in each apartment within 15 feet of any room used for sleeping.
- Put up window guards in any apartment where a child 10 years or younger lives.
- Remove any walls or thoroughly cover any walls that have peeling or lead-based paint in an apartment where a child 6 years or younger is living. Lead-based paint is found mainly in apartments built or painted before 1960.
- Make every effort to guarantee that there are no roaches, rats, mice or other vermin in your apartment.

What happens if I can't pay my rent on time?
Tell the landlord right away. If he knows you are having money problems, he may accept the rent late or insist that you pay only some of the money. As soon as you have the money, pay the landlord and get a receipt.

My landlord won't accept the late rent. What should I do?
Keep the money in a safe place. Don't spend it. You will need the back rent if the landlord tries to evict you and you fight the eviction in court.

What happens if I do not pay my rent on time or if I do things that are not allowed under my lease?
Your landlord is allowed to go to court to ask a judge to get you to move. A

need more help?

What should I do if my landlord does not provide me with heat or hot water, or if I think that I'm a victim of housing discrimination or that my rights as a tenant are being violated?

For heat or hot water complaints, call:
- The Citizen Service Center, 311

For housing discrimination and tenants rights complaints, call:
- Asian Americans for Equality (Page 96)
- Chinese-American Planning Council (Page 103)
- Flatbush Development Corporation (Page 108)
- Jacob A. Riis Neighborhood Settlement House (Page 113)
- New York City Commission on Human Rights (Page 119)
- New York State Division of Housing and Community Renewal (D.H.C.R.) (Page 123)
- Promesa (Page 125)
- Queens Legal Services (Page 126)

landlord is not allowed to just tell you to leave your apartment or to remove your furniture and clothes and keep them or throw them out on the street.

What does a landlord have to show to get me to leave the apartment?
The landlord cannot evict you. Only a sheriff or city marshal can carry out a court-ordered eviction and must show you the eviction order. For more information, go to www.housingnyc.com/resources/attygenguide.html.

Does an eviction order have to be in my native language?
Eviction notices are in English and Spanish. Court documents are in English only, though translators are available in court.

What should I do if I get an eviction order or notice to vacate?
Call a housing lawyer immediately. If the eviction notice specifies a court date, be sure to be there. If you don't appear, you may be evicted even sooner than the eviction date.

If I am undocumented, is my landlord allowed to evict me without a court order?
No matter what your immigration status, if a landlord or building superintendent locks you out of your apartment without an eviction order, you should contact the police. But you should remember that the landlord might tell the **Bureau of Immigration and Customs Enforcement**, or **B.I.C.E.**, that you are undocumented. The B.I.C.E., which is part of the United States Department of Homeland Security, has assumed some responsibilities of what had for many years been the Immigration and Naturalization Service, or I.N.S.

I can't afford even the cheap apartments I've found. Is there any alternative?
The **New York City Housing Authority (N.Y.C.H.A.)** (Page 121) provides decent housing for low-income residents, but there is a long waiting list.

How do I apply for low-income housing?
Complete an application available at any of the five Borough Application Offices.

need more help?

These organizations help tenants fight eviction:

- Eviction Intervention Services, 1-212-308-2210 (English and Spanish)
- Church Avenue Merchants Block Association (C.A.M.B.A.) (Page 103)
- Citizens Advice Bureau (C.A.B.) (Page 104)
- New York Urban League (Page 124)
- South Bronx Action Group (Page 127)

To find out where they are, call the **New York City Housing Authority** (**N.Y.C.H.A.**), 1-212-306-3000 (Page 121), or go to its Web site, **www.nyc.gov/html/ nycha/html/boroughoffices.html**.

Does it matter that I am undocumented?

When this book went to press, only one person on the household's public housing application had to be a documented immigrant. This means that one person who would live in the apartment must either have a Permanent Resident Card, also known as an Alien Registration Card and commonly known as a green card, which shows that he or she is living legally in the United States, or must be a citizen. The amount of money the city would pay toward the rent would be reduced depending on the number of undocumented immigrants living in the household. *However, policies toward immigrants change often so it is best to check with an immigration advocacy group listed in the Resource Directory at the back of this guide, or, if you can afford it, with a reputable immigration lawyer.*

How do I get a green card?

Getting a green card is often a long, complicated process, and policies affecting immigrants change often. The basic steps are given in the Lawful Status chapter, beginning on page 78. You should always seek help from an immigrant service provider listed in the Resource Directory at the end of this guide or, if you can afford it, from a reputable immigration lawyer.

I earn too much to qualify for low-income public housing, but I still can't afford the rent on a private apartment. Is there anything I can do?

There are about 125,000 city- and state-sponsored rental and co-op apartments for moderate- and middle-income people in New York City. These are known as Mitchell-Lamas. There are limits to the amount your family can earn to qualify and limits on how many people can live in an apartment.

What happens if I look and look and still can't find an apartment within my budget? Is there any emergency housing or are there other places I can go?

The city's **Department of Homeless Services** runs homeless shelters for men, women and families regardless of their immigration status, and drop-in centers that offer the homeless hot meals, clothes, medical care, showers and places to do laundry, as well as counseling, employment referrals and other social services. Its headquarters is **33 Beaver Street in Lower Manhattan**, 1-212-361-8000 (English and Spanish). To find a drop-in center near you, call the headquarters or visit the department's Web site, **www.nyc.gov/html/dhs/html/di-directions.html**.

And don't despair if you can't get to those places. Many houses of worship, clinics and social service agencies in neighborhoods throughout the city offer shelters,

need more help?

Sources of help with low-income public housing:

- City-sponsored Mitchell-Lama apartments, 1-212-863-6500 (English and Spanish)
- Information on state-sponsored apartments, 1-212-480-7343 (English and Spanish)
- Web site, www.housingnyc.com/resources/mitchell/mitchell.html

food pantries, crisis intervention and other services for those in need. The groups mentioned throughout this guide and listed in the Resource Directory at the end will be able to help you or refer you to someone who can.

■

"When I first came to this nation, I arrived at 38 Ludlow Street, a tenement building. And when I arrived to that apartment, I said, 'Where is the toilet?' I thought you pressed a button and the toilet would come out automatically. You press another button and a bathtub would come out automatically, and I had the rude awakening that evening that it wasn't so. My uncle and his wife lived in one apartment with five children. It took me years to really understand that this was what the people in the other country called the 'wonderful city' paved with gold."

— *Rafael Guzman, Dominican, 1966* [2]

LABOR AND EMPLOYMENT

"I walked the streets, you see, and saw this big building and there's a big sign, EMPLOYMENT OFFICE. So I walked in there and asked for a job. And of course he couldn't speak any Swedish and I couldn't speak much English, but I could tell him that much, that I wanted a job. So he said, 'Wait a minute, I'll get one of your countrymen.' So he got me a blacksmith foreman and he was a Swede, so he said, 'Oh, I can use a young fellow like you.'"

— *Charles T. Anderson, Swedish, 1925* [3]

■

The thought of searching for work in a new country may seem scary at first, but there are many places to look in New York and many resources to help you find a job.

How can I find a job?
- Ask friends and relatives where there might be a job or who might be hiring.
- Walk down streets where there are factories, stores or restaurants and see which ones have a HELP WANTED sign in the window. Go into the places with the sign and speak with the person in charge or the one who knows about the job.
- Check newspapers published in your language. They will have sections advertising available jobs.
- Contact an organization that helps with job search and placement.

Can I work by the day?
People who want to work as day laborers often gather on street corners and wait for those who need their services to drive up and offer them a job like cleaning, gardening or pouring concrete. Day laborers usually bargain for their hourly or daily wage. *Warning: Sometimes people who hire day laborers will refuse to pay them at the*

**❝ It is very important
to remember that if you are undocumented
and are working in the United States, you are still
protected by the same labor laws that cover people
who are documented. But you can be prosecuted
and deported if the United States government
learns that you are not documented. ❞**

*end of the day or week. If that happens, contact the police and tell them whatever you
know about the person who hired you.*

What questions is it legal for an employer to ask?

Employers may ask what skills you have and why you want to work for them. It is
illegal for employers to ask about your age, race, religion, national origin, sexual
orientation, pregnancy status or disability.

Will a physical exam be required?

You do not have to take a physical exam unless it is required of all employees. The
results of the exam are kept confidential and are not used to discriminate on the
basis of disability.

Will I be tested for drugs before I can get a job?

Many employers test for illegal drugs like marijuana and cocaine and will not hire
you if those drugs are found in a blood or urine test. If you failed the drug test but
the only drug you took was something prescribed by a doctor or bought in a
pharmacy, like cough medicine, ask to take the test again.

What documents will I need to apply for a job?

To get a job, you will need two documents, one to show who you are and one that
shows you are eligible to work. And all employers must complete an I-9 form for
each worker.

What is an I-9 form?

An I-9 form is something that all employers must fill out and sign for each employee.
The employer has to verify each employee's eligibility for employment and identity
documents. You must complete the first section of the form on your first day at work.

Will my I-9 form be sent to United States immigration authorities?

No, I-9 forms are not filed with the federal government.

What documents do I need to prove that I am legally eligible to work?
Either a Permanent Resident Card, also known as an Alien Registration Card and commonly called a green card, or an Employment Authorization Document, known as an E.A.D., will show that you are legally eligible to work.

How do I get a green card?
Getting a green card is often a long, complicated process, and policies affecting immigrants change often. The basic steps are given in the Lawful Status chapter, beginning on page 78. You should always seek help from an immigrant service provider listed in the Resource Directory at the end of this guide, or, if you can afford it, from a reputable immigration lawyer.

How long does it take to get a green card? Can I work until it arrives?
You can work if your passport has been stamped to say that your application is pending. United States law limits the number of immigrant visa numbers that are available every year. This means that even if the **United States Citizenship and Immigration Services (U.S.C.I.S.)**, a division of the **United States Department of Homeland Security**, approves an immigrant visa petition for you, you may not get an immigrant visa number immediately. You could wait 2 to 10 years or more between the time the U.S.C.I.S. approves your immigrant visa petition and an immigrant visa number becomes available. United States law also limits the number of immigrant visas available by country. You will get an approval notice in the mail and will have to go to the **U.S.C.I.S. New York City District Office, 26 Federal Plaza in Lower Manhattan**, to pick up the card. When it expires, you must fill out another application and pay the fee again. If you do not, you are working illegally.

Do I need an Employment Authorization Document (E.A.D.)?
If you are not a citizen or a lawful permanent resident, you may need to apply for an Employment Authorization Document (E.A.D.) to prove you may work in the United States. If the U.S.C.I.S. does not approve or deny your E.A.D. application within 90 days, you may request an interim E.A.D. (Asylum applicants may request an interim E.A.D. within 30 days, but they must have waited 150 days from the date when they filed their completed original asylum application to apply for an E.A.D.)

How do I get an Employment Authorization Document, or E.A.D.?
Fill out **U.S.C.I.S. Form I-765.** Read the entire application carefully and submit the right documents, photos and fee. You should apply for a renewal E.A.D. six months before your original one expires.

What happens if I get turned down? Can I appeal?
If your application for an E.A.D. is denied, you will get a letter telling you why. You

need more help?

Many groups help with job search and placement. Here are a few:

- Chinese-American Planning Council (Page 103)
- Church Avenue Merchants Block Association (C.A.M.B.A.) (Page 103)
- Citizens Advice Bureau (C.A.B.) (Page 104)
- Hellenic American Neighborhood Action Committee (H.A.N.A.C.) (Page 110)
- Jacob A. Riis Neighborhood Settlement House (Page 113)
- New York Association for New Americans (N.Y.A.N.A.) (Page 118)
- New York City Department of Education, Office of Adult and Continuing Education (Page 120)
- New York City Workforce 1 Career Center (Page 122)
- University Settlement Society of New York (Page 129)

cannot appeal to a higher authority, but you may submit a motion to reopen or reconsider to the U.S.C.I.S. office that turned down your request. A motion to reopen must state new facts that are to be provided in a reopened proceeding and must be accompanied by affidavits or other evidence. A motion to reconsider must show that the decision was based on an incorrect application of the law or of U.S.C.I.S. policy, based on the evidence that was in the file when the decision was made.

Can I get a job if I am undocumented?

Yes, you can be hired despite your immigration status, but the person or company that hires you is breaking the law. If you provide false or phony documents to get a job, you too are breaking the law. The United States has strict laws that require employers to check the immigration status of all new workers, including those who were here before 1986, when the law took effect. Policies affecting immigrants change often so it is best to check with an immigration advocacy group listed in the Resource Directory at the back of this guide, or, if you can afford it, with a reputable immigration lawyer.

What are my rights as a worker?

Whether or not you are documented, you have several basic rights:

- The right to be paid a minimum wage set by the government. As of December 2003, the minimum wage was $5.15 an hour.
- The right to a regular break. It must be a paid break only if the company has signed a contract specifying that is the case.
- The right to have your employer pay for things like disability insurance and Social Security.
- The right to basic health and safety protection, explained later in this chapter.

Must every worker be paid the minimum wage?
No, some workers are not covered by the minimum wage law, including part-time baby sitters who work in the employer's home, home care attendants who live in the home of the sick or elderly person they care for and do not do housework, taxi drivers and a few others. For a full list, call the **United States Department of Labor, Wage and Hour Division's toll-free number, 1-866-487-9243** (English and Spanish), or visit the Web site, **http://www.dol.gov/**.

Can I earn more than the minimum wage?
Yes. Your employer cannot pay you less than the minimum wage, but he or she is free to pay you more.

How many hours am I required to work before I am paid overtime?
If you are not a live-in worker, you are entitled to overtime pay for all the time that you work over 40 hours in a payroll week. (A payroll week is a seven-day week, but it does not have to be a calendar week, which is Sunday through Saturday. A payroll week can run from Monday through Sunday or Wednesday through Tuesday, etc.) If you are a live-in worker, you are entitled to overtime pay for all the time you work over 44 hours in a payroll week.

Are breaks and weekend shifts included in the total hours in a payroll week?
Meal breaks and other breaks, whether paid or unpaid, are not considered in the total hours for a payroll week. And remember, overtime is based on a 40-hour payroll week. You are not entitled to overtime just because you work more than eight hours on a given day or because you work on a Saturday or a Sunday.

What is the rate of pay for overtime?
The overtime rate is one-and-a-half times the hourly rate for each hour worked over 40 hours per week or 10 hours in a single day. So if your regular hourly rate is $6 and you work 45 hours in a week, you should receive $240 for 40 hours ($6 x 40 hours) plus $45 for 5 hours ($9 x 5 hours), for a total of $285 for the week.

I work in a garment factory where I am paid by the piece. Am I still entitled to the minimum wage and overtime?
You still must be paid at least the minimum wage, and you must be paid overtime if you work the required number of hours.

If I work as a nanny or a maid, will the family I work for know that I am entitled to overtime and other benefits?
In New York City, if you are hired through an employment agency, the agency must give you and your employer a list of your rights to overtime pay and other

benefits. The employer must sign the list to show that he or she understands what you are entitled to.

Should I work for cash?
Not if you can avoid it because it usually means your employer is not taking out money for things like taxes, Social Security and workers' compensation. Working for cash may also make it hard to prove that you worked at all and to collect benefits like Social Security and workers' compensation.

What is Social Security?
An insurance program financed by employers and workers that pays benefits when workers reach retirement age or become too ill or disabled to ever work again.

Can undocumented workers get Social Security?
No.

What is workers' compensation?
An insurance program financed by employers that provides benefits and pays for medical care for most full-time and part-time workers who are hurt on the job or who can't work and need care because of job-related injuries or illness.

Can undocumented workers get workers' compensation?
Yes. In New York State, undocumented workers are fully protected by workers' compensation laws.

Can my employer take other money out of my wages?
An employer is not allowed to deduct anything from your wages except what is required by law or government rules (like income taxes, court-ordered child support, wage garnishments) and amounts that you have authorized and that are for your benefit (like insurance premiums, union dues, money to buy United States savings bonds).

What are income taxes?
In the United States, if you make more than a certain amount of money, you must pay taxes. Both the federal government and New York State require that you send in forms, known as income tax returns, each year. These forms, which are due on April 15 each year, tell the government about the money you earned in the previous calendar year and how you spent it. When you send in the forms, you also send in the money to pay income taxes, if you owe them.

How will I know if I owe taxes?
You must pay income taxes on any income earned in the United States if your sta-

need more help?

Filling out tax forms is very complicated. If you can afford it, hire an accountant who specializes in tax law. If you do not have the money to pay an accountant, you can contact these agencies, which provide free tax preparation help. They may not do all types of returns and some have income guidelines to be eligible for their services. Most are open only during tax season, from mid-January to mid-April:

- Internal Revenue Service Taxpayer Assistance Unit, www.irs.gov for office locations. Multilingual assistance is available in every office
- Community Tax Aid, 1-212-788-7552 (English only)
- Community Food Resource Center, 1-866-WAGE-PLUS (1-866-924-3758) for English or 1-866-DOLARES (1-866-365-2737) for Spanish
- Volunteer Income Tax Assistance (VITA), 1-718-488-3655 (English only)

tus as an immigrant requires it and if your total income exceeds a minimum amount determined by your age, marital status and whether you are the head of a household.

I get tips at my job. Can my employer keep those?

An employer may not demand or accept any portion of your tips unless you work checking hats or coats. If you are a waiter or food service worker, your employer may take up to $1.85 an hour from your minimum wage if you earn that much in tips. And if you work at a banquet, party or other special function where the bill includes a certain percentage as a tip, your employer may take that tip and divide it among all the service employees who worked at the party.

If I get tips at my job, does my employer have to pay me anything else?

Yes. If you are a waiter or food service worker, you must be paid at least the minimum wage minus what you get in tips.

If I work as a janitor or building superintendent, can my employer deduct the tips I get from my wages?

Your employer (the landlord or property manager) is not allowed to deduct tips from your wages. The minimum wage for a janitor is based on the number of apartments or offices in the building, rather than on an hourly rate.

Must I wear a uniform at my job? If so, who pays for it?

Your employer can require you to wear a uniform. If you have to buy the uniform from your employer, he must pay you back for its total cost soon after you buy it. If you buy the uniform from another company, your employer has to pay you back only a portion. Your employer also has to wash or dry-clean the uniform or pay you to do so.

How often should my employer pay me?
Manual workers, like mechanics, maids and landscapers, must be paid their full wages weekly and no later than seven days after the end of the week in which they were earned. Clerical and other workers (except those who earn more than $600 a week) must be paid at least twice a month.

Do I get paid if I don't show up for work?
No. But an employer can deduct only the amount you would have been paid during the time you were absent. For example, if you miss four hours of work, your employer cannot deduct eight hours' pay.

Is there any limit to the number of hours I can work? Am I allowed any time off?
There are no restrictions on the number of work hours per day. In many places of employment, like factories, stores, restaurants and year-round hotels, workers must be given at least one day (24 consecutive hours) off in a calendar week. And remember, you must be paid overtime if you are not a live-in employee and if you work more than 40 hours in a payroll week. If you are a live-in employee, you must be paid overtime if you work more than 44 hours in a payroll week or 10 hours in a single day.

Do I get meal breaks, and does my employer have to pay me during breaks?
You are entitled to meal breaks. Employees who work a shift of more than six hours must have an uninterrupted meal period of at least half an hour. Your employer does not have to pay you for meal breaks unless the company has signed a contract to do so.

Can I take time off without pay?
Under the federal Family and Medical Leave Act of 1993, employers with more than 50 workers must allow them up to 12 weeks of unpaid leave under certain conditions. For more information, visit the **Department of Labor's** Web site at **www.dol. gov/esa/regs/statutes/whd/fmla.**

My employer pays for my health insurance. What happens if I lose my job?
If you quit or lose your job and have been covered for at least three months by health insurance offered by your employer, you must be allowed to pay for that insurance for up to 18 months under a plan known as Cobra, although Cobra insurance is much more expensive.

If you are discriminated against because you insist on these rights, you can take legal action, like filing a formal complaint or a lawsuit, but it can take years for the government or the courts to undo the illegal action taken against you.

need more help?

Many groups can explain your rights as a worker and can help if they have been violated. Here are a few:

- Asian American Legal Defense and Education Fund (Page 95)
- Chinese Staff and Workers' Association (Page 102)
- Latino Workers Center (Page 113)
- Legal Aid Society (Page 114)
- New York City Commission on Human Rights (Page 119)
- New York State Department of Labor, Division of Employment Services Office (Page 123)
- Queens Legal Services (Page 126)

Can I be treated differently because I am an immigrant?

Federal law makes it illegal for an employer to discriminate against any employee or job applicant because of that person's national origin. No one can be denied an equal chance at a job because of birthplace, ancestry or how well he or she speaks English.

Must I speak English where I work?

You must speak English only if your employer can show that English is necessary to do business.

How old must I be to work?

Students as young as 14 may get an employment certificate, commonly called working papers, but they may not work in factories. A student general employment certificate is issued to students who are 16 or 17, and a full-time employment certificate is issued to 16- and 17-year-olds who do not attend school or who are leaving school for full-time work. The number of hours that minors are allowed to work varies with their age and whether or not they attend school.

■

"My cousin has a master's degree in accounting, and he had a great job in the Dominican Republic, but he rather work here at a supermarket which he makes more money. ...My parents are another story. ...They were both professional in D.R., but they for some reason or another saw a better life here, and they also worked in supermarket for many years."

— *Irma Olivo, Dominican, 2003* [4]

CHILD CARE

"**M**ost people do not know that a settlement house is really a club combined with social service. The Hudson Guild, a five-story field of joy for slum kids, had Ping-Pong rooms and billiard rooms, a shop in which to make lamps, a theater for putting on amateur plays, a gym to box and play basketball in. There were young men who guided us as counselors whom I remember with fondness to this day. They were more like friends than adults assigned to watch over us. I still remember one helping us eat a box of stolen chocolates rather than reproaching us. Which was exactly the right thing for him to do; we trusted him after that. The Hudson Guild kept more kids out of jail than a thousand policemen."

— *Mario Puzo, son of Italian immigrants, remembering the 1930's* [5]

■

As any parent or caregiver knows, raising a child is a scary and difficult job, but it is also endlessly rewarding. Raising children in an unfamiliar city is especially stressful. This chapter will help you learn what kind of child care is available and how to find the type of care that fits how and where you and your family live and work.

What types of organized child care are available in New York City?
For young children, there are three main types:
- **Home day care**, in which children from the age of 6 weeks to 4 or 5 years are cared for in the home of someone who has either registered with or is licensed by the city's Department of Health. These homes can care for up to 12 children.
- **Day care centers**, which are usually larger than most home day care settings. The number of children cared for varies.

■ **Preschool**, which is for 4-year-olds. Children are taught basic academic and social skills to prepare them for kindergarten.

What is Head Start?

Head Start is a federal program that helps prepare young children from low-income families to start school by teaching things like numbers, colors and basic reading skills. Each local center sets age limits for children.

What is Early Head Start?

Early Head Start is a federal program that provides day care for infants from birth to 3 years and also provides prenatal care to teenage mothers from low-income families.

How can I find out if there is a Head Start or an Early Head Start center near where I live or work?

There are several ways:

■ Call the **Head Start Information and Publication Center toll free, 1-866-763-6481** (English only), and tell them your state and ZIP code. They can find the most convenient center for you.

■ Call the **New York City Administration for Children's Services Division of Child Care and Head Start, 1-718-FOR-KIDS** (Page 119).

■ Use the national Head Start program search tool at **www.acf.hhs.gov/programs/hsb/hsweb/index.jsp**.

need more help?

Contact these two main sources of information about child care in New York:
■ New York City Administration for Children's Services Division of Child Care and Head Start (Page 119)
■ New York City Child Care Resource and Referral Consortium (Page 119)

You can also contact these groups:
■ Brooklyn Chinese-American Association (Page 98)
■ Chinese-American Planning Council (Page 103)
■ Citizens Advice Bureau (C.A.B.) (Page 104)
■ Forest Hills Community House (Page 109)
■ Promesa (Page 125)
■ Southeast Bronx Neighborhood Centers (Page 127)
■ United Community Centers (Page 128)
■ University Settlement Society of New York (Page 129)

Like me, my children are undocumented. Can I still get child care for them?

Programs that receive government money, including city programs and Head Start, are supposed to require a Social Security card from a parent, so it is unlikely that your children will be able to receive care from them. Obtaining a Social Security card is explained in the Documents chapter. If you are undocumented, you can pay cash to a home-based provider to care for your child.

I work nights and sometimes weekends. Is there any way I can find someone to care for my children?

Changing work schedules and unusual job hours make it very hard to find child care because most centers and programs are open Monday through Friday from morning into early evening. In addition, financial help is provided for care only during traditional hours unless parents can provide proof, like a letter from their employer, that they must work other hours.

Some other suggestions:

■ Pay someone you know and trust, perhaps a relative or good friend, to care for your child in your home. This can work whether you work days, nights or weekends.

■ Find other people willing to care for your child in their homes. The **New York City Administration for Children's Services Division of Child Care and Head Start** (Page 119) can provide names and numbers.

■ Work alternate shifts with your partner or someone else who can care for your child.

■ Use several different child-care options, for example, a day care center when you work in the early evening and a relative when you work later.

■ Trade care with another family. For every hour that family cares for your child, you care for their child for an hour.

need more help?

Contact these organizations for information about after-school programs:

■ Alianza Dominicana (Page 95)
■ Brooklyn Chinese-American Association (Page 98)
■ Citizens Advice Bureau (C.A.B.) (Page 104)
■ The Door (Page 108)
■ Hellenic American Neighborhood Action Committee (H.A.N.A.C.) (Page 110)
■ Jacob A. Riis Neighborhood Settlement House (Page 113)
■ New York City Administration for Children's Services Division of Child Care and Head Start (Page 119)
■ New York City Child Care Resource and Referral Consortium (Page 119)
■ Y.M.C.A. of Greater New York (Page 130)

need more help?

Contact these organizations for information about summer programs:

- Alianza Dominicana (Page 95)
- Brooklyn Chinese-American Association (Page 98)
- Citizens Advice Bureau (C.A.B.) (Page 104)
- Community Association of Progressive Dominicans (Page 106)
- Hellenic American Neighborhood Action Committee (H.A.N.A.C.) (Page 110)

I've heard it's harder to find care for very young children. Is that true?
Yes, many child-care centers require that children be potty trained, which usually does not occur until they are 2 or older. Also, government-licensed family-care providers may care for only two children under the age of 2.

Is there any way that I can get someone to care for a child younger than 6?
Contact the agencies described earlier in this chapter, the **New York City Administration for Children's Services Division of Child Care and Head Start**, 1-718-FOR-KIDS (Page 119), or the **New York City Child Care Resource and Referral Consortium**, 1-888-469-5999 (Page 119).

My children will be in school most of the day. Is there any place for them to go after school?
The **Partnership for After-School Education** has an online directory of after-school programs on its Web site, **http://www.pasesetter.com//#asp_directory**. You can also call the Partnership at **1-212-571-2664** (English and Spanish).

The **New York City Department of Youth and Community Development** runs **Beacon Schools** that must be open at least six days a week. They usually stay open as late as 10 p.m. and are also open on weekends and holidays and during school vacations. They offer tutoring and help with homework, as well as English and computer classes for adults. They also have recreational and cultural activities. To find out if there is a Beacon School in your neighborhood, call **1-212-676-8255** (English and Spanish), or visit the Web site **www.nyc.gov/html/dycd/pdf/beacondirectory.pdf**.

Where can my children go during the summer when school is out?
Beacon Schools are also open in the summer for children whose parents work.

What will I be asked when I call to find out about most types of child care?
You will probably be asked several questions about your family, how much you and other family members earn, whether you receive public assistance or

❝ Finding low-cost child care can be hard. Call and visit child-care centers often so if a space opens up, everyone knows how interested you are. ❞

welfare, and whether it is more convenient for your child to be cared for near your home or your job.

If I am placed on a waiting list for low-cost child care, what should I do?

Call back often so that the people in charge know you are serious about finding child care so you can work. Visit the child-care center often to check on your status. A space might open up if everyone knows how interested you are.

What sorts of documents will I need to place my children in child care?

You will need a medical record form with each child's medical and dental information, including an immunization history. You can get the medical record form from the person running the child-care program. It must be filled out by a doctor.

You might also need proof of birth for your children (a birth certificate, baptismal record or passport); Social Security cards for family members; and your passport, birth certificate, green card or other proof that you are documented.

What do I have to bring to the person or center caring for my child?

Be sure to ask. Some providers require you to bring diapers or food, which might make that home or center too expensive.

What else should I look for in a child-care provider?

You should find out:

- If the people working in the home or center have been checked to make sure they have no criminal record.
- Who will care for the children if they leave the center on a field trip or if something happens and you do not get there in time to pick them up.
- What the center does if a child becomes sick while there.
- What children are disciplined for and how they are punished.

I don't make enough money to pay for child care. Is any help available?

In New York City, public assistance agencies are committed to trying to find you child care that you can afford. Federal money helps pay for licensed child care for low-income working families, families moving from welfare to work and families in which a parent is in a vocational or educational program, is actively looking for work or is medically or otherwise incapable of caring for a child. Call the **New York City Administration for Children's Services Division of Child Care and Head Start,**

1-718-FOR-KIDS (Page 119), or the **New York City Child Care Research and Referral Consortium, 1-888-469-5999** (Page 119), both described earlier in this chapter. For help with forms, the process or payment questions, call the **Human Resources Administration Info Line, 1-877-472-8411** (Page 111).

Can I get back any money that I pay for child care?
If you pay income taxes, you can get back some — but not all — of the money you pay for child care through tax credits.

Here are places to contact for the latest information about tax credits for child care:
- **Internal Revenue Service, 1-800-TAX-1040** (English and Spanish).
- **New York State Department of Taxation, 1-800-225-5829** (English only).

I have been told I'm not eligible for subsidized child care. What should I do?
You can appeal. Go in person to an **Office of Administrative Hearings** to ask for a fair hearing. You can go to either of two offices in the city: **330 West 34th Street, third floor,** in Midtown Manhattan, or **14 Boerum Place, first floor,** in downtown Brooklyn.

I don't think my children are getting good care at the provider I use. Is there anyone to complain to?
The day care program at the **New York City Department of Health and Mental Hygiene, 1-212-676-2444** (Page 121), monitors child-care programs and looks into all complaints about homes, centers and programs that provide child care. Call to file a complaint.

■

"**A**fter putting in some hours of work every day, I am home to receive my children when they return from school. This is much better than being away from 9 to 5. Even if I worked a regular job, its meager salary would vanish in day care costs. And who would drop and pick up my kids from day care every day?"

— *Young Queens mother, Indian, 1990's* [6]

EDUCATION

"The first school I attended was around the corner from 97 Orchard Street. We were brought to the school by a cousin of mine who lived at 90. They were really Americanized children. They brought us in, then left us there. And my first exposure was to a class of young people sitting in a disciplined manner with a teacher up front. And she stood before a blackboard and was drawing American alphabet letters that I had never seen before and I was given a notebook and a pencil, and as far as I understood I was supposed to try and copy those form letters. I didn't know what I was doing. I had never seen such forms in all my life. It was like swimming in an ocean where I didn't know how to swim. It was really overwhelming."

— *Max Mason, Russian, 1921* [7]

■

New York City offers many ways for children and adults to get an education. This chapter will explain the basics of the city's public school system. It will also deal with where adults can go to learn English.

I am undocumented. Can my children still go to school in New York?
Yes. Immigration status does not matter. All children ages 5 to 21 who live in the United States are entitled to a free public education. Attendance is required for children 6 to 17.

How do I enroll my child in school?
Children from 5 to 13 are assigned to elementary and middle schools according to where they live, and registration takes place at the assigned school. For information

about the elementary or junior high school in your neighborhood, call the **Chancellor's Parent Hot Line, 1-718-482-3777** (English and Spanish; Cantonese, Mandarin and other languages by interpreter) (Page 120), or check the **Department of Education's** Web site at **www.nycenet.edu** to locate a Learning Support Center that provides a full range of information and services near you.

Do the operators at the Department of Education speak only English?
Your call will be connected to an interpreter for most languages.

My child is older than 13. How do I enroll her in school?
Parents of students entering high school may contact the **New York City Department of Education, Chancellor's Parent Hot Line, 1-718-482-3777** (English and Spanish; Cantonese, Mandarin and other languages by interpreter) (Page 120).

How do I know what district or school my child is assigned to?
Call the **Chancellor's Parent Hot Line, 1-718-482-3777** (English and Spanish; Cantonese, Mandarin and other languages by interpreter) (Page 120).

Do all elementary, intermediate and high schools offer the same programs?
No, there are many different programs. For example, not every school has a prekindergarten program.

How old must my child be to start school?
- **Prekindergarten** A child must be 4 by Dec. 31 of the school year.
- **Kindergarten** A child must be 5 by Dec. 31 of the school year.
- **First grade** A child must be 6 by Dec. 31 of the school year.

What do I need to enroll my child in school?
A parent or legal guardian must accompany the child being enrolled and bring:
- Proof of address. If the parent or guardian is the primary tenant, take the lease or a bill from Con Edison, the phone company or another utility. If the parent or legal guardian is not the primary tenant, take *two* of the following:
- Lease and notarized letter from the primary tenant stating the address and full name of child or children being enrolled.
- Statement from employer or social service agency stating the parent's address.
- Driver's license.
- Medical insurance card.
- Birth certificate, passport or baptismal certificate (with seal and authorized signature).
- Child's last report card or transcripts if he or she has been in school before.
- Immunization record.

What if I don't have all the documents that are needed to enroll my child in school?
You can often use other forms of documentation. For example, an insurance card can take the place of a proof of address. To find out more about what is often accepted, call the **Chancellor's Parent Hot Line**, 1-718-482-3777 (English and Spanish; Cantonese, Mandarin and other languages by interpreter) (Page 120).

How do I find out what shots my child needs before she is allowed in school?
It varies according to the child's age. Again, call the **Chancellor's Parent Hot Line**, 1-718-482-3777 (English and Spanish; Cantonese, Mandarin and other languages by interpreter) (Page 120).

What if my child does not have all the shots or immunizations needed to enroll in school?
Your child can still go to school if you promise to get the shots within a certain time. You will have to show that you have a doctor's appointment to do so. If you do not get the immunizations, your child can be kept out of school.

I can't afford the shots my child needs to enroll in school. What should I do?
To receive free shots, go to one of seven immunization walk-in clinics run by the

need more help?

To find free quality English programs in your neighborhood, contact the Literacy Assistance Center's referral hot line, 1-212-803-3333 (voice mail menu only, in English and Spanish), or visit the center's Web site, www.lacnyc.org/hotline/nycalidirectory.htm. These community organizations also offer classes:

- Alianza Dominicana (Page 95)
- Brooklyn Chinese-American Association (Page 98)
- Cabrini Immigrant Services (Page 99)
- Catholic Migration Services (Page 100)
- Chinatown Manpower Project (Page 102)
- Chinese Immigrant Services (Page 102)
- Church Avenue Merchants Block Association (C.A.M.B.A.) (Page 103)
- Community Association of Progressive Dominicans (Page 106)
- Indochina Sino-American Community Center (Page 112)
- Jacob A. Riis Neighborhood Settlement House (Page 113)
- New York Association for New Americans (N.Y.A.N.A.) (Page 118)
- South Bronx Action Group (Page 127)
- United Community Centers (Page 128)
- University Settlement Society of New York (Page 129)

New York City Department of Health and Mental Hygiene (Page 121). To find out more about these clinics, call 1-212-676-2273 or visit the department's Web site at www.nyc.gov/html/doh/html/imm/imm.html.

Schools in my country were different. How will teachers here decide what grade my child is in?
Elementary school pupils are placed according to their age unless other factors show they need to be placed differently. High school students will receive some credit for courses taken in their native countries.

My child knows only a little English. How will she be able to learn in school?
When you enroll your child, you are given a Home Language Identification Survey to find out which languages are spoken in the home. Based on that, the school system will decide if your child should be given a Language Assessment Battery Test, known as the L.A.B. Test. Students who score less than 40 percent on the L.A.B. must enroll in either an English for Speakers of Other Languages (E.S.O.L.) program or a bilingual program.

Who decides which English program my child should be in?
You do.

How do the two English programs in the public schools, E.S.O.L. and bilingual education, differ?
The goal of a bilingual program is for the student to remain fluent in his native language as he learns English. In bilingual education programs, math, science and social studies are taught in the *student's* native language. The other language used, and taught, is English.

The goal of an E.S.O.L. program is for students to become fluent mainly in English. All subjects are taught in English.

Do all schools offer both bilingual and E.S.O.L. programs in my language?
Every school must have an E.S.O.L. program, but the languages offered differ.

I want my child to be in a bilingual program, but her school does not have one in our language. What can I do?
You have the right to send your child to another school in the district that does. Call the Chancellor's Parent Hot Line, 1-718-482-3777 (English and Spanish; Cantonese, Mandarin and other languages by interpreter) (Page 120).

My child has a learning disability and needs special help. Can she still go to public school?
Yes. Federal law requires that children with learning disabilities be given a chance

> **If you apply to have your child transferred to a public school outside your neighborhood, no questions will be asked about the immigration status of you or your child.**

to succeed in school in the least restrictive environment. Your child will be evaluated so school officials can see what best meets her needs. She may take some subjects in a general education classroom with appropriate support services or in a special education classroom. *No child can be placed in a special education class without a parent's consent.*

The public school near where I live is not very good. Can my child go to a better school not so close to home?
In theory yes, but it is often very hard to do. The school your child wants to transfer to must have space, so contact that school first and ask. Then fill out an application for special permission, called a variance.

Where do I get the application for a variance so that my child can go to a public school other than the one closest to where we live?
Go to the superintendent's office of the community school district where your child is enrolled and ask for a variance. To find out the location of the office, call the **Chancellor's Parent Hot Line, 1-718-482-3777** (English and Spanish; Cantonese, Mandarin and other languages by interpreter) (Page 120). Or visit the **Department of Education's Division of Food Services and Transportation** Web site at **www. opt-osfns.org/schoolinfo/Superintendents.cfm.**

Is there a yearly deadline to file the application for my child to go to a public school other than the one closest to where we live?
No. You can ask for a transfer at any time. *No questions will be asked about the immigration status of the child or the parents.*

I want to go back to school to learn English. Are there any schools for me?
There are many programs that charge money for English classes, sometimes lots of money. But there are high-quality free English classes all over the city.

Can I go to school to learn other subjects besides English?
The city offers classes to help you get your general education diploma, or G.E.D. A G.E.D. is equivalent to a high school diploma. It is required for admission to college and for many jobs. The city offers G.E.D. classes in English, Spanish and French, as well as E.S.O.L. classes.

I want to get my G.E.D., but I don't think I'm ready. Are there any classes or programs to help me prepare?

The City University of New York, known as CUNY, has free adult basic skills classes at 13 of its colleges. For more information, call 1-212-541-0390 (English only).

I really want to go back to high school, but I have a job and other responsibilities and I don't speak English very well. Is there any school that might take me?

The Manhattan Comprehensive Night and Day High School, 240 Second Avenue, 1-212-353-2010 (English, Spanish and Mandarin), is intended for students who range in age from 17 to 21, have a history of school troubles, speak little English or have other problems that make it unlikely they can pass required standardized tests and graduate in a reasonable amount of time. Classes are held during the day, at night and on weekends. Tutors, lawyers, social workers and other people are available to help students with whatever they might need, like getting eyeglasses or finding a place to live.

Are there requirements?

Yes, the school has room for only 800 students so applicants must have completed 15 high school credits. Foreign students must be literate in some language beyond a primary-school level, and there is a test for admission.

Can I take college classes at the City University of New York (CUNY)?

Yes. Many immigrants have gone to CUNY to attend classes and earn their degrees because admission is easy and tuition is very low. It has thousands of courses that meet during the day and evening at places all around the city. CUNY has a guide,

need more help?

For other educational programs and opportunities, call these agencies:

- Archdiocese of New York, Superintendent of Schools (Page 95)
- Chinese-American Planning Council (Page 103)
- The Door (Page 108)
- Forest Hills Community House (Page 109)
- Hellenic American Neighborhood Action Committee (H.A.N.A.C.) (Page 110)
- Highbridge Community Life Center (Page 111)
- New York City Department of Education, Office of Adult and Continuing Education (Page 120)
- New York City Workforce 1 Career Center (Page 122)
- People's Fire House (Page 125)

"Opportunities for Adults," written specifically to help people like you. It has information on programs, services and tuition and a list of phone numbers. It also has stories about successful adults who combined their work and family responsibilities with their studies. For a copy, call **CUNY's Office of Admission Services, 1-212-997-2869** (Page 105), or visit the admissions page of CUNY's Web site, **www.cuny.edu.**

I think I am ready to study for a degree at a CUNY college, but my English is not good enough. Is there anything I can do?
Yes. CUNY has a language immersion program to help immigrants improve their English before they start college courses. Classes are offered during the day and evening. For more information, call **CUNY's Office of Admission Services, 1-212-997-2869** (Page 105).

■

"My first school was an adult E.S.L. [English as a Second Language] school. The teacher didn't allow the students to use a dictionary in class, we had to listen to him explain the word only. To make us understand the word 'sleeping,' he lay on the ground. To teach us how to tell time, he brought an alarm clock. I still remember everything he told me because through his explaining I had a deep impression I still have now."

— *Ling Leung, Chinese, 1999* [8]

MONEY

"**W**ell, conditions being what they were, most of my countrymen soon were entrusting to my care all of their savings and not expecting any interest in return. I, in turn, invested in real estate and deposited in various banks all of their savings, and mine, too."

— *Anonymous Italian immigrant, 1887* [9]

■

You can't live for long at all in New York (or most other places) unless you understand how to save your money and how to spend it wisely on things you need and want. This chapter will, among other things, guide you through various banking systems in the city, explain how an automated teller machine, or A.T.M., works and discuss inexpensive places from which to wire money to your native country.

Where is it safe for me to keep my money in New York?
Banks and credit unions are safe places to keep money that you bring into the country, your wages or your public assistance benefits. To keep your money in a bank, you have to open an account. To keep your money in a credit union, you have to join one.

How do I open an account at a bank or credit union?
Each bank and credit union has different requirements for opening an account, so you need to ask a bank officer or an account representative. You often need to provide proof of an address where you receive mail, for example a utility bill, and a Social Security card or number. (The Documents chapter has information about getting a Social Security number and card.) You may also have to present two forms of identification, usually with photographs. Some examples are a

passport or visa, driver's license, identification card from your job, nonresident registration card, naturalization certificate, armed forces identification card or major credit card.

I don't have a driver's license and I don't have a job. Where can I get another form of identification to use to open an account and for other things?
You may get a nondriver state identification card with a photo from the **Department of Motor Vehicles**. Go to **www.nydmv.state.ny.us** for instructions. Because of increased security concerns since Sept. 11, the department often updates the list of acceptable proofs of identity and birth date on the Web site. You may also call the department at **1-212-645-5550** or **1-718-966-6155** (English and Spanish).

What is the difference between a bank and a credit union?
A bank is owned by a company, and a credit union is owned by all the people who put money into it. They are called members. Often, to belong to a credit union, you must live in a certain neighborhood or work for a company or belong to a union or social organization. Banks have many more branches than credit unions so they may be more convenient in that respect. But credit unions require only a small amount of money, usually $10 to $20, to join. Both offer similar basic services although credit unions often offer slightly lower interest rates on loans and higher ones on savings.

What should I look for when picking a bank or credit union?
Ask yourself these questions:
- Is the bank or credit union insured by the Federal Deposit Insurance Corporation (F.D.I.C.) or the National Credit Union Administration (N.C.U.A.)?
- What kinds of identification must I show to open an account?
- What are the monthly fees?
- Do I have to keep a minimum amount of money in the account?
- How long must I wait after opening an account or depositing cash or a check before I can withdraw the money?
- Are out-of-state checks treated differently?
- Is there a limit on the number of times I can put money in, take it out or write a check each month?
- Does the bank charge an extra fee if, instead of going to a branch, I use an automated teller machine?
- Can I get a credit card, and if so, what is the annual fee and interest rate?

After I pick a bank or credit union, what do I do?
Decide which accounts you want to open. The two main types are checking accounts and savings accounts.

need more help?

Here are some large banks with branches throughout the city:

- Banco Popular (Page 96)
- Cathay Bank (Page 99)
- Chase (Page 101)
- Citibank (Page 104)
- HSBC (Page 111)

Here are credit unions throughout the city:

- Bethex Federal Credit Union (Page 97)
- Bushwick Cooperative Federal Credit Union (Page 98)
- Lower East Side People's Federal Credit Union (Page 114)
- University Settlement Federal Credit Union (Page 128)

How does a bank or credit union account work?
Money that you put into a checking or a savings account is called a deposit. Money that you take out is called a withdrawal. A checking account will also allow you to write checks for the money that is in the account. A savings account will pay you a small percentage of the money you have deposited. This is called interest.

Do checking accounts pay interest?
Sometimes, but you usually have to keep several thousand dollars in them to be paid interest.

What can I use checks for?
To pay bills and other expenses, either by sending checks through the mail or taking them to the place that sent you the bill. Checks are an easy way to pay bills and keep track of what you spend for rent, groceries, telephone, gas and electricity and other things.

What happens to a check that I write?
The person or business the check is written to signs and cashes it. This means that the amount of money you wrote the check for is taken out of your account and goes to the person or business the check is written to or to their bank account.

Do I ever get back the checks I write?
Some banks send checks that have been cashed back to the person who wrote them. A check that has been cashed is called a canceled check. Other banks do

not send back the checks but do send a list of the checks you have written that have been cashed. This list is called a statement. If someone questions whether you paid a bill, your canceled check or statement listing the cashed check is proof that you did.

What else is important to know about a bank account?

- Always keep a careful record of each check you write.
- Keep a careful record of each deposit and withdrawal.
- Check each statement carefully and compare it to your own records, to make sure everything matches. Be sure to deduct any service or check fees and to add any interest you have earned.
- If you have problems or don't understand something, take your checkbook and statement to the bank and speak with a customer service representative.
- When you order checks, have your address printed on them.

Checks that I've seen have "MEMO" written in the lower left-hand corner. What does that mean?

That is where you write your account number for the bill you are paying or a note to remind you what the check was for.

What should I do if someone pays me by check?

You have to sign the check on the back, which is called endorsing it. Then cash it at a bank or check-cashing outlet and collect the money, or deposit it in your account at the bank or by using an automated teller machine, which is explained later in this chapter.

Are there rules about signing a check?

There aren't rules, but there are some precautions you should take. Always sign in ink, and always write "for deposit only" and your account number on the back of a check you endorse and intend to deposit into your account. Then, if you lose the check, no one else can cash it. If you are going to the bank to deposit the check, rather than doing it at an automated teller machine, it is a good idea not to endorse the check until you are inside the bank. Then if you lose it, no one can pretend to be you and cash it.

What happens if I write a check for more money than I have in my account?

If you write a check for more money than you have in the account, your check will bounce, which means it will be returned to your bank without being paid. Do not do this. You may be fined by the bank and by the company to which you wrote the bounced check. You will also get a bad credit rating, which will make it difficult to get a credit card, make layaway purchases, etc.

What is a savings account? How does it work?

A savings account is for money that you do not need right away. Banks pay you interest on the money in a savings account. How much interest will depend on the bank and the kind of account you choose. You can get money out of your savings account in the form of cash or a bank check. Deposits can be made in cash or by check, but you might have to wait 5 to 20 days to withdraw the money that you deposit by check.

If I don't have an account at a bank or credit union, how can I cash my paycheck and pay bills?

Check-cashing services let you cash checks and pay certain bills for a fee. Keep in mind that these fees are often much higher than fees charged by banks and credit unions for the same services.

How does a check-cashing service work?

A check-cashing service charges you money to cash paychecks and other kinds of checks. Some will cash personal checks; others may not or may charge a higher fee for them. You can also pay bills at some check-cashing services, for a fee.

If I don't have an account at a bank or a credit union, how can I send money to my family?

Money-wiring services like **Western Union, 1-800-325-6000 (or for help in Spanish, 1-800-325-4045)** (Page 129), and **MoneyGram, 1-800-926-9400** (Page 117), charge you to wire money and receive money from places around the world. You can also buy something called a money order, which can be used to pay bills and send money to people. All have different prices, identification requirements, time requirements for a check to clear or expiration dates and other rules, so shop around.

How does a money-wiring service work?

You go to a money-wiring service and fill out a form that is available only in English and Spanish. You tell a clerk how much money you are sending and give the name and address of the person you are sending it to. That person is called the recipient. You also give the clerk the amount of money you are sending and whatev-

warning!

Never send cash from any country through the United States or international mail. In the United States, it is illegal to send currency through the mail or to use international couriers like DHL and Federal Express to send currency.

> ❝ Fees for using A.T.M.'s add up quickly so try to use only those machines belonging to your bank or credit union. ❞

er fee the service charges to send it. The clerk gives you a number, usually called a control number, which you must tell to the recipient. Within a day, the money is available in the recipient's local currency or in American dollars. To get the money, the recipient must go to a branch of the money-wiring service and tell a clerk the control number.

Can I wire money to a bank account?
Yes, if you or the recipient has an account at the bank and you know the number of the account, you can use a money-wiring service to send money to that account.

How do I know which money-wiring services I can trust?
Ask other people from your country who have been successful in sending money home. They may have a reputable agent or representative who can help you. If **Western Union, 1-800-325-6000 (or for help in Spanish, 1-800-325-4045)** (Page 129), has a branch in your home country, it is probably the cheapest, most efficient way to transfer money. If the recipients have bank accounts back home, bank wire transfers are secure.

I need to send money somewhere where there are no banks or Western Union outlets. Is that possible?
Chances are there are smaller private agencies, like **Delgado Travel** (Page 107), that handle such transactions. Ask people whom you know to be reputable what agency they use. It is wise to first transfer a small amount of money as an experiment. Once you are sure the recipient has it, you can send larger amounts.

How does a money order work?
You buy a money order at a bank, check-cashing service or post office for the amount that you want to send someone or that you need to pay a bill. A money order is usually cheapest at the post office and it can be traced if it is lost or stolen before it is cashed. Not all businesses accept money orders.

What is an automated teller machine, and how does it work?
Automated teller machines, usually called A.T.M.'s, belong to banks or credit unions and allow you to do most banking functions 24 hours a day. Your bank or credit union will issue you an A.T.M. card and ask you to choose a personal identification number, or PIN, which serves as a password. Each A.T.M. has a screen that tells you

step by step how to use it, but all basically work the same way:
1. Insert or swipe your card through a slot in the A.T.M.
2. Punch your PIN on the keypad.
3. Complete your transaction. You can withdraw cash, make deposits, transfer money between accounts and learn your account balance.
4. Each time you use an A.T.M., make sure you get a receipt, a piece of paper that tells you what you did with your money. Record that in your checkbook or savings account log.

I speak little English. Will the instructions at an A.T.M. be in my language?
Most A.T.M.'s in New York City have instructions in English and Spanish. In neighborhoods with large numbers of immigrants who speak other languages, the machines will also have instructions in those languages.

Are A.T.M.'s free?
No. Usually the bank or credit union where you have an account will allow you to use its A.T.M.'s free for a certain number of deposits and withdrawals each month. But machines belonging to other banks will automatically deduct a fee, usually from 75 cents to $1.50, from your account each time you use them. These fees add up quickly so try to use few A.T.M.'s other than those belonging to your bank or credit union.

Can I use my A.T.M. card to buy things?
Only if your bank or credit union allows it and if you make enough money or have

warning!

A.T.M.'s are very convenient, but when using them, take these precautions:

- Always sign the back of your A.T.M. card as soon as you get it, to make it harder for someone else to use it if it is lost or stolen.
- Do not write your PIN on the card or on any paper that you keep with the card.
- Do not allow anyone to see you punch in your PIN or follow you from the machine after you take out money.
- Try not to visit an A.T.M. alone at night.
- Try to use an A.T.M. in a locked, well-lighted area, rather than one on the street.
- Never allow anyone, especially a stranger, to use your A.T.M. card, even if you are unsure how to use the machine and that person offers to help.
- After using an A.T.M. to take out cash, always put your card, money and receipt in your pocket or purse before leaving the lobby or machine.

deposited enough money to qualify. If you use your card this way, it is called a debit card.

How does a debit card work?
You swipe your card through a small machine at a store's checkout counter and enter your PIN. This authorizes the bank or credit union to deduct the cost of what you bought from your account, just as when you write a check. Some banks may charge a fee, just as they do for using an A.T.M.

What is a credit card?
A credit card lets you buy goods and services and pay for them later. Sometimes you can use a credit card to borrow money. This is called a cash advance.

How can I get a credit card?
First, you must have a Social Security number and a lot of other documentation. You must also fill out an application. Applications can be found at banks, stores, check-cashing services and many other places. A bank will then study all the information on your application to decide if you can afford to use such a card. If you are approved, you will be allowed to use the card to buy only a certain amount of merchandise. That amount is your credit limit. At the end of each month, the bank or credit card company will send you a statement that lists everything you bought and tells you the minimum amount you have to pay that month.

Are credit cards free?
Some are, but many charge an annual fee. And in any month that you do not pay for all the merchandise you bought or the cash you borrowed that month, you will be charged a fee for the remaining amount, known as the balance. The fee is called the interest or finance charge and can range from 5 percent to 21 percent or more on the balance.

warning!

There are always people who will lend you money for a very high price. They are called loan sharks and they are known to prey on poor immigrants who may need money very badly. They are often found hanging around factories where immigrants work and in the neighborhoods where they live. If you can avoid it, you should not borrow money from these people because you probably will not be able to pay what they charge in interest and fees, and they will then order you to do more and more things for them. Often those things are illegal or unsavory, and you will not want to do them. The loan sharks may threaten to harm you or your family if you don't do what they ask.

credit card dos and don'ts

- Do charge only that merchandise that you can afford to pay for each month if you don't want to pay interest or finance charges.
- Don't miss a payment, or your card is likely to be canceled.
- Do keep all credit card receipts so you know what you charged and the cost.
- Do check your monthly credit card statement and tell the bank or credit card company immediately if you have been charged for anything you did not buy.

I have a credit card from my own country. Can I use it here?
You usually can if it is a major card like American Express, Visa or MasterCard. Just be sure the bill is sent or forwarded to you at your address in New York.

I have a job, but I need more money. My family back home can't afford to send any, and I can't afford a credit card. What can I do?
If you qualify, a bank or credit union may lend you money, for which you pay interest. Each bank or credit union has different terms and qualifications so it is best to check with a teller or loan officer there.

■

"The first work I did was sweeping floors. My first check was for $125 for the week. I was thinking of the currency in Ecuador, where a good salary is $80 a month. So when I got a check for five days of work, I said, 'Oh God, I'm rich.' After three or four weeks I was getting down because I had to pay rent, buy tokens, buy food. I noticed I wasn't as well off as I thought at first."

— *Jose Zambrano, Ecuadorean, 2001* [10]

HEALTH CARE AND INSURANCE

*"*W*e never visited a doctor. If we sprained our wrists from skatin', we always went to Grandma. She'd take a piece of twine and pull it apart. Then she'd dip it in the white of an egg. When she set it on our wrists with a bandage, it got as hard as a cast, and it got better. She was like a chiropractor from the other side. Grandma was a real Italian grandmother. She also had certain oils she used to massage us. For temperature, she used to rub all the muscles in our hands and then pull a finger. For throat, she'd rub our glands and then pull a piece of hair. It worked."*

— *Marie Cutaia, grandchild of Italian immigrants, remembering the 1920's* [11]

■

The 21st-century American health care system has grown far beyond home remedies to gene-based disease screening, microsurgery and hospice care for the terminally ill. How much you can afford to pay for these and countless other services, either with your own money or through insurance or public assistance, determines a lot about the kind of care you will get. New York City has many different types of public and private hospitals and clinics, including those that are low cost and offer treatment to undocumented immigrants, as well as many different types of private and subsidized insurance programs.

This chapter will explain the basic kinds of health care services available in the city and refer you to agencies where you can learn more about those services, which ones you qualify for and how you can get the care and insurance you need.

What should I do if I am very sick or hurt and need medical care right away?
Get to the nearest hospital as quickly as you can.

What if I am too sick or hurt to get to a hospital or a doctor myself?
Call 911, the emergency telephone number. Tell the operator what is wrong with you and where you are. An ambulance will pick you up and take you to the emergency room of a nearby hospital.

Will the 911 emergency operator speak my language?
Operators who speak virtually any language can be available very quickly.

What if there is an emergency and I am taken to a hospital where I can't afford to pay and do not have insurance?
It is illegal for a hospital to refuse to give you emergency treatment. Ask the hospital if you are eligible for a reduced fee based on your income or ability to pay, or if you are undocumented, for emergency Medicaid. If you receive a bill, you will not have to pay it all at once. Negotiate a payment schedule with the hospital.

I speak very little English. Will the people at the hospital understand me?
The patients' bill of rights requires hospitals to provide an interpreter or a translator. Even if you bring a friend or relative to translate for you, insist that the hospital get a translator for you, too.

What if it is not an emergency but I need to stay in a hospital and do not have insurance?
The hospital where you have gone will have to find a hospital that will take you without insurance. All public hospitals must provide care regardless of insurance, immigration status or ability to pay.

I have no insurance and can't afford to pay much. What should I do if I get sick but it is not an emergency?
If you have a minor ailment or a chronic illness like diabetes, asthma or AIDS, you can still be treated in a hospital emergency room, but you will probably have a very long wait until you see a doctor. Try to avoid going to the emergency room on Saturday night, the busiest time in most emergency rooms.

If you don't have a life-threatening ailment, go to a free or low-cost clinic. You

getting treatment

When this book was printed, it was illegal for a hospital in New York to refuse to treat undocumented immigrants. New York City public hospitals have a formal policy of not reporting immigration status. Private hospitals and clinics are not required or encouraged to report your immigration status.

need more help?

These hospitals and health care organizations offer free or low-cost services:

- Bellevue Hospital Center (Page 97)
- Charles B. Wang Community Health Center (Page 101)
- Community Healthcare Network (Page 107)
- Lutheran Medical Center (Page 115)
- Morris Heights Health Center (Page 118)
- Promesa (Page 125)

can sometimes schedule appointments at clinics and not have to wait so long. Public hospitals and clinics in New York will treat patients who have no insurance and cannot afford to pay for care. A list of **public hospitals** can be found on the Web site, **www.nyc.gov/html/hhc.home/html**. They offer many types of general and specialized care, like treatment for dental problems, diabetes and substance abuse. You will be asked to share information about your income and to discuss payment options with the hospital or clinic. If you call or go to one that does not have the service you need, ask the staff to send you to one that does.

What are some of these hospitals and clinics where I can go for treatment of routine injuries, minor ailments or a chronic illness?
- Any public hospital, clinic or nursing program owned by New York City.
- School health clinics in some elementary, intermediate and high schools. These range from a nurse who visits the school once a week and gives vision and hearing tests, to full-service clinics that care for students' physical and mental health needs.
- Department of Health clinics that diagnose and treat sexually transmitted diseases and tuberculosis; administer immunizations; screen for breast cancer; care for pregnant women, new mothers and new babies; and give anonymous counseling and tests for H.I.V.

How much will I have to pay for nonemergency treatment at a hospital or a clinic if I don't have insurance?
It usually depends on your income. Ask if the hospital or clinic has a sliding scale fee, which means that the amount you are charged goes up with your income, so people with very low incomes have to pay little or nothing. If you do have to pay, you can usually spread out the payments.

Will I have to show proof of how much I earn at a hospital or clinic?
Yes. You will usually be asked to provide a recent pay stub or a letter from your

employer, although a few hospitals and clinics will accept a self-declaration form in which you say what your income is.

So do I really need health insurance?

Yes. You can't predict what your medical bills will be. If you and your family are rarely sick, your health care costs might be low. But if you or someone in your family becomes ill or is injured, your bills could be very high — too high for you to pay them yourself. If you are eligible, you should try to enroll in an insurance program.

Does every job come with health insurance?

No, but most full-time work offers some kind of health insurance. Most part-time work does not. If you can get health insurance through your job, payments for all or part of the cost will usually be deducted from your wages.

If I have insurance, does it mean that I will not have to pay anything when I visit a doctor or get a prescription filled?

Not necessarily. You may be charged a fee, usually $5 to $20, for some services, like doctor visits or prescription drugs. This is called a co-payment. Instead of a co-payment, some insurance plans require you to pay a percentage of the cost of the doctor visit or prescription.

I lost my job. What happens to my health insurance?

A federal law called Cobra allows you to pay for your group health insurance coverage for up to 18 months although Cobra insurance is much more expensive. Medicaid, which provides coverage for some low-income people who cannot afford health insurance, might also help pay for family coverage for your spouse and children.

I am covered under my spouse's insurance plan at work. What happens if we divorce or if my spouse dies?

You will be able to pay for coverage under Cobra, and other members of your family may be eligible for coverage under Medicaid.

What if my employer does not pay for health insurance, or if I'm not working and cannot afford such insurance?

You can buy your own health insurance, but private health insurance is very expensive, $300 to $500 a month or more. If you can afford to buy it, do so. In addition, many low-income individuals and families are eligible for free or low-cost health insurance programs like **Medicaid, Family Health Plus, Child Health Plus** or **Healthy NY**, which are described later in this chapter.

need more help?

These organizations provide information about how to get health insurance:

- Asian Americans for Equality (A.A.F.E.) (Page 96)
- Citizens Advice Bureau (C.A.B.) (Page 104)
- The Door (Page 108)
- Managed Care Consumer Assistance Program (M.C.C.A.P.), Community Service Society of New York (Page 115)

How can I find out what New York's free or low-cost health insurance programs offer, whether I am eligible and how to apply?

These programs are described in several answers below. To learn more basic information about them, call the city's **Human Resources Administration (H.R.A.) Info Line, 1-877-472-8411** (Page 111).

To find out if you and your family are eligible for these programs call the **Department of Health and Mental Hygiene's** automated touch-tone telephone line, **Health-Stat, 1-888-692-6116** (Page 109). You will be asked questions to determine which programs you and your family qualify for and the most convenient places for you to enroll.

In addition you can go to the offices of community organizations, social service organizations, health plans and the doctors and hospitals that are part of those plans, and city health clinics. To find locations and contact information for those places and groups, call the HealthStat line (Page 109) or visit a Web site run by the **Mayor's Office of Health Insurance Access, www.nyc.gov/html/hia/html/places.html**.

What is Medicaid?

Medicaid provides coverage for some low-income people who cannot afford health insurance.

Can undocumented immigrants get Medicaid?

Only if they are pregnant or require emergency medical treatment and meet all other eligibility requirements. Other immigrants are eligible, though. In New York, legal immigrants and those immigrants without lawful status who are known to the **United States Citizenship and Immigration Services (U.S.C.I.S.)** as Prucols may be eligible for Medicaid regardless of when they arrived in the United States. There are several categories of Prucols, including immigrants granted stays or suspensions of deportation, who are allowed to remain in the United States for an indefinite period. These immigrants must meet other eligibility standards, like income, to enroll.

The application form for Medicaid does not ask for immigration information on other family members, and New York State does not share information on the form with the federal government. The U.S.C.I.S., a division of the **United States Department of Homeland Security**, has decided that using Medicaid will not affect any family member's ability to get a green card, to become a citizen, to sponsor a family member or to travel to and from the United States.

How can I find out if I am eligible for Medicaid, and if so, where can I apply?

People receiving public assistance or welfare are automatically eligible. Other people may be eligible because they are disabled. To find out if you are eligible and where to apply, call the **HealthStat** line, **1-888-692-6116** (Page 109), or the **Human Resources Administration (H.R.A.) Info Line, 1-877-472-8411** (Page 111), or visit the Web site at **www.nyc.gov/html/hra/ html/serv_medicaid.html**.

What should I bring with me when I apply for Medicaid?

As many of the following as you can: proof of age, like a birth certificate; proof of citizenship or immigration status; proof of where you live, like a rent receipt or landlord statement; current paycheck stubs if you are working; proof of income from other sources like a Social Security check stub or bank book.

Is the application process difficult?

Yes. All Medicaid applicants face many bureaucratic challenges before they are enrolled, and immigrants must prove their lawful status. This is especially hard for Prucols because of their many different categories and all the forms and letters that are required. The important thing is to remember not to give up before you receive the benefits you are entitled to.

If I am eligible for Medicaid, what will I show my doctor or clinic to prove it?

You will receive a benefit identification card to use when you need medical services.

Will Medicaid cover all the medical care my family and I need?

No. Some services will not be covered, and you will have to check before getting certain other services to see if they are covered. This is called prior approval.

need more help?

Here are some places where you can get more information about Medicaid:

- New York State's Medicaid help line, 1-800-541-2831 (English, Spanish, Cantonese and Mandarin)
- Medical and Health Research Association of New York City (M.H.R.A.) (Page 116)
- New York City Workforce 1 Career Center (Page 122)

need more help?

These groups will help you to apply for Family Health Plus:

- Alianza Dominicana (Page 95)
- Caribbean Women's Health Association (Page 99)
- Chinese-American Planning Council (Page 103)
- Medical and Health Research Association of New York City (Page 116)

Will I have to pay anything for Medicaid or when I see a doctor who accepts Medicaid patients?

No. Benefits are free, and there are no additional costs, known as co-payments, for services.

What is Family Health Plus?

Family Health Plus is a public health insurance program for people from 19 to 64 who cannot buy health insurance on their own or through their jobs but who make too much money to qualify for Medicaid. It provides free comprehensive coverage, including prevention, primary care, hospitalization, prescriptions and other services.

Are undocumented immigrants eligible for Family Health Plus?

No, Family Health Plus is not available to undocumented immigrants.

How can I find out if I am eligible for Family Health Plus, and if so, where can I apply?

New York residents from 19 to 64 who do not have health insurance on their own or through their jobs and who are not eligible for other public health programs like Medicare or Medicaid are eligible for Family Health Plus. For locations and contact information call the **HealthStat** line, **1-888-692-6116** (Page 109), or visit the Web site at **www.nyc.gov/html/hia/html/places.html**.

Are there income limits to qualify for Family Health Plus?

How much you and your family can earn and still qualify for Family Health Plus depends on how many people are in the family.

Can my family have a bank account and apply for Family Health Plus?

Yes. There are no limits on other assets and resources.

I'm pregnant. Can I get Family Health Plus?

Yes, if you meet the income guidelines, which are somewhat higher than those for Medicaid.

What is Child Health Plus?

Child Health Plus is an insurance program sponsored by New York State for children under 19 who are uninsured.

My children are undocumented. Can they get Child Health Plus?

All children younger than 19 are eligible for Child Health Plus regardless of immigration status.

The application form for Child Health Plus does not ask for immigration information on any other family members, and New York State does not share information on the form with the federal government. The U.S.C.I.S. has decided that using Child Health Plus will not affect any family member's ability to get a green card, become a citizen, sponsor a family member or travel in and out of the United States.

Do I have to pay for Child Health Plus?

You might have to pay a small monthly fee to belong to the plan, but you will not have to pay anything when your child sees a doctor.

What is covered under Child Health Plus?

If your children are eligible for Child Health Plus, you will be asked to pick a local provider, who will decide which services you are eligible for and which doctors you can see under the plan.

How can I find out if my children are eligible, and if so, how can I apply?

Call the HealthStat line, 1-888-692-6116 (Page 109), or visit the Web site at www.nyc.gov/html/hia/html/places.html. For a list of places to enroll and for more information about Child Health Plus, call 1-800-698-4543 (English and Spanish).

What is Healthy NY?

Healthy NY is a program that offers lower-cost health insurance to working people who meet certain eligibility requirements.

How can I find out if I'm eligible for Healthy NY and if so, how can I apply?

Call the HealthStat line, 1-888-692-6116 (Page 109), or visit the Web site at www.nyc.gov/html/hia/html/places.html.

What is Medicare?

Medicare is the federal health insurance program for people 65 and older and disabled people younger than 65 who have received Social Security disability for more than 24 months. It helps to pay for certain hospital costs and medical care. It is divided into Medicare Part A and Medicare Part B.

Will my immigration status affect whether I can get Medicare?

You must be a documented immigrant but you do not have to be a citizen to get Medicare. Generally you are eligible if you are 65 or older, are a citizen or permanent resident of the United States and if you or your spouse worked for 10 years in Medicare-covered employment.

Are there any standard costs for either part of Medicare?

Each part has certain monthly fees, known as premiums, and for each part you must pay a certain amount for treatment during a time period. Medicare pays the rest. The amounts you pay are called deductibles. Both parts also have set fees you must pay for each doctor visit or hospital room. They are called co-payments.

What does Medicare Part A pay for?

Medicare Part A (Hospital Insurance) helps pay for care when you are admitted to a semiprivate room or ward in a hospital or are sent to a skilled-nursing home after a three-day hospital stay. It also pays for pints of blood you get when you are in a hospital or skilled-nursing center. It pays for a Medicare-approved hospice for people who are terminally ill and for some home health care services. It does *not* pay for a private room, private-duty nurses or a telephone or television in your room.

What does Medicare Part B pay for?

Medicare Part B (Medical Insurance) helps pay for doctors' services other than routine physical checkups; outpatient medical and surgical services and supplies; diagnostic tests and approved operations in an outpatient surgery center; blood you are given while an outpatient; and durable medical equipment like wheelchairs, hospital beds and walkers. It also covers some home health care services listed in Medicare Part A.

Medicare also pays for:

- Ambulance services when other transportation would threaten your health
- Artificial eyes and limbs and their replacement parts
- Braces for arms, legs, back and neck
- Chiropractic services limited to spine manipulation
- Emergency care
- One pair of standard eyeglass frames and appropriate lenses after cataract surgery
- Drug therapy for transplant patients covered by Medicare
- Macular eye-degeneration treatment
- Medical nutrition therapy for people with diabetes or kidney disease
- Some medical supplies
- Very few outpatient prescription drugs

- Some preventive services
- Prosthetic devices, including breast prosthesis
- Some second opinions from doctors
- Services of practitioners including clinical social workers, physician assistants and nurse practitioners
- Therapeutic shoes for people with diabetes
- Transplants performed under certain conditions and at Medicare-approved centers
- X-rays, M.R.I.'s, CAT scans, E.K.G.'s and some other diagnostic tests

How much does Medicare Part A (Hospital Insurance) cost?

Most people do not have to pay the premium for Part A because they or their spouses paid Medicare taxes while they were working. But they might have to pay other deductibles and co-payments, which can vary.

I did not pay Medicare taxes. Can I still get Medicare Part A (Hospital Insurance)?

If you or your spouse did not pay Medicare taxes while you worked and you are 65 or older, you still might be able to buy Part A. Call **1-800-633-4227** (English and Spanish), or visit the Web site **www.medicare.gov**.

How much does Medicare Part B (Medical Insurance) cost?

In early 2003 the monthly premium was $58.70. The rate changes annually; you can get the most current information by calling **1-800-633-4227** (English and Spanish) or by visiting the Web site **www.medicare.gov**.

be prepared!

Long before an emergency strikes, make a list of things you'll need to tell the doctors and nurses so you can take it to the hospital with you. It should include:

- Serious illnesses you've had
- Operations you've had
- Allergies
- Chronic conditions
- Medications you take (if you have time, bring them with you)
- Symptoms like pain, redness, nausea, numbness, swelling, etc., and when they started
- Family history of illnesses
- Date of birth
- Social Security number, if you have one
- Name, address and phone number of employer, if you work

I can't afford to pay for Medicare Part B (Medical Insurance). What should I do?

There are four programs for low-income people who need help paying Medicare premiums. Call the **Human Resources Administration Info Line, 1-877-472-8411** (Page 111).

How do I enroll in Medicare?

The city's **Department for the Aging** has a screening tool called **UNIForm** that helps you find out if you are eligible for major federal, state and city benefit programs. It is available at senior centers throughout the city. To find a center near you, call the **New York City Department for the Aging Senior Call Center, 1-212-442-1000** (English Spanish, Cantonese, Mandarin and other languages). You can also visit the Web site **home.nyc.gov/html/dfta.** You can enroll yourself through the Social Security Administration or by calling **1-800-772-1213** (English and Spanish).

I need to take medication that I can't afford. What should I do?

Many health insurance plans do not cover the cost of prescription drugs. Other plans limit the cost or the brands of drugs they will pay for. These programs might help you pay for prescriptions:

- **AIDS Drug Assistance Program (A.D.A.P.)** pays for medicine for some low-income people with H.I.V. infection and some related conditions. Call **1-800-542-2437** (English and Spanish).
- **Elder Pharmaceutical Insurance Coverage (EPIC)** is a prescription plan for low-income people over age 65. For more information and an application, call EPIC's toll-free help line, **1-800-332-3742** (English and Spanish).

I am undocumented. Do I still qualify for low-cost prescription drug programs?

Yes. You may qualify for **A.D.A.P.** and **EPIC** regardless of immigration status.

Are there income limits and co-payments for low-cost prescription drug programs?

Yes, but they are subject to change so call the numbers above to learn the current income limits and co-payments.

■

"When I came to this country eight years ago, I had no information about places I could go in case I was sick, had an emergency or for a simple checkup. And like many others, we came to this country without papers so we were afraid. But it must not be that way, since it means we put our health, and even our lives, in danger. Fortunately, many cities in the United States have very efficient, and in most cases just, health care systems. Best of all, some of the services are free, and discrimination is illegal."

— *Maricela Gonzalez, Mexican, 1999* [12]

SAFETY

"I called together our people in the community and we started the United Indian American Association. We arranged five different demonstrations. Since we took action, things are better. Before, they attacked Indians every day. They attacked over 20 different families. They broke into houses, Indian shops and stores. They attacked Indian women going shopping. They point their hand at them in the street. They beat up on them. But now it is in control. Now there is less fear when we walk down the streets."

—Hardayal Singh, Indian, 1977 [13]

■

New York is probably safer now than it has been at any time in the last two decades. Crime has been falling steadily since the mid 1990's, and has fallen even faster since the attack on the World Trade Center on Sept. 11, 2001.

Sept. 11, though, provided fresh evidence that the city itself is facing an increased threat from terrorism. And that threat has had a significant impact on the lives of many immigrants.

The Sept. 11 attack led to the creation of the **United States Department of Homeland Security**, which now carries out many functions of what had been known for years as the **Immigration and Naturalization Service**, or **I.N.S.** The department's **Bureau of Immigration and Customs Enforcement (B.I.C.E.)** actively searches for people whose visas have expired, who have not complied with deportation orders or who are not documented. Someone who has proper documents but who has been convicted of a crime is also much more likely to be deported.

This chapter will focus on your rights as an immigrant living in the United States and in New York City and on your safety. Safety includes many issues, among them how to protect yourself from certain crimes, like rape and robbery, and what to do if you are the victim not only of a crime, but also of misconduct by the police or the B.I.C.E.

Can the police come into my home and search it at any time?
No. You have a right to deny a police officer entry into your home unless the officer has a valid order, which must be signed by a judge. This order is called a warrant.

Are there times when the police are allowed to search my home without a warrant?
Yes. Police officers are allowed to enter and search your home without a warrant in an emergency situation, for example when a person is screaming for help inside your home or when the police are chasing someone.

It is possible that the United States Department of Justice will allow federal regulations enacted after Sept. 11 to be used to enable local police departments to arrest immigrants without a warrant if they are suspected of violating immigration laws. But it is not clear how local departments, including the New York Police Department, will interpret and use those regulations. In addition, policies affecting immigrants change often so it is best to check with an immigration advocacy group listed in the Resource Directory at the back of this guide, or, if you can afford it, with a reputable immigration lawyer.

What if the police have a warrant but I do not want them to search my house?
Always tell the officers that you do not consent to the search. This will limit the search to the area specified in the warrant. Ask if you can watch the search. If you can, take notes, including the names, badge numbers and agencies of the officers. Call a lawyer or an immigrant advocate as soon as possible.

What if the police force their way into my house to search it?
Do everything described above.

don't leave home without them!

Besides your immigration papers like your visa, Employment Authorization Document, arrival-departure card (I-94) or green card, always carry the name and telephone number of a reputable immigration lawyer who will take your calls. Immigration laws are hard to understand and there have been many changes since Sept. 11. More changes are likely. The Bureau of Immigration and Customs Enforcement will not explain your rights or your options. As soon as you encounter a B.I.C.E. agent, call your lawyer. If you cannot call or do not get through right away, keep trying.

need more help?

These agencies and groups provide legal counseling and referrals:

- Asian American Legal Defense and Education Fund (Page 95)
- The Bronx Defenders (Page 98)
- Caribbean Women's Health Association (C.W.H.A.) (Page 99)
- CUNY Law School — Main Street Legal Services, Immigration and Refugee Rights (Page 107)
- Legal Aid Society (Page 114)
- New York Association for New Americans (N.Y.A.N.A.) (Page 118)
- New York City Commission on Human Rights (Page 119)
- Queens Legal Services (Page 126)
- Safe Horizon (Page 126)

What happens if the police stop me on the street?

You have the right to ask the police if you are free to go. Be polite and keep your hands where the police can see them. Do not run or try to resist arrest. Do not make any statements. Do not sign anything you do not understand. Ask to see a lawyer. Contact one of the organizations listed in the box above.

What should I do if the police stop me and decide to search me?

You do not have to consent to a search. If you do not wish to consent, say clearly, "I do not consent to a search," and do everything else described in the answer above.

What should I do if a police officer injures me or violates my rights?

You have the right to ask the officer to tell you his name and badge number. If he refuses, try to remember them from the officer's uniform. As soon as you can, write down everything that happened and take photographs of your injuries, like cuts and bruises. Try to find people who saw what happened.

For legal advice, contact one of the organizations listed above and call the city's **Civilian Complaint Review Board hot line, 1-800-341-CCRB (2272)** (Page 106).

What is the Civilian Complaint Review Board?

The board, also known as the C.C.R.B., is an independent city agency not connected to the Police Department that has the authority to look into reports of police misconduct. Complaints may be filed by a victim or by a witness. You do not have to be a United States citizen or a resident of New York City. It is important to file a complaint as soon as possible because the board has only 18 months to study your complaint.

Which documents should I carry to prove my immigration status?
If you are a permanent resident, your Permanent Resident Card, also known as an Alien Registration Card and commonly known as a green card, or your passport. If you are a nonimmigrant alien, your arrival-departure card (an I-94), a notation in your passport and/or other proof of your status from the **United States Citizenship and Immigration Services (U.S.C.I.S.)**, another division of the **United States Department of Homeland Security**.

What if the police ask me to show my immigration documents?
Ask if you are free to go. If you are told you are, walk away. If you are told you are not free to go, you are being detained. This does not necessarily mean that you are being arrested. The police are allowed to "frisk" you, which means they can pat down the outside of your clothing. Do not give the police permission to search you any further. Tell the police: "I do not consent. I want to speak to my lawyer."

What if the police continue to search me after I tell them that I don't consent and that I want to contact my lawyer?
Stay calm. Do not get into a fight with the police or with agents from B.I.C.E. You could be hurt or arrested. Keep saying: "I don't consent. I want to speak to my lawyer." Get the officers' names, badge numbers and agency. You do not have to answer questions or give a statement if you are detained or even if you are arrested.

Do I have to give my name if I am detained or arrested?
Legally, you do not have to give your name unless they suspect you of a crime. But

need more help?

Call these hot lines and organizations if you or someone you know is the victim of domestic violence:

- New York State Domestic Violence Hot Line, 1-800-942-6906 (English only)
- New York State Domestic Violence Hot Line, 1-800-942-6908 (Spanish only)
- New York City Domestic Violence Hot Line, 1-800-621-4673 (English, Spanish, Cantonese and Mandarin)
- CUNY Law School — Main Street Legal Services, Immigration and Refugee Rights (Page 107)
- Park Slope Safe Homes Project (Page 124)
- Queens Legal Services (Page 126)

> ❝ If you are stopped by the police, be polite, keep your hands where the officer can see them and do not run or try to resist arrest. ❞

refusing to give your name may arouse suspicion. Be aware that the police or B.I.C.E. agents may be carrying a list of names of deportable aliens. Giving a false name is not likely to be a prosecutable crime in and of itself, but it is illegal, and the police or the B.I.C.E. may detain you if you do so.

What if I am stopped by the police while I am driving a car?
You must show your driver's license, vehicle registration and proof of insurance, but you do not have to consent to a search, although the police may be able to search your car legally anyway.

I am undocumented. Can a B.I.C.E. agent arrest me without a warrant?
Yes, a B.I.C.E. agent is allowed to arrest you without a signed order if the agent thinks that you are in the United States illegally and that you are likely to escape before an arrest warrant can be obtained.

What happens if I am arrested by a B.I.C.E. agent? Can I just be put on a plane to my native country?
In most cases, you must have a hearing in front of an immigration judge in Immigration Court. But the law does not say how long the court is allowed to wait before granting you a hearing.

Is there any way I can be deported without a hearing by an immigration judge?
Yes, if you give up or "waive" your right to a hearing, agree to leave without a hearing, have been convicted of certain crimes, were arrested at a border or have been deported before.

Can I be deported even if I have a green card and other documents?
Immigrants convicted of a crime defined by immigration law as an "aggravated felony" can be deported. A list of aggravated felonies is available on the Web at **www.newamericans.com/citizen/articles/felonieslist.html**. It is best to get legal advice about how conviction of a crime can affect immigration status.

I was convicted of a crime but did not have to go to jail. Can I still be deported?
Yes. If you have been sentenced for a crime in the United States — even if you only paid a fine and did not go to jail — it is essential that you consult an immigration lawyer or advocate before traveling abroad. (A list of groups that

immigration laws after september 11

Laws passed after the Sept. 11 terrorist attacks allow the Bureau of Immigration and Customs Enforcement, or B.I.C.E., to keep arrested immigrants in jail for weeks, months or longer. The laws do not say when an immigration judge has to hear your case. And if a judge decides you are a threat to society or might try to flee, he or she may order you to stay in jail. Also, some laws say that you cannot be released if you are charged with terrorism or have been convicted of certain crimes.

offer legal counseling is on page 63.) If you leave the country and try to re-enter and/or if you apply for citizenship, you often run the risk of deportation proceedings.

Will the B.I.C.E. really track me down for a minor offense?

There is always that risk. And even if a B.I.C.E. agent is not looking for you, you may come in contact with the agency after you serve your sentence and are applying for citizenship or other immigration benefits, or when you return to the United States after a vacation or business trip outside of the country.

If I am stopped or taken into custody by a B.I.C.E. agent, should I sign any documents?

Do not sign anything you do not understand. By signing a document given to you by a B.I.C.E. agent, you may give up certain rights or agree to return to your country. Contact an immigration lawyer or advocate.

What if a B.I.C.E. agent comes to where I work?

Again, since Sept. 11 it is more likely that the police and B.I.C.E. agents without warrants will come to a workplace looking for undocumented workers or workers suspected of terrorism or of associating with terrorists. In that case, say only that you want to speak to a lawyer or an immigrant advocate. Remember that any information you give to a B.I.C.E. agent before speaking to a lawyer may endanger your case.

What should I do if there is an emergency?

Grab the nearest phone and call 911, the police emergency response number. It is a free call. The police know automatically the location from which you are calling unless you call from a cell phone. You do not have to give your name. Operators or translators are always available to help speakers of the city's major foreign languages.

When is an emergency serious enough to call 911?
- When a crime is happening.
- When lives are in danger.
- When someone has been seriously injured or needs serious medical attention.

What do I do about less urgent complaints like noisy neighbors or people I think are selling drugs?
For these and other nonemergency situations, call the 311 Citizen Service Center. This call center, which opened in March 2003, enables you to call one easy-to-remember number — 311 — to contact most of the city's nonemergency government services, and do things like report a lack of heat or hot water in your apartment or find out when garbage is picked up in your neighborhood. The 311 Citizen Service Center is open 24 hours a day, and help is available in 170 languages.

If I don't speak English, can I still go to the police station to report a minor offense or complaint?
Police stations in precincts where many people do not speak English have bilingual receptionists who also live in the precinct. They will help you with or find someone to help you with any matters relating to Police Department programs and officers. If your problem is something that the Police Department does not deal with, a bilingual receptionist will try to find the right agency to help you, probably by calling 311.

What should I do if I'm raped?
- Rape is a crime that can be committed by a friend, a spouse, a domestic partner or a relative. Call 911 immediately and report it to the police. *The rape was not your fault even if it was done by someone you know and love. Don't be ashamed.*
- Tell the police the details of the attack, no matter how intimate, and anything you remember about your attacker.
- Do not wash or douche. Have a medical exam and an internal gynecological exam as soon as possible. Try to take a police officer with you.
- Get tested for H.I.V. and AIDS and ask the doctor immediately for anti-AIDS drugs.
- Contact an organization that provides services for victims of sexual assault.

need more help?

These organizations provide treatment and counseling to sex abuse victims:

- Bellevue Hospital Center (Page 97)
- Safe Horizon (Page 126)

Sometimes my spouse or my domestic partner slaps me or beats me. Is there anything I should do?
Yes. Physical abuse of spouses, domestic partners and children is illegal in the United States and will result in arrest. Call the police and tell them. Call an immigrant service agency or domestic violence hot line.

■

"**N**ew immigrants are easy to become the crime victim because they are strangers here. I was robbed four times the first two years I was in New York. It made me feel that New York is not a safe place for people to live. I thought that I have to find a way to solve this problem. A police officer told me a list of things I have to do for living safely such as always pay attention around myself and don't walk where there are no people. The crime came down a lot. I hope it can give new immigrants some help."

—*Pak Ping, Chinese, 1999* [14]

PUBLIC ASSISTANCE

"There was what they called home relief at that time. It's welfare today; then it was home relief. They would give you potatoes and butter, and all that stuff, you know. And I remember going down with a neighbor one time to go pick up the potatoes and the cheese. I guess that's where all the cheese boxes came from."

— *Josephine Esposito, daughter of Italian immigrants, remembering the 1930's* [15]

■

If you can't work, if you can't find a job or if your job does not pay enough, public assistance and food stamps may be able to help you pay for food, clothing, rent, gas, electricity and other utilities and household items.

What is public assistance?
Public assistance, often called welfare, refers to many different government programs that provide money and other benefits to people whose household income falls below the federal poverty level set by the government or the New York standard of need.

What is "family assistance," who is eligible, how much can you get and how long do benefits last?
Family assistance is a type of welfare or public assistance that provides cash to needy families. If you arrived in the United States after August 1996 and have lived here for less than five years, you are not eligible. Eligible adults can receive family assistance for a total of 60 months, which do not have to be consecutive.

Benefits depend on household size and income. Your household income is the money earned by all adults in the household. For example, if you live alone and earn $400 a month and the New York standard of need is $500 a month, you qualify for public assistance. But if other people are living in the household and everyone together earns $800 a month, you are above the federal poverty level and do not qualify.

Family assistance benefits are paid twice a month and are to be used for housing, food and clothing. After the 60-month limit is reached, the adult and all members of his or her household are not eligible for any more family assistance benefits.

What is "safety net assistance," who is eligible, how much can you get and how long do benefits last?

Safety net assistance is also a type of welfare or public assistance. It also provides assistance, but for those not eligible for family assistance: single adults, childless couples and new immigrants, regardless of family size, who have been in the United States less than five years. Benefits are also available to people who have exhausted their five-year eligibility for family assistance. Benefits are paid twice monthly and are to be used for housing, food and clothing.

applying for public assistance

A step-by-step guide

1. Go to a community organization where your language is spoken or to your local Human Resources Administration Income Support Center/Job Center and get an information sheet and application. H.R.A. must give you an application. To get the address of your center, call the H.R.A. Infoline, 1-877-HRA-8411 (1-877-472-8411) (Page 111).

2. If you can, fill out the application there and hand it in. If you need help, ask for it rather than making a mistake that could delay your getting benefits. If you leave with the application to fill out later, do so as soon as possible and return it to your local H.R.A. center.

3. Within seven business days, you must be interviewed. The interviewer will ask about your education, training and work history; what types of jobs you can do; your plans for future employment and your child-care needs.

4. An H.R.A. caseworker will visit your apartment to make sure that you live where you say you do and that your standard of living does not seem to be above the federal poverty level. If it is, the caseworker will think you are not telling the truth about your household income.

5. It should not take H.R.A. longer than 30 to 45 days to tell you if you qualify for public assistance, but sometimes it takes longer and you have to keep asking. If you do not get an answer in that time, do not give up. Continue going back to the office and asking what has been decided about your application.

Can I get public assistance?
You may be able to. Different programs have different eligibility guidelines and standards of need. Whether you qualify depends on your immigration status, when you arrived in the United States, your age, your health and your household income.

How can I find out about all the different public assistance benefits?
The **GovBenefits** Web site, **www.govbenefits.gov/GovBenefits/jsp/GovBenefits.jsp**, is a good tool and easy to use. You answer some questions about yourself and GovBenefits supplies a list of government programs you might be eligible for and information about how to apply.

I am undocumented. If I go to the Web site that has information about public assistance benefits, will the government be able to find out where I live and get other information about me?
No. This Web site is completely confidential. You do not have to give your name, phone number, Social Security number or any other information that could be used to identify you.

What should I do if I'm not sure I qualify for a certain public assistance program?
If you know you need a particular kind of aid, like food stamps, but are not sure you qualify, you should always apply. Laws and requirements change all the time, so don't be discouraged if you have to apply more than once and to more than one program.

Can I still work and get public assistance?
Yes, as long as your household income does not go above state and federal eligibility guidelines.

I am undocumented. Can I still get public assistance?
Eligibility requirements differ depending on the type of service you need. Many types of public assistance are available only to immigrants residing legally in the United States. However, certain kinds of assistance like emergency Medicare, pre-natal care and food from pantries or soup kitchens, are available to all New York residents regardless of immigration status. New York City agencies sometimes have to ask about status to determine whether someone is eligible for a particular program. As of this printing, they are not obligated to report your undocumented status to the United States Department of Homeland Security's **Bureau of Immigration and Customs Enforcement,** or **B.I.C.E.** (The department has taken over the duties of what was for many years the Immigration and Naturalization Service, or I.N.S.) However, policies affecting immigrants change often so it is best to check with an

immigration advocacy group listed in the Resource Directory at the back of this guide, or, if you can afford it, with a reputable immigration lawyer.

How do I apply for public assistance?
In New York City, you apply for most public assistance programs through the **Human Resources Administration (H.R.A.)**. Go to the administration's **Refugee and Immigrant Center** (Page 112). If you have trouble speaking English, you can get help in applying for public assistance, Medicaid and Medicare. The staff speaks several languages, including Spanish, Cantonese, Russian, Albanian, Vietnamese, Japanese, Arabic and several African dialects.

Can I apply for public assistance over the phone?
It is very hard because the number is always busy. It is easier and more reliable to go to an H.R.A. Income Support Center to apply.

What will I do at the center where I apply for public assistance?
You will be given an information sheet about your rights to welfare and other public assistance and asked to fill out an application.

Will everything be in English at the center where I apply for public assistance?
No. The information should be in five languages: English, Spanish, Chinese, Russian and Arabic.

How will I know if my application for public assistance has been approved or denied?
You must get a notice in writing. If you were not approved, the notice must explain why. If you are dissatisfied with the decision, you have a right to a fair hearing to contest it. A fair hearing is a chance for you to tell an administrative law judge your side of the story and why you think the refusal was wrong.

If I am denied public assistance benefits, how can I get a hearing to appeal the denial?
Go to an **Office of Administrative Hearings** to ask for a fair hearing. They are at

write it down

When applying for public assistance, make sure you write down any contact you have with the Human Resources Administration. Mark the date you turned in your application for benefits. This could help you get benefits retroactively if H.R.A. does not promptly issue benefits to which you are entitled. Also write down the name of every H.R.A. official and staff member you deal with.

> **Always apply for any kind of public assistance you need even if you think you don't qualify. Laws change often. Don't give up if you have to apply more than once or to more than one program.**

330 West 34th Street, third floor, in Midtown Manhattan, and 14 Boerum Place, first floor, in downtown Brooklyn.

What if I have been getting benefits but am told I am no longer eligible? Will the benefits continue until I get a hearing?

If you ask for a fair hearing within 10 days of the date on the top right corner of the letter from the city telling you that it is going to reduce or cut off your benefits, you have the right to get your welfare, food stamps and Medicaid until the fair hearing takes place.

If I get a hearing and am told I am entitled to benefits, will they start or resume right away?

Not necessarily. Sometimes it takes several months for benefits to arrive.

If I receive public assistance, will I have to do work for the government in return?

Some work requirements, called workfare, can be met through education. Also, you can be exempt from workfare if you are one of the following:

- disabled
- caring for a disabled person
- older than 60
- younger than 16 or younger than 19 and a full-time student
- in your last month of pregnancy
- a mother caring for a new child

How long will I be allowed to care for my baby before I must enroll in workfare so that I can continue to get public assistance?

A mother on public assistance is allowed 12 months in her lifetime to care for newborn children, but no more than 3 months per child. You can apply for an extension to the 3-month rule but not the 12-month rule.

What are food stamps and who is eligible?

Food stamps are used instead of cash to buy food and related items at participating grocery stores and supermarkets. You do not have to be destitute to qualify for food stamps, and many immigrants are eligible for them. To find out if you qualify for food stamps or to learn the location of the 20 food stamp offices in the city, call the **H.R.A.**, 1-877-472-8411 (Page 111), or visit the Human Resources Administration Web site, www.nyc.gov/html/hra/html/serv_foodstamps.html.

need more help?

For the latest public assistance regulations, contact your City Council member. If you don't know who your council member is, call the League of Women Voters Telephone Information Service, 1-212-213-5286 (English only), and tell them your address. Contact these groups for advice on getting public assistance:

- Asian American Legal Defense and Education Fund (A.A.L.D.E.F.) (Page 95)
- Asian Americans for Equality (A.A.F.E.) (Page 96)
- Brooklyn Chinese-American Association (Page 98)
- Charles B. Wang Community Health Center (Page 101)
- Chinatown Manpower Project (Page 102)
- Chinese-American Planning Council (Page 103)
- Church Avenue Merchants Block Association (C.A.M.B.A.) (Page 103)
- City Harvest Hunger Hot Line (Page 105)
- Community Association of Progressive Dominicans (Page 106)
- Forest Hills Community House (Page 109)
- Indochina Sino-American Community Center (Page 112)
- Jacob A. Riis Neighborhood Settlement House (Page 113)
- Legal Aid Society, Civil Division (Page 114)
- Legal Services for New York City (Page 114)
- Lutheran Medical Center (Page 115)
- Medical and Health Research Association of New York City (M.H.R.A.) (Page 117)
- New York Association for New Americans (N.Y.A.N.A.) (Page 118)
- New York City Neighborhood W.I.C. Program (Page 117)
- New York State Office of Temporary and Disability Assistance (Page 124)
- Queens Legal Services (Page 126)
- Southeast Bronx Neighborhood Centers (Page 127)

Can I get food stamps if I am undocumented?
There are different categories of undocumented immigrants, and many are now eligible. It is best to apply at any Human Resources Administration job center or food stamp office.

Will they speak my language at a food stamp office?
The city must provide free translated documents and interpreters in Spanish, Cantonese, Mandarin, Arabic, Russian and some other languages if needed.

Will I actually get food stamps to use in stores?
No, you get an Electronic Benefits Transfer (E.B.T.) card, a plastic debit card that

allows you to get your cash public assistance (welfare) and use food stamps in New York City.

Where will I get my E.B.T. card, and do I have to use it?
The card will be sent to you in the mail. You must use it if you receive welfare and/or food stamps. There are no exemptions or waivers.

Will my E.B.T. card have my picture on it?
Some cards have pictures on them. Others do not. Your card is valid with or without a picture.

Where can I use my E.B.T. card?
At stores and automated teller machines (A.T.M.'s) that show the Quest® sign.

What can I do with my E.B.T. card?
- Use your food stamp or cash assistance account to buy food and other things.
- Get cash from your cash account.
- Get cash back from your account at stores that allow E.B.T. users who buy things there to do so.

Must I pay a fee to use my E.B.T. card to buy food?
No. You should never be charged a fee to make a food purchase. You can make as many food purchases as you want without paying a fee as long as you have enough food stamps in your account.

Must I pay a fee to use my E.B.T. card to get cash from my account?
Not always. Any store, check-cashing service or any A.T.M. that charges a fee has to post a notice telling you that fee, and you should avoid using their services.

How can I find out where I can use my E.B.T. card and which places do not charge a fee?
Call **1-800-289-6739** (English and Spanish) to speak with someone who can tell you the location of A.T.M.'s that do not charge a fee.

How many times can I use my E.B.T. card to get cash without paying a fee?
If you use locations that do not charge a fee, you can get cash for free four times a month. After the fourth time, you will be charged 85 cents each time you get cash that month.

How will I know how much cash assistance and food stamps I have in my E.B.T. account?
Call **Citibank Customer Service's** toll-free number, **1-888-328-6399** (English and

save these numbers

Call Citibank Customer Service, 1-888-328-6399 (English and Spanish), to:

- Report and replace a lost, stolen or damaged E.B.T. card.
- Change your Personal Identification Number, or PIN, for your E.B.T. card.
- Report that you were given the wrong amount of cash assistance.
- Report problems at A.T.M.'s or stores.
- Check your current account balances and last 10 transactions.
- Report mistakes with your account.
- Call 1-800-289-6739 (English and Spanish) for the locations of A.T.M.'s that do not charge a fee.
- Call the New York City Message Center, 1-877-879-4194 (English and Spanish), to hear voice mail messages relating to your public assistance benefits case.

Spanish), for the balance of your food stamps and cash assistance and for a record of your last 10 transactions. Some A.T.M.'s and store machines print your balance on your receipt. *Save all receipts, even if a machine will not give you cash or let you pay with food stamps.*

What should I do if I lose my E.B.T. card or it is stolen?
Call **Citibank Customer Service, 1-888-328-6399**, *immediately*. If you use a touch-tone phone, a recorded voice will answer and ask you to press 1 for English or 2 for Spanish. Order a "stop payment" on your account. If someone uses your card before you order a stop payment, you will lose these benefits and will not be able to get them back.

Can I speak to a live person when I call Citibank Customer Service about my E.B.T. card?
Yes. When you call **1-888-328-6399**, a recorded voice will answer and ask you to press 1 for English or 2 for Spanish. *Do not press any buttons. Ignore all recorded instructions.* After a short wait you will be connected to someone who should help answer your questions.

Are there any other programs besides food stamps that will help me feed my family?
The Special Supplemental Nutrition Program for Women, Infants and Children, known as **W.I.C.**, provides free supplemental foods, nutrition education and referrals for health care to low-income women who are pregnant or breastfeeding and women with children up to 5 years old who are found to be at "nutritional risk," meaning they have certain medical or diet conditions. W.I.C. is available regardless of immigration status.

How do I find out if my children or I are eligible for W.I.C.?
Call New York State's toll-free Department of Health help lines: **Child and Adult Care Food Program, 1-800-942-3858** (English only); **Growing Up Healthy hot line, 1-800-522-5006** (Page 109).

■

"I can still remember going with my mother to the welfare office — the long lines, the hours of waiting and the treatment that was given to my mother. I felt the sense of humiliation in my mother's face. But there was no other way. My father worked as a dishwasher and my mother took care of us seven. I remember my mother waking up early to wait for the mailman on the 1st and the 16th of the month. We always used to get a treat when the check came. Ha ha, but if it didn't come on the day, then we were in trouble. We depended on the food stamps to buy the food and on the money assistance to help pay for the utilities. My sister Eva has worked as a case worker for many years and things have changed so much that I thank God I do not have the need to go on welfare."

— *Georgina Acevedo, daughter of Puerto Rican migrants, remembering the 1960's* [16]

LAWFUL STATUS

"The feelings which overwhelmed me when I was admitted to American citizenship, when I first voted for an American president, when I watched my eldest child being registered in a public school are ineffable. It was the breaking of a dawn after a long, dark night. The very lilt of the word 'America' gives me peace and comfort and hope."

— *Simon Finkelstein, Russian, remembering the 1890's* [17]

■

Whether you hope to live permanently in the United States, which is known as seeking lawful permanent residency or green card status, or have traveled here from abroad for a limited time or specific purpose, i.e., as a tourist or to work, your lawful status or intent is granted by the United States government through various types of visas.

As has been noted several times in the guide, after the events of Sept. 11, 2001, the **United States Department of Homeland Security** took over many functions of what had been the **Immigration and Naturalization Service**, or **I.N.S.** A division of the department, the **United States Citizenship and Immigration Services**, or **U.S.C.I.S.**, which processes benefits for immigrants, will review applications for visas and for Permanent Resident Cards, which are also known as Alien Registration Cards and are commonly called green cards. U.S.C.I.S. will also process applications from immigrants wishing to become United States citizens.

This chapter describes the most common types of visas that allow people from other countries to travel legally in the United States. It also describes a green card, and why it is important, and explains the complex and often years-long process involved in getting such a card. Finally, it describes the lengthy process to become a citizen, which is known as naturalization, some benefits of citizenship, and some sample questions that might appear on the test that must be taken by anyone seeking to become a citizen.

Since Sept. 11, another division of the Department of Homeland Security, the **Bureau of Immigration and Customs Enforcement**, or **B.I.C.E.**, has been tracking immigrants — those with documents and those without — far more closely. Immigration policies change often and are generally becoming much stricter. It is important therefore, to always be aware of whether or not you are in lawful status and the impact that that might have on what you are doing or want to do in the United States.

Libraries and immigrant advocacy groups found in the Resource Directory at the end of this guide have staff members and reference materials that explain many more details about lawful status and its importance and what is involved in getting a green card or becoming a citizen. Since policies affecting immigrants change often, it is always important to consult one of those groups or a reputable immigration lawyer.

What is a visa?

A visa is a permit to apply to enter the United States. If needed, it is normally gotten at an American consulate outside the United States. It gives the purpose of a visit, for business, tourism, etc., and is sometimes valid for several visits to the United States during a specified period of time.

Are all visas alike?

No, all visas are not alike. A **nonimmigrant visa** is given to someone who lives in another country and wishes to come temporarily to the United States for a specific purpose. Nonimmigrant visas are given to tourists, business people, students, temporary workers, diplomats, etc.

An **immigrant visa** is given to someone who intends to live and work permanently in the United States. In most cases, your relative or employer sends an application to the U.S.C.I.S. for you (the beneficiary) to be given the opportunity to become an immigrant. (Some applicants, including workers with extraordinary ability, investors and certain special immigrants, can petition on their own behalf.) Once qualified, you need to apply to become a lawful permanent resident.

Getting an immigrant visa is almost always a very complicated process that usually takes at least 2 years and can take 10 years or more. It is very important that throughout this process you are careful to stay in lawful status because you must be in lawful status to change your status, i.e., from a nonimmigrant to an immigrant visa and permanent resident status.

For many nonimmigrant visa categories, you should apply directly to an American consulate outside the United States. For all immigrant visas except those won through the Diversity Visa Lottery program (explained later in this chapter), you must first apply to the U.S.C.I.S.

The Department of State is responsible for providing visa numbers to foreign nationals interested in immigrating to the United States. To find out more about the **Department of State's visa process** visit its Web site, **http://travel.state.gov/visa _services.html**.

What is a green card?

A green card, also known as a Permanent Resident Card or Alien Registration Card, is a document that proves that an immigrant is allowed to work legally in the United States and that he or she may live here permanently. If you have a green card, you are known as a lawful permanent resident and are in lawful status.

How do I get a green card?

There are two basic processes that you can go through to become a permanent resident, the family-based process and the employment-based process. No matter which process you choose, if you are in the United States you must be in lawful status to adjust that status.

What happens if I am out of lawful status?

If you entered the United States unlawfully, if you entered with permission but did not stay in lawful status or if you worked without permission, you cannot adjust

need more help?

These groups provide reputable legal advice and counseling on immigration matters:

- Asian American Legal Defense and Education Fund (Page 95)
- Caribbean Women's Health Association (Page 99)
- Catholic Charities Office for Immigrant Services (Page 100)
- Catholic Migration Services (Page 100)
- Citizens Advice Bureau (C.A.B.) (Page 104)
- CUNY Law School — Main Street Legal Services, Immigration and Refugee Rights Program (Page 107)
- Emerald Isle Immigration Center (Page 108)
- Hebrew Immigrant Aid Society (H.I.A.S.) (Page 110)
- Hellenic American Neighborhood Action Committee (H.A.N.A.C.) (Page 110)
- Legal Aid Society, Civil Division (Page 114)

> **A green card proves that an immigrant may work legally and live permanently in the United States.**

your status unless you qualify for certain exemptions or waivers. Normally, you would have to leave the United States to apply for an immigrant visa. Be aware you may be barred from re-entry for 3 to 10 years. It is very important, therefore, that you do not travel without seeking help from a reputable immigration lawyer or from an immigrant service provider found in the Resource Directory at the back of this guide.

They can also help determine if you are eligible for an exemption or waiver that will allow you to stay in the United States as you apply for an immigrant visa.

How does the family-based process work?

This is a two-step process:

1. A citizen or lawful permanent resident files **U.S.C.I.S. Form 130, Petition for Alien Relative**, to classify you as someone who is eligible to apply for an immigrant visa.
2. Once that application is approved, you may apply to become a lawful permanent resident when a visa number becomes available.

That sounds simple. Why does it take so long?

The number of available visa numbers is limited, and it may take years until one is available. Therefore, although your first application may be approved quickly, it could take 2 to 10 years or more until a visa number is available and you are granted lawful permanent resident status.

Are there any quicker exceptions to this lengthy process?

Yes, but only if visas are immediately available, and the exceptions apply only to what are known as immediate relatives — the parents, spouses and unmarried children under 21 of United States citizens.

How does the process work for immediate relatives?

If visa numbers are available immediately for these relatives and if they are in the United States, both applications will be filed at essentially the same time. If the relatives wishing to emigrate are outside the United States, the family in the United States files and the application is sent to the United States consulate in the would-be immigrants' country, where they can apply for an immigrant visa to come here. It is best to seek advice from a reputable immigration lawyer or an immigrant service provider in the Resource Directory at the back of this guide.

need more help?

These agencies and groups provide help with citizenship applications and the naturalization process:

- Brooklyn Chinese-American Association (Page 98)
- Caribbean Women's Health Association (C.W.H.A.) (Page 99)
- Catholic Charities Office for Immigration Services (Page 100)
- Catholic Migration Services (Page 100)
- Chinese Immigrant Services (Page 102)
- Church Avenue Merchants Block Association (C.A.M.B.A.) (Page 103)
- Emerald Isle Immigration Center (Page 108)
- Hebrew Immigrant Aid Society (H.I.A.S.) (Page 110)
- Immigration Advocacy Services (Page 112)
- New York Immigration Hot Line, 1-800-566-7636 (Page 122)
- South Bronx Action Group (Page 127)
- Southside Community Mission, Immigration Program (Page 127)
- United Community Centers (Page 128)

For more information on naturalization eligibility, requirements and testing, go to the U.S.C.I.S. Web site: http://uscis.gov.

How does the employment-based process work?

In most cases, this is a three-step process and again it can take several years. When there is not a wait for visas, steps two and three can happen at essentially the same time.

1. An employer applies for labor certification, which could take 2 to 4 years.
2. When certification is granted, **U.S.C.I.S. Form I-140, Petition for Alien Worker Status**, must be filed.
3. After this is granted, an application must be filed to adjust your status to permanent resident status. You can change your status only if you are in lawful status.

Are there any quicker exceptions to this lengthy process?

Yes, if you marry an American citizen, if you are an immediate relative of an American citizen or if you fall under a law known as 245(i), which is not a blanket amnesty but a limited form of relief and applies to people who have been in the United States since Dec. 21, 2000, and filed petitions for lawful permanent resident status on or before April 30, 2001.

I have no one to sponsor me. Is there any way I can get an immigrant visa?

The Diversity Visa Lottery makes 55,000 immigrant visas available each year for people from countries that have low immigration rates to the United States. For details on how the lottery works, go to **www.immigration.gov/graphics/services /residency/divvisa.htm.**

If I am picked in the Diversity Visa Lottery, what does it mean?
It means that you may be able to apply for lawful permanent residency status.

How do I get the application for naturalization, U.S.C.I.S. Form N-400?
Call the **U.S.C.I.S. forms hot line, 1-800-870-3676** (English and Spanish). You can also order it on the Internet at **http://uscis.gov.**

If I apply for citizenship, will I be interviewed or questioned?
Yes. All applicants for citizenship must be interviewed. This is often called the naturalization interview.

When will I be interviewed in connection with my citizenship application?
In New York, interviews are usually scheduled from a year to 18 months after the U.S.C.I.S. gets your N-400 application.

How will I know when and where my citizenship interview is to take place?
You will receive a notice in the mail telling you when and where to go and what you must bring with you.

What if I miss my citizenship interview?
Do not miss your interview. Your application may be delayed for a year or more and could be denied. Seek help from an immigrant service provider in the Resource Directory at the back of this guide.

What will happen at my citizenship interview?
The U.S.C.I.S. representative will:
- Update and review information on the N-400 naturalization application.
- Review your supporting documents, including tax returns for up to the last five years, green card, birth certificate, passport, etc.
- Test your knowledge of United States history and government, and your ability to read, write and speak English, unless you qualify for a disability waiver or an exemption.

What are some reasons that I might want to become a United States citizen?
There are many reasons. Here are some important ones that immigrants have told us about:
- A citizen has the right to vote for elected federal, state and local officials. These are the people who shape the policy of the government, which can affect your daily life in New York City.

- Only a citizen has the right to hold most city, state or federal offices and certain federal, state and city jobs.
- Citizens can leave the United States and live in another country for as long as they want, and travel may be easier for United States citizens in certain countries.
- Citizens can ask for permission to bring more categories of family members to the United States.
- Citizens cannot be prevented from re-entering the United States.
- Citizens cannot be deported.
- Citizens do not have to worry about renewing their green cards every 10 years.
- Citizens who retire to many foreign countries receive all their benefits from Social Security, the retirement and disability program administered by the government. Most lawful permanent residents will receive their benefits for only six months until they return to the United States to live for a full month. There are exceptions, and there are several countries where the United States is not allowed to send Social Security payments. For a list of those exceptions and countries and for more information about the effect of immigration on Social Security benefits, go to **www.ssa.gov.immigration**. The Web site has a multilingual gateway and interpreters.
- Certain countries recognize "dual citizenship." This allows naturalized United States citizens to remain citizens of the country where they were born.
- Citizens are eligible for more public benefits and for more educational scholarships and financial aid.
- In some cases, lawful permanent residents under 18 can become citizens automatically if they live with a parent who is a citizen. This means they will not have to go through the long, complicated naturalization process later on.

Who is eligible to become a United States citizen?

These are some basic requirements:

- You must be at least 18.
- You must be a lawful permanent resident (a green card holder) for at least 5 years. Or be a lawful permanent resident for at least 3 years and be married to a United States citizen for that time and still be married to that same United States citizen when you apply for naturalization.
- You must have lived in the state where you file your citizenship application for at least three months.
- You must have paid taxes for the last 5 years.
- If you are a man between 18 and 26, you must have registered for the Selective Service.
- You must have good moral character, which can be shown through payment of taxes, registration for the Selective Service and lack of conviction for certain crimes.

- You must be able to speak, read, write and understand basic English and to show that you understand the basics of United States history and government. There are exceptions to this for older people and the disabled so you should consult with an immigration service provider in the Resource Directory at the back of this guide.
- You must have been physically in the United States for at least half of the last five years or half of the last three months.
- You cannot have left the United States for more than six months on any trip unless you have traveled with a re-entry permit from the U.S.C.I.S.
- You must intend to live permanently in the United States, although you would be allowed to travel as any other United States citizen can.
- You must disclose if you have been arrested or fined for any offense, including a traffic violation. Again it is advised that you consult a reputable immigration lawyer or an immigration service provider in the Resource Directory at the back of this guide.

What do I need to become a United States citizen?
- Many forms, including Form N-400, Application for Naturalization.
- Two color photographs, 2 inches by 2 inches (three-quarter face profile including right ear).
- Photocopy of green card, front and back.
- Application fee and fingerprint fee. These are payable by money order or personal check to the U.S.C.I.S. Write your name, address and alien registration number on the front of the check. *These fees change periodically, so ask the U.S.C.I.S. or an immigration lawyer or advocacy group what you should pay.*
- Copy of your marriage license if applicable. If you are applying as the spouse of a United States citizen, your spouse's United States passport.
- U.S.C.I.S. Form N-648, Medical Waiver, completed by a psychologist or physician if you have a mental or physical disability that makes it difficult to learn English and/or take the citizenship test.

What is the citizenship test like?
You will probably be asked 10 to 15 questions orally from a list of 100 questions.

Do I have to answer all the citizenship test questions correctly?
No, but you have to answer at least 6 out of 10 correctly.

I have lived and worked hard in the United States a long time, but I have not had the time or education to learn good English or much about the government. Does that mean I can't become a citizen?
Not necessarily. Applicants who are 65 or older and have had lawful permanent

need more help?

These groups provide help preparing for the citizenship test:

- Asian Americans for Equality (A.A.F.E.) (Page 96)
- Catholic Migration Services (Page 100)
- Community Association of Progressive Dominicans (Page 106)
- Forest Hills Community House (Page 109)
- Hellenic American Neighborhood Action Committee (H.A.N.A.C.) (Page 110)
- Indochina Sino-American Community Center (Page 112)
- New York Association for New Americans (N.Y.A.N.A.) (Page 118)
- South Bronx Action Group (Page 127)
- Southside Community Mission, Immigration Program (Page 127)

resident status in the United States for at least 20 years may be given special consideration. If you are 50 or older and have had lawful permanent resident status for at least 20 years, or are 55 or older and have had such status for at least 15 years, you have the option to take the history and government test in your native language.

What are some citizenship test questions I might be asked?
Here are five sample questions:
1. What do the stripes on the United States flag mean?
   They represent the original 13 states, or colonies.
2. What is the Constitution?
   The supreme law of the land.
3. What is the Congress?
   The Senate and the House of Representatives.
4. Why did the Pilgrims come to America?
   For religious freedom.
5. Who was Martin Luther King Jr.?
   A civil rights leader.

How can I study for the citizenship test?
Many libraries and community and immigrant advocacy groups offer tutoring and other help.

What happens if I fail to show that I can read, write and understand basic English or if I fail the citizenship test?
If you fail one or both, the U.S.C.I.S. will schedule you to come back for another

interview. At that time, you will be tested again and if you fail that time, your application for citizenship will be denied.

If my citizenship application is denied because I cannot read and write enough English or because I fail the test, can I reapply, and if so, when?
You may reapply as soon as you want. You should reapply as soon as you have learned enough English or history and government to pass the test(s).

If I think that my citizenship application was unfairly denied, is there anything I can do?
Yes. If your application is denied, you will get a letter that tells you why and also explains how to request a hearing. It will include Form N-336. You must fill out the form and return it to the U.S.C.I.S., along with the right fee, within 30 days after you receive your denial letter. At the time this guide was printed, the fee was $195. Requests sent with the incorrect amount will be returned. It is a good idea to check the U.S.C.I.S. Web site for the correct fee, **http://uscis.gov.**

What happens if I pass my citizenship test?
The U.S.C.I.S. has 120 days to approve or deny your citizenship application. You will be notified by mail if you have been approved and will be told where and when you will be sworn in as a citizen.

I have moved. How do I notify the U.S.C.I.S.?
You must give the **U.S.C.I.S.** your new address within 10 days of moving. You can alert them by telephone but only in the case of naturalization applications. The phone number is **1-800-375-5283** (English and Spanish). For legal permanent residence and other applications you must complete Form AR-11, a change of address form, and send it to every immigration office where you have filed applications or petitions. Send these forms by certified mail, return-receipt requested. And be sure to make copies for your records.

Is there any way I can check on my citizenship application?
Yes. Call the **U.S.C.I.S. National Customer Service Center, 1-800-375-5283** (English and Spanish). If you have a receipt number for an application or a petition filed at a U.S.C.I.S. service center, you can check the status of your case at the U.S.C.I.S. Web site, **http://uscis.gov.**

My children were not born in the United States. How do they become citizens?
A child younger than 18 who was not born in this country is usually eligible for citizenship when a parent becomes a citizen if the child is living with the parent and the child is a lawful permanent resident. For information regarding older children

and for answers to more specific questions regarding the citizenship of children, seek help from a reputable immigration lawyer or from an immigration service provider in the Resource Directory at the back of this guide.

Is there anything I should get to prove that my children are citizens?
A Certificate of Citizenship or a United States passport.

■

"I came because of the new religious and autocratic regime in Iran. The experience was exciting, difficult and at times unpleasant. After assimilating to the new culture and enjoying the lifestyle, I realized that I had become an American. I had gotten used to the freedom, the amenities, the people and the eclectic culture. Becoming an American citizen was a very big step for me. I asked myself why I should become a citizen. The immediate answer was convenience — carrying an American passport, job opportunities and so forth. But I have come to realize that there are more meaningful advantages. It is being part of a democracy where one can make a difference. I can contribute in preserving the American culture and ideology and to ensure a happy life for my children."

— *Kaynam Hedayat, Iranian, 2002* [18]

DOCUMENTS

Throughout this guide are references to documents that classify someone's eligibility to apply for a visa, which are essential for every immigrant to the United States, and to other documents, like phone cards, that make life easier and help you to pay less for goods and services. This chapter describes the documents that you should have and carry with you at all times.

Visas

A visa is a permit to apply to enter the United States.

A nonimmigrant visa is given to someone who lives in another country and wishes to come to the United States temporarily for a specific purpose. Nonimmigrant visas are given to people like tourists, business people, students, temporary workers, diplomats, etc.

An immigrant visa is given to someone who intends to live and work permanently in the United States and is usually a step in the process of getting a Permanent Resident or Alien Registration Card, commonly known as a green card. Most people get immigrant visas through applications filed either by relatives or prospective employers. The process can take 2 to 10 years or more and is described in more detail on page 78 in the Lawful Status chapter.

Some people may be allowed to petition on their own behalf, including abused spouses of United States citizens, juveniles who have been abused or abandoned, or aliens of extraordinary ability.

Employment Authorization Document (E.A.D.)

A document that shows you are authorized to work in the United States even if you are not a citizen or are not a lawful permanent resident who has been granted a Permanent Resident Card, also known as an Alien Registration Card and commonly called a green card.

Green Card

Certifies that you are a lawful permanent resident of the United States and are entitled to live and work here. To get a green card you must go through a very long and complicated process that could take from 2 to 10 years or more. That process is described below and in the Lawful Status chapter. Because the process is so complex, it is important that you have the help of either a reputable immigration lawyer, or one of the immigrant advocacy groups listed in the Resource Directory at the end of this guide.

These are the basic steps to getting a green card:

1. A relative (using **U.S.C.I.S. Form I-130, Petition for Alien Relative**) or an employer (using **U.S.C.I.S. Form I-140, Petition for Alien Worker**) files an immigrant petition for you with the U.S.C.I.S. to classify you as someone who may apply for an immigrant visa. Once an immigrant visa is available and you are in the United States and in lawful status, you may apply to adjust that status to that of a lawful permanent resident. If you are outside the United States, the approved petition will be forwarded to the American consulate abroad for completion of the process for you to obtain an immigrant visa.

2. You are given an immigrant visa number, even if you are already in the United States.

3. If you are already in the United States, you may apply to adjust your status to that of a legal permanent resident with **U.S.C.I.S. Form I-485, Application to Register Permanent Residence or to Adjust Status.** If you are outside the United States, go to the local United States consulate to complete processing for an immigrant visa.

WEB SITE: www.immigration.gov/graphics/howdoi/LPReligibility.htm.

PHONE: National Customer Service Center, 1-800-375-5283 (English and Spanish).

Driver's License

In most cases, you can drive in New York if you have a valid driver's license from another country. In fact, the New York State Department of Motor Vehicles (D.M.V.) recommends that you do not apply for a New York license as long as you are still a legal resident of the country that issued your license.

If you have a driver's license from another country and apply for a New York State license, you must do these things:

1. Pass a written test.
2. Take a five-hour course.
3. Pass a road test.
4. Show a green card.
5. Show a Social Security card or a letter from the Social Security Administration stating why you do not qualify for a card.

> ❝ **In most cases a valid driver's license from another country allows you to drive legally in New York.** ❞

6. Surrender your foreign driver's license, which will be destroyed by the D.M.V. within 60 days unless you ask that it be saved. If you need to get your foreign driver's license back, ask for it at the local D.M.V. office where you applied.

If you are applying for a driver's license for the first time, you must be at least 16 years old and do these things:
1. Apply for a learner's permit.
2. Pay the application fee and driver's license fee.
3. Pass a vision test and written test.
4. Practice for your road test.
5. Schedule the road test either by phone or online.
6. Pass the test.

WEB SITE: www.nydmv.state.ny.us/license.htm
PHONE: Manhattan, Bronx, 1-212-645-5550 (English and Spanish); Brooklyn, Queens, Staten Island, 1-718-966-6155 (English and Spanish).

Nondriver Photo Identification Card

If you do not have a driver's license, you may apply to the D.M.V. for a nondriver photo identification card. This card contains the same personal information, photograph, signature and protection against alteration and fraud as a driver's license. To get this card, you must provide proof of identity and date of birth.

WEB SITE: www.nydmv.state.ny.us/license.htm
PHONE: Manhattan, Bronx, 1-212-645-5550 (English and Spanish); Brooklyn, Queens, Staten Island, 1-718-966-6155 (English and Spanish).

Social Security Card

The application form for a Social Security card is known as an SS-5. It can be used by anyone who has never had a card, needs a replacement card or has changed his or her name. To get a form, call the Social Security Administration or visit its Web site.

Instructions with the form explain how to fill it out and what supporting documents are required. After you have completed the application, take or mail it, along with the original or certified copies of supporting documents, to the nearest Social Security office. Your original documents will be returned quickly. Once the Social Security office has everything it needs, it will mail you a card in about two weeks.

WEB SITE: www.ssa.gov
PHONE: 1-800-772-1213 (English and Spanish).

Electronic Benefits Transfer (E.B.T.) Card

An E.B.T. card is a plastic debit card that allows you to get cash public assistance (welfare) and use food stamps in New York City. You can apply for the card at any of the city Human Resources Administration job centers or food stamp offices. It will be sent to you in the mail, and you must use it to obtain welfare and/or food stamps.

WEB SITE: www.nyc.gov/html/hra/html/serv_foodstamps.html

PHONE: 1-877-472-8411 (English, Spanish, Cantonese and Mandarin) (Page 111).

Automated Teller Machine (A.T.M.) Card

You can get an A.T.M. card when you open a checking or savings account at a bank or credit union. The card allows you to perform banking services, like making deposits and getting cash, at an A.T.M. instead of going to a bank.

When you apply for a card, you will be asked to choose a secret personal identification number or PIN. Then, every time you put the card into an A.T.M., you will be asked to punch in your PIN before you are allowed to withdraw cash or do other banking services.

Do not allow other people to handle your A.T.M. card and do not tell other people your PIN.

Call your bank or credit union or visit its Web site to find out how to get an A.T.M. card.

MetroCard

You must use a MetroCard instead of cash to ride the subways. You can use either a MetroCard or cash to ride buses operated by New York City Transit. With a Metro-Card, your ride can cost less than the current fare for a subway or local bus ride. You also get an automatic free transfer between subways and buses and between bus lines. If you are 65 or older, or are physically or mentally disabled, you can apply for a reduced fare MetroCard, which allows you to ride for half fare.

The MetroCard system works like this: You pay a certain amount of money, which is coded onto the card, and every time you swipe the card through a subway turnstile or bus machine, the amount of the fare is deducted. When all of the money is deducted, it is time to refill your card or buy a new one.

You can buy MetroCards at subway station token booths, MetroCard vending machines, MetroCard buses and vans and at stores that display the MetroCard sign.

You can spend various amounts on a pay-per-ride (or regular) MetroCard. If you spend more than a certain amount, you will receive a bonus that will allow you to get extra rides.

You can also choose from several unlimited ride MetroCards, which cost different amounts and allow you unlimited rides within a certain time.

WEB SITE: www.mta.nyc.us/metrocard

PHONE: 1-212-638-7622 (English, Spanish, Cantonese and Mandarin)

Phone Card

If you do not have a telephone or long-distance service where you live or if you use pay telephones, it is a good idea to buy a phone card. This card allows you to pay in advance to make long-distance phone calls to many places.

You can buy the cards in many places, including bodegas, supermarkets and convenience stores. Make sure that any phone card you buy has a valid customer service number.

Generally, you pay a specific dollar amount for the card or buy a specific number of minutes.

Most prepaid phone cards come with a toll-free access telephone number and a personal identification number (PIN). To make a phone call, dial the access number and punch in your PIN. A recording will tell you to enter the number of the caller you are trying to reach.

The total cost of the call is deducted from the value of the card. You will be told how many minutes — or how many units — remain on the card.

If you have used all the minutes on your card and cannot replenish it by buying more minutes, you will have to buy a new card.

It is important to shop around and make sure you are getting a fair number of minutes for the amount of money you are spending on a card because some companies charge too much for their cards.

The Federal Trade Commission advises that you always ask these four questions before buying a phone card:

1. What is the *connection fee* for each call?
2. Is there a *service fee*?
3. Is there a *maintenance fee*?
4. Is there an *expiration date*? Do not buy a card that has a chance of expiring before you have used all the minutes.

RESOURCE DIRECTORY

Most New Yorkers will tell you that in this city, it's not what you know but whom you know. The truth, especially for newcomers, is: It's both.

There is so much to learn about the city itself: its ethnic neighborhoods, bus and subway routes, public school system, the list goes on and on. What you need to know — and what you want to know — can often seem overwhelming. They aren't.

In the text of the guide, page numbers follow the names of many agencies, groups and service providers and refer you to a page in this section, the Resource Directory. The Resource Directory provides a detailed profile of those agencies, groups and service providers that have been reviewed by fellow immigrants and found to be especially helpful and reliable.

Above each profile are symbols that refer to the issues that the resource agency, group or service provider deals with, like housing or child care.

The name of each resource agency, group or service provider is followed by its most common abbreviation.

Each profile then details the location(s) of the resource agency, group or service provider, its telephone and fax numbers, e-mail and Web addresses, services offered, language(s) spoken, and documents or other requirements, if any. A language listing followed by the symbol (P) means that the agency, group or service provider offers printed material in that language.

The Resource Directory is a very handy reference, so you might want to carry the guide as you make your way around New York City.

Key to Resource Directory symbols:

HOUSING

LABOR AND EMPLOYMENT

CHILD CARE

EDUCATION

MONEY

HEALTH CARE AND INSURANCE

SAFETY

PUBLIC ASSISTANCE

LAWFUL STATUS

Alianza Dominicana, Inc.
2410 Amsterdam Avenue, 4th Floor, New York, N.Y. 10033
Phone: 1-212-740-1960; Fax: 1-212-740-1967
Web site: http://www.alianzadom.org/index.html

What can I get help with?
- English classes, G.E.D. and computer literacy (Spanish).
- After-school tutoring and summer youth program.
- Family-focused immigrant assistance.
- Community-based health services; getting health insurance coverage.
- Bilingual/bicultural services to people affected/infected with H.I.V. or AIDS.

Whom do you help? Everyone. **In what languages can you help?** Spanish (P). **What must I bring?** ID is helpful, but not required. **Where else are you located?** 1 site in the Bronx; 10 in Manhattan. Call ahead.

Archdiocese of New York, Superintendent of Schools
1011 First Avenue, New York, N.Y. 10022
Phone: 1-212-371-1000

What can I get help with?
- Getting lists of Catholic schools in Manhattan, the Bronx and Staten Island.
- Learning how to set up appointments with individual schools and what to expect at an open house.

Whom do you help? Everyone. **In what languages can you help?** Spanish (P). **What must I bring?** Nothing. **Where else are you located?** Only location above.

Asian American Legal Defense and Education Fund (A.A.L.D.E.F.)
99 Hudson Street, New York, N.Y. 10013
Phone: 1-212-966-5932, 1-212-966-6030; Fax: 1-212-966-4303
Web site: http://www.aaldef.org

What can I get help with?
- Free advice on immigration laws and family law.
- Help with naturalization applications.
- Government benefits.

- Employment discrimination and labor rights.
- Police misconduct.

Whom do you help? Everyone. Legal services by appointment only. **In what languages can you help?** Chinese (P) (Cantonese, Mandarin, Toisanese), Bangla, Hindi, Korean, Tagalog and Urdu speakers call 1-212-966-5932 or 1-212-966-6030. **What must I bring?** Call ahead for appointment and to learn which records, documents and legal papers to bring. **Where else are you located?** Only location above.

Asian Americans for Equality (A.A.F.E.)
277 Grand Street, 3rd Floor, New York, N.Y. 10002
Phone: 1-212-680-1374; Fax: 1-212-680-1815; E-mail: info@aafe.org
Web site: http://www.aafe.org

What can I get help with?
- Basic housing rights and responsibilities; housing legal assistance and representation; homeownership counseling and access to affordable mortgages.
- Government benefits and health care counseling.
- Citizenship counseling and civics classes.
- Small business counseling and access to affordable financing.
- Computer literacy. Fully equipped computer center offers a variety of programs.

Whom do you help? Everyone. **In what languages can you help?** Spanish (P), Chinese (P) (Cantonese, Mandarin), Bengali, Korean. **What must I bring?** Depends on service needed. **Where else are you located?** 5 sites in downtown Manhattan; 1 in Queens. Call ahead.

Banco Popular
Phone: 1-800-377-0800; Web site: http://www.bancopopular.com

What can I get help with?
- Savings and checking accounts, credit, insurance, investments, loans and mortgages.

Whom do you help? Everyone. **In what languages can you help?** Spanish (P). **What must I bring?** For regular personal banking, at least two forms of ID: United States or non-United States passport, nonresident registration card with photo, naturalization certificate with photo, Armed Forces ID card, driver's license and/or major bank or credit card. **Where else are you located?** 5 sites in the Bronx; 9 in Brooklyn; 10 in Manhattan; 3 in Queens. Call ahead.

Bellevue Hospital Center
462 First Avenue, New York, N.Y. 10016
Phone: 1-212-562-4141; Web site: http://www.nyc.gov/bellevue

What can I get help with?
- Asthma, diabetes, nutrition, smoking cessation, stress management and weight management.
- Health screenings, classes and support groups.
- Rape clinic.
- Extended care for people who require ongoing medical attention.
- Preventive and primary care for all family members.
- Routine dental examinations and dental care; treatment for mouth and gum diseases.

Whom do you help? Everyone. **In what languages can you help?** Spanish (P), Chinese (Cantonese, Mandarin), Bengali, Polish, French and Russian are most popular; 135 languages available; interpreters on-site. **What must I bring?** Insurance card if available. **Where else are you located?** 5 sites in the Bronx; 6 in Brooklyn; 5 in Manhattan; 2 in Queens; 1 in Staten Island. Call ahead.

Bethex Federal Credit Union
20 East 179th Street, Bronx, N.Y. 10453
Phone: 1-718-299-9100; Fax: 1-718-294-4950; Web site: http://www.bethexfcu.org

What can I get help with?
- Checking and savings accounts; loans.

Whom do you help? Everyone. **In what languages can you help?** Spanish (P) speakers available at every branch. **What must I bring?** $20 ($10 membership fee and $10 deposit for new savings account). Proof of residence (phone or utility bill), photo ID and Social Security card or green card. **Where else are you located?** 3 sites in the Bronx; 1 in Manhattan. Call ahead.

The Bronx Defenders
860 Courtlandt Avenue, Bronx, N.Y. 10451
Phone: 1-718-838-7878; Fax: 1-718-665-0100; E-mail: shaynak@bronxdefenders.org
Web site: http://www.bronxdefenders.org

What can I get help with?
- Legal counsel for those charged with crimes; civil legal services.
- Disability and employment suspension issues.
- Substance addiction.
- Social services referrals.

Whom do you help? Those arrested or fearing arrest for crimes in the Bronx. (Not necessary to be a Bronx resident.) **In what languages can you help?** Spanish (P). **What must I bring?** Varies with service sought. **Where else are you located?** Only location above.

Brooklyn Chinese-American Association
5002 Eighth Avenue, 2nd Floor, Brooklyn, N.Y. 11220
Phone: 1-718-438-9312; Fax: 1-718-438-8303

What can I get help with?
- Citizenship counseling.
- Medicaid and food stamps.
- Translation services.
- Prekindergarten, day care, after-school and summer programs; senior citizens center.
- English, business and computer classes; Chinese language classes for children.
- Health education.

Whom do you help? Only legal residents of Brooklyn. **In what languages can you help?** Chinese (P) (Cantonese, Mandarin). **What must I bring?** Nothing. **Where else are you located?** 4 sites in Brooklyn. Call ahead.

Bushwick Cooperative Federal Credit Union
1475 Myrtle Avenue, Brooklyn, N.Y. 11237
Phone: 1-718-418-8232; Fax: 1-718-418-8252; E-mail: bushwickfcu@rbscc.org

What can I get help with?
- Checking and savings accounts; loans; financial literacy.

Whom do you help? Everyone. **In what languages can you help?** Spanish. **What must I bring?** Two forms of ID, at least one with photo; proof of address; Social Security card; insurance statement or pay stub. **Where else are you located?** Only location above.

Cabrini Immigrant Services
139 Henry Street, New York, N.Y. 10002
Phone: 1-212-791-4590; Fax: 1-212-791-4592

What can I get help with?
- Completing forms and applications; getting necessary referrals.
- English classes (requires commitment of one day a week).
- Free food.

Whom do you help? Everyone. **In what languages can you help?** Spanish (P), Chinese (P) (Mandarin). **What must I bring?** Nothing. All services are free. Register for classes in August and/or December. **Where else are you located?** Only location above.

Caribbean Women's Health Association (C.W.H.A.)
123 Linden Boulevard, Brooklyn, N.Y. 11226
Phone: 1-718-826-2942; Fax: 1-718-826-2948; Web site: http://www.cwha.org

What can I get help with?
- Legal representation in immigration courts and familiy unification and deportation hearings.
- Citizenship applications and test preparation.
- Community health; H.I.V. and AIDS services; maternal and child health and W.I.C.

Whom do you help? Everyone. **In what languages can you help?** Spanish, Haitian (P), Creole (P), French (P). For other languages, translator can be available. Call ahead. **What must I bring?** Small fees for legal assistance. Call ahead. **Where else are you located?** 2 other sites in Brooklyn; 2 in Queens. Call ahead.

Cathay Bank
Phone 1-800-9CATHAY (1-800-922-8429)

What can I get help with?
- Checking and savings accounts; I.R.A.'s and C.D.'s; auto, home equity and

mortgage loans; foreign currency exchange. **Whom do you help?** Everyone. **In what languages can you help?** Chinese (Cantonese, Mandarin) (P) **What must I bring?** At least two forms of ID: United States or non-United States passport, nonresident registration card with photo, naturalization certificate with photo, Armed Forces ID card, driver's license and/or major bank or credit card. **Where else are you located?** 1 site in Brooklyn; 1 in Manhattan; 1 in Queens. Call ahead.

Catholic Charities Office for Immigrant Services
1011 First Avenue, 12th Floor; New York, N.Y. 10022
Phone: 1-212-419-3700, 1-800-566-7636 (for assistance in languages listed below)
Fax: 1-212-751-3197; Web site: http://www.catholiccharities.org

What can I get help with?
- Legal help on immigration and refugee resettlement issues; legal representation for detained asylum seekers.
- Naturalization and citizenship documents.

In what languages can you help? Spanish (P), Chinese (Mandarin) (P), Arabic, French, Haitian Creole, Italian, Japanese, Korean, Polish, Punjabi, Russian, Serbo-Croatian, Turkish and Urdu. **Whom do you help?** Everyone. **What must I bring?** $50 service fee, though people with financial problems will not be turned away. Call ahead. **Where else are you located?** Outreach sites (monthly): Bronx and Staten Island. Call ahead.

Catholic Migration Services
1258 65th Street, Brooklyn, N.Y. 11219
Phone: 1-718-236-3000; Fax: 1-718-256-9707; E-mail: migration@aol.com
Web site: www.catholicimmigration.org

What can I get help with?
- Legal help with immigration issues.
- Evening English classes (all levels); citizenship classes.
- Training in basic computer skills, culinary arts, residential and workplace cleaning.

Whom do you help? Everyone. **In what languages can you help?** Spanish (P), Albanian, Greek, Italian, Haitian Creole and Polish. Call ahead. **What must I bring?** Small fee for services. Call ahead. **Where else are you located?** 1 site in Queens.

Charles B. Wang Community Health Center
268 Canal Street, New York, N.Y. 10013
Phone: 1-212-379-6998; Fax: 1-212-379-6930

What can I get help with?
- Primary care, women's health, obstetrics, gynecology, cancer screening, internal medicine, pediatrics, pediatric cardiology, adolescent care, allergy, dental care, eye care, urology, acupuncture, specialty care, mental health, health education, disease prevention.
- Child Health Plus and Family Health Plus enrollment.
- Social services, W.I.C.

Whom do you help? Everyone. **In what languages can you help?** Chinese (Cantonese, Mandarin, Toisanese, Shanghainese and Taiwanese). Call ahead. **What must I bring?** Proof of Medicaid and third-party insurance coverage; proof of ability to pay like pay stubs and tax receipts; whatever documentation you have. Sliding scale fees of $20 to $60 are charged based on ability to pay. **Where else are you located?** 1 other site in Lower Manhattan; 1 in Queens.

Chase
Phone: 1-800-CHASE24 (1-800-242-7324); Web site: http://www.chase.com

What can I get help with?
- Checking and savings accounts, credit cards, investments, insurance, mortgages and other loans.

Whom do you help? United States citizens with a United States postal address and valid Social Security number. **In what languages can you help?** ServiceLine (English, Spanish; from 212, 516, 585, 914, 718 only) 935-9999. ServiceLine (English, Chinese) 1-212-809-6464. ServiceLine (bilingual Korean) 1-212-809-3737. **What must I bring?** Proof of date of birth, mother's maiden name, employment information, driver's license or state ID number. **Where else are you located?** Call for nearest branch.

Chinatown Manpower Project, Inc.
70 Mulberry Street, New York, N.Y. 10003
Phone: 1-212-571-1690; Fax: 1-212-571-1686; Web site: www.cmpny.org

What can I get help with?
- English, citizenship and job-skills development classes.
- Vocational training in computerized bookkeeping and accounting, basic office technology and computer operation.
- Entrepreneurial training, financial packaging, business consultation and technical assistance to individuals and small businesses.
- Benefits counseling.

Whom do you help? New York City residents. **In what languages can you help?** Chinese (Cantonese, Mandarin). **What must I bring?** Green card or Social Security card; proof of address. Call ahead. **Where else are you located?** 1 site in Brooklyn; 1 other site in Lower Manhattan. Call ahead.

Chinese Immigrant Services
133-54 41st Avenue, 4th Floor, Flushing, N.Y. 11355
Phone: 1-718-353-0195; Fax: 1-718-359-5065

What can I get help with?
- Chinese immigrant support groups and groups for young people.
- Counseling and mediation for families with conflicts.
- Information, referral and advice on various social and legal issues.
- English classes and programs about United States culture and institutions.

Whom do you help? New York City residents. **In what languages can you help?** Chinese (P) (Cantonese, Mandarin). **What must I bring?** Nothing. **Where else are you located?** Only location above.

Chinese Staff and Workers' Association
15 Catherine Street, 2nd Floor, New York, N.Y. 10038
Phone: 1-212-619-7979; Fax: 1-212-374-1506

What can I get help with?
- Legal advice on regulations and labor standards in restaurants, garment and

service industries; worker education and leadership development.
Whom do you help? Everyone. **In what languages can you help?** Chinese (P) (Cantonese, Mandarin, Fukienese). **What must I bring?** Nothing. **Where else are you located?** 1 site in Brooklyn. Call ahead.

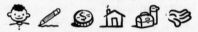

Chinese-American Planning Council (C.P.C.)
150 Elizabeth Street, New York, N.Y. 10012
Phone: 1-212-941-0920; Fax: 1-212-966-8581; Web site: http://www.cpc-nyc.org

What can I get help with?
- Employment training for apparel, hotel, clerical and multimedia businesses.
- Adult literacy classes and transitional employment for mature workers.
- Case management and counseling services for those affected by Sept. 11, 2001.
- Child Health Plus, Family Health Plus, food stamps and other benefits.
- Fair housing.
- Asian child care resources and referrals and family services.
- Health services to parents of the developmentally disabled.
- Help with H.I.V., AIDS and drug prevention.

Whom do you help? Everyone, but mainly Asian immigrants and Asian-Americans living in Chinatown, the Lower East Side, Flushing and Sunset Park. **In what languages can you help?** Chinese (P) (Cantonese, Mandarin). **What must I bring?** ID is useful. **Where else are you located?** 11 day care centers, 2 senior centers, 2 walk-in case management sites, 1 employment and training site and 1 youth employment program site in Manhattan; branch offices, 1 employment and training site and 3 youth services sites in Brooklyn; branch offices, 1 day care center and 1 senior center in Queens. Call ahead.

Church Avenue Merchants Block Association, Inc. (C.A.M.B.A.)
1720 Church Avenue, 2nd Floor, Brooklyn, N.Y. 11226
Phone: 1-718-287-2600; Fax: 1-718-287-0857; Web site: http://www.camba.org

What can I get help with?
- Advice, representation and emergency assistance for those facing eviction and denial of benefits.
- Immigration legal services; services for refugees and those seeking asylum; naturalization and citizenship workshops.
- Job training and placement.
- English and computer classes.

Whom do you help? Everyone. Must be documented for job-placement services. **In what languages can you help?** Spanish (P), Albanian (P), Russian (P), French, Arabic, Bosnian, Haitian Creole. **What must I bring?** Specific documents needed for job placement and refugee services. Call ahead. **Where else are you located?** 13 sites in Brooklyn. Call ahead. **Legal services:** 885 Flatbush Avenue, 2nd Floor, Brooklyn, N.Y. 11226, Phone 1-718-287-0010. **Job placement and refugee services:** 2211 Church Avenue, Room 202, Brooklyn, N.Y. 11226, Phone 1-718-282-0108.

Citibank
Phone: 1-800-627-3999; Web site: http://www.citibank.com

What can I get help with?
■ Checking and savings accounts, insurance, investment, credit cards, mortgages and other loans.

Whom do you help? Everyone. **In what languages can you help?** Spanish (P). **What must I bring?** At least two forms of ID: United States or non-United States passport, non-resident registration card with photo, naturalization certificate with photo, Armed Forces ID card, driver's license and/or major bank or credit card. **Where else are you located?** Call to find nearest branch.

Citizens Advice Bureau (C.A.B.)
2054 Morris Avenue, Bronx, N.Y. 10453
Phone: 1-718-365-0910; Fax: 1-718-365-0697; Web site: http://www.cabny.org

What can I get help with?
■ Day care, after-school and summer camp programs for children and teens, and senior centers (including food, exercise and games).
■ Advice on immigration, citizenship and other legal issues.
■ E.S.O.L. and civics classes.
■ Employment assistance.
■ Eviction prevention, counseling for homeless people and families.
■ Health insurance advice.
■ Counseling and case management for people with AIDS.

Whom do you help? Everyone. **In what languages can you help?** Spanish (P). **What must I bring?** Nothing. **Where else are you located?** More than 20 sites throughout the Bronx. Call ahead.

City Harvest Hunger Hot Line
575 Eighth Avenue, 4th Floor, New York, N.Y. 10018
Phone: 1-917-351-8700; Fax: 1-917-351-8720; Web site: http://www.cityharvest.org

What can I get help with?
■ Emergency food programs.
Whom do you help? Everyone in need. **In what languages can you help?** Spanish. **What must I bring?** ID and proof of address. Call ahead. **Where else are you located?** Serves hundreds of agencies in all five boroughs.

City University of New York (CUNY)
1114 Avenue of the Americas, New York, N.Y. 10036
Phone: 1-212-997-CUNY (2869); Web site: http://www.cuny.edu/

What can I get help with?
■ English classes to prepare for CUNY admission and T.O.E.F.L. exam.
■ Undergraduate and graduate programs at all colleges in liberal arts and sciences, business, health sciences, public affairs and community and social services, engineering, architecture and related technologies, law, library science, teacher education.
■ Advice on various programs and institutions.
■ Financial assistance.
■ Honors and weekend programs.
■ Continuing education and professional development certificate programs.
Whom do you help? Everyone. **In what languages can you help?** Varies by campus. **What must I bring?** Completed application form, $40 fee, translated secondary school diploma/certificate and/or transcripts. Exact immigration status and visa, current or expired. T.O.E.F.L. scores and SAT scores if applicable. T.O.E.F.L. exam determines language ability to study at CUNY. **Where else are you located?** 20 campuses: 4 in Brooklyn, 3 in the Bronx, 7 in Manhattan, 5 in Queens, 1 in Staten Island.

Civilian Complaint Review Board (C.C.R.B.)
40 Rector Street, 2nd Floor, New York, N.Y. 10006
Phone: 1-212-442-8833 or 1-800-341-2272; Fax: 1-212-442-9109;
Web site: http://www.nyc.gov/ccrb

What can I get help with?
■ Complaints against New York City Police Department officers for excessive or unnecessary force, abuse of authority, discourtesy or offensive language.
Whom do you help? Everyone. **In what languages can you help?** Chinese (P) (Cantonese, Mandarin), Spanish (P), Arabic (P), French, Russian (P), Polish (P), Korean (P) and Italian. For other languages, state the requested language and your phone number. Translator will call back. **What must I bring?** As much information as you have about an incident. C.C.R.B. will ask for date, time, location and a detailed description of the incident and the officers involved. Other useful information includes: license plate numbers, an arrest number, a court docket number and telephone numbers. You do not need to know the name or badge number of the officer(s) involved. **Where else are you located?** Only location above.

Community Association of Progressive Dominicans
3940 Broadway, 2nd Floor, New York, N.Y. 10032
Phone: 1-212-781-5500; Fax: 1-212-927-6089; Web site: http://home.att.net/~acdpinc/

What can I get help with?
■ Legal representation and advice about eviction and landlord issuse and low-income housing.
■ English, computer and citizenship classes and summer camp.
■ Counseling and help filling out applications for food stamps and public assistance.
Whom do you help? Must be documented and have low income. **In what languages can you help?** Spanish (P). **What must I bring?** Green card and/or employment authorization/working papers; family size requirements to qualify for housing only. Call ahead. **Where else are you located?** 1 site in the Bronx; 5 in Upper Manhattan. Call ahead.

Community Healthcare Network, Bronx Center
975 Westchester Avenue, Bronx, N.Y. 10459
Phone: 1-718-991-9250/51; Fax: 1-212-991-3829; Web site: http://www.chnnyc.org

What can I get help with?
- Primary medical care for adults, children and those with H.I.V.; family planning and prenatal care; school physicals; asthma screening; mental health care; nutritional services; social services.

Whom do you help? Everyone. **In what languages can you help?** Spanish (P), Chinese (P) at Lower Manhattan; French, Haitian Creole available at Brooklyn sites. **What must I bring?** Pay stub or letter from employer indicating wages and need for reduced fee or insurance card. Teenagers need ID. **Where else are you located?** 4 sites in Brooklyn; 3 in Manhattan; 1 in Queens. Call ahead.

CUNY Law School
Main Street Legal Services, Immigration and Refugee Rights Program
65-21 Main Street, Flushing, N.Y. 11367
Phone: 1-718-340-4300; Fax: 1-718-340-4478; Web site: http://www.law.cuny.edu

What can I get help with?
- Citizenship and immigration legal services, including asylum and family petitions; domestic violence issues; elder law.

Whom do you help? Everyone. **In what languages can you help?** Spanish, Chinese (Cantonese) and Bengali. Depends on the students enrolled each semester. Call ahead. **What must I bring?** Call ahead. **Where else are you located?** Only location above.

Delgado Travel
7908 Roosevelt Avenue, Jackson Heights, N.Y. 11372
Phone: 1-718-426-0500; Fax: 1-718-397-0347

What can I get help with?
- Money-wiring; shipping packages; international phone calls; travel arrangements.

Whom do you help? Everyone. **In what languages can you help?** Spanish (P). **What must**

I bring? Depends on services sought. **Where else are you located?** 4 sites in the Bronx; 4 in Brooklyn; 5 in Manhattan; 12 in Queens. Call ahead.

The Door
121 Avenue of the Americas, New York, N.Y. 10013
Phone: 1-212-941-9090; Fax: 1-212-941-0714; Web site: http://www.door.org

What can I get help with?
- Comprehensive youth development services, health care, counseling, education, legal services, the arts and recreation.

Whom do you help? Any New York City resident from 12 to 21. **In what languages can you help?** Spanish and Chinese (Cantonese and Mandarin). Web site available in English, Spanish and Chinese. **What must I bring?** Nothing. **Where else are you located?** Only location above.

Emerald Isle Immigration Center
59-26 Woodside Avenue, Woodside, N.Y. 11377
Phone: 1-718-478-5502; Fax: 1-718-446-3727; Web site: http://www.eiic.org

What can I get help with?
- Immigration and other legal services, paperwork, green cards, citizenship exam preparation and referrals.
- Job search and placement.

Whom do you help? Everyone. **In what languages can you help?** Spanish, French. **What must I bring?** Depends on services sought. **Where else are you located?** 1 site in the Bronx. Call ahead.

Flatbush Development Corporation
1616 Newkirk Avenue, Brooklyn, N.Y. 11226
Phone: 1-718-859-3800; Fax: 1-718-859-4632

What can I get help with?
- Housing, tenant and landlord workshops, tenant associations.

Whom do you help? Depends on services sought. Call ahead. **In what languages can you help?** Spanish (P), Chinese (Mandarin), Cambodian, French and Haitian

Creole (P), Thai. **What must I bring?** Photo ID, proof of address, Social Security card if available. **Where else are you located?** Only location above.

Forest Hills Community House
108-25 62nd Drive, Forest Hills, N.Y. 11375
Phone: 1-718-592-5757; Fax: 1-718-592-2933; Web site: http://www.fhch.org

What can I get help with?
- English citizenship classes for youth and adults.
- Computer classes and job training.
- Benefits counseling, food/nutrition and housing services.
- Mental health, senior citizens program and adult day care.
- Early childhood programs.

Whom do you help? Queens residents. **In what languages can you help?** Spanish (P), Arabic, American Sign Language, French, Haitian Creole, Hebrew, Korean and Russian. **What must I bring?** Depends on services sought. Call ahead. **Where else are you located?** 15 sites in Queens. Call ahead.

Growing Up Healthy Hot Line
Phone: 1-800-522-5006

What can I get help with?
- Food stamps; grocery coupons for parents with a child under the age of 5 through W.I.C.
- Medicaid family planning and health information.
- Income maintenance.
- Senior citizens services.

Whom do you help? Referrals only. **In what languages can you help?** Interpreters available for many languages.

HealthStat
See New York City Department of Health and Mental Hygiene (Page 121)

Hebrew Immigrant Aid Society (H.I.A.S.)
333 Seventh Avenue, New York, N.Y. 10001
Phone: 1-212-967-4100; Fax: 1-212-760-1833; E-mail: info@hias.org
Web site: http://www.hias.org

What can I get help with?
■ Visa and immigration qualifications, document applications, questions and legal representation; food and housing for refugees and immigrants; preparation for naturalization exam and interview.
Whom do you help? Everyone. Appointments required; call ahead. **In what languages can you help?** Spanish, Russian (P), Yiddish and French. **What must I bring?** Nothing. **Where else are you located?** Only location above.

Hellenic American Neighborhood Action Committee (H.A.N.A.C.)
49 West 45th Street, 4th Floor, New York, N.Y. 10036
Phone: 1-212-840-8005 or 1-212-996-3949; Fax: 1-212-840-8384;
E-mail: info@hanac.org; Web site: http://www.hanac.org

What can I get help with?
■ Legal representation, counseling services and advocacy.
■ Employment workshops, job preparation, job placement.
■ Basic education, G.E.D. instruction, internship placements.
■ English classes and preparation for citizenship exams.
■ Community outreach, family therapy, crisis intervention, couples counseling, foster placement prevention and senior citizen services.
■ Tutoring, mentoring and financial counseling
■ After-school and Beacon programs; summer day camp and youth employment programs.
Whom do you help? Documented low-income immigrants. **In what languages can you help?** Spanish, Greek and Hindi. **What must I bring?** Depends on services sought. **Where else are you located?** 2 sites in Manhattan; 2 in Queens. Call ahead.

Highbridge Community Life Center
979 Ogden Avenue, Bronx, N.Y. 10452
Phone: 1-718-681-2222; Fax: 1-718-681-4137 or 1-718-992-3481

What can I get help with?
- English classes and literacy classes in Spanish; basic education and G.E.D. classes; after-school programs.
- Food pantry and mobile meals.
- Employment services.

Whom do you help? Everyone. **In what languages can you help?** Spanish. **What must I bring?** Nothing. Must register in January, June and/or September. **Where else are you located?** Only location above.

HSBC Bank USA
Phone: 1-800-975-HSBC (1-800-975-4722); Web site: http://us.hsbc.com/

What can I get help with?
- Checking and savings accounts, insurance, investments, credit cards, mortgages and other loans.

Whom do you help? United States residents with a United States address and a valid Social Security number or those in the process of obtaining one; foreign exchange students. **In what languages can you help?** ServiceLine (English) 1-800-975-HSBC (1-800-975-4722); ServiceLine (Spanish) 1-888-433-4722; ServiceLine (Most Asian languages, including Cantonese and Mandarin) 1-800-711-8001. **What must I bring?** Social Security number or Tax Identification Number (non-United States citizens need green card or visa). Must provide date of birth, mother's maiden name, employment information, driver's license or state ID number; utility bill or major credit card as proof of address. **Where else are you located?** Call to find the nearest branch, or visit the Web site and use branch locator.

Human Resources Administration (H.R.A.)
Phone: 1-877-HRA-8411 (1-877-472-8411)

What can I get help with?
- Food stamps and Medicaid eligibility.
- Child care and safety issues.

Whom do you help? Everyone. **In what languages can you help?** Spanish, Chinese (Cantonese, Mandarin), Russian and Vietnamese.

Human Resources Administration (H.R.A.), Refugee and Immigrant Center
2 Washington Street, New York, N.Y. 10004
Phone: 1-212-495-7050; Fax: 1-212-495-7604

What can I get help with?
- Applying for public assistance, Medicaid and Medicare if you have trouble speaking English.

Whom do you help? Eligibility is based on need. **In what languages can you help?** Spanish (P) speakers at both offices; Chinese speakers (P) (Cantonese, Mandarin) at the Manhattan office only. Interpreters and printed materials in Cambodian, French, Russian, Haitian Creole, Vietnamese, Albanian and Arabic. **What must I bring?** Some form of ID. **Where else are you located?** 1 site in Brooklyn. Call ahead.

Immigration Advocacy Services
24-40 Steinway Street, Astoria, N.Y. 11103
Phone: 1-718-956-8218; Fax: 1-718-274-1615
Web site: www.immigrationadvocacy.com

What can I get help with?
- Any immigration, naturalization and citizenship issue.

Whom do you help? Everyone. **In what languages can you help?** Spanish (P), Chinese (Cantonese, Mandarin), Arabic (P), Greek, Italian, Portuguese and Urdu. **What must I bring?** Nothing. **Where else are you located?** Only location above.

Indochina Sino-American Community Center
170 Forsyth Street, New York, N.Y. 10002
Phone: 1-212-226-0317; Fax: 1-212-925-0327
E-mail: isacenter@netzero.net

What can I get help with?
- Determining eligibility for social services and where to apply.
- English and citizenship classes.

- Translation services.
- Job training and employment.
- Senior citizens programs.

Whom do you help? New York City residents. **In what languages can you help?** Chinese (P) (Cantonese, Mandarin, Fukienese) and Vietnamese. **What must I bring?** Registration and materials fee for classes. **Where else are you located?** Only location above. Call ahead.

Jacob A. Riis Neighborhood Settlement House, Inc.
10-25 41st Avenue, Long Island City, N.Y. 11101
Phone: 1-718-784-7447; Fax: 1-718-784-1964; E-mail: jriis@unhny.org
Web site: http://www.riissettlement.org

What can I get help with?
- Immigration documents, employment services, housing issues and benefits.
- After-school program, teen program, summer youth camp.
- Special programs for girls and young women.
- Senior center with transportation available for those 60 and older.
- Computer literacy and English classes.

Whom do you help? Depends on services sought. **In what languages can you help?** Spanish (P). **What must I bring?** Nothing. **Where else are you located?** Only location above.

Latino Workers Center
191 East Third Street, New York, N.Y. 10009
Phone: 1-212-473-3936
Fax: 1-212-473-6103

What can I get help with?
- Employee rights, occupational health and safety; getting compensation for injury and loss of pay.

Whom do you help? Everyone. **In what languages can you help?** Spanish (P). **What must I bring?** Nothing. **Where else are you located?** Only location above.

Legal Aid Society, Civil Division
199 Water Street, 3rd Floor, New York, N.Y. 10038
Phone: 1-212-440-4300; Fax: 1-212-509-8941; Web site: http://www.legal-aid.org

What can I get help with?
- Legal assistance with immigration, housing, government benefits, Social Security, consumer, bankruptcy, employment, unemployment, family and health issues.

Whom do you help? All immigrants. **In what languages can you help?** All languages. **What must I bring?** All court and government documents you have. **Where else are you located?** Neighborhood offices in all five boroughs and in Housing Courts. For office locations, go to Web site listed above.

Legal Services for New York City
350 Broadway, 6th Floor (Central Office), New York, N.Y. 10013
Phone: 1-212-431-7200; Fax: 1-212-431-7232; Web site: http://www.lsny.org/

What can I get help with?
- Free legal services for family, housing, benefits, consumer, health, employment, economic development and education issues.

Whom do you help? United States citizens and documented immigrants. Does not serve prisoners. **In what languages can you help?** English only. **What must I bring?** Noncitizens must bring green cards, proof of income and any documents relevant to the service sought. **Where else are you located?** 3 sites in the Bronx; 8 in Brooklyn; 3 in Manhattan; 2 in Queens; and a Staten Island outreach project. Call ahead.

Lower East Side People's Federal Credit Union
37 Avenue B, New York, N.Y. 10009-7441
Phone: 1-212-529-8197; Fax: 1-212-529-8368; E-mail: lespfcu@lespfcu.org
Web site: http://www.lespfcu.org/index.html

What can I get help with?
- Savings and checking accounts, direct deposit, A.T.M. access and loans.

Whom do you help? People who live or work on the Lower East Side (from East 14th Street to the Brooklyn Bridge, and Third Avenue/Bowery to the East River), or who are affiliated with a Lower East Side organization; relatives of current members. **In what languages can you help?** Spanish. **What must I bring?** Two current ID cards, including one with photo and signature; Social Security card or proof of Social Security number; minimum of $30; proof of Lower East Side residency or employment, or a letter from Lower East Side organization with which you are affiliated. **Where else are you located?** Free A.T.M.'s throughout Manhattan and Brooklyn.

Lutheran Medical Center
150 55th Street, Brooklyn, N.Y. 11220
Phone: 1-718-630-7000/7210; Fax: 1-718-492-5090
Web site: http://www.lutheranmedicalcenter.com

What can I get help with?
- Medical, mental health and primary care; H.I.V., AIDS and cancer; stroke center.
- Social services and domestic violence.
- Government benefits and food/nutrition counseling.
- Information on immigration and other legal issues.

Whom do you help? Everyone. Discounted services for Brooklyn residents. **In what languages can you help?** Spanish (P), Chinese (P) (Cantonese, Mandarin), Russian (P) and Arabic (P). **What must I bring?** ID; proof of address; proof of income to receive discount. **Where else are you located?** 4 sites in Brooklyn. Call ahead.

Managed Care Consumer Assistance Program (M.C.C.A.P.)
Community Service Society of New York
105 East 22nd Street, New York, N.Y. 10010
Phone: 1-212-614-5400 (Central help line); Fax: 1-212-614-5305
Web site: http://www.mccapny.org

What can I get help with?
- Choosing and using a managed health care plan, including information for people with chronic health conditions like H.I.V. and AIDS, physical, cognitive and developmental disabilities, and chronic mental illness.
- Free or low-cost health insurance, including Medicaid, Medicare, Child Health Plus, Family Health Plus and commercial insurance.

Whom do you help? New York City residents. **In what languages can you help?** English and Spanish through the central help line. Through subcontracting agencies, Chinese (Cantonese, Mandarin), Korean, Russian, Arabic, Yiddish and Haitian Creole.

What must I bring? Nothing. **Where else are you located?** 5 referral agency sites in the Bronx; 3 in Brooklyn; 14 in Manhattan; 3 in Queens; 1 in Staten Island.

Medical and Health Research Association of New York City, Inc. (M.H.R.A.)
Health Insurance Enrollment Project (H.I.E.P.)
40 Worth Street, Suite 720, New York, N.Y. 10013
Phone: 1-212-285-0220, ext. 130; Fax: 1-212-385-0565; Web site: http://www.mhra.org

What can I get help with?
- Choosing a managed health care plan.
- Getting and recertifying free or low-cost health insurance, including Medicaid, Child Health Plus B, Family Health Plus and P.C.A.P.

Whom do you help? Everyone. **In what languages can you help?** Spanish, Chinese (Cantonese, Mandarin), Russian, Arabic, Polish, Hebrew, Italian. **What must I bring?** Proof of income (four recent pay stubs or a letter from your employer; income tax return only if self-employed); proof of address; ID: birth or religious certificate, passport or green card; Social Security card (for Medicaid and Family Health Plus only; not necessary for Child Health Plus B). Proof of citizenship status (green card or application for green card, letter from U.S.C.I.S., visa; not necessary for Child Health Plus B). **Where are you located?** 4 sites in Brooklyn; 1 other site in Manhattan; 3 in Queens.

Medical and Health Research Association of New York City, Inc. (M.H.R.A.)
M.I.C.-Women's Health Services
225 Broadway, 17th Floor, New York, N.Y. 10007
Phone: 1-212-267-0900; Fax: 1-212-571-5641; Web site: http://www.mhra.org

What can I get help with?
- Cancer screening; S.T.D. and H.I.V. education, counseling and testing; family planning; preventive dental care.
- Prenatal care; enrollment of qualified women in the Prenatal Care Assistance Program (P.C.A.P.) and other Medicaid programs.

Whom do you help? All women. Medicaid, commercial insurance and cash accepted. Fees are based on patients' ability to pay. **In what languages can you help?** Spanish, French and Creole at all centers; Chinese (Cantonese, Mandarin) at Fort Greene and Jamaica; Punjabi, Russian and Urdu at Astoria; Arabic at Fort Greene; Tagalog at Jamaica and Manhattan; Guyanese and Greek at Bushwick;

Romanian at Eastern Parkway. **What must I bring?** Insurance information if you are insured. If not, ID (passport, birth certificate or Social Security card); proof of address (utility bill in your name or letter from your landlord or from a friend or relative with whom you live, stating that you live there) and proof of income. Staff can help with documentation if you are not sure what to bring. **Where else are you located?** 1 site in the Bronx; 4 in Brooklyn; 1 additional site in Manhattan; 2 in Queens.

Medical and Health Research Association of New York City, Inc. (M.H.R.A.)
New York City Neighborhood W.I.C. Program
40 Worth Street, Suite 720, New York, N.Y. 10013
Phone: 1-212-766-4240; Fax:1-212-260-6200

What can I get help with?
- Nutrition education and counseling; counseling and instruction on breastfeeding; referral to other health and human services providers.
- Voter registration.

Whom do you help? Pregnant women, breastfeeding and nonbreastfeeding postpartum women, infants and children to the age of 5 who are New York State residents. Income limit is 185 percent of the federal poverty level. **In what languages can you help?** Spanish, Chinese (Cantonese), French-Creole, Russian, Italian, Polish, Bengali, Yiddish, Tagalog, Arabic and Urdu. **What must I bring?** Physician referral; proof of address; proof of income (except for Medicaid recipients). **Where else are you located?** 2 sites in the Bronx; 7 in Brooklyn; 2 in Manhattan; 7 in Queens.

MoneyGram
Phone: 1-800-926-9400; Web site: http://www.moneygram.com

What can I get help with?
- Wiring money.

Whom do you help? Everyone. **In what languages can you help?** Spanish (P). Other languages vary by location. **What must I bring?** Cash to be wired and fee; photo ID if wiring more than $900. **Where else are you located?** Throughout New York City. Call main number above and enter your 10-digit phone number to find nearest location.

Morris Heights Health Center
85 West Burnside Avenue, Bronx, N.Y. 10453
Phone: 1-718-716-4400; Fax: 1-718-294-6912; Web site: http://www.morrisheights.org

What can I get help with?
- Primary health care; family planning and reproductive health care for pregnant women, health care for newborns; school physicals; asthma screening and care; mental health care; nutritional services; social services; and special teen services.

Whom do you help? Everyone. **In what languages can you help?** Spanish (P), Chinese (Cantonese — limited), French and Russian. Will find interpreter for others. **What must I bring?** Birth certificate or driver's license; proof of low-income status. Fees are based on ability to pay. **Where else are you located?** 2 additional sites in the Bronx. Call ahead.

New York Association for New Americans, Inc. (N.Y.A.N.A.)
17 Battery Place, New York, N.Y. 10004
Phone: 1-212-425-2900/5051; Legal Services: 1-212-898-4180; Fax: 1-212-425-7260
Web site: http://www.nyana.org

What can I get help with?
- U.S.C.I.S. documents, relative petitions, employment-based visas and applications for permanent residency; naturalization, citizenship and exam preparation.
- Counseling for drug abuse.
- Obtaining government benefits.
- Job search and placement.
- English classes.

Whom do you help? New immigrants. **In what languages can you help?** Spanish (P), Chinese (Cantonese, Mandarin, Taiwanese) and Russian (P). Chinese not available at Queens location. **What must I bring?** Working papers are required for job placement. Fees vary with complexity of issue. No fee for phone consultation with a paraprofessional. **Where else are you located?** 1 site in Brooklyn; 1 in Queens. Call ahead.

New York City Administration for Children's Services
Division of Child Care and Head Start
66 John Street, New York, N.Y. 10038
Phone: 1-718-FOR-KIDS (1-718-367-5437); Fax: 1-212-361-6023

What can I get help with?
■ Information about neighborhood day care and after-school care; financial help for child care; training for contracted provider agencies.

Whom do you help? All callers. Eligibility for subsidized child care depends on income and reason for care. **In what languages can you help?** Spanish (P). **What must I bring?** Social Security card or green card, birth certificate, proof of address and income. **Where else are you located?** 1 site each in the Bronx, Brooklyn, Manhattan and Queens. Call ahead.

New York City Child Care Resource and Referral Consortium
Phone: 1-888-469-5999

What can I get help with?
■ Resource and referral services for day care, after-school care and financial help; training for child care providers.
■ Health and safety information.

Whom do you help? Everyone. **In what languages can you help?** Will try to provide assistance in any language. **What must I bring?** Proof of income. Call ahead.

New York City Commission on Human Rights
40 Rector Street, New York, N.Y. 10006
Phone: 1-212-306-5070; Fax: 1-212-306-7474
Web site: http://www.ci.nyc.ny.us/html/cchr/home.html

What can I get help with?
■ Discrimination complaints; fair housing, employment and bias-related harassment issues.

Whom do you help? Everyone. **In what languages can you help?** Spanish (P), Chinese (Cantonese, Mandarin) (P) and French (P). **What must I bring?** Must have an interview appointment. To make appointment, call 1-212-306-7450. **Where else are you**

located? The commission maintains Community Service Centers throughout the city. Call ahead.

New York City Department of Education, Chancellor's Parent Hot Line
Phone: 1-718-482-3777; Web site: http://www.nycenet.edu

What can I get help with?
- All information that relates to the education of a child in the public schools
- Referrals to district learning support centers for issues not resolved at the school level or to take care of school-business matters, including registration and transportation.

Whom do you help? Everyone. **In what languages can you help?** Spanish, Chinese (Cantonese, Mandarin) and other languages by interpreter. **What must I bring?** Call ahead. **Where else are you located?** Learning Support Centers: 2 sites in the Bronx; 4 in Brooklyn; 2 in Manhattan; 4 in Queens; 1 in Staten Island.

New York City Department of Education, Office of Adult and Continuing Education
42-15 Crescent Street, Long Island City, N.Y. 11101
Phone: 1-718-609-2770; Fax: 1-718-392-4768

What can I get help with?
- G.E.D., E.S.O.L., basic education and computer training; vocational training in electrical repair, auto mechanics, phlebotomy (drawing blood), administering E.K.G.'s and nursing.
- Job search, résumé writing and interview skills help for students who have completed a course.

Whom do you help? Must be 21 or older and take placement exam. G.E.D. or high school diploma required for some training courses. Child care available at Brooklyn and Manhattan Learning Centers. Call ahead. **In what languages can you help?** All classes are offered in English. G.E.D. is only class offered in Spanish. Call ahead. **What must I bring?** Fee required for nursing program and some related health courses. **Where else are you located?** Classes are in all five boroughs. Call ahead.

New York City Department of Health and Mental Hygiene
125 Worth Street, New York, N.Y. 10013
Phone: 1-212-442-9666 (English and Spanish voice menu. Call can be directed to an
interpreter for most languages)
AIDS Hot Line: 1-800-TALK-HIV (Calls can be directed to an interpreter for most languages)
Bureau of Day Care: 1-212-676-2444 (English and Spanish)
Bureau of School Health: 1-212-676-2500 (English only)
HealthStat: 1-888-692-6116 (Spanish and Mandarin)
Immunization Hot Line: 1-212-676-2273 (English and Spanish)
Immunization Hot Line Referrals: 1-800-325-CHILD (2445) (If necessary, you will
receive a call back from someone who speaks your language)
Spanish Immunization Referrals: 1-800-945-6466
Women's Health Line: 1-212-230-1111 (English and Spanish voice menu. Calls can be
directed to an interpreter for most languages)
Fax: 1-212-442-5670; Web site: http://www.nyc.gov/html/doh

What can I get help with?
- Maternal, reproductive and infant health program; women's health program; free flu and pneumonia shots; free immunizations if required for school attendance; birth and death records.
- Enrolling in free and low-cost public health insurance.
- Complaints about day care homes, centers and programs.
- Rodent and health violation complaints.

Whom do you help? Everyone. **In what languages can you help?** Any language available through interpreters. **What must I bring?** Proof of address for prenatal care program. **Where else are you located?** Only location above.

New York City Housing Authority (N.Y.C.H.A.)
250 Broadway, New York, N.Y. 10007
Phone: 1-212-306-3000 (Central number for all boroughs); 1-212-828-7100 (Manhattan
application office); Web site: http://www.nyc.gov/html/nycha

What can I get help with?
- Finding affordable housing; Section 8 rental housing program.
- Social services.
- Educational and recreational programs.
- Job training.

Whom do you help? Low-income New York City residents. Priority given to shelter residents. **In what languages can you help?** Spanish (P), Chinese (Cantonese, Mandarin, Toisanese). For more information call the Language Bank at Equal Opportunity, 1-212-306-4443. **What must I bring?** When you call, have your Social Security number ready. **Where else are you located?** 1 site in each borough. Call ahead.

New York City Workforce 1 Career Center
168-46 91st Avenue, 2nd Floor, Jamaica, N.Y. 11432
Phone: 1-718-557-6756
Web site: http://www.nyc.gov/html/wia/html/career_centers.html

What can I get help with?
- Education assessment and student financial aid applications.
- E.S.O.L., G.E.D. and adult literacy information.
- Job search, training and placement; résumé and cover letter preparation; computer skills assessment and workshops.
- Government work-support benefits like child care, Medicaid and other free or low-cost health insurance.

Whom do you help? New York City residents. **In what languages can you help?** Spanish (P). Translation services available. **What must I bring?** Depends on service sought. **Where else are you located?** 1 site in the Bronx, 1 in Upper Manhattan.

New York Immigration Hot Line
Phone: 1-800-566-7636

What can I get help with?
- Information and referrals on immigration law, including relative petitions, visas, citizenship, political asylum, temporary protected status, deportation and exclusion, and special waivers.
- Referrals to city and state services.
- Employment and housing discrimination.

Whom do you help? Everyone. **In what languages can you help?** Spanish, Chinese (Mandarin), French, Polish, Russian, Macedonian, Indian, Arabic, Haitian Creole, Hindi, Albanian, Turkish, Korean and Serbo-Croatian.

New York State Department of Labor, Division of Employment Services Office
138-60 Barclay Avenue, Flushing, N.Y. 11355
Phone: 1-718-321-6307, 1-888-209-8124 (New York State number for general informa-
tion); Fax: 1-718-461-8572; Web site: http://www.labor.state.ny.us/index.html

What can I get help with?
■ Finding a job, learning your rights as a worker, collecting unemployment
insurance if you have been fired.
Whom do you help? Residents by location. **In what languages can you help?** Spanish
(P), Chinese (Cantonese, Mandarin) (P), Creole. **What must I bring?** Résumé,
proof of citizenship, Social Security card if available. Call ahead. **Where else are**
you located? 3 sites in the Bronx; 3 in Brooklyn; 4 in Manhattan; 4 in Queens.
Call ahead.

New York State Department of Labor, Division of Labor Standards
345 Hudson Street, New York, N.Y. 10014
Phone: 1-212-352-6700; Fax: 1-212-352-6593

What can I get help with?
■ State labor laws, child labor, minimum wage, unpaid wages, payment of wages,
wage supplements, work-hour rules governing garment and farm industries.
Whom do you help? Victims of labor law violations in all five boroughs. **In what lan-**
guages can you help? Spanish (P). For other languages, bring your own interpreter.
What must I bring? Varies with service sought. Call ahead. **Where else are you locat-**
ed? 1 site in Lower Manhattan, 1 in Upper Manhattan. Call ahead.

New York State Division of Housing and Community Renewal (D.H.C.R.)
38-40 State Street, Albany, N.Y. 12207
Phone: 1-866-ASK-DHCR (1-866-275-3427); Fax: 1-518-474-5752
E-mail: DHCRInfo@dhcr.state.ny.us; Web site: http://www.dhcr.state.ny.us

What can I get help with?
■ Housing applications, rental history, Section 8 housing, housing discrimination.
Whom do you help? Everyone. **In what languages can you help?** Spanish. Translation
service available for other languages. **What must I bring?** Varies with service sought.

Where else are you located? 1 site each in the Bronx, Brooklyn, Queens and Staten Island; 2 sites in Manhattan. Call ahead.

New York State Office of Temporary and Disability Assistance
Phone: 1-800-342-3009; Web site: www.otda.state.ny.us

What can I get help with?
- Food stamps and Home Energy Assistance Program (HEAP).
- Request a fair hearing by using online services.

Whom do you help? Call to determine eligibility for programs. Provides refugee and immigrant information and service referrals to network of nonprofit agencies around the state through the Bureau of Refugee and Immigration Affairs (B.R.I.A.), 1-800-566-7636; 1-800-232-0212. **In what languages can you help?** Spanish.

New York Urban League
204 West 136th Street, New York, N.Y. 10030
Phone: 1-212-926-8000, ext. 39; Fax: 1-212-283-4948; E-mail: nyulexec@aol.com
Web site: http://www.nyul.org

What can I get help with?
- Counseling on evictions, homelessness, and substandard and inadequate housing; finding housing; tenant/landlord mediation; housing discrimination complaints; information and support for home ownership.
- Counseling on social service benefits.

Whom do you help? Everyone. **In what languages can you help?** Spanish. **What must I bring?** Varies with service sought. Call ahead. **Where else are you located?** 1 site in the Bronx; 2 sites each in Brooklyn, Manhattan, Queens and Staten Island. Call ahead.

Park Slope Safe Homes Project
P.O. Box 150429, Brooklyn, N.Y. 11215
Phone: 1-718-499-2151; Fax: 1-718-369-6151

What can I get help with?
- Services, shelter, counseling and support groups for battered women and their children.

■ Services for victims of women-to-women violence.
Whom do you help? Domestic violence victims and their children. **In what languages can you help?** Spanish (P) and Arabic (P). **What must I bring?** Nothing. Call ahead. **Where else are you located?** Only location above.

People's Fire House
113 Berry Street, Brooklyn, N.Y. 11211
Phone: 1-718-388-4696; Fax:1-718-218-7367

What can I get help with?
■ Tenant counseling and advice for people looking for housing.
■ Computer literacy.
Whom do you help? Everyone. **In what languages can you help?** Spanish (P); Polish (P). **What must I bring?** Any kind of ID and/or Social Security card. Call ahead. **Where else are you located?** Only location above.

Promesa, Inc.
1776 Clay Avenue, Bronx, N.Y. 10457
Phone: 1-718-960-7500; Fax: 1-718-299-0463; Web site: http://www.promesa.org

What can I get help with?
■ Primary and behavioral health care; substance abuse rehabilitation; H.I.V. and AIDS services, including primary care, counseling, testing, referral and adult day care for people with AIDS.
■ Affordable housing; drop-in center for homeless.
■ Day care.
■ Services for runaway youths.
In what languages can you help? Spanish (P). **Whom do you help?** Everyone. Housing assistance requires income limits. **What must I bring?** Green card or proof of citizenship and Social Security number. **Where else are you located?** 15 Program Services Offices in the Bronx.

Queens Legal Services
8900 Sutphin Boulevard, Jamaica, N.Y. 11435
Phone: 1-718-657-8611; Fax: 1-718-526-5051
Web site: http://www.queenslegalservices.org

What can I get help with?
- Free legal help with housing, government benefits, consumer rights, labor rights, public school education and family law problems.
- Legal services for special problems faced by older people, victims of domestic violence and people with disabilities, H.I.V. or AIDS.

Whom do you help? Citizens and documented immigrants living in Queens. Some services based on income. **In what languages can you help?** Spanish. **What must I bring?** Proof of income, green card and any documents associated with case, like court papers. **Where else are you located?** 1 additional site in Queens. Call ahead.

Safe Horizon
2 Lafayette Street, New York, N.Y. 10007
Phone: 1-212-577-7700; 24-hour hot line: 1-800-621-HOPE (1-800-621-4673)
Fax: 1-212-385-0331; E-mail: feedback@safehorizon.org
Web site: http://www.safehorizon.org

What can I get help with?
- Financial help, crisis counseling and referrals for crime and abuse victims.
- General victims' services hot line, referral and service network.
- Counseling, group counseling, advocacy and help in dealing with the police.
- Victims' services and counseling for torture victims in Jackson Heights.
- Rape awareness counseling in Brooklyn.
- Emergency and short-term counseling, advocacy and services for sexual assault survivors and secondary victims.

Whom do you help? New York City residents. Male and female rape and assault victims age 13 and up. **In what languages can you help?** Spanish (P), Chinese (Cantonese, Mandarin), French, Haitian Creole, Hindi, Korean, Polish, Russian and Urdu. **What must I bring?** Police reports or anything regarding case. Fees for complex legal issues only are based on ability to pay. Call for appointment. **Where else are you located?** 75 programs throughout the five boroughs. Call ahead.

South Bronx Action Group
384 East 149th Street, Suite 220, Bronx, N.Y. 10455
Phone: 1-718-993-5869; Fax: 1-718-993-7904; E-mail: sbaginc@aol.com

What can I get help with?
- Counseling on basic housing rights and responsibilities; housing court services, advocacy and workshops; referrals to real estate agents to find housing.
- Citizenship and E.S.O.L. classes.
- Immigration and naturalization services.

Whom do you help? Everyone. **In what languages can you help?** Spanish (P). **What must I bring?** Nothing. **Where else are you located?** Only location above.

Southeast Bronx Neighborhood Centers
955 Tinton Avenue, Bronx, N.Y. 10456
Phone: 1-718-542-2727; Fax: 1-718-589-2927; E-mail: dymcenter@aol.com
Web site: http://www.sebnc.org

What can I get help with?
- Child care, day care and after-school programs; teen services; senior center that includes home health care.
- Food stamp referral and registration.
- Computer technology courses and career counseling services.
- Help for people with disabilities.

Whom do you help? Must have Social Security card. **In what languages can you help?** Spanish. **What must I bring?** Child-care services require Social Security card. Fees are based on ability to pay. **Where else are you located?** 3 sites in the Bronx. Call ahead.

Southside Community Mission, Immigration Program
250 Hooper Street, Brooklyn, N.Y. 11211
Phone: 1-718-387-3803; Fax: 1-718-387-3739

What can I get help with?
- Immigration forms, family petitions, status adjustments, naturalization, employment authorization, residency visas/conditional residency.

- Citizenship applications and classes.
- Legal representation.

Whom do you help? Everyone. Minimal fee on first visit. **In what languages can you help?** Spanish. **What must I bring?** Minimal fee depends on service. Call ahead. **Where else are you located?** 1 other site in the Bronx.

United Community Centers
613 New Lots Avenue, Brooklyn, N.Y. 11207
Phone: 1-718-649-7979; Fax: 1-718-649-7256; E-mail: uccinc@mindspring.com
Web site: http://www.unhny.org

What can I get help with?
- Day care and after-school programs.
- Basic education and E.S.O.L. classes.
- Computer hardware job-training program for adults.
- Immigration, deportation and citizenship issues.

Whom do you help? Everyone. **In what languages can you help?** Spanish (P), Haitian Creole. **What must I bring?** Nothing. Call for appointment for legal and deportation issues. Day care program for children ages 2 to 4 is based mainly on income and residency. **Where else are you located?** Only location above.

University Settlement Federal Credit Union
184 Eldridge Street, 4th Floor, New York, N.Y. 10002
Phone: 1-212-674-9120; Fax: 1-212-254-5334
Web site: http://www.universitysettlement.org

What can I get help with?
- Savings and low-interest loans.

Whom do you help? Low-income residents. **In what languages can you help?** Spanish. **What must I bring?** Call ahead. **Where else are you located?** Call ahead.

University Settlement Society of New York
184 Eldridge Street, New York, N.Y. 10002
Phone: 1-212-674-9120; Fax: 1-212-475-3278; E-mail: info@universitysettlement.org
Web site: http://www.universitysettlement.org

What can I get help with?
- Infant and early childhood and day care services, after-school programs, day and summer camps.
- Literacy programs, youth employment services.
- Adolescent pregnancy services, counseling and clinical services.
- Social services, nutrition and escort and telephone reassurance programs for the elderly.
- Services for formerly homeless families.

Whom do you help? Immigrants and low-income New Yorkers. **In what languages can you help?** Chinese (P) (Cantonese, Mandarin), Spanish (P), Russian and Bengali. **What must I bring?** A few programs have a sliding scale fee based on family income. Call ahead. **Where else are you located?** Call ahead.

Western Union
Phone: 1-800-325-6000, 1-800-325-4045 (Spanish)
Web site: http://www.westernunion.com

What can I get help with?
- Wiring money.

Whom do you help? Everyone. **In what languages can you help?** Varies by location, but hot line has Spanish operators available at all times. **What must I bring?** Cash to be wired and fee; photo ID if wiring more than $1,000. **Where else are you located?** Call or check Web site.

Y.M.C.A. of Greater New York
333 Seventh Avenue, 15th Floor, New York, N.Y. 10001
Phone: 1-212-630-9600

100 Hester Street (Chinatown branch), New York, N.Y. 10002
Phone: 1-212-219-8393; Fax: 1-212-941-9046
Web site: http://www.ymcanyc.org

What can I get help with?
- Parent workshops, family counseling (Chinatown branch only), after-school programs and programs for teens.

Whom do you help? Chinatown branch provides counseling to families with a child from 4 to18. Main branch offers other programs and referrals to neighborhood Y.M.C.A.'s. **In what languages can you help?** Chinese (P) (Cantonese, Mandarin) and Spanish (P). **What must I bring?** Call ahead. **Where else are you located?** 2 sites in the Bronx; 9 in Brooklyn; 4 in Manhattan; 7 in Queens; 4 in Staten Island.

INDEX

ENDNOTES

[1] Ewen, Elizabeth, *Immigrant Women in the Land of Dollars*, New York: Monthly Review Press, 1985, p. 61. [2] Oral History with Rafael Guzman, Collection of the Lower East Side Tenement Museum. [3] Charles T. Anderson interviewed by Dana Gumb, Interview #005. Voices from Ellis Island: An Oral History of American Immigration, A Project of the Statue of Liberty–Ellis Island Foundation. [4] Interview with Irma Olivo by Lisa Chice, 2002. [5] *The Italian-American Catalog*. Joseph Giordano (editor). Garden City, N.Y.: Doubleday, 1986. [6] Khandelwal, Madhulika S., *Becoming American, Being Indian: An Immigrant Community in New York City*, Ithaca, N.Y.: Cornell University Press, 2002, p. 130. [7] Oral History with Max Mason, Collection of the Lower East Side Tenement Museum. [8] Ling Leung, unpublished paper, 1999. [9] Male immigrant, called Padrone, from Italy, in *America, the Dream of My Life: Selections from the Federal Writers' Project's New Jersey Ethnic Survey*. David Steven Cohen (editor). New Brunswick, N.J.: Rutgers University Press, 1990. [10] Oral History with Jose Zambrano, Collection of the Lower East Side Tenement Museum. [11] Kisseloff, Jeff, *You Must Remember This: An Oral History of Manhattan from the 1890s to World War II*. New York: Harcourt Brace Jovanovich, 1989. p. 562. [12] Maricela Gonzalez, unpublished paper, 1999. [13] Hardayal Singh, "Being Indian in New Jersey," in *Asian American Experiences in the United States*. Joann Faung Jean Lee (editor), Jefferson, N.C.: McFarland and Company, 1991. [14] Pak Ping, unpublished paper, 1999. [15] Oral History with Josephine Esposito, Collection of the Lower East Side Tenement Museum. [16] Interview with Georgina Acevedo by Lisa Chice, 2002. [17] *Spiritual Autobiographies*. Louis Finkelstein (editor), New York, NY: Harper and Brothers, 1952. [18] Interview with Kaynam Hedayat by Lisa Chice, 2002.

LA GUÍA PARA INMIGRANTES EN LA CIUDAD DE NUEVA YORK DEL NEW YORK TIMES

Joan P. Nassivera

*Con la Participación Conjunta
del Lower East Side Tenement Museum*

CONTENIDO

INTRODUCCIÓN Y RECONOCIMIENTOS

"A lo largo de los años muchas personas han comprendido nuestras necesidades y problemas y han tratado de remediarlos. Ahora, queremos ofrecerle algo real, basado en nuestras propias experiencias.

Al llegar a un nuevo país, suele ser muy difícil para los nuevos inmigrantes obtener información. Todo les resulta extraño. No saben dónde acudir para matricularse en la escuela, dónde encontrar trabajo, dónde están ubicados los hospitales, cómo obtener atención de salud con seguro, etc. Incluso nosotros hemos pagado por servicios que podríamos haber obtenido gratis y hemos sido explotados por nuestros patrones porque no conocíamos nuestros derechos.

Hemos dedicado la suma de nuestros esfuerzos para ayudar a los nuevos inmigrantes. Queremos compartir nuestras historias para que los inmigrantes recién llegados cuenten con la orientación que nunca tuvimos y no cometan los mismos errores."

Estas son las palabras de inmigrantes que se han asentado recientemente en la ciudad de Nueva York, hombres y mujeres de China, México, la República Dominicana, Hong Kong, Ecuador, Madagascar y El Salvador.

Quizás sean personas como usted, o como lo era su madre hace una década, o su abuelo hace una generación. Dejaron sus países de origen en busca de una vida mejor en una ciudad de posibilidades infinitas. Algunos tenían familiares o amigos aquí; otros llegaron sin conocer a nadie.

Muchos de estos inmigrantes vienen de pueblos y ciudades en donde la policía y los funcionarios gubernamentales representan, a veces, una fuerza de represión, y por consiguiente se rehusaron a buscar ayuda en los organismos oficiales o a solicitar información a funcionarios del gobierno que podrían haberlos encaminado en la dirección correcta. Otros buscaron asistencia y fueron rechazados o enviados al lugar o a la persona incorrecta, hallando sólo desaliento. Pero a pesar de todas estas dificultades estaban decididos a triunfar en su nuevo destino. Y esa determinación se refleja en cada una de estas páginas.

Estos inmigrantes comparten sus sueños, los sueños de todo neoyorquino: un trabajo que pague un sueldo decente, un lugar seguro para vivir, funcionarios gubernamentales que no sean corruptos o abusivos, la oportunidad de obtener una buena educación, atención médica a cargo de médicos y enfermeras capacitados.

Nueva York ofrece todo esto y mucho más. Pero para la mayoría de los inmigrantes, lograr una vida mejor significa descifrar el laberinto confuso y complejo de la ciudad. Cada día surgen nuevas preguntas: ¿Cómo puedo encontrar un lugar para vivir a un precio accesible? ¿Hay alguna guardería que pueda cuidar a mi hijo para que yo pueda trabajar de noche? ¿Me atenderá un médico si estoy enfermo y no tengo dinero? ¿Dónde puedo aprender inglés? ¿Podré obtener ayuda en una emergencia si no hablo el idioma? ¿Cómo me convierto en ciudadano americano?

En estas páginas, el New York Times y el Lower East Side Tenement Museum contestan estas preguntas y cientos de preguntas más que los inmigrantes tienen a diario.

Durante más de 150 años, el Times ha sido parte vibrante y vital del panorama en constante evolución de los inmigrantes en Nueva York. Es un órgano de la prensa que goza del respeto y confianza de los lectores, y como tal, es un elemento esencial de estas comunidades donde los recién llegados de Europa se asentaron a principios de los años 1900 y donde los inmigrantes de América Latina, Asia y otros lugares del mundo están estableciendo hoy en día sus raíces.

El museo, ubicado en una casa de vecindad del Lower East Side que entre 1863 y 1935 albergó a unos 7,000 inmigrantes de más de 20 países, proporciona una perspectiva histórica de la amplia gama de experiencias migratorias en un vecindario que continúa siendo el primer punto de partida para miles de recién llegados a los Estados Unidos. El museo también suple las necesidades de los inmigrantes actuales de varias maneras, ofreciendo incluso clases de inglés gratis que permiten a los nuevos inmigrantes conocer las historias de aquellos que llegaron antes que ellos.

Los artículos originales, informativos y útiles son un sello distintivo del Times. Escuchamos atentamente a los inmigrantes que asistían a las clases del museo como a los que encontramos a través de la ciudad, describir lo que necesitaban para establecerse y mejorar sus vidas en Nueva York.

En una de las clases, los estudiantes se enteraron cómo los inmigrantes del Siglo XIX que llegaron a Ellis Island fueron recibidos por voluntarios que hablaban su idioma y los ayudaron con sus necesidades básicas. Esta información hizo que un estudiante exclamara: "Nadie nos estaba esperando en el Aeropuerto Kennedy. ¡Nadie!" Ahora, el Times y el museo participan en forma conjunta para crear la primera guía completa para inmigrantes en un volumen práctico y fácil de usar.

Otro recurso que está al alcance de los recién llegados a la ciudad de Nueva York es la Oficina del Alcalde para Asuntos de Inmigración (Mayor's Office of Immigrant Affairs), cuyo objetivo es el de fomentar la participación de los inmigrantes en todos los aspectos de la vida de la ciudad alentando la comunicación y el contacto entre los organismos municipales y las comunidades de inmigrantes. Visite el sitio Web de la oficina en www.nyc.gov/immigrants.

Cada uno de los capítulos de la guía ha sido revisado por inmigrantes que asisten a las clases del Tenement Museum, así como por expertos que integran grupos de derechos para inmigrantes y proveedores de servicios, incluyendo la New York Association for New Americans, la New York Immigration Coalition and University Settlement. Sus tareas no se han limitado solamente a la verificación de datos, sino que han puesto todo su empeño para asegurar que la guía responda completamente y con precisión a las necesidades de este público: inmigrantes actuales, sus patrones y las personas que los ayudan a encontrar su camino, en ésta, la ciudad más fascinante del mundo.

Una obra como esta requiere la colaboración de muchos. En primer lugar deseamos agradecer a Alyse Myers del Times y Ruth J. Abram del Tenement Museum, cuya visión y comprensión de las comunidades de inmigrantes en Nueva York fueron el catalizador para el éxito de este proyecto.

Meighan Meeker and Tessa Rosario del Times y Liz Ševčenko del Tenement Museum fueron los directores del proyecto que supervisaron cada una de sus fases y cuya tarea más valiosa, frustrante y casi constante fue la de recordarme que la frase "fecha de entrega" también tiene significado fuera de la sala de prensa.

Alison Bowles, Lisa Chice and Michael Sant' Ambrogio del Tenement Museum supervisaron las actividades de investigación y las evaluaciones de los expertos en inmigración, una tarea gigantesca a cargo de Ms. Bowles, Ms. Chice, Geovanny Fernandez, Jana Hasprunova, Sushma Joshi, Stephen Morton, Marilyn Ordoñez, Elizabeth Rivera y Rosten Woo.

Entre los proveedores de servicios para inmigrantes y sus agencias que brindaron generosamente su tiempo y sugerencias cabe mencionar a: John Albert, Safe Horizon; Asian Americans for Equality; Emily Blank, Cypress Hills Advocates for Education; Sister Mary Burns, The Maura Clarke–Ita Ford Center; Maria Contreras-Collier, Ethel Cordova and Idalia Garcia, Cypress Hills Family Day Care Program/Cypress Hills Child Care Network; Ellen Davidow, Administrative Services Unit, New York State Department of Labor, Division of Labor Standards; Sara Dunne, Hard Work Disabilities Project of St. Barbara's Church; Andrew Friedman, Make the Road by Walking; Roberta Herche, N.Y.A.N.A. (New York Association for New Americans); Steve Jenkins, Make the Road by Walking and Workplace Justice Project; Wasim Lone, G.O.L.E.S. (Good Old Lower East Side); Jacqueline Lugo, La Providencia; David Morales, Banco Popular; Melissa Mowery, C.A.M.B.A. (Church Avenue Merchants Block Association); y Jimmy Yan, Advocates for Children. Margie McHugh y Dan Smulian, the New York Immigration Coalition.

La realización de *la Guía para Inmigrantes en la Ciudad de Nueva York del New York Times* fue posible gracias al apoyo generoso de Louis and Anne Abrons Foundation, Altman Foundation, Carnegie Corporation of New York, la Nathan Cummings Foundation, Furthermore: un programa de J.M. Kaplan Fund, y Wolfensohn Family Foundation.

Nuestro especial agradecimiento a: Susan Chira, Deborah Hartnett, Nancy Lee, Diane McNulty, Jennifer Pauley, Lee Riffaterre, Susan Rose, Arlene Schneider, Katherine Snider, Gabrielle Stoller y Fran Straus.

Por último, pero no menos importante, están los inmigrantes cuyo entusiasmo, sugerencias y persistencia guiaron este proyecto: *Argentina:* Julia Justo, Fernando

Salamone; *Brasil:* Marli Silva; *China:* May Chen, Pak Ping Ng; *Ecuador:* Laura Pilozo, Judith Tagle; *El Salvador:* Ernesto Ibañez; *Guinea:* Aminato Conde Diallo; *Hong Kong:* Ling Leung; *Irán:* Doran Gowhari; *Lituania:* Zoya Shterenberg; *Madagascar:* Sophie Herivelomalala; *México:* Gilela Bello, Maricela Gonzalez, Alicia Julian, Enriqueta Ramirez, Anselmo Zanes; *Polonia:* Karolina Gorak, Ilya Seldinas; *Puerto Rico:* Mercy Alves, Carmen Diaz, Judith Marinez, Placida Rodriguez; *República Dominicana:* Nayib Ega, Andrea Hernandez, Rosalba Jimenez, Paulenia Ortiz, Yleana Paulino, Esther Pestituyo, Rosalina Rodriguez, Victoria Rosario; *Rusia:* Inna Kaminskaya, Marina Lebedeva, Olga Seldina; y Ucrania: Marik Davydov.

Estos hombres y mujeres brindaron la descripción más elocuente de sus sueños para esta guía: "Esperamos que este proyecto no sea el final sino un buen comienzo para los nuevos inmigrantes, con la ayuda de otras personas que están interesadas en el bienestar de aquellos que vienen a Nueva York en busca de una vida mejor."

Joan P. Nassivera
Ciudad de Nueva York, Diciembre de 2003

CÓMO USAR LA GUÍA

El objetivo principal de esta guía es que le sea útil a usted, el inmigrante, a sus patrones y a los funcionarios gubernamentales y proveedores de servicios sociales cuya tarea es prestarle ayuda durante el período de adaptación a su nuevo hogar, la ciudad de Nueva York. A continuación le ofrecemos algunas sugerencias para que pueda aprovechar esta guía al máximo.

Encontrar información según el tema

La guía está dividida en capítulos. Los encabezamientos de cada capítulo y las descripciones en el Contenido reflejan temas generales que pueden serle de utilidad durante su primera etapa en la nueva ciudad. Por ejemplo, la sección Vivienda incluye, entre otros datos, cómo encontrar un lugar para vivir; la sección Trabajo y empleo incluye sugerencias sobre cómo encontrar trabajo e información acerca de cuánto es el salario mínimo por ley. En la sección Educación, puede averiguar cómo matricular a su hijo en una escuela pública y dónde puede ir para aprender inglés.

Cómo encontrar las respuestas que busca

Cada capítulo contiene las preguntas que nuestros contribuyentes/revisores inmigrantes consideraron eran las más importantes, y a veces las más difíciles de responder, durante las primeras semanas y meses en la ciudad. Cada respuesta ofrece información básica y con frecuencia incluye el nombre de una agencia y un número de teléfono para llamar si desea más información. Muchas de las respuestas también incluyen sitios Web útiles.

Cómo obtener más ayuda

Cada capítulo tiene recuadros sombreados con los nombres de grupos comunitarios y agencias de servicios sociales que proporcionan más información y asistencia. Cuando el nombre de un grupo o una agencia está indicado con un número de página, significa que nuestros contribuyentes/revisores inmigrantes consideraron que dicho grupo o agencia es tan útil y confiable que merece una descripción más extensa en el Directorio de recursos al final de esta guía.

En el directorio, aparecen símbolos arriba de cada descripción y hacen referencia al tema del que se ocupa tal agencia de recursos, grupo o proveedor de servicios, por ejemplo vivienda o guarderías infantiles.

Siempre que corresponda, se proporciona la abreviatura común de cada agencia de recursos, grupo o proveedor de servicios.

Cada descripción detalla además la ubicación de la agencia de recursos, del grupo o proveedor de servicios, el número de teléfono y números de fax, dirección de correo electrónico y dirección Web, servicios que ofrece, idioma(s) hablado(s), documentos y otros requisitos, si los hay.

Formato multilingüe

La guía completa se imprimirá primero en inglés, luego en español y por último en chino.

Nuestros revisores, tanto inmigrantes como proveedores de servicios, subrayaron que cierta información es tan importante que debería aparecer más de una vez en la guía. Como por ejemplo, los pasos básicos para obtener una Tarjeta de Residencia Permanente, también conocida como Tarjeta de Registro de Extranjeros y comúnmente llamada tarjeta verde, un documento que cumple un papel esencial en muchos aspectos de la vida de un inmigrante, como lo son la vivienda y el empleo, sólo para nombrar dos. Por lo tanto, encontrará estos pasos descritos en el capítulo titulado Estado legal y se mencionarán también en los capítulos dedicados a Vivienda, Trabajo y empleo, y Documentos.

Además, teniendo en cuenta que el objetivo de cada respuesta es el de responder de modo completo a cada pregunta, cierta información específica importante como por ejemplo, las dos divisiones principales que forman parte de un organismo federal relativamente nuevo, y que son respectivamente el Departamento de Seguridad Interna (Department of Homeland Security), la Oficina de Inmigración y Aduanas (Bureau of Immigration and Customs Enforcement — B.I.C.E.) y El Servicio de Ciudadanía e Inmigración — U.S.C.I.S.), se introducen y explican varias veces en diferentes contextos.

Se ha puesto todo el empeño posible para asegurar que la información que aparece en esta guía sea correcta y esté actualizada a la fecha de impresión. Pero es importante recordar que las leyes y políticas de inmigración que afectan a los inmigrantes se modifican con frecuencia, especialmente desde los ataques del 11 de septiembre del 2001. Además, otras agencias gubernamentales, así como grupos de servicios sociales y proveedores de servicios para inmigrantes también cambian sus políticas y programas. Por consiguiente, siempre es conveniente contactarse con un grupo o una agencia que aparece en el Directorio de Recursos al final de esta guía, o consultar con un abogado de inmigración de buena reputación para obtener la información más reciente sobre los temas que se describen en esta guía.

Esperamos que la guía despierte el interés suficiente y obtengamos el financiamiento necesario a fin de que podamos actualizarla e imprimirla en otros idiomas. Le invitamos a enviarnos sus comentarios y sugerencias por correo electrónico y para idiomas adicionales a **immigrantguide@nytimes.com**. No podremos responder a sus correos electrónicos, pero tendremos en cuenta sus comentarios al compilar la próxima edición.

VIVIENDA

"La luz del sol y el aire fresco de la montaña de mi pueblo se convirtieron en cuatro paredes y personas por doquier. El silencio y la luz del sol quedaron atrás, el presente consistía de un nuevo panorama urbano. Las calles empedradas. La hileras monótonas e interminables de casas de alquiler que impedían ver el cielo. El tráfico de carretas, carretillas y carruajes, y el sonar de las herraduras de caballos que lanzaban chispas en la noche. El repiqueteo de campanas y el sonido estridente de las sirenas que anunciaban un incendio en el vecindario. Corredores húmedos. Largas escaleras de madera y el baño en el pasillo".

— *Leonard Covello, italiano, 1910* [1]

■

En la ciudad de Nueva York hay una escasez de viviendas, especialmente viviendas para residentes de ingresos bajos y moderados. Esto significa que para la mayoría de los inmigrantes la búsqueda de vivienda será larga y difícil, pero ciertamente no imposible. Si bien nunca ha sido fácil conseguir una vivienda a un precio accesible, los inmigrantes siempre han logrado su objetivo. Durante siglos se han establecido en Nueva York, configurando y reconfigurando la ciudad.

¿Cómo hago para encontrar un apartamento en Nueva York?

■ Póngase en contacto con un grupo comunitario que ayuda a los inmigrantes a encontrar vivienda.

■ Pregunte a un miembro del clero o a miembros de su congregación o solicite información en iglesias del vecindario donde quiere vivir.

■ Busque letreros en lugares públicos, como por ejemplo bodegas, lavaderos o iglesias, que anuncian una habitación o un apartamento en alquiler.

> ❝ No se fíe de lo que le ha prometido el dueño salvo que esté escrito en un contrato de arrendamiento firmado por ambos. El propietario no puede cambiar lo que dice el contrato hasta su vencimiento. ❞

- Coloque sus propios anuncios en un lugar público ("Busco habitación. Puedo pagar $500 por mes").
- Busque en diarios y periódicos comunitarios anuncios para compartir una habitación o un apartamento y listas de apartamentos en alquiler. Mire en periódicos gratis como The Village Voice y LOOT. Es posible que estos anuncios hayan sido colocados por un corredor o un agente inmobiliario. La tarea de estas personas y cuánto cobran se explica más adelante.

¿Qué debo hacer si veo un anuncio para un apartamento a un precio razonable?
Actúe con rapidez. Llame al número anunciado y haga una cita para ver el apartamento de inmediato.

¿Qué comisiones pueden cobrar legalmente los dueños de edificios (landlords), los corredores de propiedad inmobiliaria y los agentes intermediarios?
El dueño puede cobrarle un depósito de garantía, que por lo general es equivalente a un mes de alquiler. Por ayudarle a encontrar el apartamento, un corredor de propiedad inmobiliara puede cobrarle una comisión, por lo general del 12 al 15 por ciento del alquiler del primer año. No debe pagar la comisión hasta tener en sus manos un contrato de arrendamiento firmado por el dueño. Una agencia intermediaria puede cobrarle una comisión por proporcionarle una lista de apartamentos disponibles. Pero la agencia debe reembolsarle toda la comisión menos un cargo de $15 si usted no alquila un apartamento de esa lista.

¿Qué comisiones no pueden cobrar por ley los dueños de edificios, los corredores de propiedad inmobiliaria y los agentes intermediarios?
Es ilegal que le exijan pagar una prima sobre el alquiler legal y el depósito de garantía. Por lo general esta prima se denomina "llave."

Cuando un aviso en un periódico o anuncio de alquiler de apartamento dice "sin comisión" ¿qué significa?
Significa que usted no tiene que pagar dinero extra además del depósito de garantía.

¿Qué sucede con el depósito de garantía que le doy al dueño del edificio?
El dueño se puede quedar con el depósito de garantía sólo si usted se muda sin pagar el alquiler o si el apartamento ha sufrido tantos daños que el dueño tiene que

hacer reparaciones después que usted se muda. Si usted ha pagado todo el alquiler y el apartamento está en buenas condiciones, el dueño deberá reembolsarle el depósito de garantía cuando usted se muda.

¿Qué es un contrato de arrendamiento? Indica:

■ Cuánto tiene que pagar por mes de alquiler.
■ Cuánto tiempo puede vivir en el apartamento.
■ Quién paga los servicios públicos, como por ejemplo la electricidad, el gas, la calefacción y el teléfono.

¿Es necesario tener un contrato de arrendamiento?

No, no es obligatorio, pero sin un contrato de arrendamiento usted tiene muy pocos derechos, y son difíciles de probar en el tribunal.

¿Tengo que pagar los servicios públicos?

Sí, el inquilino generalmente tiene la responsabilidad de poner la electricidad y el gas a su nombre y pagarlos. Esto significa que tiene que llamar a las compañías de servicios públicos y decirles que se mudará al apartamento en una fecha determinada y que a partir de dicha fecha le deben enviar la factura a usted. La mayoría de los apartamentos tienen el cableado necesario para instalar el teléfono, pero por lo general el inquilino debe aportar el aparato del teléfono y elegir una compañía telefónica local, una compañía telefónica de larga distancia y un plan de llamadas.

Todos los planes de llamadas de larga distancia me parecen caros. ¿Cómo puedo llamar a mi país y a otros lugares a un precio razonable?

Muchos inmigrantes compran tarjetas de llamadas. El tipo de tarjeta y el precio determinan dónde puede llamar y cuánto tiempo puede hablar. Muchos recomiendan las tarjetas telefónicas internacionales porque son más baratas que llamar desde la casa con un plan de llamadas internacionales.

¿necesita más ayuda?

Estos grupos ofrecen consejos sobre cómo encontrar vivienda:

■ Asian Americans for Equality (A.A.F.E.) (Página 241)
■ Chinese-American Planning Council (Página 249)
■ Flatbush Development Corporation (Página 255)
■ Hellenic American Neighborhood Action Committee (H.A.N.A.C.) (Página 257)
■ People's Fire House (Página 273)

¿Dónde puedo comprar tarjetas de llamadas?
En bodegas, quioscos de periódicos, tiendas especiales que venden tarjetas de llamadas y en algunos lugares donde canjean cheques.

¿Puede el dueño negarse a alquilarme el apartamento?
Sí. El propietario de una vivienda decide a quién se la alquila, y usted puede ser rechazado si por ejemplo, el propietario piensa que usted no podrá pagar el alquiler. Pero el propietario no puede negarse a alquilar en base a su edad, raza, religión, lugar de origen, tipo de trabajo, orientación sexual, estado civil, si está embarazada o sufre una incapacidad o según el número de hijos que tiene.

El dueño de mi apartamento quiere saber cuánto gano. ¿Debo decirle?
Sí, y también tiene derecho a ver el talón de su cheque de sueldo u otra prueba de sus ingresos, para asegurarse que gana lo suficiente para pagar el alquiler.

¿Cuándo puede el propietario aumentar mi alquiler y por cuánto?
El propietario puede aumentar el alquiler cuando se termina su contrato de arrendamiento. Este aumento se basa en la **Junta de Normas de Alquiler (Rent Guidelines Board)**. Para obtener más información, puede llamar a la junta al **1-212-385-2934** (Solamente en inglés) o visitar su sitio Web en **www.housingnyc.com**.

Creo que el propietario de mi apartamento me está cobrando demasiado. ¿Qué puedo hacer?
Llame a la **Oficina de Administración de Alquileres (Office of Rent Administration)** al **1-718-739-6400** (inglés y español), y pida una copia de los antecedentes de alquiler del apartamento. Puede hacerlo cuando está negociando su primer contrato de arrendamiento o cuando debe pagar el primer aumento de alquiler.

Pago mi alquiler en efectivo. ¿Cómo puedo probar que pagué el alquiler todos los meses?
Es muy importante que obtenga un recibo del propietario con la fecha, la cantidad que pagó, su nombre y la dirección del apartamento. La persona que recoge el alquiler debe firmar el recibo e indicar cuál es su cargo/puesto.

¿Quién puede vivir conmigo en el apartamento, y tiene el propietario derecho a saber quién vive conmigo?
Pueden vivir con usted los miembros de su familia directa, así como un compañero de cuarto y los hijos menores de edad de éste. Pero hay normas del Departamento de Salud que prohíben el exceso de ocupantes. Puede encontrarlas en **www.housingnyc.com/index.html**. El dueño del apartamento tiene derecho a preguntarle quién vive con usted, pero no puede preguntarle la relación que esa persona tiene con usted.

Una persona con la que vivo firmó el contrato de arrendamiento. A pesar de esto, ¿puedo vivir en el apartamento?

Sí, pero sólo mientras la persona que firmó el contrato de arrendamiento viva allí. Si en el apartamento no queda ninguna persona que firmó el contrato, el propietario puede desalojar a los ocupantes. Sólo un inquilino original puede renovar un contrato de arrendamiento.

Si se rompe algo en el apartamento ¿qué debo hacer?

Si no lo rompió usted, no es su responsabilidad repararlo o pagar para que sea arreglado. Pídale al propietario o al encargado que lo arregle. Si lo rompió usted, es su responsabilidad arreglarlo o pagar para que sea arreglado.

Según la ley, ¿cuáles son las responsabilidades del dueño del edificio?

- Proporcionar agua caliente (por lo menos 120 grados Fahrenheit) en todo momento.
- Proporcionar calefacción del 1 de oct. al 31 de mayo. Si la temperatura afuera cae por debajo de los 55 grados Fahrenheit, desde las 6 de la mañana hasta las 10 de la noche la temperatura dentro del apartamento debe ser de por lo menos 68 grados Fahrenheit. Desde las 10 de la noche hasta la 6 de la mañana, si la temperatura afuera cae por debajo de los 40 grados Fahrenheit, la temperatura dentro del apartamento debe ser de por lo menos 55 grados Fahrenheit.

¿necesita más ayuda?

¿Qué debo hacer si el propietario no me proporciona calefacción o agua caliente, o si pienso que soy víctima de discriminación en la vivienda o que se han violado mis derechos como inquilino?

Para quejas sobre calefacción o agua caliente, llame al:
- Centro de Servicios para Ciudadanos al 311 (Citizen Service Center)

Para quejas sobre discriminación de vivienda y derechos del inquilino, llame a:
- Asian Americans for Equality (Página 241)
- Chinese-American Planning Council (Página 249)
- Flatbush Development Corporation (Página 255)
- Jacob A. Riis Neighborhood Settlement House (Página 260)
- New York City Commission on Human Rights (Página 267)
- New York State Division of Housing and Community Renewal (D.H.C.R.) (Página 271)
- Promesa (Página 273)
- Queens Legal Services (Página 273)

- Poner una alarma contra incendio en cada apartamento a una distancia de 15 pies de cualquier habitación que se use para dormir.
- Poner protección en las ventanas en todo apartamento donde viva un niño de 10 años o menor.
- Quitar cualquier pared o cubrir cuidadosamente cualquier pared descascarada o pintada con pintura a base de plomo en un apartamento donde vida un niño de 6 años o menor. La pintura a base de plomo se encuentra por lo general en apartamentos construidos o pintados antes de 1960.
- Hacer todos los esfuerzos posibles para garantizar que no haya cucarachas, ratas, ratones u otras pestes en su apartamento.

¿Qué sucede si no puedo pagar el alquiler a tiempo?
Informe al propietario de inmediato. Si sabe que tiene problemas de dinero puede aceptar su pago tardío o insistir que pague parte del dinero. Tan pronto tenga el dinero pague al propietario y obtenga un recibo.

El propietario no acepta que pague tarde, ¿qué debo hacer?
Guarde el dinero en un lugar seguro. No lo gaste. Necesitará el alquiler retrasado si el propietario trata de desalojarlo y usted apela el desalojo en un tribunal.

¿Qué sucede si no pago el alquiler a tiempo o hago cosas que no se permiten según el contrato de arrendamiento?
El propietario puede ir al tribunal y pedirle al juez que lo oblige a mudarse. El propietario no puede decirle simplemente que se vaya del apartamento o sacar sus muebles y su ropa del apartamento y guardarlos o arrojarlos a la calle.

¿Qué debe probar el propietario para obligarme a irme del apartamento?
El propietario no puede desalojarlo. Sólo un alguacil puede ejecutar una orden judicial de desalojo y debe mostrarle la orden de desalojo. Para más información, visite **www.housingnyc.com/resources/attygenguide.html.**

¿necesita más ayuda?

Estas organizaciones ayudan a apelar un desalojo:

- Eviction Intervention Services, 1-212-308-2210 (inglés y español)
- Church Avenue Merchants Block Association (C.A.M.B.A.) (Página 250)
- Citizens Advice Bureau (C.A.B.) (Página 251)
- New York Urban League (Página 272)
- South Bronx Action Group (Página 275)

La orden de desalojo, ¿tiene que estar en mi idioma nativo?

Las órdenes de desalojo están en inglés y español. Los documentos del tribunal están solamente en inglés, pero hay intérpretes en el tribunal.

¿Qué debo hacer si recibo una orden de desalojo o notificación para dejar el apartamento?

Llame de inmediato a un abogado especializado en viviendas. Si la orden de desalojo especifica una fecha de presentación en el tribunal, recuerde asistir. Si no se presenta, puede ser desalojado incluso antes de la fecha de desalojo.

Si soy indocumentado, ¿puede el dueño del edificio desalojarme sin una orden del tribunal?

No importa cuál sea su estado legal, si el propietario o encargado le impide ingresar a su apartamento sin una orden del tribunal, debe llamar a la policía. Pero debe tener en cuenta que el propietario puede informar a la **Oficina de Inmigración y Aduanas o B.I.C.E. (Bureau of Immigration and Customs Enforcement)** que usted está indocumentado. La B.I.C.E., que es parte del Departamento de Seguridad Interna (Department of Homeland Security), ha asumido ciertas responsabilidades que previamente pertenecían al Servicio de Inmigración y Naturalización (Immigration and Naturalization Service — I.N.S.).

No me alcanza el dinero ni siquiera para los apartamentos más baratos. ¿Existe alguna alternativa?

La **Comisión de Vivienda para la Ciudad de Nueva York (New York City Housing Authority — N.Y.C.H.A.)**, (Página 269), ofrece viviendas decentes para residentes de bajos ingresos, pero hay una larga lista de espera.

¿Cómo puedo solicitar vivienda para personas de bajos ingresos?

Complete un formulario de solicitud que puede obtener en cualquiera de las Oficinas de Solicitud de los cinco distritos. Para averiguar dónde quedan, llame a la **Comisión de Vivienda para la Ciudad de Nueva York (New York City Housing Authority — N.Y.C.H.A.)**, 1-212-306-3000 (Página 269) o visite el sitio Web, www. nyc.gov/html/nycha/html/boroughoffices.html.

¿Importa que esté indocumentado?

A la fecha de impresión de esta guía, sólo una persona en el formulario de solicitud de vivienda pública tenía que ser un inmigrante documentado. Es decir, una de las personas que va a vivir en el apartamento tiene que tener una Tarjeta de Residencia Permanente o Tarjeta de Registro de Extranjeros (conocida comúnmente como tarjeta verde), que muestra que él o ella está viviendo legalmente en los estados Unidos, o debe ser ciudadana. El porcentaje del alquiler que pagará la ciudad se reducirá

¿necesita más ayuda?

Recursos para ayuda con vivienda pública para personas de bajos ingresos:

■ Apartamentos Mitchell-Lama patrocinados por la ciudad, 1-212-863-6500 (inglés y español)

■ Información sobre apartamentos patrocinados por el estado, 1-212-480-7343 (inglés y español)

■ Sitio Web, www.housingnyc.com/resources/mitchell/mitchell.html

según el número de inmigrantes indocumentados que vivan en la vivienda. *Sin embargo, las normas con respecto a los inmigrantes cambian con frecuencia, por lo tanto es mejor consultar con un grupo de apoyo a los inmigrantes que aparece en el Directorio de Recursos al final de esta guía, o, si puede pagarlo, consultar con un abogado de inmigración de buena reputación.*

¿Cómo puedo obtener una tarjeta verde?

Con frecuencia, el proceso para obtener una tarjeta verde es largo y complicado, y las normas que afectan a los inmigrantes cambian con frecuencia. Los pasos básicos se indican en el capítulo titulado Estado legal, que comienza en la página 222. Siempre debe procurar la ayuda de uno de los proveedores de servicios para inmigrantes que aparecen en el Directorio de Recursos al final de esta guía, o si puede pagarlo, consulte con un abogado de inmigración confiable.

Mis ingresos son demasiado altos para calificar para vivienda pública de bajos ingresos, pero aún así no puedo pagar el alquiler de un apartamento privado. ¿Hay algo que pueda hacer?

En la ciudad de Nueva York hay cerca de 125,000 apartamentos patrocinados por la ciudad y el estado para personas de ingresos moderados a medianos. Se conocen como los Mitchell Lama. Hay límites con respecto a los ingresos familiares y límites con respecto a cuánta gente puede vivir en el apartamento.

¿Qué pasa si busco y busco y no puedo encontrar un apartamento que pueda pagar? ¿Hay viviendas de emergencia o algún otro lugar al que pueda ir?

El **Departamento de Servicios para Desamparados (Department of Homeless Services)** de la ciudad administra refugios para hombres, mujeres y familias sin tener en cuenta su estado legal, y centros que ofrecen a los desamparados comida, ropa, atención médica, duchas y lugares para lavar, así como asesoramiento, referencias para empleo y otros servicios sociales. La sede está en **33 Beaver Street en el Bajo Manhattan, 1-212-361-8000** (inglés y español). Para encontrar un centro drop-in cerca de usted, llame a la sede o visite el sitio Web del departamento, **www.nyc.gov/html/dhs/html/di-directions.html.**

Y no se desespere si no puede acudir a estos lugares. Muchas iglesias, clínicas y agencias de servicios sociales en vecindarios de toda la ciudad ofrecen refugios, cocinas comunitarias, intervención en situaciones críticas y otros servicios para aquellos que los necesitan. Los grupos que se mencionan a lo largo de esta guía y se enumeran en el directorio de recursos al final, podrán ayudarle o referirlo a alguien que pueda.

■

"**C**uando recién llegué a este país, fui a 38 Ludlow Street, una casa de vecindad. Y cuando llegué al apartamento, pregunté, '¿dónde está el baño?' Pensé que bastaba apretar un botón y el inodoro aparecería automáticamente, que apretabas otro botón y que aparecería una bañera automáticamente, pero ese día me enteré que la realidad era otra. Mi tío y su esposa vivían en un apartamento con cinco niños. Me tomó muchos años entender que éste era el lugar que las personas de otros países llamaban la "ciudad maravillosa tapizada en oro"

— *Rafael Guzman, dominicano, 1966* [2]

TRABAJO Y EMPLEO

"**C**aminé por las calles hasta que me encontré frente a un gran edificio que tenía un gran cartel que decía: Oficina de empleos. Entré y pedí trabajo. Por supuesto él no hablaba sueco y yo apenas hablaba inglés, pero alcancé a decirle que buscaba un empleo. 'Espere un minuto, dijo él 'voy a buscar a un compatriota suyo.' Llegó con un herrero sueco, que me miró y dijo, 'Oh, yo necesito a alguien como usted.'"

— *Charles T. Anderson, sueco, 1925* [3]

■

La sola idea de buscar trabajo en un nuevo país puede resultar intimidante al principio, pero en Nueva York hay muchos grupos y recursos para ayudarle a encontrar trabajo.

¿Cómo puedo encontrar trabajo?

- Pregunte a sus amigos y familiares si saben de algún puesto de trabajo o si conocen a alguien que esté contratando personal.
- Camine por vecindarios donde haya fábricas, tiendas o restaurantes y observe cuáles tienen un cartel en la ventana que diga HELP WANTED (SE NECESITAN TRABAJADORES). En estos lugares, pida hablar con la persona a cargo o la persona que tiene información sobre el empleo.
- Lea los periódicos en español. En la sección de clasificados encontrará ofertas de trabajo.
- Póngase en contacto con una organización que ayuda a buscar y conseguir empleo.

¿Puedo trabajar y cobrar por día?

Las personas que quieren trabajar como jornaleros por lo general se reúnen en las esquinas y esperan que aquellos que necesitan sus servicios se acerquen y les ofrezcan trabajo de limpieza, jardinería o para vertido de hormigón. Los jornaleros por lo general negocian su paga por hora o por día. *Advertencia: A veces las personas que contratan a jornaleros se niegan a pagarles al finalizar el día o la semana. Si esto ocurre, comuníquese con la policía y proporcione toda la información que tiene sobre la persona que lo contrató.*

Según la ley, ¿qué preguntas tiene derecho a hacerme el patrón?

Los patrones pueden preguntarle qué tipo de destrezas tiene usted y por qué quiere trabajar para él/ella. Es ilegal que los patrones hagan preguntas sobre la edad, la raza, la religión, el lugar de origen, la orientación sexual, el embarazo o la incapacidad.

¿Tendré que hacerme un examen médico?

No tendrá que hacerse un examen médico, salvo que este requisito se exija a todos los empleados. Los resultados del examen serán confidenciales y no se usarán para discriminar sobre la base de incapacidad.

¿Tendré que hacerme una prueba de drogas?

Muchos patrones exigen una prueba para detectar la presencia de drogas ilícitas, como por ejemplo marihuana y cocaína y no lo contratarán si se encuentran rastros de estas drogas en su prueba de sangre u orina. Si su prueba de drogas da positiva, pero lo que ha tomado es un medicamento que le ha recetado el médico o que compró en la farmacia, por ejemplo un medicamento contra la tos, pida que le tomen la prueba nuevamente.

¿Qué documentos necesitaré?

Para conseguir trabajo, necesitará dos documentos, uno que demuestre quién es y el otro que indique que tiene permiso para trabajar. Todos los patrones deben completar un formulario I-9 para cada empleado.

¿Qué es un formulario I-9?

Es un formulario que todos los patrones deben completar y firmar para cada empleado. El patrón debe verificar la identidad y el permiso de trabajo de cada empleado. Usted debe completar la primera sección del formulario el primer día de trabajo.

¿Se enviará el formulario I-9 a los funcionarios de inmigración de los Estados Unidos?

No es necesario que el formulario I-9 se presente ante el gobierno federal.

¿Qué documentos necesito para probar que puedo trabajar legalmente?

La Tarjeta de Residencia Permanente, también conocida como Tarjeta de Registro de Extranjeros y comúnmente llamada tarjeta verde, o un Documento de Permiso

> **❝ Es muy importante**
> **recordar que si está indocumentado**
> **y trabaja en los Estados Unidos, está protegido**
> **por las mismas leyes laborales que cubren a las personas**
> **documentadas. Pero puede ser enjuiciado y deportado**
> **si el gobierno de los Estados Unidos descubre**
> **que usted está indocumentado. ❞**

de Trabajo, conocido como E.A.D. (por sus siglas en inglés) probarán que usted puede trabajar legalmente.

¿Cómo puedo obtener una tarjeta verde?

Con frecuencia, el proceso para obtener una tarjeta verde es largo y complicado, y las normas que afectan a los inmigrantes cambian con frecuencia. Los pasos básicos se indican en el capítulo titulado Estado legal, que comienza en la página 222. Siempre debe procurar la ayuda de uno de los proveedores de servicios para inmigrantes que aparecen en el Directorio de Recursos al final de esta guía, o si puede pagarlo, consulte con un abogado de inmigración confiable.

¿Cuánto demora conseguir una tarjeta verde? ¿Puedo trabajar hasta que la reciba?

Puede trabajar si se ha colocado un sello en su pasaporte que indica que la solicitud está pendiente. La ley de los Estados Unidos limita la cantidad de números de visas de inmigrante que se extienden todos los años. Esto significa que aunque el **Servicio de Ciudadanía e Inmigración de los Estados Unidos (U.S.C.I.S.),** una división del **Departamento de Seguridad Interna de los Estados Unidos,** apruebe su petición para una visa de inmigrante, es posible que no obtenga de inmediato un número de visa de inmigrante. Existe la posibilidad que tenga que esperar de 2 a 10 años o más desde el momento que el U.S.C.I.S. apruebe su petición de visa de inmigrante y haya un número de visa de inmigrante disponible. La ley de los Estados Unidos también limita el número de visas de inmigrante que otorga por país. Usted recibirá un aviso de aprobación por correo y tendrá que ir a la **Oficina de Distrito de la Ciudad de Nueva York del U.S.C.I.S., 26 Federal Plaza en el Bajo Manhattan,** a recoger su tarjeta. Cuando venza, tendrá que completar otra solicitud y volver a pagar el cargo. Si no lo hace, estará trabajando ilegalmente.

¿Necesito un Permiso de Trabajo (E.A.D., sus siglas en inglés)?

Si usted no es ciudadano o un residente permanente legal, tiene que solicitar un permiso de trabajo (Employment Authorization Document o E.A.D.) para probar que tiene derecho a trabajar en los Estados Unidos. Si el U.S.C.I.S. no aprueba o deniega su solicitud para un permiso de trabajo dentro de un plazo de 90 días, puede solicitar un permiso temporal. (Las personas que solicitan asilo pueden solicitar un permiso de trabajo temporal dentro de un plazo de 30 días, pero deben haber esperado 150 días desde la fecha en que presentaron su solicitud de asilo original para solicitar un permiso de trabajo).

¿Cómo puedo obtener un permiso de trabajo, o E.A.D.?
Complete el **Formulario I-765 de el U.S.C.I.S.** Lea la solicitud completa cuidadosamente y presente los documentos apropiados, fotos y honorarios. Debe solicitar una renovación del permiso de trabajo seis meses antes de que venza el original.

¿Qué pasa si rechazan mi solicitud? ¿Puedo apelar?
Si su solicitud de permiso de trabajo es denegada, recibirá una carta que le explica el motivo. No puede apelar a una autoridad superior, pero puede presentar ante la oficina de el U.S.C.I.S. que denegó su solicitud una petición para reabrir o reconsiderar su caso. Una moción para reabrir el caso debe estipular nuevos datos que deben presentarse en la audiencia de reapertura y debe estar acompañada de declaraciones juradas u otra evidencia. Una moción para reconsiderar debe mostrar que la decisión se basó en una aplicación incorrecta de la ley o de las normas de el U.S.C.I.S., en base a la evidencia que figuraba en el expediente cuando se tomó la decisión.

¿Puedo conseguir un trabajo si estoy indocumentado?
Sí, lo pueden contratar a pesar de su estado legal pero la persona o compañía que lo contrata está violando la ley. Si usted proporciona documentos falsos para conseguir un trabajo, también está violando la ley. Estados Unidos tiene leyes estrictas que exigen a los patrones verificar que un nuevo trabajador tiene permiso de trabajo, incluyendo aquellos que fueron contratados antes de 1986, cuando entró en vigencia la ley. Las políticas que afectan a los inmigrantes cambian con frecuencia, por lo tanto es recomendable consultar con uno de los grupos de defensa de los inmigrantes que aparecen en el Directorio de Recursos al final de esta guía, o si lo puede pagar, consulte con un abogado de inmigración de buena reputación.

¿Cuáles son mis derechos como trabajador?
Tenga o no los documentos necesarios, usted tiene varios derechos básicos:
- El derecho de recibir un salario mínimo establecido por el gobierno. Al mes de diciembre de 2003, el salario mínimo era de $5.15 por hora.
- El derecho a un descanso regular pago. Debe ser un descanso pago sólo si la compañía firmó un contrato especificando que éste es el caso.

¿necesita más ayuda?

Hay muchos grupos que ofrecen ayuda para la búsqueda de trabajo y colocaciones. Estos son algunos de ellos:

- Chinese-American Planning Council (Página 249)
- Church Avenue Merchants Block Association (C.A.M.B.A.) (Página 250)
- Citizens Advice Bureau (C.A.B.) (Página 251)
- Hellenic American Neighborhood Action Committee (H.A.N.A.C.) (Página 257)
- Jacob A. Riis Neighborhood Settlement House (Página 260)
- New York Association for New Americans (N.Y.A.N.A.) (Página 265)
- New York City Department of Education, Office of Adult and Continuing Education (Página 267)
- New York City Workforce 1 Career Center (Página 269)
- University Settlement Society of New York (Página 277)

- El derecho a que su patrón pague ciertos beneficios tales como seguro por incapacidad y Seguro Social.
- El derecho a protección básica de salud y seguridad, que se explica más adelante en este capítulo.

¿Se debe pagar a todos los trabajadores el salario mínimo?

No, algunos trabajadores no están cubiertos por la ley de salario mínimo, incluyendo las personas que cuidan niños a tiempo parcial en el hogar del patrón, aquellas que brindan atención y viven en el hogar de la persona anciana o enferma que cuidan y no hacen tareas de limpieza, conductores de taxi y otros trabajadores que están en esta categoría. Para obtener una lista completa, llame al número gratis del **Departamento de Trabajo de los Estados Unidos, División de Trabajadores Asalariados y por Hora (United States Department of Labor, Wage and Hour Division)** al 1-866-487-9243 (inglés y español), o visite el sitio Web: **http://www. dol.gov/**.

¿Puedo ganar más que el salario mínimo?

Sí. Su patrón no puede pagarle menos que el salario mínimo, pero él o ella puede pagarle más.

¿Cuántas horas debo trabajar antes de recibir horas extra?

Si usted no es un trabajador que vive en la casa del patrón, tiene derecho a recibir horas extras por cualquier hora de trabajo que excede las 40 horas de trabajo en una semana de nómina. (Una semana de nómina es una semana de siete días, pero no tiene que ser necesariamente una semana calendario, que es de domingo a sábado.

Una semana de nómina puede ser de lunes a domingo o de miércoles a martes, etc.) Si usted vive en la casa de su patrón, tiene derecho a recibir horas extra por cada hora que trabaja en exceso de 44 horas en una semana de nómina.

¿Se incluyen en el total de horas en una semana de nómina los períodos de descanso y turnos de fin de semana?

El tiempo que se toma para comer y otros descansos, ya sean pagos o impagos, no se consideran en el total de horas para una semana de nómina. Y recuerde, las horas extra se basan en una semana de nómina de 40 horas. Usted no tiene derecho a recibir horas extra simplemente porque trabaja más de ocho horas en un día determinado o porque trabaja un sábado o un domingo.

¿Cómo se calcula el pago de las horas extra?

Las horas extras se calculan de la siguiente manera: 1 1/2 veces su tarifa por hora por cada hora que excede las 40 horas de trabajo por semana o 10 horas en un solo día. Por lo tanto, si su tarifa regular por hora es de $6 y usted trabaja 45 horas en una semana, debería recibir $240 por 40 horas ($6 x 40 horas) más $45 por 5 horas ($9 x 5 horas), para un total de $285 la semana.

¿Tengo derecho a recibir el salario mínimo y horas extra si trabajo en una fábrica donde me pagan por pieza, como por ejemplo una fábrica textil?

Le deben pagar por lo menos el salario mínimo, y horas extra si trabaja el número de horas requeridas.

Si trabajo como niñera o empleada doméstica, ¿sabrá la familia que tengo derecho a horas extras y otros beneficios?

En la ciudad de Nueva York, si la contratan a través de una agencia de empleo, la agencia tiene que darle a usted y a su empleador una lista de sus derechos a cobrar horas extra y otros beneficios. El empleador debe firmar la lista para demostrar que él o ella entiende a lo que usted tiene derecho.

¿Debería cobrar en efectivo por mi trabajo?

No si puede evitarlo, porque significa que su patrón no le está descontando impuestos, Seguro Social e Indemnización para Trabajadores. Si le pagan en efectivo le será muy difícil probar que de hecho ha trabajado y en tal caso no podrá obtener beneficios como el Seguro Social o indemnización laboral.

¿Qué es el Seguro Social?

Es un programa de seguro financiado por los patrones y los trabajadores que paga beneficios cuando los trabajadores se jubilan o están demasiado enfermos o incapacitados para volver a trabajar.

¿necesita más ayuda?

El proceso para completar la declaración de impuestos es complicado. Si puede pagarlo, contrate a un contador que se especialice en derecho tributario. Si no tiene el dinero para pagar un contador, puede ponerse en contacto con estas agencias que ofrecen ayuda gratis para preparar los impuestos. Es posible que no hagan todo tipo de declaraciones de impuestos y algunas tienen límites de ingresos para calificar para estos servicios. La mayoría sólo funcionan durante la temporada de impuestos, desde mediados de enero hasta mediados de abril.

- Internal Revenue Service Taxpayer Assistance Unit, visite el sitio Web para información sobre dónde están ubicadas las oficinas, www.irs.gov. Se ofrece asistencia multilingüe en todas las oficinas
- Community Tax Aid, 1-212-788-7552 (inglés solamente)
- Community Food Resource Center, 1-866-WAGE-PLUS (924-3758) para inglés 1-866-DOLARES (1-866-365-2737) para español.
- Volunteer Income Tax Assistance (VITA), 1-718-488-3655 (inglés solamente)

Los trabajadores indocumentados, ¿pueden recibir Seguro Social?
No.

¿Qué es el programa de indemnización para trabajadores (worker's compensation)?
Es un programa de seguro financiado por los patrones que provee beneficios y paga los costos médicos cuando los trabajadores se lesionan en el trabajo o no pueden trabajar y necesitan atención debido a lesiones o enfermedades relacionadas con el trabajo.

Los trabajadores indocumentados, ¿pueden recibir worker's compensation?
Sí. Los trabajadores indocumentados están protegidos por las leyes de worker's compensation.

¿Puede mi patrón descontar otro dinero de mi salario?
El patrón no puede descontar nada de su salario salvo lo que la ley o las reglas gubernamentales estipulan, (como por ejemplo, impuestos sobre la renta, manutención para menores decretada por el tribunal, embargo del salario) y montos que usted ha autorizado para su beneficio (como primas de seguro, cuotas del sindicato, dinero para comprar bonos de ahorro de los Estados Unidos).

¿Qué son los impuestos sobre la renta?
En los Estados Unidos, si gana más de una cierta cantidad de dinero, tiene que pagar

impuestos. Tanto el gobierno federal como el estado de Nueva York exigen que usted presente todos los años formularios conocidos como declaraciones de impuestos. Estos formularios que deben presentarse antes del 15 de abril de cada año indican el dinero que usted ha ganado durante el año calendario previo y cómo lo gastó. Si se determina que tiene que pagar impuestos sobre la renta, tendrá que enviar dinero conjuntamente con los formularios para pagar dichos impuestos.

¿Cómo sé si tengo que pagar impuestos?

Debe pagar impuestos sobre la renta sobre cualquier cantidad ganada en los Estados Unidos si su categoría como inmigrante lo exige y si sus ingresos totales exceden el monto mínimo que se calcula conforme a su edad, estado civil y si es jefe de familia.

En mi trabajo recibo propinas. ¿Puede mi patrón quedarse con ellas?

Un patrón no puede exigir o aceptar ninguna porción de sus propinas salvo que trabaje en el guardarropas. Si trabaja como camarero o sus funciones incluyen servir comida, su empleador puede deducirle hasta $1.85 por hora de su salario mínimo si gana esa cantidad en propinas. Y si trabaja en un banquete, fiesta u otra recepción especial donde la factura incluye cierto porcentaje como propina, el patrón podrá tomar la propina y dividirla entre todos los empleados de servicio de restauración que trabajaron en la fiesta.

Si recibo propinas, ¿debe mi patrón pagarme algo más?

Sí. Si usted trabaja como camarero o sus funciones incluyen servir comida, debe recibir por lo menos el salario mínimo menos lo que recibe en propinas.

¿Qué pasa si trabajo como portero o conserje (superintendent) de un edificio?

Su patrón (el landlord o el encargado de la propiedad) no puede deducir las propinas de su salario. El salario mínimo para un portero se basa en el número de apartamentos u oficinas en el edificio, más que en la tarifa por hora.

¿Tengo que usar uniforme? De ser así, ¿quién lo paga?

Su patrón puede exigirle que use uniforme. Si usted debe comprar el uniforme que le entrega su patrón, éste debe reintegrarle el costo total después que lo compra. Si compra el uniforme en otra compañía, el patrón sólo tendrá que reintegrarle una porción. Su patrón también tiene que hacerse cargo del costo de lavar o enviar a la tintorería el uniforme o pagarle para que usted lo haga.

¿Con cuánta frecuencia debería recibir la paga?

Los que realizan trabajos manuales, tales como mecánicos, empleadas de limpieza y jardineros, deben recibir el salario semanalmente y no más tarde de siete días después de finalizar la semana en que devengaron el sueldo. Los empleados de

¿necesita más ayuda?

Muchos grupos pueden explicarle cuáles son sus derechos y ayudarle si piensa que sus derechos han sido violados. Estos son algunos de ellos:

- Asian American Legal Defense and Education Fund (Página 241)
- Chinese Staff and Workers' Association (Página 249)
- Latino Workers Center (Página 260)
- Legal Aid Society (Página 260)
- New York City Commission on Human Rights (Página 267)
- New York State Department of Labor, Division of Employment Services Office (Página 270)
- Queens Legal Services (Página 273)

oficina y otros (excepto aquellos que ganan más de $600 por semana) deben recibir el salario quincenalmente.

¿Recibiré mi paga si no me presento a trabajar?

No. Pero el patrón sólo puede deducir la cantidad que usted hubiera recibido durante el tiempo que estuvo ausente. Por ejemplo, si falta cuatro horas de trabajo, su patrón no puede deducirle ocho horas de trabajo.

¿Hay un límite en el número de horas que puedo trabajar? ¿Puedo tomarme tiempo libre?

No hay restricciones sobre el número de horas que puede trabajar por día. En muchos lugares de empleo, tales como fábricas, tiendas, restaurantes y hoteles abiertos todo el año, los trabajadores deben recibir por lo menos un día (24 horas consecutivas) libre en una semana calendario. Y recuerde, deben pagarle horas extra si usted es un trabajador que no vive en la casa de su patrón y trabaja más de 40 horas en una semana de nómina. Si es un trabajador que vive en la casa de su empleador deben pagarle horas extra si trabaja más de 44 horas en una semana de nómina o diez horas en un solo día.

¿Qué pasa con los descansos para comer, tiene que pagarme mi empleador por estos descansos?

Usted tiene derecho a tomarse un descanso para comer. Los empleados que trabajan un turno de más de seis horas deben tener un período de almuerzo sin interrupciones de por lo menos media hora. Su empleador no tiene que pagarle por los descansos para comer salvo que la compañía ha firmado un contrato que así lo estipula.

¿Puedo tomarme tiempo libre sin paga?

Según la ley Federal de Licencias por Cuestiones Médicas o Familiares de 1993

(Federal Family and Medical Leave Act), los empleadores que tienen más de 50 trabajadores deben permitirles hasta 12 semanas de licencia sin goce de sueldo en ciertas circunstancias. Para más información, visite el sitio Web del **Departamento de Trabajo** en **www.dol.gov/esa/regs/statutes/whd/fmla.**

Mi patrón paga por mi seguro de salud. ¿Qué pasa si pierdo el trabajo?

Si se va o pierde su trabajo y ha estado cubierto por lo menos durante 3 meses por el seguro de salud que ofrece su patrón, usted podrá continuar pagando el seguro por hasta 18 meses bajo un plan conocido como Cobra, aunque el seguro Cobra es mucho más costoso.

Si sufre discriminación porque insiste en estos derechos, puede presentar una queja o demanda legal, pero suele demorar años hasta que el gobierno o el tribunal corrija la acción ilegal de la que fue víctima.

¿Me pueden tratar de forma diferente porque soy un/a inmigrante?

Las leyes federales establecen que es ilegal que un patrón discrimine contra un empleado o una persona que solicita trabajo debido a su lugar de origen. No se puede denegar a nadie la igualdad de oportunidades en el trabajo debido a su lugar de nacimiento, raza o su nivel de fluidez al hablar inglés.

¿Tengo que hablar inglés donde trabajo?

Sólo si su patrón puede demostrar que el inglés es necesario para su actividad comercial.

¿Qué edad debo tener para trabajar?

Los estudiantes tan jóvenes como de 14 años pueden conseguir un certificado de trabajo, comúnmente llamado permiso de trabajo, pero no pueden trabajar en fábricas. Se emite un certificado de trabajo general a estudiantes de 16 ó 17 años, y un certificado de trabajo a tiempo completo a los jóvenes de 16 y 17 años que no asisten a la escuela o que dejan la escuela para trabajar a tiempo completo. El número de horas que se autoriza a los menores a trabajar varía según la edad y si asisten o no a la escuela.

■

"Mi primo tiene una maestría en contabilidad, y tenía un trabajo excelente en la República Dominicana, pero prefiere trabajar aquí en un supermercado porque gana más dinero....Mis padres también tienen su historia....Ambos eran profesionales en la República Dominicana, pero por algún motivo u otro pensaron que podían tener una vida mejor en este país, y también trabajaron en un supermercado durante años."

— *Irma Olivo, Dominicana, 2003* [4]

GUARDERÍAS INFANTILES

"La mayoría de las personas no sabe que un centro social comunitario es en realidad una especie de club combinado con servicios sociales. El Hudson Guild, un mundo de diversión de cinco pisos para niños pobres, tenía salas de ping-pong y de billar, un taller en el que se podían fabricar lámparas, un teatro para montar obras de teatro aficionado, un gimnasio para boxear y jugar al básquetbol. Había hombres jóvenes que actuaban como consejeros a los que aún recuerdo con cariño hoy en día. Eran más bien amigos que adultos cuya tarea era supervisarnos. Todavía recuerdo a uno de ellos ayudándonos a comer una caja de chocolates robados en vez de castigarnos. Fue sin lugar a dudas una buena decisión, pues a partir de esa fecha confiamos en él. El Hudson Guild mantenía más chicos fuera de la cárcel que mil policías."

— *Mario Puzo, hijo de inmigrantes italianos, recordando los años 1930* [5]

Como lo sabe todo padre o tutor, criar un niño es una tarea difícil y compleja, pero las recompensas son inmensas. Criar niños en una ciudad que uno apenas conoce es especialmente estresante. En este capítulo encontrará información sobre las opciones que existen para el cuidado de niños y cómo encontrar el lugar que mejor responde a sus necesidades en el vecindario donde usted y su familia viven o trabajan.

¿Qué programas existen en la ciudad de Nueva York para el cuidado de niños?

Para niños pequeños hay tres opciones principales:

■ **Atención en el hogar de una persona autorizada.** Esta alternativa ofrece la posibilidad de dejar a los niños entre las edades de 6 semanas y 4 ó 5 años en la casa de una persona que está registrada en el Departamento de Salud de la ciudad o tiene permiso de esa dependencia. Pueden atender hasta 12 niños.

- **Guarderías.** Por lo general, son más grandes que los centros que funcionan en el hogar de una persona. El número de niños varía.
- **Preescolar,** para niños de 4 años. Se enseña a los niños destrezas escolares y sociales básicas a fin de prepararlos para el jardín de infantes.

¿Qué es Head Start?

Head Start es un programa federal que ayuda a preparar a los niños de familias de bajos ingresos para ingresar a la escuela enseñándoles números, colores y destrezas básicas de lectura. Los centros en cada localidad establecen el límite de edad.

¿Qué es Early Head Start?

Early Head Start es un programa federal que ofrece guarderías para bebés desde su nacimiento hasta los 3 años y también proporciona cuidados prenatales para madres adolescentes de familias de bajos ingresos.

¿Cómo puedo averiguar si hay un centro Head Start o Early Head Start cerca de donde vivo o trabajo?

Puede hacerlo de varias maneras:

- Llame gratis al **Centro de Publicaciones e Información de Head Start (Head Start Information and Publication Center)** al 1-866-763-6481 (inglés solamente), e indíqueles su estado y código postal. Ellos pueden ubicar el centro más conveniente para usted.
- Llame a la **Administración de Servicios para Niños de la Ciudad de Nueva York División de Cuidado de Niños y Head Start (New York City Administration for Children's Services Division of Child Care and Head Start)** al 1-718-FOR-KIDS (Página 266).
- Use la herramienta de búsqueda del programa nacional de Head Start en **www. acf.hhs.gov/programs/hsb/hsweb/index.jsp.**

Al igual que yo, mis hijos están indocumentados. ¿A pesar de ello, puedo tener acceso a programas para el cuidado de niños?

Se supone que los programas que reciben dinero del gobierno, incluyendo los programas de la ciudad y Head Start, requieren que uno de los padres tenga tarjeta del Seguro Social, por lo tanto es poco probable que sus hijos tengan acceso a los servicios que se ofrecen. Cómo obtener una tarjeta de Seguro Social se explica en el capítulo denominado Documentos. Si usted está indocumentado, puede pagarle en efectivo a una persona que atiende niños en su hogar.

Trabajo por la noche y a veces los fines de semana. ¿Podré encontrar a alguien para cuidar a mis hijos?

Si su turno de trabajo cambia o debe trabajar en un horario poco habitual, es proba-

❝ Encontrar una guardería infantil de bajo costo puede ser difícil. Llame y visite con frecuencia las guarderías para que sepan que usted está muy interesada y le avisen si se abre un espacio. ❞

ble que le resulte difícil encontrar una alternativa para el cuidado de niños, porque la mayoría de los centros y programas están abiertos de lunes a viernes, desde la mañana hasta la tarde. Además, sólo se ofrece ayuda financiera para el cuidado de niños durante horas regulares, salvo que los padres puedan proporcionar evidencia, como por ejemplo, una carta del empleador que estipula que deben trabajar en otro horario.

Otras sugerencias:

- Contrate los servicios de una persona que conoce y en la que confía, quizás un familiar o un buen amigo, para que cuide a su hijo en su casa. Esto es una alternativa posible ya sea que trabaje durante el día, la noche o los fines de semana.
- Busque otras personas que estén dispuestas a cuidar a su hijo en la casa de ellos. Puede obtener nombres y números de teléfono de la **Administración de Servicios para Niños de la Ciudad de Nueva York División de Cuidado de Niños y Head Start (New York City Administration for Children's Services Division of Child Care and Head Start)** (Página 266).
- Alterne los turnos de trabajo con su pareja u otra persona que pueda cuidar a su hijo.
- Utilice diferentes opciones, por ejemplo, una guardería cuando trabaja por la tarde y un familiar cuando tiene que trabajar más tarde.
- Intercambie tareas de cuidado de niños con otra familia. Por cada hora que la familia cuida a su hijo, usted cuida al hijo de ellos por una hora.

Me han dicho que es difícil encontrar guarderías para niños pequeños, ¿es cierto?

Sí, muchas guarderías exigen que los niños sepan ir al baño solos, lo que generalmente no ocurre hasta la edad de 2 años o más. Además, las personas licenciadas por el gobierno que cuidan a niños en sus hogares no pueden cuidar a más de dos niños menores de 2 años.

¿Hay alguna manera de conseguir que alguien cuide a un niño menor de 6 años?

Comuníquese con las agencias que se describen previamente en este capítulo, la **New York City Administration for Children's Services Division of Child Care and Head Start**, 1-718-FOR-KIDS (Página 266), o el **New York City Child Care Resource and Referral Consortium**, 1-888-469-5999 (Página 266).

Mis hijos estarán en la escuela la mayor parte del día, ¿hay algún lugar al que puedan ir después de la escuela?

En el sitio Web de la **Asociación para Actividades Después de la Escuela (Partnership** for **After-School Education**) encontrará un directorio en línea para programas después de la escuela, **http://www.pasesetter.com//#asp_directory.** También puede llamar a la Asociación al **1-212-571-2664** (inglés y español).

El **Departamento de Jóvenes y Desarrollo Comunitario de la Ciudad de Nueva York** (**New York City Department of Youth and Community Development**) administra las **Escuelas Beacon** que deben estar abiertas por lo menos seis días por semana. Por lo general, permanecen abiertas hasta las 10 de la noche y también abren los fines de semana y feriados y durante las vacaciones escolares. Ofrecen clases privadas y ayuda con las tareas escolares, así como cursos de inglés y computación para adultos. Asimismo, cuentan con actividades recreativas y culturales. Para averiguar si hay una Escuela Beacon en su vecindario, llame al **1-212-676-8255** (inglés y español), o visite el sitio Web **www.nyc.gov/html/dycd/pdf/beacondirectory.pdf.**

¿Qué actividades pueden hacer los niños durante las vacaciones escolares?
Las Escuelas Beacon están abiertas en verano para los niños cuyos padres trabajan.

¿Qué preguntas me harán cuando llame para obtener información sobre guarderías infantiles?
Lo más probable es que le hagan preguntas sobre su familia, cuánto gana usted y otros miembros de su familia, si recibe asistencia pública o ayuda de bienestar social y si es más conveniente para usted encontrar una guardería cerca de su hogar o de su trabajo.

Si me ponen en una lista de espera para una guardería de bajo costo, ¿qué debería hacer?
Llame con frecuencia para que las personas a cargo sepan que está realmente interesada en encontar un lugar para su hijo. Visite la guardería con frecuencia para ver si ha avanzado en la lista de espera. Es posible que se abra un lugar si todos saben que usted está muy interesada.

¿necesita más ayuda?

Comuníquese con estas organizaciones para obtener información sobre programas de verano:

- Alianza Dominicana (Página 240)
- Brooklyn Chinese-American Association (Página 243)
- Citizens Advice Bureau (C.A.B.) (Página 251)
- Community Association of Progressive Dominicans (Página 253)
- Hellenic American Neighborhood Action Committee (H.A.N.A.C.) (Página 257)

¿necesita más ayuda?

Comuníquese con las siguientes organizaciones para obtener información sobre programas después de la escuela:

- Alianza Dominicana (Página 240)
- Brooklyn Chinese-American Association (Página 243)
- Citizens Advice Bureau (C.A.B.) (Página 251)
- The Door (Página 254)
- Hellenic American Neighborhood Action Committee (H.A.N.A.C.) (Página 257)
- Jacob A. Riis Neighborhood Settlement House (Página 260)
- New York City Administration for Children's Services Division of Child Care and Head Start (Página 266)
- New York City Child Care Resource and Referral Consortium (Página 266)
- Y.M.C.A. of Greater New York (Página 278)

¿Qué tipo de documentos necesitaré para poner a mis hijos en una guardería infantil?

Necesitará un formulario de historial clínico con la información médica y dental de cada niño, incluyendo un registro de vacunas. Puede solicitar el formulario de historial clínico a la persona que dirige la guardería infantil. El médico debe llenar el formulario con la información requerida.

Es posible que también necesite prueba del nacimiento de su hijo (un certificado de nacimiento, registro bautismal o pasaporte); tarjetas de Seguro Social de los miembros de la familia y su pasaporte, certificado de nacimiento, tarjeta verde u otra prueba de que está documentado.

¿Qué debo llevar a la guardería o a la casa de la persona que cuidará a mi hijo?

Recuerde preguntar. Algunos proveedores requieren que lleve pañales o comida, lo que puede aumentar los costos de esa guardería.

¿Qué otros factores debo tener en cuenta cuando busco un lugar para dejar a mi hijo?

Debe averiguar lo siguiente:

- Si se ha verificado que las personas que trabajan en la casa o en la guardería no tienen antecedentes penales.
- Quién cuidará de los niños si salen en un paseo organizado o si algo sucede y usted no llega a tiempo para recogerlos.
- Qué medidas toma la guardería si un niño se enferma mientras está allí.
- Qué medidas disciplinarias se utilizan.

No gano suficiente dinero para pagar una guardería. ¿Hay otro tipo de ayuda disponible?
En la ciudad de Nueva York, las agencias que brindan asistencia pública ponen todo su empeño en tratar de ayudarle a encontrar una guardería que usted pueda pagar. El dinero que aporta el gobierno federal ayuda a pagar el costo de una guardería infantil autorizada a las familias trabajadoras de bajos ingresos, a las familias que están en el período de transición de recibir asistencia pública a empezar a trabajar, y a las familias donde uno de los padres está en un programa educativo o vocacional, está buscando trabajo activamente o no puede cuidar al niño debido a una incapacidad médica o de otro tipo. Llame a la **New York City Administration for Children's Services Division of Child Care and Head Start, 1-718-FOR-KIDS** (Página 266), o al **New York City Child Care Research and Referral Consortium, 1-888-469-5999** (Página 266), ambas se mencionan previamente en este capítulo. Para obtener ayuda con los formularios, el trámite o con preguntas sobre pago, llame a la **Línea de Información de la Administración de Recursos Humanos (Human Resources Administration Info Line)** al 1-877-472-8411 (Página 258).

¿Puedo recibir un reembolso del dinero que pago por una guardería infantil?
Si paga impuestos sobre la renta, puede recibir un reembolso parcial, pero no total del dinero que paga para el cuidado de los niños a través de créditos tributarios.

¿necesita más ayuda?

Póngase en contacto con estas dos fuentes principales de información sobre guarderías en Nueva York:

- Administración de Servicios para Niños de la Ciudad de Nueva York División de Cuidado de Niños y Head Start (New York City Administration for Children's Services Division of Child Care and Head Start) (Página 266)
- Comisión de Referencia y Recursos para el Cuidado de Niños en la Ciudad de Nueva York (New York City Child Care Resource and Referral Consortium) (Página 266)

También puede llamar a estos grupos:

- Brooklyn Chinese-American Association (Página 243)
- Chinese-American Planning Council (Página 249)
- Citizens Advice Bureau (C.A.B.) (Página 251)
- Forest Hills Community House (Página 255)
- Promesa (Página 273)
- Southeast Bronx Neighborhood Centers (Página 275)
- United Community Centers (Página 276)
- University Settlement Society of New York (Página 277)

He aquí algunos lugares que puede contactar para obtener la información más reciente sobre créditos tributarios para el cuidado de niños.

■ Servicio de Rentas Internas (Internal Revenue Service), 1-800-TAX-1040 (inglés y español).

■ Departamento de Tributación del Estado de Nueva York (New York State Department of Taxation), 1-800-225-5829 (inglés solamente).

Me han informado que no califico para una guardería subsidiada. ¿Qué puedo hacer?

Puede apelar. Vaya en persona a la **Oficina de Audiencias Administrativas (Office of Administrative Hearings)** para solicitar una audiencia imparcial. Puede dirigirse a cualquiera de las dos oficinas ubicadas en la ciudad: **330 West 34th Street, tercer piso, en Midtown Manhattan,** o **14 Boerum Place, primer piso, en downtown Brooklyn.**

Pienso que mis hijos no reciben buena atención en la guardería que utilizo. ¿Puedo presentar una queja?

El programa de guardería diurno del **Departamento de Salud e Higiene Mental de la Ciudad de Nueva York (New York City Department of Health and Mental Hygiene), 1-212-676-2444 (Página 268),** evalúa los programas de guardería e investiga todas las quejas acerca de centros de cuidado de niños en el hogar, fuera del hogar y programas infantiles. Llame para presentar una queja.

■

"**D**espués de trabajar varias horas por día, estoy en casa para esperar a mis hijos cuando regresan de la escuela. Esto es mucho mejor que estar fuera de la casa de 9 a 5. Aunque tuviera un horario de trabajo regular, no me quedaría con mucho después de pagar los costos de una guardería. ¿Y quién se encargaría de llevarlos y traerlos de la guardería todos los días?"

— *Joven madre de Queens, India, años 1990* [6]

EDUCACIÓN

"La primera escuela a la que asistí quedaba a la vuelta de 97 Orchard Street. Un primo mío que vivía en el número 90 de Orchard era el encargado de llevarnos. Eran niños realmente americanizados. Nos llevaban hasta la escuela y allí nos depositaban. Mi primer recuerdo es de una clase de jóvenes sentados de un modo disciplinado y una maestra al frente. Estaba parada frente a una pizarra y estaba dibujando letras del alfabeto americano que nunca había visto antes y me dieron un cuaderno y un lápiz, y según entendí se suponía que tenía que tratar de copiar esas letras. No sabía lo que estaba haciendo. Nunca había visto ese estilo de escritura en toda mi vida. Era como nadar en un océano sin saber nadar. Realmente fue abrumador."

— Max Mason, ruso, 1921[1]

■

La ciudad de Nueva York ofrece muchas oportunidades para que los niños y los adultos puedan obtener una educación. En este capítulo se ofrece información básica sobre el sistema de escuelas públicas de la ciudad y también se dan sugerencias para que los adultos sepan dónde pueden ir para aprender inglés.

Soy indocumentado. ¿Pueden mis hijos asistir a la escuela en Nueva York?
Sí. Su estado legal no importa. Todos los niños de 5 a 21 años que viven en los Estados Unidos tienen derecho a una educación pública gratis. La asistencia es obligatoria para niños de 6 a 17 años.

¿Cómo matriculo a mi hijo en la escuela?
Se asigna a los niños de 5 a 13 años a escuelas primarias y secundarias según el lugar

donde viven, y la matriculación tiene lugar en la escuela asignada. Para obtener información sobre la escuela primaria o secundaria en su vecindario, llame a la **línea de información del Chancellor's Parent**, al 1-718-482-3777 (inglés y español; cantonés, mandarín y otros idiomas con intérprete) (Página 267), o visite el sitio web del **Departamento de Educación** en **www.nyce.edu** para localizar un Centro de Apoyo de Enseñanza que ofrezca la información y los servicios cerca de su domicilio.

¿Las personas que contestan el teléfono en el Departamento de Educación hablan sólo inglés?

Se conectará la llamada a un intérprete para la mayoría de los idiomas.

Mi hijo tiene más de 13 años. ¿Cómo lo inscribo en la escuela?

Los padres de estudiantes que están por ingresar a la escuela secundaria pueden llamar al **Departamento de Educación de la Ciudad de Nueva York, Chancellor's Parent Hot Line**, 1-718-482-3777 (Página 267).

¿Cómo sé a qué distrito o escuela ha sido asignado mi hijo?

Llame a la **línea de información del Chancellor's Parent** al 1-718-482-3777 (inglés y español; cantonés, mandarín y otros idiomas con intérprete) (Página 267).

¿Todas las escuelas primarias y del primero y segundo ciclo del secundario ofrecen los mismos programas?

No, hay muchos programas diferentes. Por ejemplo, no todas las escuelas tienen un programa de preescolar.

¿Qué edad debe tener mi hijo para empezar la escuela?

- **Preescolar** El niño debe cumplir 4 años antes del 31 de diciembre del año escolar.
- **Jardín de infantes** El niño debe tener 5 años antes del 31 de diciembre del año escolar.
- **Primer grado** El niño debe tener 6 años antes del 31 de diciembre del año escolar.

¿Qué necesito para matricular a mi hijo en la escuela?

El padre/madre o tutor legal debe acompañar al niño para matricularlo y llevar:

- Comprobante de domicilio. Si el padre/madre o tutor es el inquilino principal, lleve el contrato de alquiler o la factura de Con Edison, del teléfono u otro servicio público. Si el padre o tutor legal no es el inquilino principal, lleve dos de los siguientes:
- Contrato de alquiler y carta legalizada del inquilino principal que indique la dirección y el nombre completo del niño o niños que se inscriben.

- Declaración del empleador o agencia de servicios sociales que estipule la dirección del padre/madre.
- Licencia de conducir.
- Tarjeta de seguro médico.
- Certificado de nacimiento, pasaporte o certificado bautismal (con sello y firma autorizada)
- El último boletín de calificaciones o certificado de estudios si el niño ha asistido antes a la escuela.
- Registro de vacunas.

¿Qué pasa si no tengo todos los documentos que hacen falta para matricular a mi hijo?
Puede usar otras formas de documentación. Por ejemplo, una tarjeta de seguro puede reemplazar el comprobante de domicilio. Para averiguar cuáles son los documentos que se aceptan habitualmente, llame a la **línea de información de Chancellor's Parent** al **1-718-482-3777** (inglés, español; cantonés, mandarín y otros idiomas con intérprete) (Página 267).

¿Cómo averiguo qué vacunas necesita mi hijo antes de inscribirse en la escuela?
Depende de la edad del niño. Nuevamente, llame a la **línea de información del Chancellor's Parent** al **1-718-482-3777** (inglés, español; cantonés, mandarín y otros idiomas con intérprete) (Página 267).

¿Qué sucede si mi hijo no tiene las vacunas o inmunizaciones necesarias para matricularlo en la escuela?
Su hijo puede ir a la escuela si promete vacunarlo dentro de un plazo determinado. Debe mostrar que tiene una cita con el médico para vacunar a su hijo. Si no lo vacuna, la escuela podría prohibir el acceso a su hijo.

No puedo pagar las vacunas que mi hijo necesita para la escuela. ¿Qué puedo hacer?
Para vacunas gratis, vaya a una de las siete clínicas de la ciudad administradas por el **Departamento de Salud e Higiene Mental de la Ciudad de Nueva York** (**New York City Department of Health and Mental Hygiene**) (Página 268). No necesita cita previa. Para obtener más información sobre estas clínicas, llame al **1-212-676-2273** o visite el sitio Web del departamento en **www.nyc.gov/html/doh/html/imm/imm.html**.

Las escuelas en mi país son diferentes, ¿cómo decidirán los maestros en qué grado tiene que estar mi hijo?
A los alumnos de la escuela primaria se les asigna el grado según la edad, salvo que exista alguna razón para hacerlo de otra manera. Los estudiantes de la escuela

secundaria recibirán ciertas equivalencias por los cursos que tomaron en sus países de origen.

Mi hija sólo habla un poquito de inglés. ¿Cómo aprenderá en la escuela?

Cuando matricula a su hija, le darán una Encuesta de Identificación de Idioma en el Hogar para averiguar qué idiomas hablan en su casa. Según los resultados de la encuesta, el sistema educativo decidirá si su hija debe tomar una prueba de evaluación de idioma (Language Assessment Battery Test), conocida como prueba L.A.B. Los estudiantes que sacan un puntaje inferior al 40 por ciento en la prueba L.A.B., deberán inscribirse en el programa de Inglés para Personas que Hablan Otros Idiomas (English for Speakers of Other Languages — E.S.O.L) o un programa bilingüe.

¿Quién decide en qué programa de inglés debe participar mi hijo?

Usted decide.

¿En qué se diferencian los dos programas de inglés en las escuelas públicas, E.S.O.L y la educación bilingüe?

El objetivo de un programa bilingüe es que los chicos sigan hablando su idioma nativo con fluidez a medida que aprenden inglés. En los programas de educación bilingüe, matemáticas, ciencias y estudios sociales se enseñan *en el idioma nativo del estudiante*. El otro idioma que se usa y enseña es el inglés.

El objetivo de un programa E.S.O.L. es que los estudiantes aprendan el inglés con fluidez. Todas las materias se enseñan en inglés.

¿Todas las escuelas ofrecen tanto programas bilingües como E.S.O.L. en mi idioma?

Todas las escuelas deben tener un programa E.S.O.L, pero los idiomas que se ofrecen varían.

Me gustaría que mi hijo estuviera en un programa bilingüe, pero su escuela no ofrece uno en nuestro idioma. ¿Qué puedo hacer?

Usted tiene derecho a enviar a su hijo a otra escuela en el distrito que sí ofrece uno. Llame a la **línea de información del Chancellor's Parent**, 1-718-482-3777 (inglés y español; cantonés, mandarín y otros idiomas con intérprete) (Página 267).

Mi hija tiene una incapacidad de aprendizaje y necesita ayuda especial. ¿Puede asistir a una escuela pública?

Sí. La ley federal exige que los niños que tienen una incapacidad de aprendizaje tengan la oportunidad de lograr un buen rendimiento en la escuela en un entorno menos restrictivo. Su hija será evaluada por los funcionarios de la escuela para analizar sus necesidades particulares. Puede tomar ciertas materias en una clase de educación general con los servicios de apoyo apropiados o en una clase de educación especial. *No se puede colocar a ningún niño en una clase de educación especial sin el consentimiento de los padres.*

La escuela pública cerca de donde vivo no es muy buena. ¿Puedo mandar a mi hija a una escuela mejor pero más lejos?
En teoría sí, pero por lo general es difícil. La escuela a la que su hija quiere asistir debe tener espacio, por lo tanto llame primero a la escuela y pregunte. Luego, complete una solicitud para un permiso especial, llamado varianza (variance).

¿Dónde puedo obtener la solicitud para una variante para que mi hijo pueda ir a una escuela un poco más alejada de nuestra casa?
Vaya a la oficina del director del distrito escolar de la comunidad en donde está inscrito su hijo y pida una variante. Para averiguar la ubicación de la oficina, llame a la **línea de información del Chancellor's Parent**, 1-718-482-3777 (inglés, español; cantonés, mandarín y otros idiomas con intérprete) (Página 267). También puede visitar el sitio Web de la **División de Servicios de Alimentos y**

¿necesita más ayuda?

Para encontrar programas gratis de enseñanza de inglés de buena calidad, llame a la línea de referencia del Centro de Asistencia de Alfabetización (Literacy Assistance Center) al 1-212-803-3333 (mensaje grabado, sólo en inglés y español), o visite el sitio Web del centro, www.lacnyc.org/hotline/nycalidirectory.htm. Estas organizaciones comunitarias también ofrecen clases:

- Alianza Dominicana (Página 240)
- Brooklyn Chinese-American Association (Página 243)
- Cabrini Immigrant Services (Página 244)
- Catholic Migration Services (Página 246)
- Chinatown Manpower Project (Página 248)
- Chinese Immigrant Services (Página 248)
- Church Avenue Merchants Block Association (C.A.M.B.A.) (Página 250)
- Community Association of Progressive Dominicans (Página 253)
- Indochina Sino-American Community Center (Página 259)
- Jacob A. Riis Neighborhood Settlement House (Página 260)
- New York Association for New Americans (N.Y.A.N.A.) (Página 265)
- South Bronx Action Group (Página 275)
- United Community Centers (Página 276)
- University Settlement Society of New York (Página 277)

Transporte del Departamento de Educación (Department of Education's Division of Food Services and Transportation) en **www.opt-osfns.org/schoolinfo/Superintendents.cfm.**

¿Hay una fecha límite anual para presentar la solicitud para que mi hijo vaya a una escuela pública diferente de la que está más cerca de casa?
No. Puede hacer la transferencia en cualquier momento. *No le harán ninguna pregunta sobre el estado legal de los padres o del niño.*

Quiero volver a la escuela para aprender inglés. ¿Hay alguna escuela para mí?
Hay muchos programas que cobran por enseñar inglés, a veces mucho dinero. Pero también hay muy buenas clases de inglés gratis en toda la ciudad.

¿Puedo ir a la escuela a aprender otras materias además de inglés?
La ciudad ofrece clases para ayudarle a obtener su diploma de educación general, o G.E.D. El G.E.D. es el equivalente de un diploma de escuela secundaria. Se requiere para ingresar a la universidad y muchos trabajos lo exigen. La ciudad ofrece clases de G.E.D. en inglés, español y francés, así como clases de E.S.O.L.

Quiero obtener mi G.E.D., pero me parece que no estoy listo. ¿Hay clases o programas que puedan ayudar a prepararme?
La **Universidad de la Ciudad de Nueva York** o CUNY, ofrece clases gratis de destrezas básicas para adultos en 13 de sus instituciones universitarias. Para obtener más información, llame al **1-212-541-0390** (inglés solamente).

¿necesita más ayuda?

Para averiguar acerca de otros programas educacionales y oportunidades, llame a estas agencias:

- Archdiocese of New York, Superintendent of Schools (Página 240)
- Chinese-American Planning Council (Página 249)
- The Door (Página 254)
- Forest Hills Community House (Página 255)
- Hellenic American Neighborhood Action Committee (H.A.N.A.C.) (Página 257)
- Highbridge Community Life Center (Página 257)
- New York City Department of Education, Office of Adult and Continuing Education (Página 267)
- New York City Workforce 1 Career Center (Página 269)
- People's Fire House (Página 273)

> **Si usted solicita que su hijo sea transferido a una escuela pública fuera de su vecindario no le harán ninguna pregunta sobre su estado legal ni el de su hijo.**

Realmente me gustaría volver a estudiar, pero trabajo y tengo otras responsabilidades y además no hablo inglés muy bien. ¿Podré ingresar a alguna escuela?

La Manhattan Comprehensive Night and Day High School, 240 Second Avenue, 1-212-353-2010 (inglés, español y mandarín), está orientada hacia aquellos estudiantes de 17 a 21 años, que han tenido una serie de problemas en la escuela, no hablan mucho inglés o tienen otros problemas que limitan las probabilidades de que pasen las pruebas estándares requeridas y se gradúen en un período de tiempo razonable. Las clases tienen lugar durante el día, la noche y los fines de semana. Hay tutores, abogados, trabajadores sociales y otras personas dispuestas para ayudar a los estudiantes con lo que necesitan, como por ejemplo, conseguir anteojos o encontrar un lugar para vivir.

¿Cuáles son los requisitos?

La escuela tiene lugar sólo para 800 estudiantes, por lo tanto es necesario que los candidatos hayan completado 15 créditos de la escuela secundaria. Los estudiantes extranjeros deben superar el nivel de escuela primaria en algún idioma, y hay una prueba de admisión.

¿Puedo tomar cursos universitarios en la Universidad de la Ciudad de Nueva York (CUNY)?

Sí. Muchos inmigrantes han asistido a clases en CUNY y han obtenido sus diplomas porque el ingreso es fácil y el costo de la enseñanza es bajo. La universidad ofrece miles de cursos durante el día y la noche en diferentes establecimientos de la ciudad. CUNY tiene una guía, "Oportunidades para adultos," escrita específicamente para ayudar a personas como usted. Proporciona información sobre programas, servicios y costos de matrícula y una lista de números de teléfono. Asimismo, incluye relatos de adultos que se han superado, trabajando, estudiando y atendiendo al mismo tiempo sus responsabilidades familiares.

Para obtener una copia, llame a la **Oficina de Servicios de Admisión de CUNY (CUNY's Office of Admission Services)**, al **1-212-997-2869** (Página 251), o visite la página de admisiones del sitio Web de CUNY, **www.cuny.edu**.

Pienso que estoy preparado para obtener una licenciatura en una universidad de la Ciudad de Nueva York, pero mi inglés no es lo suficientemente bueno. ¿Puedo hacer algo al respecto?

Sí. CUNY tiene un programa de inmersión de idioma para ayudar a los inmigrantes a mejorar su inglés antes de comenzar los cursos universitarios. Las clases se ofrecen durante el día y la noche. Para más información, llame a la **Oficina de Servicios de Admisión de CUNY** al **1-212-997-2869** (Página 251).

■

"Mi primera escuela fue una escuela para adultos E.S.L. (Inglés como segundo idioma). El maestro no permitía que los estudiantes usaran un diccionario en la clase, teníamos que escuchar cuando él explicaba lo que significaba la palabra. Para hacernos entender la palabra 'sleeping' se acostó en el suelo. Para enseñarnos la hora trajo un reloj despertador. Todavía recuerdo todo lo que nos enseñó, porque dejó una profunda impresión en mí."

— *Ling Leung, chino, 1999* [8]

DINERO

"Dada la situación, al poco tiempo la mayoría de mis paisanos me estaban confiando sus ahorros sin esperar ningún tipo de interés a cambio. Yo, a la vez, invertí en bienes inmuebles y deposité en varios bancos todos sus ahorros y los míos también."

— *Inmigrante italiano anónimo, 1887* [9]

No se puede vivir durante mucho tiempo en Nueva York (o en ningún otro lugar) sin entender cómo ahorrar dinero y cómo gastarlo de manera inteligente en las cosas que uno necesita y le gustaría tener. El propósito de este capítulo, entre otras cosas, es guiarlo a través de los diferentes sistemas bancarios de la ciudad, explicarle cómo funciona un cajero automático, o A.T.M., y comentar sobre agencias de bajo costo para enviar dinero a su país de origen.

¿Qué lugares seguros hay en Nueva York para guardar el dinero?
Los bancos y las cooperativas de crédito son lugares seguros para guardar el dinero que trae con usted de su país, su sueldo u otras prestaciones. Para guardar el dinero en un banco tiene que abrir una cuenta. Para guardar el dinero en una cooperativa de crédito debe hacerse miembro.

¿Qué debo hacer para abrir una cuenta en un banco o cooperativa de crédito?
Cada banco y cooperativa de crédito tiene requisitos diferentes para abrir una cuenta, por lo tanto tendrá que consultar con el funcionario del banco o con el representante de cuenta. Por lo general, tendrá que proporcionar prueba del domicilio donde recibe el correo, por ejemplo, una factura de un servicio público y una tarjeta o número del Seguro Social. (El capítulo titulado Documentos ofrece

información sobre cómo conseguir una tarjeta o número del Seguro Social). Es probable que también tenga que mostrar dos formas de identificación, por lo general con foto. Algunos ejemplos son un pasaporte o visa, licencia de conducir, tarjeta de identificación de su trabajo, tarjeta de registro de no residente, certificado de naturalización, tarjeta de identificación de las fuerzas armadas o una tarjeta de crédito reconocida.

No tengo una licencia de conducir y no tengo trabajo. ¿Dónde puedo obtener una forma de identificación que pueda usar para abrir una cuenta y hacer otro tipo de trámites?

El **Departamento de Vehículos Automotores (Department of Motor Vehicles)** emite una tarjeta de identificación del estado con foto, no válida para conducir, pero que sirve como forma de identificación. Visite **www.nydmv.state.ny.us** para obtener instrucciones. Debido a las medidas de seguridad adicionales que se han implementado a partir del 11 de septiembre, el departamento con frecuencia actualiza en su sitio Web la lista de documentos aceptables para probar la identidad y fecha de nacimiento. También puede llamar al departamento al **1-212-645-5550** ó **1-718-966-6155** (inglés y español).

¿En qué se diferencia un banco de una cooperativa de crédito?

Un banco es propiedad de una compañía, una cooperativa de crédito es propiedad de todas las personas que tienen dinero depositado allí. Estas personas se llaman miembros. Por lo general, para ser miembro de una cooperativa de crédito, debe vivir en un vecindario específico o trabajar para una compañía o estar afiliado a un sindicato u organización social. Los bancos suelen tener más sucursales que las cooperativas de crédito y pueden resultar más convenientes en ese aspecto. Pero en las cooperativas de crédito sólo necesita una cantidad de dinero pequeña para abrir una cuenta, generalmente de $10 a $20. Ambos ofrecen servicios básicos similares si bien las cooperativas de créditos con frecuencia ofrecen tasas de interés un poco más bajas sobre los préstamos y más altas para los ahorros.

¿Qué características debo buscar en un banco o en una cooperativa de crédito?

Hágase estas preguntas:

- ¿Está el banco o la cooperativa de crédito asegurado por la Corporación de Protección al Ahorro Federal (F.D.I.C.) o la Administración Nacional de Cooperativas de Crédito (N.C.U.A.)?
- ¿Qué tipo de identificación debo mostrar para abrir una cuenta?
- ¿Cuáles son los cargos mensuales?
- ¿Debo mantener una cantidad mínima en la cuenta?
- ¿Cuánto tengo que esperar desde que abro la cuenta o deposito dinero o un cheque hasta poder retirar el dinero?

- ¿Hay requisitos diferentes para los cheques emitidos fuera del estado?
- ¿Hay límites para depositar dinero, hacer retiros y escribir cheques todos los meses?
- ¿Cobra el banco dinero extra si en vez de ir al banco, saco dinero de un cajero automático?
- ¿Me darán una tarjeta de crédito, y de ser así, cuál será el cargo anual y la tasa de interés?

Después que elijo un banco o una cooperativa de crédito, ¿qué debo hacer?
Decida qué tipo de cuenta quiere abrir. Los dos tipos principales son una cuenta corriente (o cuenta de cheques) y cuenta de ahorro.

¿Cómo funciona una cuenta de banco o de una cooperativa de crédito?
El dinero que usted pone en una cuenta corriente o de ahorro se llama un depósito. El dinero que usted saca se llama retiro de fondos. Una cuenta corriente le permitirá escribir cheques por la cantidad de dinero que tiene en la cuenta. Una cuenta de ahorro le pagará un pequeño porcentaje sobre el dinero que tiene depositado. Esto se llama interés.

¿Pagan interés las cuentas corrientes?
A veces, pero por lo general tiene que tener depositado varios miles de dólares para que le paguen interés.

¿Para qué puedo utilizar cheques?
Para pagar facturas y otros gastos, ya sea enviando cheques por correo o pagando en el lugar que le envió la factura. Los cheques son una manera fácil de pagar las cuentas y mantener un control de lo que gasta en alquiler, comida, teléfono, gas, electricidad y otras cosas.

¡advertencia!

Siempre hay personas dispuestas a prestarle dinero a un precio muy alto. Se llaman usureros y suelen aprovecharse de los inmigrantes pobres que están desesperados por dinero. Por lo general se los encuentra alrededor de las fábricas donde trabajan los inmigrantes y en los vecindarios donde viven. Si puede evitarlo, no debe tomar dinero prestado de estas personas porque es muy probable que no pueda pagar el interés y las comisiones que cobran, y en tal caso le ordenarán que haga más y más cosas para ellos. Generalmente son cosas ilegales o desagradables, y no querrá hacerlas. Los usureros pueden amenazar con causarle daño a usted o su familia si no hace lo que le piden.

¿Qué pasa con los cheques que escribo?

La persona o negocio a nombre de quien se escribe el cheque lo firma y lo cobra. Esto quiero decir que la cantidad de dinero que usted escribió en el cheque se saca de su cuenta y se paga a la persona o negocio a nombre de quien se escribió el cheque o a la cuenta de banco de éstos.

¿Recibiré de vuelta los cheques que escribo?

Algunos bancos envían los cheques cobrados de vuelta a la persona que los escribió. Un cheque que ha sido cobrado se llama cheque pagado. Otros bancos no le devuelven los cheques pero le envían una lista de los cheques que usted ha escrito y que han sido cobrados. Esta lista se llama estado de cuenta. Si le cuestionan el pago de una factura, su cheque pagado o el estado de cuenta que enumera los cheques pagados es una prueba de que usted ha pagado.

¿Qué otra cosa importante debo saber sobre una cuenta de banco?

- Siempre mantenga un registro cuidadoso de cada cheque que escribe.
- Mantenga un registro cuidadoso de cada depósito y retiro de fondos.
- Revise detenidamente cada estado de cuenta y compárelo con sus propios registros, para estar seguro de que todo corresponde. Recuerde deducir cualquier comisión por servicios o por cheque y agregar los intereses devengados.
- Si tiene problemas o hay algo que no entiende, lleve su libreta de cheques y estado de cuenta al banco y hable con un representante de atención al cliente.
- Cuando solicite cheques, pídalos con su dirección impresa en el cheque.

¿necesita más ayuda?

A continuación le ofrecemos una lista con algunos de los bancos más grandes con sucursales en toda la ciudad:

- Banco Popular (Página 242)
- Cathay Bank (Página 245)
- Chase (Página 247)
- Citibank (Página 250)
- HSBC (Página 258)

He aquí las cooperativas de crédito en la ciudad:

- Bethex Federal Credit Union (Página 243)
- Bushwick Cooperative Federal Credit Union (Página 244)
- Lower East Side People's Federal Credit Union (Página 261)
- University Settlement Federal Credit Union (Página 277)

He visto cheques que dicen "MEMO" en el extremo inferior izquierdo. ¿Qué quiere decir?

Allí es donde escribe el número de cuenta de la factura que está pagando o una nota para recordar el propósito del cheque.

¿Qué debo hacer si alguien me paga con un cheque?

Tiene que firmar el cheque atrás. Este proceso se llama endosar. Luego, cóbrelo en el banco o centro de canje de cheques, o deposítelo en su cuenta en el banco o a través de un cajero automático, que se explica más adelante en este capítulo.

¿Existen reglas acerca de firmar un cheque?

No hay reglas, pero hay ciertas precauciones que debería tomar. Siempre firme con tinta, y siempre escriba "para depósito solamente" y su número de cuenta al dorso de un cheque que endosa y tiene la intención de depositar en su cuenta. De esta manera, si pierde el cheque, ninguna otra persona lo puede cobrar. Si piensa ir al banco a depositar el cheque, en vez de hacerlo en un cajero automático, es mejor no endosar el cheque hasta estar dentro del banco. De esta manera si lo pierde, nadie puede hacerse pasar por usted y cobrarlo.

¿Qué pasa si escribo un cheque por una cantidad mayor a la que tengo en mi cuenta?

Si escribe un cheque por una cantidad mayor a la que tiene en la cuenta, el cheque será devuelto sin haber sido pagado. No haga esto. El banco y la compañía, a la que le escribió el cheque con fondos insuficientes, podrán cobrarle un cargo. Además aparecerá en sus antecedentes de crédito, y le resultará más difícil obtener una tarjeta de crédito, hacer compras a plazos, etc.

¿Qué es una cuenta de ahorro y cómo funciona?

Una cuenta de ahorro es útil para el dinero que no necesita de inmediato. En una cuenta de ahorro el banco le paga interés sobre su dinero. La cantidad de interés dependerá del banco y el tipo de cuenta que tenga. Puede sacar dinero de una cuenta de ahorro ya sea en efectivo o mediante un cheque del banco. Los depósitos se pueden hacer en efectivo o por cheque, pero es posible que tenga que esperar de 5 a 20 días para retirar el dinero que deposita mediante un cheque.

Si no tengo una cuenta en un banco o cooperativa de crédito, ¿cómo puedo cobrar mi cheque de sueldo y pagar las facturas?

Los centros de canje de cheques le permiten cobrar el cheque y pagar ciertas facturas, pero tendrá que pagar una comisión. Recuerde que estas comisiones suelen ser mucho más altas que aquellas que cobra un banco o cooperativa de crédito por los mismos servicios.

¡advertencia!

Nunca envíe dinero a otro país a través del correo de los Estados Unidos o internacional. En los Estados Unidos, es ilegal enviar dinero a través del correo o utilizar servicios de correo internacionales como DHL y Federal Express para enviar dinero.

¿Cómo funciona un centro de canje de cheques?

Un centro de canje de cheques le cobra una comisión por canjear su cheque de sueldo y otros tipos de cheques. Algunos canjean cheques personales; otros no o podrán cobrarle una comisión más alta. En algunos centros de canje de cheques también se puede pagar algunas facturas, pero tendrá que pagar una comisión.

Si no tengo una cuenta en un banco o cooperativa de crédito, ¿cómo podré enviar dinero a mi familia?

Las agencias de transferencia de dinero como **Western Union, 1-800-325-6000 (o para ayuda en español, 1-800-325-4045) (Página 278),** y **MoneyGram, 1-800-926-9400 (Página 264),** le cobran una comisión por enviar y recibir dinero internacionalmente. También puede comprar lo que se llama un giro postal, que puede utilizarse para pagar facturas y enviar dinero. Todos estos servicios tienen diferentes precios, requisitos de identificación, plazos para la compensación del cheque o fecha de vencimiento y otras reglas. Por lo tanto, es conveniente fijarse en los diferentes servicios antes de elegir.

¿Cómo funciona una agencia de transferencia de dinero?

Usted debe ir a una agencia de transferencia de dinero y completar un formulario disponible sólo en inglés y español. Le informa al empleado cuánto dinero desea enviar y el nombre de la persona que lo recibirá. Esa persona se llama destinatario. También deberá entregarle al empleado la cantidad de dinero que envía y la comisión que le cobran por enviar el dinero. El empleado le dará un número, generalmente llamado número de control, que usted debe indicar al destinatario. En un día, el dinero estará disponible en la moneda local del destinatario o en dólares americanos. Para recibir el dinero, el destinatario debe ir a la sucursal de la agencia de transferencia de dinero y dar el número de control al empleado.

¿Puedo transferir dinero a una cuenta de banco?

Sí, si usted o el destinatario tiene una cuenta en el banco y sabe el número de la cuenta, puede usar una agencia de transferencia de dinero para enviar dinero a esa cuenta.

¿Cómo sé en qué agencia de transferencia de dinero puedo confiar?

Pregunte a otras personas de su país que hayan enviado dinero sin problemas. Es posible que conozcan a una agencia de confianza o un representante que pueda ayudarle. Si **Western Union, 1-800-325-6000 (o para ayuda en español, 1-800-325-4045)** (Página 278), tiene una sucursal en su país de origen, probablemente es la manera más efectiva y más barata para transferir dinero. Si el destinatario tiene una cuenta de banco en su país, las transferencias bancarias son seguras.

Necesito enviar dinero a un lugar donde no hay bancos o sucursales de Western Union. ¿Cómo lograrlo?

Es posible que haya agencias privadas más pequeñas, como **Delgado Travel** (Página 254) que se encarguen de estas transacciones. Pregunte a otras personas si conocen una agencia confiable que puedan recomendar. Siempre es conveniente enviar primero una pequeña cantidad de dinero como prueba. Una vez que está seguro que el destinatario la ha recibido, puede enviar una cantidad mayor.

¿Cómo funciona un giro postal?

Usted compra un giro postal en un banco, centro de canje de cheques u oficina postal por la cantidad que quiere enviar o que necesita para pagar una factura. Por lo general, los giros postales son más baratos en el correo y se pueden rastrear en caso de robo o extravío antes de ser cobrados. No todos los negocios aceptan giros postales.

¿Qué es un cajero automático y cómo funciona?

Los cajeros automáticos, generalmente llamados A.T.M., son propiedad de un banco o cooperativa de crédito y le permiten hacer transacciones bancarias las 24 horas del día. Su banco o cooperativa de crédito le dará una tarjeta de A.T.M y le pedirá que

¡advertencia!

Los A.T.M. son muy convenientes pero cuando los utilice tenga estas precauciones:

- Siempre firme al dorso de su tarjeta de A.T.M. tan pronto la reciba, para que en caso de robo o extravío sea más difícil utilizarla.
- No escriba su PIN en la tarjeta o en ningún papel que guarda con la tarjeta.
- No permita que nadie vea cuando oprime su PIN o lo siga después que retira dinero.
- Trate de no ir a un A.T.M. por la noche si está solo.
- Trate de usar los A.T.M. que están en un sitio cerrado y bien iluminado, en vez de usar los que están en la calle
- Nunca permita que nadie, especialmente un extraño, utilice su tarjeta de A.T.M., aunque no esté seguro cómo usar el cajero y la persona se ofrezca a ayudarle.
- Después de usar un A.T.M. para sacar dinero, siempre guarde la tarjeta, el dinero y el recibo en su bolsillo o cartera antes de salir del vestíbulo o dejar el cajero.

elija un número de identificación personal o PIN, que sirve de contraseña. Cada A.T.M. tiene una pantalla que le explica paso por paso cómo usarlo, pero básicamente todos funcionan de la misma manera:

1. Inserte o deslice la tarjeta por la ranura del A.T.M.
2. Oprima en el teclado su PIN.
3. Complete la transacción. Puede retirar dinero, hacer depósitos, transferir dinero entre cuentas y obtener información sobre su saldo.
4. Cada vez que utiliza un A.T.M. recuerde solicitar un recibo, un pedazo de papel que indica qué transacción efectuó. Anote la transacción en su libreta de cheques o registro de la cuenta de ahorro.

No hablo muy bien inglés. ¿Tiene el cajero automático instrucciones en mi idioma?

La mayoría de los cajeros automáticos de la ciudad de Nueva York tienen instrucciones en inglés y español. En vecindarios con un gran número de inmigrantes que hablan otros idiomas, los cajeros también tendrán instrucciones en esos idiomas.

¿Son gratis los cajeros automáticos?

No. Por lo general un banco o una cooperativa de crédito donde tiene una cuenta le permitirá usar los A.T.M. gratis para efectuar un cierto número de depósitos y retiros de fondos cada mes. Pero los cajeros que pertenecen a otros bancos automáticamente le deducirán un cargo, por lo general de 75 centavos a $1.50 de su cuenta cada vez que los utilice. Estos cargos se acumulan rápidamente, por lo tanto trate de usar con poca frecuencia los cajeros automáticos que no pertenecen a su banco o cooperativa de crédito.

¿Puedo usar mi tarjeta de A.T.M. para hacer compras?

Sólo si su banco o cooperativa de crédito lo autoriza y si usted gana el dinero suficiente o tiene suficiente dinero depositado para poder hacerlo. Si utiliza su tarjeta de esta manera se llama una tarjeta de débito.

detalles sobre tarjetas de crédito

- Sólo compre con la tarjeta la mercancía que puede pagar cada mes si no quiere pagar intereses o cargos por financiamiento.
- Pague puntualmente o pueden cancelarle la tarjeta.
- Guarde todos los recibos de la tarjeta de crédito para saber qué compró y cuánto pagó.
- Revise el estado de cuenta mensual de la tarjeta de crédito e informe de inmediato al banco o a la tarjeta de crédito si le han cobrado por algo que no compró.

> **Los cargos por el uso de los cajeros automáticos se acumulan rápidamente, por lo tanto trate de usar únicamente los cajeros automáticos que pertenecen a su banco o cooperativa de crédito.**

¿Cómo funciona una tarjeta de débito?

Usted desliza su tarjeta en una pequeña máquina en la caja de la tienda e ingresa su PIN. Esto autoriza al banco o a la cooperativa de crédito a deducir el costo de lo que compró de su cuenta, como si escribiera un cheque. Algunos bancos cobran una comisión, al igual que con un cajero automático.

¿Qué es una tarjeta de crédito?

Una tarjeta de crédito le permite comprar bienes y servicios y pagar luego. A veces puede usar una tarjeta de crédito para tomar dinero en préstamo. Esto se llama adelanto en efectivo.

¿Cómo puedo obtener una tarjeta de crédito?

Primero debe tener un número de Seguro Social y mucha otra documentación. También tiene que llenar una solicitud. Puede recoger una solicitud en un banco, tienda, centro de canje de cheques y en otros lugares. El banco analizará toda la información en su solicitud y decidirá si cuenta con los recursos suficientes para tener una tarjeta de crédito. Si su solicitud es aprobada, podrá usar la tarjeta para comprar sólo una cantidad determinada de productos. Esa cantidad es su límite de crédito. Al final de cada mes, el banco o la compañía de la tarjeta de crédito le enviará un estado de cuenta en donde se enumera todo lo que ha comprado y le indica la cantidad mínima que debe pagar ese mes.

¿Son gratis las tarjetas de crédito?

Muchas sí, pero algunas cobran un cargo anual. Y cada mes que usted no paga el monto total de la mercancía que compró o el dinero en efectivo que tomó prestado ese mes, se le cobrará un cargo sobre la cantidad restante, llamada saldo. El cargo se llama interés o cargo por financiamiento y puede oscilar del 5 al 21 por ciento o más sobre el saldo.

¿Tengo una tarjeta de crédito de mi país, puedo usarla aquí?

Por lo general sí, si es una tarjeta de crédito de renombre como por ejemplo American Express, Visa o MasterCard. Asegúrese de que la factura le llegue a usted en su dirección en Nueva York.

Tengo trabajo pero necesito más dinero. Mi familia no puede enviarme dinero y yo no califico para una tarjeta de crédito. ¿Qué puedo hacer?

Si usted reúne los requisitos necesarios, un banco o una cooperativa de crédito puede prestarle dinero, sobre el que pagará interés. Cada banco o cooperativa de crédito tiene diferentes términos y requisitos, por lo tanto es conveniente consultar con un cajero o funcionario del banco.

■

"Mi primer trabajo fue barrer pisos. Mi primer cheque fue de $125 por semana. Estaba pensando en la moneda de Ecuador donde un buen salario es de $80 por mes. Por eso cuando me dieron un cheque por cinco días de trabajo, pensé 'Díos mío, soy rico.' Después de tres o cuatro semanas me di cuenta que tenía que pagar el alquiler, comprar 'tokens' para el metro y comida y me di cuenta que no era tanto dinero como pensaba."

— *Jose Zambrano, ecuatoriano, 2001*[10]

ATENCIÓN DE SALUD Y SEGURO

"Nunca fuimos al médico. Si nos torcíamos la muñeca patinando, nos curaba la abuela. Agarraba un pedazo de cordel y lo separaba. Luego, lo metía en una clara de huevo batida. Cuando nos vendaba la muñeca con este material, se ponía duro como el yeso, y nos mejorábamos. Era como un quiropráctico del antiguo mundo. Era una verdadera abuela italiana. También nos hacía masajes con aceites especiales. Cuando teníamos fiebre, nos frotaba todos los músculos del cuerpo y nos tiraba un dedo. Para el dolor de garganta, nos frotaba las glándulas y nos tiraba el cabello. Siempre funcionaba."

— *Marie Cutaia, nieta de inmigrantes italianos,*
recordando los años 1920[11]

El sistema de atención de salud del Siglo XXI en los Estados Unidos ha evolucionado en gran medida, a partir de los remedios caseros hasta la evaluación de enfermedades basada en el análisis de los genes, microcirugía y atención en establecimientos especiales para enfermos terminales. Lo que puede pagar según sus recursos por estos y muchos otros servicios, ya sea con su dinero o a través del seguro o asistencia pública, determina en gran medida el tipo de atención que recibirá. La ciudad de Nueva York tiene muchos hospitales y clínicas diferentes, públicos y privados, incluyendo algunos gratis y que ofrecen tratamiento a inmigrantes indocumentados, así como muchos programas de seguro privados y subsidiados.

En este capítulo se explican los diferentes servicios de atención de salud básicos en la ciudad y se mencionan agencias a las que puede acudir para obtener más información sobre estos servicios, para cuáles reúne las condiciones exigidas y cómo obtener la atención y el seguro que necesita.

¿Qué debo hacer si estoy muy enfermo o herido y necesito atención médica de inmediato?
Vaya al hospital más cercano lo más rápido posible.

¿Qué pasa si estoy demasiado enfermo o lesionado para llegar a un hospital o médico por mi cuenta?
Llame al 911, el número de teléfono de emergencia. Informe al operador cuáles son sus síntomas y dónde está. Una ambulancia lo recogerá y lo llevará a la sala de emergencia de un hospital cercano.

¿El operador del 911 hablará mi idioma?
Se puede tener acceso muy rápido a operadores que hablan virtualmente cualquier idioma.

¿Qué pasa si hay una emergencia y me llevan a un hospital que no puedo pagar y no tengo seguro?
Es ilegal para un hospital rehusarse a brindarle tratamiento de emergencia. Pregunte en el hospital si puede pagar una tarifa reducida basada en sus ingresos o capacidad de pago, o si es indocumentado, si tiene derecho a Medicaid de emergencia. Si recibe una factura no tendrá que pagarla toda de una sola vez. Negocie un plan de pago con el hospital.

Hablo muy poco inglés. ¿Me entenderán en el hospital?
La declaración de derechos de los pacientes requiere a los hospitales proporcionar un intérprete o traductor. Aunque le acompañe un amigo o pariente que puede traducir para usted, insista que el hospital además le asigne un intérprete.

¿Qué pasa si no es una emergencia pero tengo que quedarme en el hospital y no tengo seguro?
El hospital al que ha acudido tendrá que encontrar un hospital que lo admita sin seguro. Todos los hospitales públicos deben brindar atención sin tener en cuenta si tiene seguro, su situación como inmigrante o su capacidad de pago.

recibiendo tratamiento

A la fecha en que se imprimió esta guía, era ilegal para un hospital en Nueva York rehusarse a atender a inmigrantes indocumentados. Los hospitales públicos de la Ciudad de Nueva York tienen una política formal de no informar sobre su situación legal como inmigrante. A los hospitales y clínicas privadas no se les obliga ni se les recomienda informar sobre su situación legal como inmigrante.

¿necesita más ayuda?

Estos hospitales y organizaciones de atención de salud ofrecen servicios gratis o de bajo costo:

- Bellevue Hospital Center (Página 242)
- Charles B. Wang Community Health Center (Página 247)
- Community Healthcare Network, Bronx Center (Página 253)
- Lutheran Medical Center (Página 262)
- Morris Heights Health Center (Página 265)
- Promesa (Página 273)

No tengo seguro y no puedo pagar mucho. ¿Qué debo hacer si me enfermo pero no es una emergencia?

Si tiene una lesión menor o una enfermedad crónica como diabetes, asma o SIDA, puede recibir tratamiento en una sala de emergencia de un hospital, pero probablemente tenga que esperar mucho hasta ver a un médico. Trate de no ir a la sala de emergencia un sábado por la noche, el momento de más actividad en la mayoría de las salas de emergencia.

Si no tiene una enfermedad que hace peligrar su vida, vaya a una clínica gratis o de bajo costo. A veces puede hacer una cita en una clínica y no tendrá que esperar mucho. En Nueva York , las clínicas y los hospitales públicos atienden a pacientes que no tienen seguro y no pueden pagar el costo de la atención médica. Puede encontrar una lista de **hospitales públicos** en el siguiente sitio Web: **www.nyc. gov/html/hhc.home/html.** Éstos ofrecen muchos tipos de atención general y especializada, como por ejemplo tratamiento de problemas dentales, diabetes y abuso de sustancias. En el hospital o clínica le harán preguntas sobre sus ingresos y tendrá la oportunidad de conversar sobre los diferentes planes de pago. Si llama o va a un hospital o clínica que no ofrece el servicio que usted necesita, pregunte al personal que le indique a qué lugar debe dirigirse para obtener ese servicio.

¿Cuáles son algunos de estos hospitales y clínicas a los que puedo ir para tratamiento de lesiones de rutina, dolencias leves o una enfermedad crónica?

- Cualquier hospital público, clínica o programa de enfermería que son propiedad de la ciudad de Nueva York.
- Clínicas de salud en algunas escuelas primarias y secundarias. Los servicios abarcan desde una enfermera que visita la escuela una vez por semana y proporciona pruebas de la vista y la audición, hasta clínicas de servicios completos que atienden las necesidades de salud físicas y mentales de los estudiantes.
- Clínicas del Departamento de Salud que diagnostican y tratan enfermedades de

transmisión sexual y tuberculosis; vacunan; hacen pruebas del cáncer del seno; atienden a las mujeres embarazadas, madres primerizas y sus bebés; y brindan asesoramiento anónimo y pruebas del V.I.H.

¿Cuánto tendré que pagar por tratamiento no de emergencia en un hospital o una clínica si no tengo seguro?

Por lo general, depende de sus ingresos. Pregunte si los precios del hospital o de la clínica se basan en una escala móvil, lo que significa que la cantidad que le cobran aumenta según sus ingresos, de manera que las personas de ingresos muy bajos pagan muy poco o nada. Si tiene que pagar, por lo general tiene la opción de pagar a plazos.

¿Tendré que mostrar prueba de lo que gano en un hospital o clínica?

Sí. Por lo general, le pedirán que presente el recibo de su cheque de sueldo o una carta de su empleador, si bien algunos hospitales y clínicas aceptan un formulario de autodeclaración en el que usted indica cuánto gana.

Entonces, ¿necesito realmente seguro de salud?

Sí. Realmente no puede predecir cuál será el monto de su factura médica. Si usted y su familia se enferman en raras ocasiones, sus costos de atención de salud pueden ser bajos. Pero si usted o alguien en su familia se enferma o lesiona, los costos podrían ser muy altos, demasiado altos para que usted pueda pagarlos. Si reúne los requisitos, debe tratar de inscribirse en un programa de seguro.

¿Todos los trabajos ofrecen seguro de salud?

No, pero la mayoría de los trabajos a tiempo completo ofrecen algún tipo de beneficios de salud, en cambio la mayoría de los trabajos a tiempo parcial, no. Si puede obtener seguro de salud a través de su trabajo, los pagos para pagar todo o parte del seguro serán deducidos automáticamente de su cheque de sueldo.

Si tengo seguro, ¿significa que no tendré que pagar nada cuando voy al médico o compro un medicamento con receta?

No necesariamente. Es posible que tenga que pagar de $5 a $20 por algunos servicios, tales como visitas al médico o cuando compre un medicamento con receta. Esto se llama un copago. En vez de copagos, algunos planes de seguro le exigen pagar un porcentaje del costo de la visita al médico o del medicamento con receta.

Perdí mi trabajo. ¿Qué pasa con mi seguro de salud?

Una ley federal llamada Cobra le permite pagar su cobertura de seguro de salud de grupo por hasta 18 meses, pero el seguro en virtud de Cobra es mucho más caro. Medicaid, que ofrece cobertura para algunas personas de bajos ingresos que no pueden pagar un seguro de salud, puede ayudarle a pagar la cobertura de familia para su cónyuge y sus hijos.

¿necesita más ayuda?

Estas organizaciones le ofrecen información sobre cómo obtener seguro de salud:

- Asian Americans for Equality (A.A.F.E.) (Página 241)
- Citizens Advice Bureau (C.A.B.) (Página 251)
- The Door (Página 254)
- Managed Care Consumers Assistance Program (M.C.C.A.P.), Community Service Society of New York (Página 262)

Estoy cubierto por el plan de seguro en el trabajo de mi cónyuge. ¿Qué pasa si nos divorciamos o mi cónyuge fallece?
Podrá pagar la cobertura en virtud de Cobra, y otros miembros de su familia pueden calificar para cobertura bajo Medicaid.

¿Qué pasa si mi empleador no ofrece seguro de salud, o si no estoy trabajando y no puedo pagar un seguro de salud?
Puede comprar su propio seguro de salud, pero el seguro de salud privado es muy caro, de $300 a $500 por mes o más. Si puede comprarlo, hágalo. Además, muchos individuos y familias de bajos recursos tienen derecho a participar en programas de seguros de salud gratis o de bajo costo como por ejemplo, **Medicaid, Family Health Plus, Child Health Plus** o **Healthy NY**, que se describen más adelante en este capítulo.

¿Cómo puedo averiguar lo que ofrecen los programas de seguro de salud gratis o de bajo costo en Nueva York, si puedo solicitarlos y cómo inscribirme?
Estos programas se describen en varias respuestas a continuación. Para obtener información básica sobre ellos, llame a la línea de información de la **Administración de Recursos Humanos (Human Resources Administration — H.R.A.)** al 1-877-472-8411 (Página 258).

Para averiguar si usted y su familia reúnen los requisitos de elegibilidad para estos programas, llame a la línea de teléfono de tono automática del **Departamento de Salud e Higiene Mental (Department of Health and Mental Hygiene), HealthStat** al 1-888-692-6116 (Página 268). Le harán preguntas para determinar cuáles son los programas a los que usted y su familia pueden tener acceso y los lugares más convenientes en los que se puede inscribir.

Además, puede ir a las oficinas de organizaciones comunitarias, organizaciones de servicios sociales, planes de salud y a los médicos y hospitales que son parte de estos planes, y clínicas de salud de la ciudad. Para obtener información sobre dónde están ubicados estos lugares y grupos llame a la línea HealthStat (Página 256) o visite el sitio Web administrado por la **Oficina de Acceso a Seguros de**

Salud del Alcalde (Mayor's Office of Health Insurance Access, www.nyc.gov/html/hia/html/places.html).

¿Qué es Medicaid?

Medicaid proporciona cobertura a algunas personas de bajos ingresos que no pueden pagar el costo de un seguro de salud.

¿Pueden los inmigrantes indocumentados recibir Medicaid?

Sólo las personas que están embarazadas o requieren tratamiento médico de emergencia y cumplen con todos los demás requisitos de elegibilidad. No obstante, otros inmigrantes sí califican. En Nueva York, los inmigrantes legales y aquellos inmigrantes con estado legal conocido como Prucol (personas residentes bajo apariencia legal) para el **Servicio de Inmigración y Ciudadanía de los Estados Unidos (United States Citizenship and Immigration Services — U.S.C.I.S.)**, pueden tener derecho a recibir Medicaid independientemente de cuándo llegaron a los Estados Unidos. Hay varias categorías de Prucol, incluyendo inmigrantes que han recibido suspensiones de deportación y que tienen autorización a quedarse en los Estados Unidos por un período indefinido. Estos inmigrantes deben cumplir con otros estándares de elegibilidad, como por ejemplo ingresos, para poder inscribirse.

El formulario de solicitud de Medicaid no pide información sobre el estado legal de los demás miembros de la familia, y el estado de Nueva York no comparte la información que aparece en el formulario con el gobierno federal. El U.S.C.I.S, una división del **Departamento de Seguridad Interna de los Estados Unidos,** ha decidido que el uso de Medicaid no afectará la capacidad de ningún miembro de la familia de obtener una tarjeta verde, hacerse ciudadano, patrocinar a un miembro de la familia o entrar y salir de los Estados Unidos.

¿Cómo puedo averiguar si tengo derecho a recibir Medicaid, y de ser así, cómo me inscribo?

Las personas que reciben asistencia pública o prestaciones sociales tienen derecho automáticamente. Otros pueden reunir los requisitos de elegibilidad porque están incapacitados. Para averiguar si califica y dónde inscribirse, llame a la **línea HealthStat** al 1-888-692-6116 (Página 256), o a la línea de información de la (**Human Resources Administration — H.R.A.**), 1-877-472-8411 (Página 258), o visite el sitio Web en www.nyc.gov/html/hra/html/serv_medicaid.html.

¿Qué debo llevar conmigo cuando vaya a inscribirme en Medicaid?

De los documentos que mencionamos a continuación, tantos como sea posible, prueba de edad, como por ejemplo un certificado de nacimiento; prueba de ciudadanía o estado legal; prueba de su domicilio, tal como el recibo del alquiler o una

¿necesita más ayuda?

He aquí algunos lugares donde puede ir para obtener más información sobre Medicaid:

- Línea de ayuda de Medicaid del estado de Nueva York, 1-800-541-2831 (inglés, español, cantonés y mandarín)
- Medical and Health Research Association of New York City (M.H.R.A.) (Página 263)
- New York City Workforce 1 Career Center (Página 269)

carta del dueño de su apartamento; recibo actual de su cheque de sueldo si trabaja; prueba de ingresos de otras fuentes, como por ejemplo, recibo del cheque del Seguro Social o libreta de cheques.

¿Es difícil el trámite de solicitud?

Sí. Todas las personas que solicitan Medicaid deberán confrontar retos burocráticos antes de inscribirse, y los inmigrantes deben mostrar prueba de su situación legal. Esto es especialmente difícil para aquellos que califican como Prucol debido a las diferentes categorías y a todos los formularios y cartas que se requieren. Lo importante es no darse por vencido antes de recibir los beneficios a los que tiene derecho.

Si califico para Medicaid, ¿qué debo mostrarle al médico o clínica para probarlo?

Recibirá una tarjeta de identificación de beneficios para usar cuando necesite servicios médicos.

¿Cubrirá Medicaid el costo de toda la atención médica que mi familia y yo necesitamos?

No. Algunos servicios no estarán cubiertos, y tendrá que verificar antes de obtener ciertos servicios para ver si están cubiertos. Esto se llama autorización previa.

¿Tendré que pagar algo por Medicaid o cuando vea a un médico que acepta pagos de Medicaid?

No. Los beneficios son gratis, y no hay costos adicionales, conocidos como copagos, por estos servicios.

¿Qué es Family Health Plus?

Family Health Plus es un programa de seguro de salud público para personas de 19 a 64 años de edad que no pueden comprar seguro de salud por cuenta propia o a través de sus trabajos, que sus ingresos exceden los límites establecidos para recibir Medicaid. Ofrece cobertura completa gratis, incluyendo prevención, atención primaria, hospitalización, recetas y otros servicios.

¿Pueden los inmigrantes indocumentados participar del programa Family Health Plus?
No, Family Health Plus no se ofrece a los inmigrantes indocumentados.

¿Cómo puedo averiguar si califico para Family Health Plus, y de ser así, dónde puedo inscribirme?
Los residentes de la ciudad de Nueva York de 19 a 64 años de edad que no tienen seguro de salud por cuenta propia o a través de sus trabajos y que no califican para otros programas de salud pública como Medicare o Medicaid, califican para Family Health Plus. Para averiguar localidades y obtener lugares para ponerse en contacto llame a la línea HealthStat al 1-888-692-6116 (Página 256), o visite el sitio Web en www.nyc.gov/html/hia/html/places.html.

¿Hay límites de ingresos para calificar para Family Health Plus?
Usted y su familia pueden tener ingresos y aún calificar para Family Health Plus depende de cuántas personas hay en su familia.

¿Puede tener mi familia una cuenta de banco y solicitar Family Health Plus?
Sí. No hay límites sobre otros activos y recursos.

Estoy embarazada. ¿Califico para Family Health Plus?
Sí, pero debe reunir los requisitos de ingresos, que son más altos que para Medicaid.

¿Qué es Child Health Plus?
Child Health Plus es un programa de seguro patrocinado por el estado de Nueva York para menores de 19 años que no tienen seguro.

Mis hijos están indocumentados. ¿Puedo recibir Child Health Plus?
Todos los niños menores de 19 años tienen derecho a Child Health Plus sin importar su estado legal.
El formulario de solicitud de Child Health Plus no pide información sobre el estado legal de ningún miembro de la familia, y el estado de Nueva York no com-

¿necesita más ayuda?

Estos grupos ayudarán con los trámites para solicitar Family Health Plus:

- Alianza Dominicana (Página 240)
- Caribbean Women's Health Association (Página 245)
- Chinese-American Planning Council (Página 249)
- Medical and Health Research Association of New York City (Página 263)

parte la información que aparece en el formulario con el gobierno federal. La U.S.C.I.S. ha decidido que usar el programa Child Health Plus no afectará la capacidad de ningún miembro de la familia de obtener la tarjeta verde, hacerse ciudadano, patrocinar a un miembro de la familia o entrar y salir de los Estados Unidos.

¿Tengo que pagar por Child Health Plus?

Es posible que tenga que pagar un cargo mensual bajo para participar en el plan, pero no tendrá que pagar nada cuando su hijo va al médico.

¿Qué servicios cubre Child Health Plus?

Si sus hijos califican para Child Health Plus, tendrá que elegir a un proveedor local, que decidirá a qué servicios tiene derecho y a qué médicos puede ver bajo el plan.

¿Cómo puedo averiguar si mis hijos califican, y de ser así, cómo los inscribo?

Llame a la línea HealthStat al 1-888-692-6116 (Página 256), o visite el sitio Web en www.nyc.gov/html/hia/html/places.html. Para una lista de los lugares donde se puede inscribir y para obtener más información sobre Child Health Plus, llame al 1-800-698-4543 (inglés y español).

¿Qué es Healthy NY?

Healthy NY es un programa que ofrece seguro de salud de bajo costo para las personas que trabajan y reúnen ciertos requisitos de elegibilidad.

¿Cómo puedo averiguar si califico para Healthy NY y de ser así, cómo puedo inscribirme?

Llame a la línea HealthStat al 1-888-692-6116 (Página 256), o visite el sitio Web en www.nyc.gov/html/hia/html/places.html.

¿Qué es Medicare?

Medicare es un programa de seguro federal para personas mayores de 65 años y personas incapacitadas menores de 65 años que han recibido beneficios por incapacidad del Seguro Social por más de 24 meses. Ayuda a pagar ciertos costos de hospital y atención médica. Está dividido en Medicare Parte A y Medicare Parte B.

¿Mi estado legal como inmigrante afectará si puedo o no conseguir Medicare?

Usted debe ser un inmigrante legal pero no es necesario que sea ciudadano para recibir Medicare. Por lo general, reúne los requisitos si tiene 65 años de edad o más, es ciudadano o residente permanente de los Estados Unidos y si usted o su cónyuge han trabajado por 10 años en un empleo cubierto por Medicare.

¿Hay costos estándares para Medicare Parte A y Medicare Parte B?

Tanto Medicare Parte A como Parte B cobran cargos mensuales, conocidos como primas, y por cada parte debe pagar una cierta cantidad por el tratamiento recibido durante un período de tiempo. Medicare paga el resto. La cantidad que usted paga se llama deducible. Ambas partes tienen honorarios fijos que usted debe pagar por cada consulta médica o sala en el hospital. Esto se llama copago.

¿Qué cubre Medicare Parte A?

Medicare Parte A (Seguro de hospital) ayuda a pagar los costos cuando usted es internado en un hospital y ocupa una habitación semiprivada o pabellón o es enviado a un centro de enfermería especializada después de una hospitalización de tres días. También paga las transfusiones sanguíneas que usted recibe cuando está en un hospital o centro de enfermería especializada. Paga la internación en un establecimiento aprobado por Medicare para pacientes terminales y por algunos servicios de atención de salud en el hogar. *No* paga por una habitación privada, enfermeras privadas, o un teléfono o televisión en la habitación.

¿Qué cubre Medicare Parte B?

Medicare Parte B (seguro médico) ayuda a pagar los servicios de los médicos además de los exámenes físicos de rutina; servicios médicos ambulatorios y servicios y suministros quirúrgicos; pruebas de diagnóstico y operaciones autorizadas en un centro de cirugía ambulatorio; transfusiones sanguíneas que recibe como paciente externo; y equipo médico durable, como por ejemplo, sillas de ruedas, camas de hospital y andadores. Asimismo, cubre algunos servicios de atención de salud en el hogar enumerados en Medicare Parte A.

Medicare también paga:

- Los servicios de ambulancia cuando otros medios de transporte podrían poner en peligro su salud
- Ojos y miembros artificiales y sus partes de repuesto
- Aparatos ortopédicos para los brazos, las piernas, la espalda y el cuello
- Servicios de quiropráctico limitados a la manipulación de la espina dorsal
- Atención de emergencia
- Un par de marcos de anteojos estándar y lentes apropiados después de una operación de cataratas
- Tratamiento con fármacos para pacientes de transplantes cubiertos por Medicare
- Tratamiento para la degeneración macular
- Tratamiento médico nutritivo para personas con diabetes o enfermedades del riñón
- Algunos suministros médicos
- Muy pocos medicamentos recetados para pacientes externos
- Algunos servicios preventivos

- Dispositivos prostéticos, incluyendo prótesis del seno
- Algunas segundas opiniones médicas
- Servicios de profesionales, incluyendo trabajadores sociales clínicos, asistentes de médicos y enfermeras diplomadas
- Zapatos terapéuticos para personas con diabetes
- Transplantes realizados bajo ciertas condiciones y en centros autorizados por Medicare
- Radiografías, imágenes por resonancia magnética (M.R.I.), tomografías computadas (CAT scans), electrocardiograma (E.K.G.) y algunas pruebas de diagnóstico.

¿Cuánto cuesta Medicare Parte A (Seguro de hospital)?

La mayoría de los individuos no tienen que pagar la prima por la Parte A porque ellos o sus cónyuges pagaron impuestos de Medicare mientras trabajaban. Pero es posible que tengan que pagar otros deducibles y copagos, que pueden variar.

No pagué impuestos de Medicare. ¿Puedo obtener Medicare Parte A (Seguro de hospital)?

Si usted o su cónyuge no pagó impuestos de Medicare mientras trabajó y tiene 65 años de edad o más, es posible que aún así pueda comprar la Parte A. Llame al **1-800-633-4227** (inglés y español), o visite el sitio Web **www.medicare.gov**.

¿Cuánto cuesta Medicare Parte B (Seguro médico)?

A principios del 2003, la prima mensual era de $58.70. El costo cambia anualmente; puede obtener la información más reciente llamando al **1-800-633-4227** (inglés y español) o visitando el sitio Web en **www.medicare.gov**.

No puedo pagar Medicare Parte B (Seguro médico). ¿Qué puedo hacer?

Hay cuatro programas para personas de bajos ingresos que necesitan ayuda para pagar las primas de Medicare. Llame a la **línea de información de la Administración de Recursos Humanos (Human Resources Administration)** al 1-877-472-8411 (Página 258).

¿Cómo me inscribo en Medicare?

El **Departamento para las Personas de la Tercera Edad** de la ciudad (**Department for the Aging**) tiene una herramienta de evaluación llamada **UNIForm** que le ayuda a averiguar si califica para los principales programas de beneficios federales, estatales y municipales. Está disponible en los centros para personas de la tercera edad en toda la ciudad.

Para encontrar un centro cercano a usted, llame al **Centro de Llamadas del Departamento para las Personas de la Tercera Edad de la Ciudad de Nueva York**

(New York City Department for the Aging Senior Call Center) al **1-212-442-1000** (inglés, español, cantonés, mandarín y otros idiomas). También puede visitar el sitio Web en **home.nyc.gov/html/dfta.** Asimismo, puede inscribirse a través de la Administración del Seguro Social o llamando al **1-800-772-1213** (inglés y español).

Tengo que tomar medicamentos que no puedo pagar. ¿Qué puedo hacer?

Muchos planes de seguro de salud, no cubren el costo de los medicamentos con receta. Otros planes tienen limitaciones con respecto al costo o las marcas de medicamentos que cubren. Los programas que siguen a continuación pueden ayudarle a pagar los medicamentos con receta:

■ **AIDS Drug Assistance Program (A.D.A.P.)** cubre el costo de los medicamentos para algunas personas de bajos ingresos con la infección del V.I.H. y otras afecciones relacionadas. Llame al **1-800-542-2437** (inglés y español).

■ **Elder Pharmaceutical Insurance Coverage (EPIC)** es un plan de medicamentos con receta para personas de bajos ingresos de más de 65 años. Para obtener más información y un formulario de solicitud, llame a la línea de información gratis de EPIC al **1-800-332-3742** (inglés y español).

Soy indocumentado. ¿Califico para un programa de medicamentos con receta de bajo costo?

Sí. Puede calificar para **A.D.A.P.** y **EPIC** independientemente de su estado legal como inmigrante.

¡esté preparado!

Antes de que ocurra una emergencia, haga una lista de lo que tiene que informar a los médicos y enfermeras y téngala a mano para llevarla con usted al hospital. Debe incluir:

■ Enfermedades graves que ha tenido
■ Operaciones
■ Alergias
■ Afecciones crónicas
■ Medicamentos que toma (si tiene tiempo, llévelos con usted)
■ Síntomas, tales como dolor, enrojecimiento, náuseas, adormecimiento, inflamación, etc., y cuándo comenzaron
■ Antecedentes familiares de enfermedades
■ Fecha de nacimiento
■ Número de seguro social, si tiene uno
■ Nombre, dirección y número de teléfono del empleador, si trabaja

¿Existen límites de ingresos y copagos para los programas de medicamentos con receta de bajo costo?

Sí, pero están sujetos a cambio. Por lo tanto, llame a los números que aparecen previamente para averiguar los límites actuales de ingresos y los copagos.

■

"Cuando llegué a este país hace ocho años, no tenía información acerca de dónde ir si estaba enferma, tenía una emergencia o para un simple examen regular. Y como muchos otros, llegué a este país sin documentos y tenía miedo. Pero no es necesario que sea así, porque no debemos poner nuestra salud e incluso nuestras vidas en peligro. Afortunadamente, la mayoría de las ciudades en los Estados Unidos tienen sistemas de atención de salud muy eficientes. Y lo que es aún mejor, muchos de estos servicios son gratis y la discriminación es ilegal."

— *Maricela Gonzalez, mexicana, 1999* [12]

SEGURIDAD

"**C**onvoqué a las personas de la comunidad y fundamos la Asociación India Americana Unida. Organizamos cinco manifestaciones. Desde que tomamos medidas, las cosas han mejorado. Antes, atacaban a los indios todos los días. Atacaron a más de 20 familias. Entraban a las casas, a las tiendas y negocios indios todos los días. Atacaban a las mujeres indias cuando salían de compras. Las señalaban con el dedo en la calle, las golpeaban. Pero ahora está bajo control. Ahora hay menos temor al caminar por las calles."

— *Hardayal Singh, indio, 1977* [13]

■

La ciudad de Nueva York es más segura hoy en día que en las últimas dos décadas. El índice de delitos ha bajado en forma constante desde mediados de los años 1990 y ha caído aún más drásticamente después de los ataques del 11 de septiembre de 2001.

Sin embargo, el 11 de septiembre fue un claro ejemplo de que la ciudad debe confrontar la amenaza cada vez mayor del terrorismo. Y esta amenaza tiene un impacto considerable en la vida de muchos inmigrantes.

El 11 de septiembre llevó a la creación del **Departamento de Seguridad Interna de los Estados Unidos**, que ahora es responsable de muchas de las funciones de las que previamente se encargaba el **Servicio de Inmigración y Naturalización**, o I.N.S. La **Oficina de Inmigración y Aduanas (Bureau of Immigration and Customs Enforcement — B.I.C.E.)** del departamento busca a las personas que están en el país con una visa vencida, aquellos que no han acatado las órdenes de deportación o que están indocumentados. Una persona que tiene la documentación apropiada pero que ha cometido un delito, también corre un riesgo mayor de ser deportada.

El tema central de este capítulo es el de sus derechos como inmigrante que vive en los Estados Unidos y en la ciudad de Nueva York y su seguridad. La seguridad abarca muchos temas, entre ellos cómo protegerse de diferentes delitos, tales como violación y robo, y qué hacer si es la víctima no sólo de un delito, sino de conducta inapropiada de parte de un policía o de la B.I.C.E.

¿Puede la policía entrar en mi casa en cualquier momento y hacer un registro?

No. Usted tiene el derecho a denegar el ingreso a cualquier oficial de policía salvo que el agente tenga una orden válida firmada por un juez. Esto se llama orden de allanamiento.

¿Hay veces que la policía está autorizada a entrar en mi casa sin una orden de allanamiento?

Sí. La policía puede entrar a su casa y hacer un registro sin una orden de allanamiento en una situación de emergencia, por ejemplo cuando una persona está gritando pidiendo auxilio dentro de su casa o cuando la policía está persiguiendo a alguien.

Existe la posibilidad de que el Departamento de Justicia de los Estados Unidos autorice que las normas promulgadas después del 11 de septiembre sean utilizadas por los departamentos de policía locales para arrestar a inmigrantes sin un mandamiento judicial si se sospecha que han violado leyes de inmigración. Pero no está claro cómo los departamentos locales, incluyendo el departamento de policía de Nueva York interpretarán y utilizarán estas normas. Además, las normas que afectan a los inmigrantes cambian con frecuencia, por lo tanto es recomendable consultar con un grupo de defensa de los inmigrantes que se menciona en el Directorio de Recursos al final de esta guía, o si puede pagarlo, consulte con un abogado de inmigración de buena reputación.

¿Qué pasa si la policía tiene una orden de allanamiento pero yo no quiero que entren en mi casa?

Siempre diga a los agentes de policía que usted no está de acuerdo con el registro. Esto limitará la inspección a una zona especificada en la orden de allanamiento. Pregunte si puede presenciar el registro. Si se lo autorizan, tome notas, incluyendo los nombres, los números en la insignia y las agencias de los oficiales. Llame a un abogado o a un defensor de los inmigrantes cuanto antes.

¿Qué pasa si la policía entra por la fuerza en mi casa y hace un registro?

Haga todo lo que se menciona previamente.

¿Qué pasa si la policía me para en la calle?

Tiene derecho a preguntarle a la policía si está libre para irse. Sea amable y mantenga las manos donde la policía se las pueda ver. No corra ni se resista al arresto. No haga ninguna declaración. No firme nada que no entiende. Pida ver a un abogado. Comuníquese con una de las organizaciones que se mencionan en el recuadro abajo.

¿Qué debo hacer si la policía me detiene y decide hacer un registro?

Usted no está obligado a consentir el registro. Si no quiere consentir, diga claramente, "No consiento el registro," y haga todo lo que se describe en la respuesta previamente.

¿Qué debo hacer si un agente de policía me lesiona o viola mis derechos?

Usted tiene derecho a pedirle al policía que le diga su nombre y número de insignia. si se rehusa, trate de recordarlos del uniforme. Tan pronto pueda escriba todo lo que sucedió y tome fotografías de sus lesiones, cortes y hematomas. Trate de encontrar testigos del acto.

Para obtener asesoramiento legal, póngase en contacto con las organizaciones que se mencionan a continuación y llame a la **Línea de Información de la Junta de Evaluación de Quejas Civiles (Civilian Complaint Review Board)** al **1-800-341-CCRB (2272)** (Página 252).

¿Qué es la Junta de Evaluación de Quejas Civiles?

La junta, también conocida como C.C.R.B. por sus siglas en inglés, es un organismo independiente de la ciudad que no está relacionado con el Departamento de Policía y que está autorizado a evaluar los informes sobre abusos policiales. Las quejas pueden ser presentadas por la víctima o un testigo. No tiene que ser ciudadano de los

¿necesita más ayuda?

Estas agencias y grupos proporcionan asesoramiento legal y referencias:

- Asian American Legal Defense and Education Fund (Página 241)
- The Bronx Defenders (Página 243)
- Caribbean Women's Health Association (C.W.H.A.) (Página 245)
- CUNY Law School — Main Street Legal Services, Immigration and Refugee Rights (Página 254)
- Legal Aid Society (Página 260)
- New York Association for New Americans (N.Y.A.N.A.) (Página 265)
- New York City Commission on Human Rights (Página 267)
- Queens Legal Services (Página 273)
- Safe Horizon (Página 274)

> **❝ Si lo para la policía, sea amable y mantenga las manos donde la policía se las pueda ver. No corra ni se resista al arresto. ❞**

Estados Unidos o residente de la ciudad de Nueva York. Es importante presentar una queja cuanto antes porque la junta tiene sólo 18 meses para examinar su queja.

¿Qué documentos debo mostrar para probar mi estado legal?

Si es un residente permanente, su Tarjeta de Residencia Permanente o Tarjeta de Registro de Extranjeros, comúnmente llamada tarjeta verde, o su pasaporte. Si es un extranjero no inmigrante, su tarjeta de llegada-salida (I-94), una notación en su pasaporte u otra prueba de su estado del **Servicio de Inmigración y Ciudadanía de los Estados Unidos, o U.S.C.I.S.**, otra división del Departamento de Seguridad Interna.

¿Qué pasa si la policía me pide mis documentos de inmigración?

Pregunte si está libre para irse. Si le dicen que sí, aléjese. Si le dicen que no, usted está siendo detenido. Esto no quiere decir necesariamente que es un arresto. La policía tiene derecho a "registrarlo," es decir que pueden tocarle el cuerpo por encima de la ropa. No autorice a la policía a un registro más intenso. Dígale a la policía: "No consiento. Quiero hablar con mi abogado."

¿Qué pasa si la policía continúa con el registro después que les digo que no consiento y que quiero hablar con mi abogado?

Conserve la calma. No discuta con la policía o con los agentes del (B.I.C.E.) Podrían lastimarlo y arrestarlo. Siga diciendo: "No consiento. Quiero hablar con mi abogado." Obtenga los nombres, el número de insignia y la agencia de los policías. No tiene que contestar preguntas ni hacer una declaración si lo detienen e incluso si lo arrestan.

¿Tengo que dar mi nombre si me detienen o arrestan?

Legalmente, no tiene que dar su nombre salvo que sospechen que cometió un delito. Pero rehusarse a dar su nombre puede despertar sospechas. Recuerde que la policía o los agentes de la B.I.C.E. pueden tener una lista de nombres de extranjeros sujetos a deportación. Es probable que dar un nombre falso no sea un delito enjuiciable por sí mismo, pero es ilegal, y la policía o la B.I.C.E. pueden detenerlo si lo hace.

¿Qué pasa si la policía me detiene cuando estoy conduciendo?

Debe mostrar su licencia de conducir, registro del vehículo y prueba de seguro, pero no tiene que aceptar un registro, si bien la policía puede tener derecho a inspeccionar su coche legalmente.

¡no deje su casa sin ellos!

Además de sus documentos de inmigración tales como la visa, permiso de trabajo, tarjeta de ingreso/salida del país (I-94) o la tarjeta verde, siempre lleve el nombre y número de teléfono de un abogado de inmigración de confianza que responderá a su llamada. Las leyes de inmigración son difíciles de entender y han ocurrido muchos cambios desde el 11 de septiembre. Es posible que haya más cambios. La Oficina de Inmigración y Aduanas no le explicará sus derechos o sus opciones. Tan pronto se encuentre con un agente de la B.I.C.E, llame a su abogado. Si no puede llamar o no puede comunicarse de inmediato, siga intentándolo.

Soy indocumentado. ¿Puede arrestarme un agente de la B.I.C.E. sin un mandamiento judicial?

Sí, un agente de la B.I.C.E. está autorizado a arrestarlo sin una orden firmada si el agente piensa que usted está en los Estados Unidos ilegalmente y que puede escapar antes de obtener un mandamiento judicial.

¿Qué sucede si me arresta un agente de la B.I.C.E.? ¿Me pueden poner en un avión de regreso a mi país?

En la mayoría de los casos, deben concederle una audiencia ante un juez de inmigración en un Tribunal de Inmigración. Pero la ley no estipula un plazo para que el tribunal le conceda la audiencia.

¿Me pueden deportar sin una audiencia ante un juez de inmigración?

Sí, si usted "renuncia" a su derecho a una audiencia, acepta irse sin una audiencia, ha sido condenado por ciertos delitos, fue arrestado en la frontera o ha sido deportado antes.

¿Me pueden deportar aunque tenga una tarjeta verde y otros documentos?

Los inmigrantes condenados por un delito definido por la ley de inmigración como un "delito grave" pueden ser deportados. Puede encontrar una lista de delitos graves en la Web en **www.newamericans.com/citizen/articles/felonieslist.html.** Es recomendable obtener asesoramiento legal sobre cómo la condena por un delito puede afectar el estado legal de un inmigrante.

Fui hallado culpable por un delito pero no tuve que ir a la cárcel. ¿Me pueden deportar?

Sí. Si ha sido condenado por un delito en los Estados Unidos — aunque sólo haya pagado una multa y no fue encarcelado — Es esencial que usted consulte con un abogado de inmigración o defensor de inmigrantes antes de viajar al extranjero (En la página 206 se mencionan varios grupos que ofrecen asesoramiento legal). Si sale del país y trata de volver a entrar y/o si solicita la ciudadanía, con frecuencia corre el riesgo de procedimientos de deportación.

¿Realmente me buscará la B.I.C.E. por una ofensa menor?

Siempre existe ese riesgo. Y aunque un agente de la B.I.C.E. no lo esté buscando, puede entrar en contacto con la agencia después de cumplir su sentencia y está solicitando su ciudadanía u otros beneficios de inmigración, o cuando regresa a los Estados Unidos después de una vacación o viaje de negocios fuera del país.

Si un agente de la B.I.C.E. me detiene o me pone bajo custodia, ¿debo firmar algún documento?

No firme nada que no entiende. Al firmar un documento que le presenta un agente de la B.I.C.E., es posible que esté renunciando a ciertos derechos o aceptando volver a su país. Comuníquese con un abogado o defensor de inmigrantes.

¿Qué pasa si un agente de la B.I.C.E. viene a mi lugar de trabajo?

Desde el 11 de septiembre es más probable que la policía o los agentes de la B.I.C.E. vayan a un lugar de trabajo sin un mandamiento judicial buscando trabajadores indocumentados o trabajadores que se sospecha son terroristas o están asociados con terroristas. En tal caso, diga solamente que quiere hablar con un abogado o un defensor de inmigrantes. Recuerde que la información que le da a un agente de la B.I.C.E. antes de hablar con un abogado puede poner en peligro su caso.

¿Qué debo hacer si hay una emergencia?

Diríjase al teléfono más cercano y llame al 911, el número de respuesta de la policía para casos de emergencia. La llamada es gratis. La policía sabrá automáticamente de dónde está llamando salvo que llame de un teléfono celular. No es necesario que dé su nombre. Siempre hay operadores e intérpretes disponibles para ayudar en los principales idiomas que hablan los habitantes de la ciudad.

leyes recientes de inmigración

Las leyes promulgadas después de los ataques terroristas del 11 de septiembre permiten a la Oficina de Inmigración y Aduanas, o B.I.C.E., mantener a los inmigrantes arrestados en la cárcel durante semanas, meses o más. Las leyes no especifican cuándo un juez de inmigración tiene que oír su caso. Y si el juez decide que usted es una amenaza para la sociedad o puede tratar de escapar, él o ella puede ordenar que usted permanezca encarcelado. Además, algunas leyes dicen que usted no puede ser puesto en libertad si ha sido acusado de terrorismo o ha sido condenado por ciertos delitos.

¿Cuándo es una emergencia lo suficientemente grave como para llamar al 911?

- Cuando está ocurriendo un delito.
- Cuando hay vidas en peligro.
- Cuando alguien ha sufrido una lesión seria o necesita atención médica por un problema grave.

¿Qué se puede hacer para quejas menos urgentes, como vecinos que hacen ruido o personas que venden drogas?

Para estas situaciones no de emergencia, llame al 311 al Centro de Servicios para Ciudadanos. Este centro de llamadas, abierto en marzo del 2003, le permite llamar a un solo número fácil de recordar — 311 — para ponerse en contacto con la mayoría de los servicios gubernamentales no de emergencia, e informar sobre situaciones tales como falta de calefacción y agua caliente en su apartamento o averiguar cuándo recogen la basura en su vecindario. El Centro de Servicios para Ciudadanos 311 está abierto las 24 horas del día, y ofrece ayuda en 170 idiomas.

Si no hablo inglés, ¿puedo ir a la estación de policía para informar sobre una ofensa menor o queja?

Las estaciones de policía en precintos donde no mucha gente habla inglés tienen recepcionistas bilingües que también viven en el precinto. Le ayudarán o buscarán a alguien que pueda ayudarle con asuntos relacionados con los programas y oficiales del Departamento de Policía. Si su problema es un asunto que no concierne al Departamento de Policía, un recepcionista bilingüe tratará de informarle cuál es la agencia que puede ayudarle, probablemente llamando al 311.

¿Qué debo hacer si me violan?

- La violación es un crimen que puede ser perpetrado por un amigo, cónyuge, pareja o familiar. Llame al 911 de inmediato e informe a la policía. *La violación no fue su culpa a pesar de que el agresor haya sido una persona que conoce y ama. No se sienta avergonzada.*
- Informe a la policía los detalles del ataque, no importa cuán íntimos sean, y cualquier cosa que recuerde del agresor.

¿necesita más ayuda?

Estas organizaciones proporcionan tratamiento y asesoramiento para víctimas del abuso sexual:

- Bellevue Hospital Center (Página 242)
- Safe Horizon (Página 274)

¿necesita más ayuda?

Llame a estas líneas de información y organizaciones si conoce a una persona que es víctima de la violencia doméstica.

- New York State Domestic Violence Hot Line, 1-800-942-6906 (inglés solamente)
- New York State Domestic Violence Hot Line, 1-800-942-6908 (español solamente)
- New York City Domestic Violence Hot Line, 1-800-621-4673 (inglés, español, cantonés y mandarín)
- CUNY Law School — Main Street Legal Services, Immigration and Refugee Rights (Página 254)
- Park Slope Safe Homes Project (Página 272)
- Queens Legal Services (Página 273)

- No se lave ni utilice duchas vaginales. Sométase cuanto antes a un examen médico y un examen ginecológico interno tan pronto sea posible. Trate de que la acompañe un agente de policía.
- Hágase una prueba del V.I.H. y SIDA y pídale al médico de inmediato medicinas anti-SIDA.
- Llame a una organización que ofrece servicios para víctimas de ataques sexuales.

A veces mi cónyuge o compañero me pega o da cachetadas. ¿Hay algo que pueda hacer?

Sí, el abuso sexual del cónyuge, compañera y niños es ilegal en los Estados Unidos y puede resultar en un arresto. Llame a la policía e informe sobre la situación. Asimismo, comuníquese con la línea de información de una agencia de servicios para inmigrantes o de violencia doméstica.

*

"Es fácil que un nuevo inmigrante sea víctima de un delito porque son extranjeros en la ciudad. Durante mis dos primeros años en Nueva York me asaltaron cuatro veces. Me hizo sentir que la ciudad de Nueva York no era un lugar seguro para vivir. Decidí que tenía que encontrar una manera de resolver este problema. Un agente de policía me dio una lista de cosas que tengo que hacer para vivir más seguro, como por ejemplo prestar atención a la gente que tengo a mi alrededor, no caminar por lugares desiertos. Los delitos disminuyeron mucho. Espero que favorezca a los nuevos inmigrantes."

— *Pak Ping, chino, 1999* [14]

ASISTENCIA PÚBLICA

"**E**n ese entonces se llamaba asistencia para el hogar. Hoy en día es bienestar social. Te daban papas y mantequilla, ese tipo de cosas. Y recuerdo que fui con mi vecino a recoger las papas y el queso. Supongo que de allí vienen todas las cajas de queso."

— *Josephine Esposito, hija de inmigrantes*
italianos, recordando los años, 1930 [15]

■

Si no puede trabajar, no puede encontrar trabajo o su trabajo no paga lo suficiente, la asistencia pública y los cupones de comida podrán ayudarle a pagar la comida, la ropa, el alquiler, el gas, la electricidad y otros servicios públicos y artículos para el hogar.

¿Qué es la asistencia pública?

La asistencia pública, con frecuencia llamada bienestar social, abarca muchos programas diferentes del gobierno que proporcionan dinero y otros beneficios a las personas cuyo ingreso familiar está por debajo del nivel de pobreza que el gobierno federal establece o del estándar de necesidad fijado por el estado de Nueva York.

¿Qué es el programa de "asistencia para la familia" (family assistance), quiénes reúnen los requisitos, cuánto dinero se recibe y cuánto duran los beneficios?

El programa de asistencia para la familia es un tipo de prestación social o asistencia pública que ofrece dinero a las familias necesitadas. Si usted llegó a los Estados Unidos después de agosto de 1996 y ha vivido aquí por menos de cinco años, no califica. Los adultos que reúnen los requisitos pueden recibir asistencia para la familia por un total de 60 meses, que no tienen que ser consecutivos.

Los beneficios dependen del número de miembros en la familia y del nivel de ingresos. El ingreso familiar es el dinero que ganan todos los adultos que conforman una familia. Por ejemplo, si usted vive solo y gana $400 por mes y el estándar de necesidad fijado por el estado de Nueva York es de $500 por mes, califica para asistencia pública. Pero si vive con otros miembros de su familia y conjuntamente ganan $800 por mes, se considera que los ingresos de la unidad familiar superan el nivel de pobreza federal y no calificará.

Los beneficios que ofrece el programa de asistencia para la familia se pagan dos veces por mes y se deben utilizar para gastos de vivienda, alimentos y ropa. Después que termina el período de 60 meses, los adultos y todos los miembros de la unidad familiar dejarán de recibir los beneficios del programa de asistencia para la familia.

¿Qué es el programa de "asistencia de seguridad" (safety net assistance), quiénes reúnen los requisitos, cuánto dinero se recibe y cuánto duran los beneficios?

El programa de asistencia de seguridad también es un tipo de prestación social o asistencia pública. Proporciona asistencia, pero para aquellos que no califican para el programa de asistencia para la familia: adultos solteros, parejas sin hijos y nuevos inmigrantes, independientemente del número de miembros que conforman la unidad familiar y que han estado en los Estados Unidos por menos de cinco años. Asimismo, se ofrecen beneficios a las personas que han agotado su elegibilidad de cinco años para recibir asistencia familiar. Los beneficios se pagan dos veces por mes y se utilizan para vivienda, comida y ropa.

¿Puedo obtener asistencia pública?

Es posible. Los programas tienen diferentes requisitos de elegibilidad y estándares. Si califica o no dependerá de su estado legal como inmigrante, cuándo llegó a los Estados Unidos, su edad, su salud y los ingresos de su unidad familiar.

¿Cómo puedo obtener información sobre todos los beneficios de asistencia pública diferentes?

El sitio Web GovBenefits, www.govbenefits.gov/GovBenefits/jsp/GovBenefits.jsp, es una buena herramienta y fácil de usar. Usted contesta algunas preguntas brindando cierta información personal y GovBenefits le proporcionará una lista de los programas de gobierno para los que usted podría calificar e información sobre cómo aplicar.

Soy indocumentado. Si voy al sitio Web que tiene información sobre beneficios de asistencia pública, ¿podrá el gobierno averiguar dónde vivo y obtener otra información sobre mí?

No. Este sitio Web es completamente confidencial. No tiene que dar su nombre, número de teléfono, número de Seguro Social o ninguna otra información que podría utilizarse para identificarle.

¿Qué debo hacer si no estoy seguro si reúno los requisitos para un programa de asistencia pública determinado?

Si sabe que necesita un tipo de ayuda específica, como por ejemplo, cupones para comida, pero no está seguro si califica, siempre es conveniente presentar una solicitud. Las normas y los requisitos cambian continuamente, por lo tanto no se desaliente si tiene que presentar una solicitud más de una vez y a más de un programa.

¿Puedo trabajar y recibir asistencia pública?

Sí, siempre y cuando el ingreso de su unidad familiar no supere las normas de elegibilidad federales y estatales.

cómo solicitar asistencia pública

Una guía paso por paso:

1. Vaya a una organización comunitaria donde hablen su idioma o al Centro de Apoyo de Ingresos/Centro de Trabajo (Income Support Center/Job Center) de la Administración de Recursos Humanos (Human Resources Administration) de su localidad y recoja una hoja de información y un formulario de solicitud. La H.R.A. debe darle un formulario de solicitud. Para obtener la dirección de su centro, llame a la línea de información de la H.R.A., al 1- 877-HRA-8411 (1-877-472-8411) (Página 258).

2. Si puede, complete el formulario de solicitud allí y entréguelo. Si necesita ayuda, pídala en vez de cometer un error que podría demorar sus beneficios. Si se lleva la solicitud para llenarla después, hágalo lo antes posible y entréguela en el centro de H.R.A. de su localidad.

3. En un plazo de siete días hábiles debería tener una entrevista. El entrevistador le preguntará sobre su educación, capacitación y antecedentes de trabajo; qué tipo de trabajo puede hacer; sus planes de empleo futuros y las necesidades de guardería para sus hijos.

4. Un asistente social de la H.R.A. visitará su apartamento para asegurarse de que vive donde usted dice y ver si su estándar de vida no supera el nivel de pobreza federal. Si vive por encima del estándar de pobreza, la asistente social pensará que usted no está diciendo la verdad sobre los ingresos que percibe su familia.

5. La H.R.A. no debería tardar más de 30 a 45 días en decirle si califica para asistencia pública, pero a veces tarda más y tiene que seguir insistiendo. Si no recibe una respuesta en ese plazo, no se dé por vencido. Siga yendo a la oficina y preguntando qué pasa con su solicitud.

Soy indocumentado, ¿puedo obtener asistencia pública?

Los requisitos de elegibilidad varían según el tipo de servicio que necesita. Muchos tipos de asistencia pública se ofrecen únicamente a los inmigrantes que viven legalmente en los EE.UU. No obstante, ciertos tipos de asistencia, como por ejemplo Medicaid de emergencia, atención prenatal y comida de ollas populares o comedores de beneficencia están al alcance de todos los residentes de Nueva York sin tener en cuenta su estado legal. A veces, las agencias de la ciudad de Nueva York deben preguntar acerca del estado legal para determinar si una persona califica para un programa específico. A la fecha de esta publicación, no estaban obligadas a informar sobre su estado legal si está indocumentado a la **Oficina de Inmigración y Aduana (Bureau of Immigration and Customs Enforcement - B.I.C.E.)** del Departamento de Seguridad Interna de los Estados Unidos. (El departamento ha asumido las responsabilidades que previamente pertenecían al Servicio de Inmigración y Naturalización, o I.N.S.) Sin embargo, las normas que afectan a los inmigrantes cambian con frecuencia, por lo tanto es recomendable consultar con uno de los grupos de defensa de inmigrantes que se mencionan en el Directorio de Recursos al final de esta guía, o si puede pagarlo, consulte con un abogado de inmigración confiable.

¿Cómo solicito asistencia pública?

En la ciudad de Nueva York, debe aplicar para los programas de asistencia pública a través de la **Administración de Recursos Humanos (Human Resources Administration — H.R.A.)** Vaya al Centro de **Refugiados e Inmigrantes (Refugee and Inmigrant Center)** (Página 258). Si no habla bien inglés, puede obtener ayuda para solicitar asistencia pública, Medicaid y Medicare. El personal habla varios idiomas, incluyendo español, cantonés, ruso, albanés, vietnamita, japonés, árabe y varios dialectos africanos.

¿Se puede solicitar asistencia pública por teléfono?

Es muy difícil porque el número siempre da ocupado. Es más fácil y más confiable ir directamente a un Centro de Apoyo de Ingresos (Income Support Center) de la H.R.A.

¿Qué debo hacer en el centro donde voy para solicitar asistencia pública?

Le darán una hoja de información sobre sus derechos a recibir prestaciones sociales y otro tipo de asistencia pública y le pedirán que complete un formulario de solicitud.

En el centro donde voy a solicitar asistencia pública, ¿estará todo en inglés?

No. La información está en cinco idiomas: Inglés, español, chino, ruso y árabe.

¿Cómo sabré si mi solicitud para asistencia pública ha sido aprobada o denegada?

Tienen que enviarle un aviso por escrito. Si no fue aprobada, el aviso debe explicar por qué. Si no está satisfecho con la decisión, tiene derecho a una audiencia imparcial para apelar. Una audiencia imparcial le ofrece la oportunidad de presentarse ante un juez de derecho administrativo y explicarle su situación y por qué piensa que el rechazo está equivocado.

Si me niegan los beneficios de asistencia pública, ¿cómo puedo obtener una audiencia para apelar?

Vaya a la **Oficina de Audiencias Administrativas** para solicitar una audiencia imparcial. Está en **330 West 34th Street, tercer piso, en Midtown Manhattan**, y en **14 Boerum Place, primer piso, en downtown Brooklyn**.

¿Qué pasa si estuve recibiendo beneficios pero me dicen que ya no califico?
¿Continuaré recibiendo los beneficios hasta poder presentarme a una audiencia?

Si solicita una audiencia imparcial dentro de los 10 días de la fecha que aparece en el extremo superior derecho de la carta en la que se le informa que se reducirán o terminarán sus beneficios, tiene derecho a continuar recibiendo las prestaciones sociales, cupones de comida y Medicaid hasta que tenga lugar la audiencia imparcial.

Si me dan una audiencia y me dicen que tengo derecho a recibir los beneficios, ¿comenzarán o se reanudarán de inmediato?

No necesariamente. A veces los beneficios tardan varios meses en llegar.

Si recibo asistencia pública, ¿tendré que trabajar para el gobierno?

Algunos requisitos de trabajo, llamados "workfare," trabajo a cambio de asistencia, pueden satisfacerse a través de la educación. Además, puede estar exento de workfare si está en una de las siguientes categorías:

- incapacitado
- cuida a una persona incapacitada
- mayor de 60

tome notas

Cuando solicita asistencia pública, recuerde anotar todo contacto que tiene con la Administración de Recursos Humanos. Marque la fecha en que entregó su solicitud de beneficios. Esto puede ayudarle a obtener beneficios retroactivamente si la H.R.A. no le suministra con prontitud los beneficios a los que tiene derecho. También escriba el nombre de todos los funcionarios de la H.R.A. y miembros del personal con los que tiene contacto.

> **❝ Siempre solicite cualquier tipo de asistencia pública aunque piense que no reúne los requisitos. Las leyes cambian con frecuencia. No se desaliente si tiene que presentar una solicitud más de una vez y a más de un programa. ❞**

- menor de 16 o menor de 19 y estudiante a tiempo completo
- en su último mes de embarazo
- una madre que está cuidando a un recién nacido

¿Cuánto tiempo puedo cuidar a mi bebé antes de tener que participar en el programa de trabajo para los que reciben asistencia pública (workfare) para poder continuar recibiendo asistencia pública?

Una madre que recibe asistencia pública tiene derecho a 12 meses a lo largo de toda su vida para cuidar a niños recién nacidos, pero no más de 3 meses por niño. Puede solicitar una extensión a la regla de 3 meses pero no a la de 12 meses.

¿Qué son los cupones de comida y cómo sé si reúno los requisitos?

Los cupones de comida se usan en vez de efectivo para comprar alimentos y artículos relacionados en tiendas y supermercados que los aceptan. Usted no tiene que ser indigente para tener derecho a recibir cupones de comida y muchos inmigrantes califican. Para averiguar si califica para los cupones de comida o para averiguar dónde están las 20 oficinas de cupones de comida en la ciudad, llame a la **Administración de Recursos Humanos (H.R.A.)** al 1-877-472-8411 (Página 258), o visite el sitio Web de la H.R.A., **www.nyc.gov/html/hra/html/ serv_foodstamps.html.**

¿Puedo recibir cupones de comida si soy indocumentado?

Hay diferentes categorías de inmigrantes indocumentados, y ahora muchos reúnen los requisitos. Es mejor solicitarlos en cualquier centro de trabajo de la Administración de Recursos Humanos o en una oficina de cupones de comida.

¿Hablarán mi idioma en una oficina de cupones de comida?

La ciudad debe proporcionar informes traducidos gratis e intérpretes en español, cantonés, mandarín, árabe, ruso y algunos otros idiomas si es necesario.

¿Me darán cupones de comida para usar en las tiendas?

No, recibirá una tarjeta de Transferencia de Beneficios Electrónica (E.B.T., por sus siglas en inglés), es una tarjeta de débito de plástico que le permite obtener el dinero de asistencia pública (bienestar social) y usar cupones de comida en la ciudad de Nueva York.

¿Dónde me dan la tarjeta E.B.T.? ¿Tengo que usarla?

La tarjeta se la enviarán por correo. Debe utilizarla si recibe asistencia pública y/o cupones de comida. No se hace ninguna excepción.

¿Tendrá mi foto la tarjeta de E.B.T.?

Algunas sí, otras no. Su tarjeta es válida con o sin foto.

¿Dónde puedo usar mi tarjeta de E.B.T.?

En tiendas y cajeros automáticos (A.T.M.) que tienen el símbolo de Quest.®

¿Qué puedo hacer con mi tarjeta E.B.T.?

- Use su cupón de comida o cuenta de asistencia en efectivo para comprar comida y otros artículos.
- Sacar dinero de su cuenta de efectivo.
- Recibir un reintegro de dinero de su cuenta en las tiendas que autorizan a los usuarios de E.B.T. que hacen compras allí.

¿Debo pagar un cargo para usar mi tarjeta E.B.T. para comprar comida?

No. Nunca deben cobrarle un cargo por comprar comida. Puede hacer todas las compras de comida que quiera sin tener que pagar un cargo, siempre y cuando tenga el número suficiente de cupones de comida en su cuenta.

¿Debo pagar un cargo para usar mi tarjeta E.B.T. para sacar dinero en efectivo de mi cuenta?

No siempre. Cualquier tienda, servicio de canje de cheques o cualquier cajero automático que cobra un cargo debe indicarlo, y usted debe evitar utilizar estos servicios.

¿Cómo puedo averiguar dónde puedo usar mi tarjeta de E.B.T. y qué lugares no cobran un cargo?

Llame al 1-800-289-6739 (inglés y español) para hablar con un representante que puede informarle la ubicación de los cajeros que no cobran cargos.

¿Cuántas veces puedo usar mi tarjeta de E.B.T. para sacar efectivo sin pagar un cargo?

Si la usa en localidades que no cobran un cargo, puede sacar efectivo gratis cuatro veces al mes. Después de la cuarta vez, le cobrarán 85 centavos cada vez que saca dinero ese mes.

¿Cómo sé cuánto dinero de asistencia y cupones de comida tengo en mi cuenta de E.B.T.?

Llame a la línea telefónica gratis de atención al cliente de Citibank al 1-888-328-

6399 (inglés y español), para obtener el saldo de sus cupones de comida y dinero de asistencia y para un registro de sus últimas 10 transacciones. Algunos ATMs y cajeros de tiendas imprimen el saldo en el recibo. *Guarde todos los recibos, aunque el cajero no le dé efectivo ni lo deje pagar con cupones de comida.*

¿Qué debo hacer si pierdo mi tarjeta de E.B.T. o me la roban?

Llame al **Servicio de Atención al Cliente de Citibank** al **1-888-328-6399** *de inmediato.* Si utiliza un teléfono de tono, le contestará un mensaje grabado y le pedirá

¿necesita más ayuda?

Para obtener información sobre las normas más actualizadas sobre asistencia pública comuníquese con un miembro del Concejo Municipal. Si no sabe quién es el miembro de su Concejo Municipal, llame al Servicio de Información Telefónica de la Liga de Mujeres Votantes (League of Women Voters Telephone Information Service) al 1-212-213-5286 (Inglés solamente), e indique su dirección. Póngase en contacto con estos grupos para obtener asesoramiento sobre cómo conseguir asistencia pública:

- Asian American Legal Defense and Education Fund (A.A.L.D.E.F.) (Página 241)
- Asian Americans for Equality (A.A.F.E.) (Página 241)
- Brooklyn Chinese-American Association (Página 243)
- Charles B. Wang Community Health Center (Página 247)
- Chinatown Manpower Project (Página 248)
- Chinese-American Planning Council (Página 249)
- Church Avenue Merchants Block Association (C.A.M.B.A.) (Página 250)
- City Harvest Hunger Hot Line (Página 251)
- Community Association of Progressive Dominicans (Página 253)
- Forest Hills Community House (Página 255)
- Indochina Sino-American Community Center (Página 259)
- Jacob A. Riis Neighborhood Settlement House (Página 260)
- Legal Aid Society, Civil Division (Página 260)
- Legal Services for New York City (Página 261)
- Lutheran Medical Center (Página 262)
- Medical and Health Research Association of New York City (M.H.R.A.) (Página 263)
- New York Association for New Americans (N.Y.A.N.A.) (Página 265)
- New York City Neighborhood W.I.C. Program (Página 264)
- New York State Office of Temporary and Disability Assistance (Página 271)
- Queens Legal Services (Página 273)
- Southeast Bronx Neighborhood Centers (Página 275)

guarde estos números

Llame al Servicio de Atención al Cliente de Citibank al 1-888-328-6399 (inglés y español), para:

- Informar y reemplazar una tarjeta de E.B.T. perdida, robada o dañada.
- Cambiar su Número de Identificación Personal, o PIN, para su tarjeta de E.B.T.
- Informar que le dieron la cantidad equivocada de asistencia en efectivo.
- Informar sobre problemas en los cajeros automáticos o tiendas.
- Ver el saldo actual de su cuenta y las últimas 10 transacciones.
- Informar sobre errores en su cuenta.
- Llame al 1-800-289-6739 (inglés y español) para las localidades de cajeros automáticos que no cobran un cargo.
- Llame al Centro de Mensajes de la Ciudad de Nueva York (New York City Message Center) al 1-877-879-4194 (inglés y español), para escuchar mensajes grabados relacionados con su caso de beneficios de asistencia pública.

que oprima 1 para inglés y 2 para español. Solicite una "suspensión de pago" sobre su cuenta. Si alguien usa su tarjeta antes de la orden de suspensión de pago, perderá los beneficios y no podrá recobrarlos.

¿Puedo hablar con un representante cuando llame al Servicio de Atención al Cliente de Citibank sobre mi tarjeta de E.B.T.?
Sí. Cuando llama al 1-888-328-6399, le contestará un mensaje grabado y le pedirá que oprima 1 para inglés y 2 para español. *No oprima ningún botón. Ignore todas las instrucciones grabadas.* Después de una breve espera le conectarán con un representante que le ayudará con sus preguntas.

¿Hay algún programa además de cupones de comida que me ayuden a alimentar a mi familia?
El Programa Suplemental de Nutrición para Mujeres, Bebés y Niños, conocido como W.I.C., ofrece alimentos suplementarios gratis, educación sobre nutrición y referencias para la atención de salud a mujeres de bajos ingresos que están embarazadas o amamantando y a mujeres con niños de hasta 5 años que se considera necesitan una nutrición especial debido a ciertas condiciones médicas o dietéticas. W.I.C. está disponible sin importar el estado legal del solicitante.

¿Cómo puedo averiguar si mis hijos califican para el programa W.I.C.?
Llame gratis a la líneas informativas del Departamento de salud del Estado de Nueva York: Child and Adult Care Food Program (Programa de alimentos para

niños y adultos), 1-800-942-3858 (inglés solamente); **Growing Up Healthy (Un desarrollo sano), 1-800-522-5006** (Página 256).

∎

"**A**ún recuerdo cuando acompañaba a mi madre a la oficina de bienestar social — las filas largas, las horas de espera y cómo trataban a mi madre. Veía la humillación en la cara de mi madre. Pero no había otra salida. Mi padre trabajaba lavando platos y mi madre nos cuidaba a nosotros siete. Recuerdo que mi madre se levantaba temprano para esperar al cartero el día 1ero y 16 del mes. Siempre nos compraba algo pequeño cuando llegaba el cheque. Pero si no llegaba ese día, ¡sálvese quién pueda! Dependíamos de los cupones de comida para comprar los alimentos y en el dinero de asistencia para ayudar a pagar los servicios públicos. Mi hermana Eva ha trabajado como trabajadora social durante muchos años y las cosas han cambiado tanto que le doy gracias a Dios que no necesito asistencia pública."

— *Georgina Acevedo, hija de trabajadores migratorios*
de Puerto Rico, recordando los años 1960 [16]

ESTADO LEGAL

"**R**ealmente no tengo palabras para explicar lo que sentí cuando me dieron la ciudadanía estadounidense, cuando voté por primera vez por un presidente americano, cuando matriculé a mi hijo mayor en una escuela pública. Era como ver el amanecer después de una larga y oscura noche. La simple cadencia de la palabra "América" me da paz, seguridad y esperanza".

— *Simon Finkelstein, ruso, recordando los años 1890* [17]

∎

Ya sea que quiere vivir de modo permanente en los Estados Unidos, es decir procurar residencia legal permanente u obtener la tarjeta verde, o viene de un país extranjero por un período de tiempo limitado o para un propósito específico, por ejemplo como turista o para trabajar, su estado legal o lícito lo determina el gobierno de los Estados Unidos a través de varios tipos de visas.

Según se indica en varias ocasiones a lo largo de la guía, después de los eventos del 11 de septiembre de 2001, el **Departamento de Seguridad Interna de los Estados Unidos** asumió muchas de las funciones que antes eran responsabilidad del **Servicio de Inmigración y Naturalización**, o **I.N.S.** Una división del departamento, el **Servicio de Inmigración y Ciudadanía de los Estados Unidos**, o **U.S.C.I.S.** (sus siglas en inglés), que tramita beneficios para inmigrantes, se encarga de evaluar las solicitudes de visa y de Tarjeta de Residente Permanente, conocidas también como Tarjetas de Registro de Extranjeros y comúnmente llamadas tarjetas verdes. El U.S.C.I.S. también procesa las solicitudes de inmigrantes que desean convertirse en ciudadanos de los Estados Unidos.

En este capítulo se describen los tipos de visa más comunes que le permiten a las personas de otros países viajar legalmente a los Estados Unidos. También se describe la tarjeta verde, por qué es importante y explica el proceso complejo, que con frecuencia demora varios años, de obtener esta tarjeta. Por último, se describe el largo proceso para convertirse en ciudadano de los Estados Unidos, llamado naturalización, así como algunos de los beneficios de la ciudadanía y ejemplos de preguntas que pueden aparecer en la prueba que debe tomar cualquier persona que desea hacerse ciudadano.

A partir del 11 de septiembre, otra división del Departamento de Seguridad Interna de los Estados Unidos, la **Oficina de Inmigración y Aduanas,** o **B.I.C.E.** (por sus siglas en inglés), sigue el rastro de los inmigrantes, de aquellos documentados e indocumentados, mucho más de cerca. Las políticas de inmigración cambian con frecuencia y por lo general se hacen más estrictas. Por lo tanto es importante saber si uno está de modo legal en los Estados Unidos y el impacto que esto puede tener en lo que está haciendo o quiere hacer en los Estados Unidos.

Las bibliotecas y grupos de defensa de inmigrantes que se mencionan en el Directorio de Recursos al final de esta guía cuentan con personal y material de referencia que explican en más detalle lo referente al estado legal y su importancia y lo que se necesita para obtener una tarjeta verde o hacerse ciudadano. Como las normas que afectan a los inmigrantes cambian con frecuencia, siempre es mejor consultar con uno de estos grupos o con un abogado de inmigración confiable.

¿Qué es una visa?

Una visa es un permiso para solicitar el ingreso en los Estados Unidos. Si es necesario, por lo general se pide en un consulado estadounidense fuera de los Estados Unidos. La visa establece el propósito de la visita, como por ejemplo negocios, turismo, etc., y puede en ciertos casos tener vigencia para varias visitas a los Estados Unidos durante un período de tiempo específico.

¿Todas las visas son iguales?

No, todas las visas no son iguales. Una **visa de no inmigrante** se otorga a una persona que vive en otro país y desea visitar los Estados Unidos temporalmente para un fin específico. Las visas de no inmigrante se conceden a turistas, gente de negocios, estudiantes, trabajadores temporales, diplomáticos, etc.

Una **visa de inmigrante** se otorga a una persona que tiene la intención de vivir y trabajar en forma permanente en los Estados Unidos. En la mayoría de los casos, un familiar o su empleador envía una solicitud al U.S.C.I.S. en su nombre (el beneficiario) para que le otorguen la oportunidad de poder ser un inmigrante. (Algunos solicitantes, incluyendo trabajadores con una capacidad extraordinaria, inversionistas y ciertos inmigrantes especiales pueden hacer la petición por cuenta propia). Una vez que es aceptado, necesita presentar el formulario de solicitud correspondiente para convertirse en un residente legal permanente.

Por lo general, el proceso para obtener una visa de inmigrante es muy complicado

> **❝ Una tarjeta verde demuestra que un inmigrante puede trabajar legalmente y vivir permanentemente en los Estados Unidos. ❞**

y puede demorar por lo menos 2 años y hasta 10 años o más. Es muy importante que durante este proceso mantenga su estado legal, porque es necesario que esté legalmente en el país para solicitar un cambio de visa, por ejemplo de una visa de no inmigrante a una visa de inmigrante y residente permanente.

Para muchas de las categorías de visa de no inmigrante deberá aplicar directamente en un consulado fuera de los Estados Unidos. Para todas las visas de inmigrante a excepción de aquellas que se obtuvieron a través del programa de Lotería de visas (que se explica posteriormente en este capítulo), deberá presentar la solicitud ante el U.S.C.I.S.

El Departamento de Estado es el órgano responsable de proporcionar números de visa a los extranjeros interesados en emigrar a los Estados Unidos. Para obtener más información sobre el **proceso de visas del Departamento de Estado,** visite el sitio Web en **http://travel.state.gov/visa_services.html.**

¿Qué es la tarjeta verde?

La tarjeta verde, conocida como Tarjeta de Residencia Permanente o Tarjeta de Registro de Extranjeros, es un documento que prueba que un inmigrante tiene permiso para trabajar legalmente en los Estados Unidos y que él o ella puede vivir aquí de modo permanente. Si usted tiene la tarjeta verde se considera que es un residente legal permanente y está en el país legítimamente.

¿Cómo se puede obtener una tarjeta verde?

Hay dos procesos básicos para convertirse en un residente legal permanente, el proceso basado en la familia y el proceso basado en el empleo. No importa cuál opción elija, si usted está en los Estados Unidos, tiene que estar en el país legalmente para poder solicitar la residencia permanente.

¿Qué sucede si no estoy en el país legalmente?

Si usted ingresó al país ilegalmente, si ingresó con permiso pero no mantuvo su estado legal o si trabajó sin permiso, no puede cambiar su estado de residencia salvo que reúna los requisitos para ciertas exenciones. Por lo general, tendría que salir de los Estados Unidos para solicitar una visa de inmigrante. Es importante recordar que podrían prohibirle la entrada al país por un período de 3 a 10 años. Por lo tanto, es muy importante que no viaje sin antes procurar ayuda de un abogado de inmigración confiable o de un proveedor de servicios para inmigrantes que aparece en el Directorio de Recursos al final de esta guía.

Ellos también pueden ayudarle a determinar si reúne los requisitos para una exención que le permita quedarse en los Estados Unidos mientras solicita la visa de inmigrante.

¿Cómo funciona el proceso basado en la familia?
Ese es un proceso en dos etapas:
1. Un ciudadano o residente legal permanente presenta ante el **U.S.C.I.S. el formulario 130, Petición para un familiar extranjero,** para clasificarlo como alguien que reúne los requisitos para solicitar una visa de inmigrante.
2. Una vez que la solicitud es aprobada, puede solicitar convertirse en un residente legal permanente cuando haya un número de visa disponible.

Parece bastante simple. ¿Por qué toma tanto tiempo?
La cantidad de números de visa disponibles es limitada, y puede tardar varios años hasta que haya uno disponible. Por lo tanto, si bien su primera solicitud puede ser aprobada rápidamente, puede tomar de 2 a 10 años o más hasta que haya un número de visa disponible y se le otorgue su residencia permanente.

¿Hay alguna exención que acelere este largo proceso?
Sí, pero sólo si hay visas disponibles de inmediato, y las exenciones se aplican solamente a las personas consideradas familiares inmediatos, es decir los padres, los cónyuges y niños solteros menores de 21 años de ciudadanos de los Estados Unidos.

¿necesita más ayuda?

Estos grupos ofrecen asesoramiento legal confiable para asuntos relacionados con la inmigración:

- Asian American Legal Defense and Education Fund (Página 241)
- Caribbean Women's Health Association (Página 245)
- Catholic Charities Office for Immigrant Services (Página 246)
- Catholic Migration Services (Página 246)
- Citizens Advice Bureau (C.A.B.) (Página 251)
- CUNY Law School — Main Street Legal Services, Immigration and Refugee Rights Program (Página 254)
- Emerald Isle Immigration Center (Página 255)
- Hebrew Immigrant Aid Society (H.I.A.S.) (Página 256)
- Hellenic American Neighborhood Action Committee (H.A.N.A.C.) (Página 257)
- Legal Aid Society, Civil Division (Página 260)

¿necesita más ayuda?

Estas agencias y grupos proporcionan ayuda con las solicitudes de ciudadanía y el proceso de naturalización:

- Brooklyn Chinese-American Association (Página 243)
- Caribbean Women's Health Association (C.W.H.A.) (Página 245)
- Catholic Charities Office for Immigration Services (Página 246)
- Catholic Migration Services (Página 246)
- Chinese Immigrant Services (Página 248)
- Church Avenue Merchants Block Association (C.A.M.B.A.) (Página 250)
- Emerald Isle Immigration Center (Página 255)
- Hebrew Immigrant Aid Society (H.I.A.S.) (Página 256)
- Immigration Advocacy Services (Página 259)
- New York Immigration Hot Line, 1-800-566-7636 (Página 270)
- South Bronx Action Group (Página 275)
- Southside Community Mission, Immigration Program (Página 276)
- United Community Centers (Página 276)

Para obtener más información sobre los requisitos de elegibilidad para la naturalización y exámenes pertinentes, visite el sitio Web de el U.S.C.I.S.: www.uscis.gov.

¿Cómo funciona el proceso para los familiares inmediatos?

Si hay números de visa disponibles de inmediato para estos familiares y si se encuentran en los Estados Unidos, ambas solicitudes se presentarán esencialmente a la misma vez. Si los parientes que desean emigrar están fuera de los Estados Unidos, la familia en los Estados Unidos presenta la solicitud y ésta se envía al consulado estadounidense del país en el que residen las personas que desean emigrar, donde podrán solicitar una visa de inmigrante para entrar a los Estados Unidos. Es conveniente procurar asesoramiento de un abogado de inmigración confiable o consultar con uno de los proveedores de servicios que aparecen en el Directorio de Recursos al final de esta guía.

¿Cómo funciona el proceso basado en el trabajo?

En la mayoría de los casos, es un proceso que consta de tres pasos y puede demorar varios años. Cuando no hay que esperar para las visas, los pasos dos y tres pueden tener lugar casi simultáneamente.

1. Un empleador solitica la certificación de trabajo, que puede demorar de 2 a 4 años.
2. Cuando se otorga la certificación, se debe presentar el Formulario 1-140 del

U.S.C.I.S., Petición de un trabajador extranjero.
3. Después que se aprueba esta petición, es necesario presentar una solicitud para cambiar su visa a residencia permanente. Sólo puede solicitar este cambio si está legamente en el país.

¿Hay alguna exención que acelere este largo proceso?

Sí, si se casa con un ciudadano estadounidense, si es un familiar inmediato de un ciudadano estadounidense, o si reúne los requisitos para ampararse bajo la ley conocida como 245(i), que no es una amnistía general sino un recurso limitado al que tienen derecho las personas que han estado en los Estados Unidos desde el 21 de diciembre de 2000, y que presentaron una solicitud para convertirse en residentes legales permanentes en o antes del 30 de abril de 2001.

Si no tengo a nadie que me patrocine. ¿Hay alguna manera de obtener una visa de inmigrante?

Sí, a través del programa de Lotería de Visas Diversificado, que concede 55,000 visas de inmigrante cada año a los países que tienen un índice bajo de inmigración a los Estados Unidos. Para obtener información detallada sobre cómo funciona la lotería, visite **www.immigration.gov/graphics/services/residency/divvisa.htm**

Si salgo seleccionado en la Lotería de Visas, ¿qué significa?

Significa que puede presentar una solicitud para convertirse en un residente legal permanente.

¿Cómo obtengo el formulario de solicitud para la naturalización, Formulario N-400 del U.S.C.I.S.?

Llame a la línea de información sobre formularios de el **U.S.C.I.S.** al 1-800-870-3676 (**inglés y español**). También lo puede solicitar en Internet en **www.uscis.gov**.

¿Si solicito la ciudadanía, seré entrevistado o me harán preguntas?

Sí. Todas las personas que solicitan la ciudadanía serán entrevistadas. Esto se llama generalmente la entrevista de naturalización.

¿Cuándo seré entrevistado en relación con mi solicitud de ciudadanía?

En Nueva York, las entrevistas se conciertan de un año a 18 meses después que el **U.S.C.I.S.** recibe su solicitud N-400.

¿Cómo sabré dónde y cuándo tendrá lugar mi entrevista de ciudadanía?

Recibirá una notificación por correo indicándole cuándo y dónde debe ir y qué debe llevar.

¿Qué pasa si pierdo la entrevista de ciudadanía?

No falte a su entrevista. Su solicitud podría verse demorada por hasta un año o más y podría ser denegada. Consulte con uno de los proveedores de servicios para inmigrantes que aparecen en el Directorio de Recursos al final de esta guía.

¿Qué sucederá durante la entrevista de ciudadanía?

El representante U.S.C.I.S.:

- Actualizará y revisará la información en la solicitud de naturalización N-400.
- Revisará la demás documentación, incluyendo declaraciones de impuestos de los últimos cinco años, tarjeta verde, certificado de nacimiento, pasaporte, etc.
- Evaluará sus conocimientos de la historia y el gobierno de los Estados Unidos, su capacidad de leer, escribir y hablar inglés, salvo que califique para una exención por incapacidad.

¿Cuáles son algunos de los motivos por los cuales me conviene hacerme ciudadano estadounidense?

Hay muchos motivos. A continuación mencionamos algunos que son importantes según la opinión de otros inmigrantes:

- Un ciudadano tiene derecho a votar por los funcionarios federales, estatales y locales. Estas son las personas que dictan la política del gobierno, que puede afectar su vida cotidiana en la ciudad de Nueva York.
- Sólo un ciudadano puede presentarse como candidato a un puesto municipal, estatal o federal y para ciertos trabajos municipales, estatales y federales.
- Los ciudadanos pueden dejar los Estados Unidos y vivir en otro país por el tiempo que deseen, y viajar en ciertos países puede ser más fácil con un pasaporte de los Estados Unidos.
- Los ciudadanos pueden solicitar permiso para traer a otros miembros de su familia a los Estados Unidos.
- A los ciudadanos estadounidenses no se les puede prohibir el reingreso a los Estados unidos.
- Los ciudadanos no pueden ser deportados.
- Los ciudadanos no tienen que preocuparse de renovar su tarjeta verde cada 10 años.
- Los ciudadanos que se jubilan y se van a vivir a otro país pueden recibir todos los beneficios del Seguro Social, el programa de jubilación e incapacidad administrado por el gobierno. La mayoría de los residentes permanentes legales sólo recibirán sus beneficios por un período de seis meses hasta que regresan a los Estados Unidos para vivir un mes entero. Existen excepciones, y hay varios países donde los Estados Unidos no está autorizado a enviar pagos del Seguro Social. Para obtener una lista de estas excepciones y países, y para más información sobre el efecto de la inmigración sobre los beneficios del Seguro

Social, visite **www.ssa.gov.immigration**. El sitio Web tiene un portal multi-lingüe e intérpretes.

- Algunos países reconocen la "doble nacionalidad". Esto permite que los ciudadanos naturalizados estadounidenses pueden seguir siendo ciudadanos del país donde nacieron.
- Los ciudadanos tienen derecho a más beneficios públicos y a más becas educativas y ayuda financiera.
- En algunos casos, los residentes permanentes legales menores de 18 años pueden convertirse en ciudadanos automáticamente si viven con su padre o madre que es ciudadano. Esto quiere decir que no tendrán que atravesar el largo y complicado proceso de naturalización en el futuro.

¿Quién reúne los requisitos para convertirse en ciudadano de los Estados Unidos?

Estos son algunos de los requisitos básicos:

- Debe tener por lo menos 18 años de edad.
- Debe ser un residente permanente legal (tener la tarjeta verde) por lo menos durante 5 años, o ser un residente permanente legal por lo menos durante 3 años y estar casado con un ciudadano de los Estados Unidos durante ese tiempo y seguir casado con ese mismo ciudadano estadounidense cuando presente la solicitud de naturalización.
- Debe haber vivido por lo menos durante tres meses en el estado donde presenta su solicitud de ciudadanía.
- Tiene que haber pagado impuestos durante los últimos cinco años.
- Si es un hombre entre los 16 y 26 años, haberse registrado para el Servicio Selectivo.
- Debe ser una persona que tiene valores morales, lo que queda en evidencia a través del pago de los impuestos, registro en el Servicio Selectivo y no haber sido condenado por ciertos delitos.
- Debe poder hablar, leer, escribir y entender inglés básico y mostrar que entiende las nociones básicas de la historia y el gobierno de los Estados Unidos. Existen excepciones a esta regla para las personas de edad e incapacitadas, por lo tanto es conveniente que consulte con uno de los proveedores de servicios que aparecen en el Directorio de Recursos al final de esta guía.
- Tiene que haber estado físicamente en los Estados Unidos por lo menos durante la mitad de los últimos cinco años o la mitad de los últimos tres meses.
- No puede haber salido de los Estados Unidos por más de seis meses en ningún viaje salvo que haya viajado con un permiso de reingreso del U.S.C.I.S.
- Su intención tiene que ser la de vivir permanentemente en los Estados Unidos, si bien estará autorizado a viajar como lo hace cualquier otro ciudadano de los Estados Unidos.
- Debe informar si ha sido arrestado o multado por cualquier transgresión,

inclusive una infracción de las reglas de tráfico. Una vez más, le recomendamos consultar con un abogado de inmigración confiable o con uno de los proveedores de servicios para inmigrantes que aparecen en el Directorio de Recursos al final de esta guía.

¿Qué necesito para convertirme en ciudadano de los Estados Unidos?

- Unas cuantas solicitudes incluyendo el formulario N-400, o solicitud de naturalización.
- Dos fotografías a color, de 2 pulgadas por 2 pulgadas (tres cuartos de perfil incluyendo la oreja derecha).
- Fotocopia de la tarjeta verde, anverso y reverso.
- Cargo para presentar el formulario de solicitud y huellas dactilares, pagadero mediante giro postal o cheque personal al U.S.C.I.S. Escriba su nombre, dirección y número de registro de extranjero en el anverso del cheque. *Estos cargos cambian periódicamente, por lo tanto consulte con el U.S.C.I.S., un abogado de inmigración o un grupo de defensa de inmigrantes cuánto debe pagar.*
- Copia de su certificado de matrimonio, si corresponde. Si solicita la ciudadanía como cónyuge de un ciudadano estadounidense, el pasaporte de su cónyuge estadounidense.
- Una fotocopia del formulario N-648 del U.S.C.I.S., Exención médica, que ha sido llenado por un psicólogo o médico si es que tiene una incapacidad física o mental que le dificulta el aprendizaje del inglés y/o tomar la prueba de ciudadanía.

¿Cómo es la prueba de ciudadanía?

Probablemente le harán de 10 a 15 preguntas orales de una lista de 100 preguntas.

¿necesita más ayuda?

Estos grupos ofrecen asistencia para prepararlo para la prueba de ciudadanía:

- Asian Americans for Equality (A.A.F.E.) (Página 241)
- Catholic Migration Services (Página 246)
- Community Association of Progressive Dominicans (Página 253)
- Forest Hills Community House (Página 255)
- Hellenic American Neighborhood Action Committee (H.A.N.A.C.) (Página 257)
- Indochina Sino-American Community Center (Página 259)
- New York Association for New Americans (N.Y.A.N.A.) (Página 265)
- South Bronx Action Group (Página 275)
- Southside Community Mission, Immigration Program (Página 276)

¿Tengo que contestar correctamente todas las preguntas de la prueba de ciudadanía?

No, pero tiene que contestar correctamente por lo menos 6 de 10 preguntas.

He vivido y trabajado duro en los Estados Unidos durante mucho tiempo, pero no he tenido tiempo ni la preparación para aprender mucho inglés o sobre el gobierno. ¿Quiere decir que no puedo hacerme ciudadano?

No necesariamente. Las personas que tienen 65 años o más y han vivido en los Estados Unidos como residentes permanentes legales por lo menos durante 20 años pueden recibir consideración especial. Si tiene 50 años o más y ha sido residente legal permanente por lo menos durante 20 años, o tiene 55 años o más y ha tenido estado legal por lo menos durante 15 años, puede tomar la prueba de historia y del gobierno en su idioma.

¿Cuáles son algunas de las preguntas que me harán?

A continuación le ofrecemos cinco ejemplos:

1. ¿Qué significan las franjas en la bandera de los Estados Unidos?
   Representan los 13 estados o colonias originales.
2. ¿Qué es la Constitución?
   La ley suprema de la nación.
3. ¿Qué es el Congreso?
   El Senado y la Cámara de Diputados.
4. ¿Por qué vinieron los peregrinos a América?
   En busca de libertad religiosa.
5. ¿Quién fue Martin Luther King Jr.?
   Un líder del movimiento de derechos civiles.

¿Cómo puedo prepararme para la prueba de ciudadanía?

Muchas bibliotecas y grupos comunitarios y de defensa de los inmigrantes ofrecen clases y ayuda.

¿Qué pasa si no puedo demostrar que leo, escribo y entiendo inglés básico o si no paso la prueba de ciudadanía?

Si falla en uno o en ambos, el U.S.C.I.S. concertará otra entrevista. En esa fecha, le volverán a tomar la prueba y si falla esta vez su solicitud de ciudadanía será denegada.

Si mi solicitud de ciudadanía es denegada porque no leo ni escribo suficiente inglés o porque no pasé la prueba, ¿puedo volver a presentar la solicitud, y de ser así, cuándo?

Puede volver a presentar la solicitud tan pronto quiera. Debe volver a hacerlo tan pronto haya aprendido suficiente inglés o historia y gobierno para pasar la(s) prueba(s).

Si pienso que mi solicitud de ciudadanía se denegó injustamente, ¿hay algo que puedo hacer?

Sí. Si su solicitud es denegada, recibirá una carta que le explica por qué y también le indica cómo solicitar una audiencia. Incluirá un Formulario N-336. Debe completar el formulario y enviarlo al U.S.C.I.S. junto con el cargo apropiado, dentro de un plazo de 30 días después de haber recibido la carta de rechazo. A la fecha en que se publicó la guía, el cargo era de $195. Las solicitudes que se envían con la cantidad incorrecta serán devueltas. Es recomendable consultar el sitio Web del U.S.C.I.S. para verificar el cargo correcto, www.uscis.gov.

¿Qué ocurre si paso mi prueba de ciudadanía?

El U.S.C.I.S. tiene 120 días para aprobar o denegar su solicitud de ciudadanía. Será notificado por correo si ha sido aprobado y le informarán cuándo y dónde tendrá lugar el juramento para convertirse en ciudadano de los EE.UU.

Me he mudado. ¿Cómo notifico al U.S.C.I.S..?

Debe indicar al U.S.C.I.S. su nueva dirección dentro de los 10 días de mudarse. Puede informarles por teléfono pero sólo en el caso de solicitudes de naturalización. El número de teléfono es 1-800-375-5283 (inglés y español). Para la residencia legal permanente y otras solicitudes debe completar el formulario AR-11, un formulario de cambio de dirección y enviarlo a todas las oficinas de inmigración donde ha presentado solicitudes o peticiones. Envíe estos formularios por correo certificado con aviso de retorno. Y recuerde hacer copias para sus archivos.

¿Hay alguna manera que puedo verificar el estado de mi solicitud de ciudadanía?

Sí. Llame al **Centro Nacional de Atención al Cliente del U.S.C.I.S.** al 1-800-375-5283 (inglés y español). Si tiene un número de recibo para la solicitud o petición que se presentó en un centro de servicios del U.S.C.I.S., puede verificar el estado de su caso en el sitio Web del U.S.C.I.S., http://uscis.gov.

Mis hijos no nacieron en los Estados Unidos. ¿Cómo pueden hacerse ciudadanos?

Un menor de 18 años que no nació en este país por lo general reúne los requisitos para hacerse ciudadano cuando el padre/madre se hace ciudadano si el hijo está viviendo con el padre/madre y es un residente legal permanente. Para obtener información sobre hijos mayores y para respuestas a preguntas más específicas sobre la ciudadanía de los hijos, consulte con un abogado de inmigración confiable o con uno de los proveedores de servicios de inmigración que aparecen en el Directorio de Recursos al final de esta guía.

¿Debo obtener algún documento para probar que mis hijos son ciudadanos?
Un Certificado de Ciudadanía o un pasaporte de los Estados Unidos.

■

"Vine a este país escapando del nuevo gobierno autocrático y religioso en Irán. La experiencia fue estimulante, difícil y a veces desagradable. Después de asimilarme a la nueva cultura y disfrutar del estilo de vida, me di cuenta que me había convertido en un americano. Me había acostumbrado a la libertad, las comodidades, la gente y la cultura ecléctica. Convertirme en ciudadano de los Estados Unidos fue una decisión difícil. Me pregunté varias veces por qué debía hacerme ciudadano. La respuesta inmediata fue conveniencia — tener un pasaporte americano, oportunidades de trabajo, etc. Pero me he dado cuenta de que hay ventajas más significativas. Es convertirse en parte de una democracia donde uno puede hacer que las cosas sean diferentes. Puedo contribuir en preservar la cultura e ideología americana y asegurar un futuro feliz para mis hijos."

— *Kaynam Hedayat, iraní, 2002* [18]

DOCUMENTOS

A lo largo de esta guía se hace referencia a ciertos documentos que clasifican la elegibilidad de una persona para solicitar una visa, que son esenciales para todos los inmigrantes que llegan a los Estados Unidos, y se mencionan otras formas de documentación, como por ejemplo las tarjetas de llamadas, que le facilitan la vida y le ayudan a pagar menos por bienes y servicios.

Visas
Una visa es un permiso para solicitar ingreso a los Estados Unidos.

Una visa de no inmigrante se concede a una persona que vive en otro país y desea venir a los Estados Unidos temporalmente con un propósito específico. Las visas de no inmigrantes se extienden a turistas, gente de negocios, estudiantes, trabajadores temporales, diplomáticos, etc.

Una visa de inmigrante se otorga a una persona cuya intención es vivir y trabajar de modo permanente en los Estados Unidos y por lo general es un paso en el proceso de obtener la Residencia Permanente o la Tarjeta de Registro de Extranjeros, comúnmente llamada tarjeta verde. La mayoría de la gente obtiene una visa de inmigrante cuando sus parientes o patrones presentan la solicitud correspondiente. Este proceso puede tardar de 2 a 10 años o más y se describe en más detalle en la página 222 en el capítulo titulado Estado legal.

En algunos casos se permite que las personas presenten una solicitud en su propio nombre, tales como cónyuges de ciudadanos estadounidenses que fueron abusados, menores que han sido abusados o abandonados o extranjeros con aptitudes extraordinarias.

Permiso de trabajo (E.A.D., sus siglas en inglés)
Un documento que muestra que usted está autorizado. Le permite trabajar en los Estados Unidos aunque no sea ciudadano o residente legal permanente que ha

recibido una Tarjeta de Residencia Permanente, también conocida como Tarjeta de Registro de Extranjeros y llamada comúnmente tarjeta verde.

Tarjeta verde

Certifica que usted es un residente legal permanente de los Estados Unidos y tiene derecho a vivir y trabajar aquí. Para obtener la tarjeta verde hay que seguir un proceso de tramitación largo y complicado que podría tardar de 2 a 10 años o más. El proceso se describe a continuación y en el capítulo titulado Estado legal. En vista de que el proceso es tan complejo, es importante contar con la ayuda de un abogado de inmigración confiable, o de uno de los grupos de defensa de los inmigrantes que aparecen en el Directorio de Recursos al final de esta guía.

Estos son los pasos básicos para obtener una tarjeta verde:

1. Un pariente (utilizando el **Formulario I-130 del U.S.C.I.S., Petición para un familiar extranjero**) o un empleador (utilizando el Formulario I-140 del U.S.C.I.S., Petición para un trabajador extranjero) presenta una petición de inmigración en su nombre ante el U.S.C.I.S. para clasificarlo como una persona que puede solicitar una visa de inmigrante. Una vez que hay una visa de inmigrante disponible y usted está en los Estados Unidos legalmente, puede solicitar cambiar su estado legal al de un residente legal permanente. Si está fuera de los Estados Unidos, la petición aprobada será enviada al consulado estadounidense en el extranjero para que se complete el proceso de su visa de inmigrante.

2. Le darán un número de visa de inmigrante aunque ya esté en los Estados Unidos.

3. Si ya está en los Estados Unidos, puede solicitar modificar su estado al de un residente legal permanente completando el **Formulario I-485, Solicitud para Ajuste a Residente Permanente) del U.S.C.I.S.** Si está fuera de los Estados Unidos, diríjase al consulado de los Estados Unidos de su localidad para solicitar una visa de inmigrante.

SITIO WEB: www.immigration.gov/graphics/howdoi/LPReligibility.htm

TELÉFONO: Centro Nacional de Atención al Cliente, 1-800-375-5283 (inglés y español)

Licencia de conducir

En la mayoría de los casos, puede conducir en Nueva York si tiene una licencia de conducir válida de otro país. De hecho, El Departamento de Vehículos Automotores del Estado de Nueva York (D.M.V., sus siglas en inglés) recomienda que no solicite una licencia de Nueva York mientras siga siendo residente legal del país que emitió su licencia de conducir.

Si tiene una licencia de conducir de otro país y solicita una licencia del estado de Nueva York, debe hacer lo siguiente:

1. Pasar un examen escrito.
2. Tomar una clase de cinco horas.

" En la mayoría de los casos puede conducir en Nueva York si tiene una licencia de conducir válida de otro país. "

3. Pasar un examen de manejo.

4. Mostrar su tarjeta verde.

5. Mostrar una tarjeta del Seguro Social o una carta de la Administración de Seguro Social que diga por qué no califica para la tarjeta.

6. Entregar su tarjeta de conducción extranjera, que será destruida por el D.M.V. en un plazo de 60 días, salvo que solicite que se guarde. Si necesita recuperar su licencia de conducir extranjera, solicítela en la oficina del D.M.V. donde presentó la solicitud.

Si es la primera vez que solicita una licencia de conducir, debe tener por lo menos 16 años y cumplir con los siguientes requisitos.

1. Solicitar un permiso de aprendizaje.

2. Pagar el cargo de la solicitud y los derechos de la licencia de conducir.

3. Pasar un examen de la vista y una prueba escrita.

4. Practicar para el examen de manejo.

5. Hacer una cita para la prueba de manejo por teléfono o en línea.

6. Aprobar la prueba.

SITIO WEB: www.nydmv.state.ny.us/license.htm

TELÉFONO: Manhattan, Bronx, 1-212-645-5550 (inglés y español); Brooklyn, Queens, Staten Island, 1-718-966-6155 (inglés y español)

Tarjeta de identificación con foto no válida para conducir

Si no tiene una licencia de conducir, debe solicitar al D.M.V. una tarjeta de identificación con foto no válida para conducir. Esta tarjeta contiene la misma información personal, fotografía, firma y protección contra alteraciones y fraude que una licencia de conducir. Para obtener esta tarjeta, debe mostrar prueba de identidad y fecha de nacimiento.

SITIO WEB: www.nydmv.state.ny.us/license.htm

TELÉFONO: Manhattan, Bronx, 1-212-645-5550 (inglés y español); Brooklyn, Queens, Staten Island, 1-718-966-6155 (inglés y español)

Tarjeta del Seguro Social

El formulario de solicitud para una tarjeta de Seguro Social se conoce como SS-5. Puede ser utilizado por toda persona que nunca ha tenido una tarjeta, necesita una tarjeta de reemplazo o ha cambiado su nombre. Para obtener un formulario, llame a la Administración del Seguro Social o visite su sitio Web. Las instrucciones que recibirá conjuntamente con el formulario explican cómo llenarlo y qué documentos adicionales necesita. Después de completar el formulario, llévelo o envíelo por correo a la oficina más próxima del Seguro Social, junto con las copias originales o certificadas de los documentos que sirven de evidencia. Le devolverán sus documentos originales rápidamente. Una vez que la oficina del Seguro Social tiene todo lo que necesita, le enviará la tarjeta en dos semanas.

SITIO WEB: www.ssa.gov

TELÉFONO: 1-800-772-1213 (inglés y español).

Tarjeta de transferencia de beneficios electrónicos (E.B.T., sus siglas en inglés)

Una tarjeta de E.B.T. es una tarjeta de débito de plástico que le permite recibir asistencia pública en efectivo (beneficios de bienestar social) y utilizar cupones de comida en la ciudad de Nueva York. Puede solicitar la tarjeta en cualquiera de los centros de trabajo de la Administración de Recursos Humanos de la ciudad u oficinas de cupones de alimentos. Se la enviarán por correo, y debe utilizarla para obtener beneficios de bienestar social y/o cupones de comida.

SITIO WEB: www.nyc.gov/html/hra/html/serv_foodstamps.html

TELÉFONO: 1-877-472-8411 (inglés, español, cantonés y mandarín) (Página 258)

Cajero automático (A.T.M.)

Puede obtener una tarjeta A.T.M. cuando abre una cuenta corriente o de ahorro en un banco o en una cooperativa de crédito. La tarjeta le permite hacer transacciones bancarias, como por ejemplo depósitos y retiros de efectivo en un A.T.M. en vez de tener que ir al banco.

Cuando solicita una tarjeta, le pedirán que elija un número de identificación personal secreto o PIN. Cada vez que use la tarjeta en un A.T.M. tendrá que oprimir el PIN en el teclado del cajero, antes de poder sacar dinero o hacer otras operaciones bancarias.

No deje que otros usen su tarjeta de A.T.M. y no le diga a otros su PIN.

Llame a su banco o cooperativa de crédito o visite el sitio Web para averiguar cómo obtener una tarjeta A.T.M.

MetroCard

Para usar el metro de la ciudad debe usar una MetroCard en vez de efectivo. Para usar los autobuses que pertenecen al New York Transit puede usar la MetroCard o dinero. Si usa la MetroCard, su viaje puede costar menos que la tarifa actual del metro o autobús. También puede obtener una transferencia gratis automática entre el metro y los autobuses y entre diferentes líneas de autobuses. Si tiene 65 años o más, o sufre una incapacidad física o mental, puede solicitar una MetroCard con tarifa reducida, que le permite viajar por la mitad de precio.

El sistema de MetroCard funciona de la siguiente manera: Usted paga una cierta cantidad de dinero que se codifica en la tarjeta y cada vez que la desliza por el molinete del metro o autobús, se deduce el monto del viaje de la tarjeta. Cuando se deduce todo el dinero, tiene que volver a recargar la tarjeta o comprar una nueva.

Puede comprar MetroCards en las estaciones del metro, las máquinas de venta automática de MetroCards, en los autobuses y minibuses que utilizan metrocards y en las tiendas que muestran el símbolo de MetroCard.

Puede comprar MetroCards de varios precios. Si compra una por un valor que excede una cierta cantidad, recibirá una bonificación que le permitirá hacer viajes extra.

También puede elegir entre varias MetroCards ilimitadas, que cuestan diferentes precios y le permiten viajes ilimitados dentro de un período de tiempo específico.

SITIO WEB: www.mta.nyc.us/metrocard

TELÉFONO: 1-212-638-7622 (inglés, español, cantonés y mandarín)

Tarjeta de llamadas

Si no tiene teléfono o servicio de larga distancia donde vive o si utiliza teléfonos públicos, es una buena idea comprar una tarjeta de llamadas. Esta tarjeta le permite pagar por adelantado para hacer llamadas de larga distancia a diferentes lugares.

Puede comprar las tarjetas en varios lugares, incluyendo bodegas, supermercados y tiendas de artículos variados. Asegúrese que la tarjeta de llamadas que compra tenga un número de servicio al cliente válido.

Por lo general, paga una cantidad específica por la tarjeta o compra un número específico de minutos.

La mayoría de las tarjetas de llamadas prepagadas tienen un número de teléfono de acceso gratis y un número de identificación personal (PIN). Para hacer una llamada, marque el número de acceso y oprima su PIN. Un mensaje grabado le indicará que ingrese el número de la persona a la que quiere llamar.

El costo total de la llamada se deducirá del valor de la tarjeta. Le indicarán cuántos minutos o cuántas unidades quedan en la tarjeta.

Si utilizó todos los minutos en la tarjeta y no la puede recargar comprando más minutos, tendrá que comprar una nueva tarjeta.

Es importante hacer comparaciones y asegurarse que está recibiendo un número de minutos justo por la cantidad de dinero que ha pagado por la tarjeta, porque algunas compañías cobran demasiado por sus tarjetas.

La Comisión Federal de Comercio aconseja hacer estas cuatro preguntas antes de comprar una tarjeta de llamadas:

1. ¿Cuál es el *cargo de conexión* por cada llamada?
2. ¿Hay un *cargo por servicio*?
3. ¿Hay un *cargo de mantenimiento*?
4. ¿Hay *fecha de vencimiento*? No compre una tarjeta que podría vencer antes de que haya tenido tiempo de utilizar todos los minutos.

DIRECTORIO DE RECURSOS

Muchos neoyorquinos le dirán que en esta ciudad lo que importa no es lo que se sabe sino a quién se conoce. La verdad, especialmente para los recién llegados, es que ambas cosas importan.

Hay tanto que conocer en la ciudad: sus vecindarios étnicos, las rutas de los autobuses y del metro, el sistema de escuelas públicas, y la lista es interminable. Lo que necesita saber y lo que quiere saber a veces resulta abrumador. Pero no tiene que serlo.

En el texto de la guía, el nombre de muchas agencias, grupos y proveedores de servicios está acompañado por un número de página que lo referirá a una página en esta sección, el Directorio de Recursos. El Directorio de Recursos ofrece una descripción detallada de estas agencias, grupos y proveedores de servicios que otros inmigrantes han evaluado y determinado que son especialmente útiles y confiables.

Siempre que corresponda, se proporciona la abreviatura de cada agencia de recursos, grupo o proveedor de servicios.

En el directorio, sobre cada descripción aparecen símbolos que hacen referencia al tema del que se ocupa tal agencia de recursos, grupo o proveedor de servicios, por ejemplo vivienda o cuidado de niños.

Cada descripción detalla además la ubicación de la agencia de recursos, del grupo o proveedor de servicios, el número de teléfono y números de fax, dirección de correo electrónico y dirección Web, servicios que ofrece, idioma(s) hablado(s), documentos y otros requisitos, si los hay. Los idiomas que aparecen enumerados seguidos por el símbolo (P) significan que esa agencia, grupo o proveedor de servicios ofrece material impreso en ese idioma.

El Directorio de Recursos es una referencia muy útil, por lo tanto es aconsejable llevar la guía con usted cuando recorre la ciudad.

Temas principales de la Guía de Recursos:

VIVIENDA

TRABAJO Y EMPLEO

GUARDERÍAS INFANTILES

EDUCACIÓN

DINERO

ATENCIÓN DE SALUD Y SEGURO

SEGURIDAD

ASISTENCIA PÚBLICA

ESTADO LEGAL

Alianza Dominicana, Inc.
2410 Amsterdam Avenue, 4th Floor, New York, N.Y. 10033
Teléfono: 1-212-740-1960; Fax: 1-212-740-1967
Sitio Web: http://www.alianzadom.org/index.html

¿Qué tipo de ayuda ofrecen?

■ Clases de inglés, G.E.D. (diploma equivalente de escuela secundaria); cursos básicos de computación (español).

■ Clases de refuerzo después de la escuela y programa para jóvenes durante el verano.

■ Asistencia para inmigrantes orientada a la familia.

■ Servicios de salud en la comunidad; cómo obtener cobertura de seguro.

■ Servicios bilingües/biculturales para las personas infectadas/afectadas con el V.I.H. o SIDA.

¿A quiénes ayudan? A todos. **¿En qué idiomas ofrecen ayuda?** Español (P). **¿Qué debo llevar?** Un documento de identidad es útil, pero no necesario. **¿Tienen algún otro centro?** Hay 1 centro en el Bronx; 10 en Manhattan. Llame para hacer una cita antes de venir.

Archdiocese of New York, Superintendent of Schools
1011 First Avenue, New York, N.Y. 10022
Teléfono: 1-212-371-1000

¿Qué tipo de ayuda ofrecen?

■ Podemos suministrarle una lista de escuelas católicas en Manhattan, el Bronx y Staten Island.

■ Enseñarle cómo hacer una cita con cada escuela y qué esperar en un "open house" (evento que se organiza para que los padres y sus hijos visiten la escuela).

¿A quiénes ayudan? A todos. **¿En qué idiomas ofrecen ayuda?** Español (P). **¿Qué debo llevar?** Nada. **¿Tienen algún otro centro?** Sólo el centro que se menciona previamente.

Asian American Legal Defense and Education Fund (A.A.L.D.E.F.)
99 Hudson Street, New York, N.Y. 10013
Teléfono: 1-212-966-5932; 1-212-966-6030; Fax: 1-212-966-4303
Sitio Web: http://www.aaldef.org

¿Qué tipo de ayuda ofrecen?

- Asesoramiento gratis sobre las leyes de inmigración y el derecho de familia.
- Ayuda con solicitudes de naturalización.
- Beneficios del gobierno.
- Discriminación en el trabajo y derecho laboral.
- Abuso policial.

¿A quiénes ayudan? A todos. Para los servicios legales debe hacer una cita previa. **¿En qué idiomas ofrecen ayuda?** Chino (P) (cantonés, mandarín, toisanés), las personas que hablan bangla, hindi, coreano, tagalog y urdu por favor llamen al 1-212-966-5932 ó 1-212-966-6030. **¿Qué debo llevar?** Llame con anterioridad para hacer una cita y averiguar qué expedientes, documentos y papeles legales tiene que traer. **¿Tienen algún otro centro?** Sólo el centro que se menciona previamente.

Asian Americans for Equality (A.A.F.E.)
277 Grand Street, 3rd Floor, New York, N.Y. 10002
Teléfono: 1-212-680-1374; Fax: 1-212-680-1815
Correo electrónico: info@aafe.org; Sitio Web: http://www.aafe.org

¿Qué tipo de ayuda ofrecen?

- Responsabilidades y derechos básicos sobre la vivienda; asistencia y representación legal para casos relacionados con la vivienda; asesoramiento sobre posibilidades de compra de vivienda y acceso a hipotecas de bajo costo.
- Beneficios del gobierno y asesoramiento sobre atención de salud.
- Asesoramiento sobre temas relacionados con la ciudadanía y clases de educación cívica.
- Asesoramiento para pequeñas empresas y acceso a financiamiento de bajo costo.
- Cursos de computación. Un centro de computación totalmente equipado ofrece una variedad de programas.

¿A quiénes ayudan? A todos. **¿En qué idiomas ofrecen ayuda?** Español (P), chino (P) (cantonés, mandarín), bengali, coreano. **¿Qué debo llevar?** Depende de los servicios que necesita. **¿En dónde tienen otros centros?** Hay 5 en downtown Manhattan; 1 en Queens. Llame para hacer una cita antes de venir.

Banco Popular
Teléfono: 1-800-377-0800; Sitio Web: http://www.bancopopular.com

¿Qué tipo de ayuda ofrecen?
- Cuentas corrientes (de cheques) y de ahorro, crédito, seguro, inversiones, préstamos e hipotecas.

¿A quiénes ayudan? A todos. **¿En qué idiomas ofrecen ayuda?** Español (P). **¿Qué debo llevar?** Para operaciones de banco personales, por lo menos dos formas de identificación: pasaporte de los EE.UU. o extranjero, tarjeta de registro de no residente con fotografía, certificado de naturalización con foto, documento de las Fuerzas Armadas, licencia de conducir y/o una tarjeta de crédito o de banco de una institución reconocida. **¿En dónde tienen otros centros?** Hay 5 sucursales en el Bronx; 9 en Brooklyn; 10 en Manhattan; 3 en Queens. Llame para hacer una cita antes de venir.

Bellevue Hospital Center
462 First Avenue, New York, N.Y. 10016
Teléfono: 1-212-562-4141; Sitio Web: http://www.nyc.gov/bellevue

¿Qué tipo de ayuda ofrecen?
- Asma, diabetes, nutrición, programas para dejar de fumar, control de estrés y del peso.
- Exámenes médicos, clases y grupos de apoyo.
- Clínica para casos de violación.
- Atención prolongada para aquellas personas que necesitan atención médica constante.
- Atención preventiva y primaria para todos los miembros de la familia.
- Exámenes dentales de rutina y cuidado dental; tratamiento para problemas de la boca y las encías.

¿A quiénes ayudan? A todos. **¿En qué idiomas ofrecen ayuda?** El español (P), chino (cantonés, mandarín), bengali, polaco, francés y ruso son los idiomas más populares; 135 idiomas disponibles; intérpretes en el lugar. **¿Qué debo llevar?** Tarjeta de seguro si la tiene. **¿En dónde tienen otros centros?** Hay 5 centros en el Bronx; 6 en Brooklyn; 5 en Manhattan; 2 en Queens; 1 en Staten Island. Llame para hacer una cita antes de venir.

Bethex Federal Credit Union
20 East 179th Street, Bronx, N.Y. 10453
Teléfono: 1-718-299-9100; Fax: 1-718-294-4950; Sitio Web: http://www.bethexfcu.org

¿Qué tipo de ayuda ofrecen?
■ Cuentas corrientes (de cheques) y de ahorro; préstamos.
¿A quiénes ayudan? A todos. **¿En qué idiomas ofrecen ayuda?** Hay personas que hablan español (P) en todas las sucursales. **¿Qué debo llevar?** $20 (cargo de inscripción de $10 y un depósito de $10 para la nueva cuenta de ahorro). Prueba de domicilio (factura de Teléfono: o de otro servicio público), documento de identidad con foto y tarjeta del Seguro Social o tarjeta verde. **¿En dónde tienen otros centros?** Hay 3 centros en el Bronx; 1 en Manhattan. Llame para hacer una cita antes de venir.

The Bronx Defenders
860 Courtlandt Avenue, Bronx, N.Y. 10451
Teléfono: (718)1-718- 838-7878; Fax: (718) 1-718-665-0100
Correo electrónico: shaynak@bronxdefenders.org
Sitio Web: http://www.bronxdefenders.org

¿Qué tipo de ayuda ofrecen?
■ Asesoramiento legal para aquellos acusados de delitos; servicios legales civiles.
■ Asuntos relacionados con la incapacidad y suspensión de empleo.
■ Abuso de drogas y/o alcohol.
■ Referencias para servicios sociales.
¿A quiénes ayudan? A aquellos que han sido arrestados o temen ser arrestados por delitos en el Bronx. (No es necesario ser residente del Bronx.) **¿En qué idiomas ofrecen ayuda?** Español (P). **¿Qué debo llevar?** Depende del servicio que solicita. **¿Tienen algún otro centro?** Sólo el centro que se menciona previamente.

Brooklyn Chinese-American Association
5002 Eighth Avenue, 2nd Floor, Brooklyn, N.Y. 11220
Teléfono: 1-718-438-9312; Fax: 1-718-438-8303

¿Qué tipo de ayuda ofrecen?
■ Asesoramiento para asuntos relacionados con la obtención de la ciudadanía.

- Medicaid y cupones de comida.
- Servicios de traducción.
- Preescolar, guarderías diurnas, programas para después de la escuela y durante el verano; centro para jubilados.
- Clases de inglés, negocios y computación; clases en chino para niños.
- Educación de la salud.

¿A quiénes ayudan? Sólo a residentes legales de Brooklyn. **¿En qué idiomas ofrecen ayuda?** Chino (P) (cantonés, mandarín). **¿Qué debo llevar?** Nada. **¿En dónde tienen otros centros?** Hay 4 centros en Brooklyn. Llame para hacer una cita antes de venir.

Bushwick Cooperative Federal Credit Union
1475 Myrtle Avenue, Brooklyn, N.Y. 11237
Teléfono: 1-718-418-8232; Fax: 1-718-418-8252
Correo electrónico: bushwickfcu@rbscc.org

¿Qué tipo de ayuda ofrecen?
- Cuentas corrientes (de cheques) y de ahorro; préstamos; cursos para aprender conceptos financieros básicos.

¿A quiénes ayudan? A todos. **¿En qué idiomas ofrecen ayuda?** Español. **¿Qué debo llevar?** Dos documentos de identificación, al menos uno con foto; prueba de domicilio; tarjeta del Seguro Social; estado de cuenta del seguro o talón del cheque de sueldo. **¿Tienen algún otro centro?** Sólo el centro que se menciona previamente.

Cabrini Immigrant Services
139 Henry Street, New York, N.Y. 10002
Teléfono: 1-212-791-4590; Fax: 1-212-791-4592

¿Qué tipo de ayuda ofrecen?
- Para completar formularios y solicitudes; obtener las referencias necesarias.
- Clases de inglés (es necesario que se comprometa a asistir una vez por semana).
- Comida gratis.

¿A quiénes ayudan? A todos. **¿En qué idiomas ofrecen ayuda?** Español (P), chino (P) (mandarín). **¿Qué debo llevar?** Nada. Todos los servicios son gratis. Inscríbase para clases en agosto y/o diciembre. **¿Tienen algún otro centro?** Sólo el centro que se menciona previamente.

Caribbean Women's Health Association (C.W.H.A.)
123 Linden Boulevard, Brooklyn, N.Y. 11226
Teléfono: 1-718-826-2942; Fax: 1-718-826-2948; Sitio Web: http://www.cwha.org

¿Qué tipo de ayuda ofrecen?
- Representación legal en tribunales de inmigración y en audiencias de casos de unificación familiar y deportación.
- Solicitudes de ciudadanía y preparación para la prueba.
- Salud comunitaria; servicios del V.I.H. y SIDA; salud para madres y sus bebés y el programa W.I.C. (mujeres, bebés y niños)

¿A quiénes ayudan? A todos. **¿En qué idiomas ofrecen ayuda?** Español, haitiano (P), creole (P), francés (P). Para otros idiomas, se utilizan los servicios de un intérprete. Llame para hacer una cita antes de venir. **¿Qué debo llevar?** Cargos bajos para asistencia legal. Llame para hacer una cita antes de venir. **¿En dónde tienen otros centros?** Hay 2 centros más en Brooklyn; 2 en Queens. Llame para hacer una cita antes de venir.

Cathay Bank
Teléfono: 1-800-9CATHAY (1-800-922-8429)

¿Qué tipo de ayuda ofrecen?
- Cuentas corrientes (de cheques) y de ahorro; Cuentas de Jubilación Individual (I.R.A.) y Certificados de Depósito (CD), préstamos para la compra de automóviles, sobre el valor adquirido de una vivienda (home equity) e hipotecarios; cambio de moneda extranjera.

¿A quiénes ayudan? A todos. **¿En qué idiomas ofrecen ayuda?** Chino (cantonés, mandarín) (P) **¿Qué debo llevar?** Por lo menos dos formas de identificación: pasaporte de los EE.UU. o extranjero, tarjeta de registro de no residente con fotografía, certificado de naturalización con foto, documento de las Fuerzas Armadas, licencia de conducir y/o una tarjeta de crédito o de banco de una institución reconocida. **¿En dónde tienen otros centros?** Hay 1 sucursal en Brooklyn; 1 en Manhattan; 1 en Queens. Llame para hacer una cita antes de venir.

Catholic Charities Office for Immigrant Services
1011 First Avenue, 12th Floor, New York, N.Y. 10022
Teléfono: 1-212-419-3700, 1-800-566-7636 (para ayuda en los idiomas que se mencionan a continuación); Fax: 1-212-751-3197
Sitio Web: http://www.catholiccharities.org

¿Qué tipo de ayuda ofrecen?
■ Ayuda legal para asuntos relacionados con la inmigración y el reasentamiento de refugiados; representación legal para detenidos que procuran asilo.
■ Documentos para la naturalización y la ciudadanía.
¿En qué idiomas ofrecen ayuda? Español (P), chino (mandarín) (P), árabe, francés, creole haitiano, italiano, japonés, coreano, polaco, punjabi, ruso, servocroata, turco y urdu. ¿A quiénes ayudan? A todos. ¿Qué debo llevar? $50 para pagar el cargo de servicio. No dejaremos de atender a las personas que tienen problemas financieros. Llame para hacer una cita antes de venir. ¿En dónde tienen otros centros? Centros de extensión (mensual): Bronx y Staten Island. Llame para hacer una cita antes de venir.

Catholic Migration Services
1258 65th Street, Brooklyn, N.Y. 11219
Teléfono: 1-718-236-3000; Fax: 1-718-256-9707
Correo electrónico: migration@aol.com; Sitio Web: www.catholicimmigration.org

¿Qué tipo de ayuda ofrecen?
■ Ayuda legal para asuntos relacionados con la inmigración.
■ Clases de inglés por las tardes (todos los niveles); clases de preparación para la ciudadanía.
■ Capacitación en destrezas básicas de computación, clases de cocina, limpieza de casas residenciales y oficinas.
¿A quiénes ayudan? A todos. ¿En qué idiomas ofrecen ayuda? Español (P), albanés, griego, italiano, creole haitiano y polaco. Llame para hacer una cita antes de venir. ¿Qué debo llevar? Un cargo bajo por servicios. Llame para hacer una cita antes de venir. ¿Tienen algún otro centro? Hay 1 centro en Queens.

Charles B. Wang Community Health Center
268 Canal Street, New York, N.Y. 10013
Teléfono: 1-212-379-6998; Fax: 1-212-379-6930

¿Qué tipo de ayuda ofrecen?

- Atención primaria, salud para la mujer, obstetricia, ginecología, evaluación de cáncer, medicina interna, pediatría, cardiología pediátrica, atención de adolescentes, alergia, atención dental, cuidado de los ojos, urología, acupuntura, atención especializada, salud mental, educación de la salud, prevención de enfermedades. Inscripción en Child Health Plus y Family Health Plus.
- Servicios sociales, programa W.I.C. (mujeres, bebés y niños)

¿A quiénes ayudan? A todos. **¿En qué idiomas ofrecen ayuda?** Chino (cantonés, mandarín, toisanés, shanganés y taiwanés). Llame para hacer una cita antes de venir. **¿Qué debo llevar?** Prueba de Medicaid y cobertura de seguro de tercero; prueba de su capacidad de pago, como por ejemplo, talón del cheque de sueldo y recibos de impuestos; cualquier documentación que tenga. Se cobran honorarios basados en una escala móvil de $20 a $60 según su capacidad de pago. **¿Tienen algún otro centro?** Otro centro en el Bajo Manhattan y uno en Queens.

Chase
Teléfono: 1-800-CHASE24 (1-800-242-7324); Sitio Web: http://www.chase.com

¿Qué tipo de ayuda ofrecen?

- Cuentas corrientes (de cheques) y de ahorro, tarjetas de crédito, inversiones, seguro, hipotecas y otros préstamos.

¿A quiénes ayudan? A ciudadanos de los Estados Unidos con una dirección postal en los Estados Unidos y un número válido de Seguro Social. **¿En qué idiomas ofrecen ayuda?** ServiceLine (inglés, español; de las siguientes área de código solamente 212, 516, 585, 914, 718) 935-9999. ServiceLine (inglés y chino) 1-212-809-6464. ServiceLine (coreano bilingüe) 1-212-809-3737. **¿Qué debo llevar?** Prueba de fecha de nacimiento, nombre de soltera de la madre, información de empleo, número de la licencia de conducir o número de identificación del estado. **¿En dónde está ubicado?** Llame para averiguar cuál es la sucursal más cercana.

Chinatown Manpower Project, Inc.
70 Mulberry Street, New York, N.Y. 10003
Teléfono: 1-212-571-1690; Fax: 1-212-571-1686; Sitio Web: www.cmpny.org

¿Qué tipo de ayuda ofrecen?
- Clases de inglés, de preparación para la ciudadanía y para el desarrollo de destrezas de trabajo.
- Capacitación vocacional en contabilidad computarizada, tecnología básica de oficina y operaciones de computación.
- Capacitación empresarial, recursos de financiamiento, consultas comerciales y asistencia técnica para individuos y pequeñas empresas.

¿A quiénes ayudan? A residentes de la ciudad de Nueva York. **¿En qué idiomas ofrecen ayuda?** Chino (cantonés, mandarín). **¿Qué debo llevar?** Tarjeta verde o tarjeta del Seguro Social; prueba de domicilio. Llame para hacer una cita antes de venir. **¿En dónde tienen otros centros?** Hay 1 centro en Brooklyn y otro en el Bajo Manhattan. Llame para hacer una cita antes de venir.

Chinese Immigrant Services
133-54 41st Avenue, 4th Floor, Flushing, N.Y. 11355
Teléfono: 1-718-353-0195; Fax: 1-718-359-5065

¿Qué tipo de ayuda ofrecen?
- Grupos de apoyo para inmigrantes chinos y grupos para jóvenes.
- Asesoramiento y mediación para familias con conflictos.
- Información, referencias y asesoramiento sobre diversos asuntos sociales y legales.
- Clases de inglés y programas sobre la cultura y las instituciones de los Estados Unidos.

¿A quiénes ayudan? A residentes de Nueva York. **¿En qué idiomas ofrecen ayuda?** Chino (P) (cantonés, mandarín). **¿Qué debo llevar?** Nada. **¿Tienen algún otro centro?** Sólo el centro que se menciona previamente.

Chinese Staff and Workers' Association
15 Catherine Street, 2nd Floor, New York, N.Y. 10038
Teléfono: 1-212-619-7979; Fax: 1-212-374-1506

¿Qué tipo de ayuda ofrecen?
- Asesoramiento legal sobre reglamentos y normas laborales en la industria de restaurantes, ropa y servicios; educación para trabajadores y desarrollo de destrezas de liderazgo.

¿A quiénes ayudan? A todos. **¿En qué idiomas ofrecen ayuda?** Chino (P) (cantonés, mandarín, fukianés). **¿Qué debo llevar?** Nada. **¿En dónde tienen otros centros?** Hay 1 centro en Brooklyn. Llame para hacer una cita antes de venir.

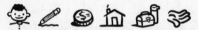

Chinese-American Planning Council (C.P.C.)
150 Elizabeth Street, New York, N.Y. 10012
Teléfono: 1-212- 941-0920; Fax: 1-212- 966-8581; Sitio Web: http://www.cpc-nyc.org

¿Qué tipo de ayuda ofrecen?
- Capacitación para empleo en la industria de ropa, hotelería, servicios administrativos y multimedia. Clases de alfabetización para adultos y empleos transicionales para trabajadores adultos. Servicios de asesoramiento y orientación para aquellos afectados por el 11 de septiembre.
- Child Health Plus, Family Health Plus, cupones de comida y otros beneficios.
- Vivienda justa.
- Recursos de guarderías infantiles para niños asiáticos, referencias y servicios para la familia.
- Servicios de salud a los padres de los niños que tienen problemas de desarrollo.
- Ayuda con el V.I.H., SIDA y prevención del uso de drogas.

¿A quiénes ayudan? A todos, pero especialmente a inmigrantes asiáticos y asiáticos-americanos que viven en Chinatown, el Lower East Side, Flushing y Sunset Park. **¿En qué idiomas ofrecen ayuda?** Chino (P) (cantonés, mandarín). **¿Qué debo llevar?** Un documento de identidad es útil. **¿En dónde tienen otros centros?** 11 guarderías infantiles, 2 centros para jubilados, 2 centros de manejo de casos en los que no se necesita cita previa, 1 centro de empleo y capacitación y 1 centro de programas para jóvenes en Manhattan; sucursales, 1 centro de empleo y capacitación y 3 centros de servicios para jóvenes en Brooklyn; sucursales, 1 guardería y 1 centro para jubilados en Queens. Llame para hacer una cita antes de venir.

Church Avenue Merchants Block Association, Inc. (C.A.M.B.A.)
1720 Church Avenue, 2nd Floor, Brooklyn, N.Y. 11226
Teléfono: 1-718- 287-2600; Fax: 1-718-287-0857; Sitio Web: http://www.camba.org

¿Qué tipo de ayuda ofrecen?
- Asesoramiento, representación y asistencia de emergencia para aquellos que confrontan un desalojo y la denegación de beneficios.
- Servicios legales para inmigrantes; servicios para refugiados y aquellos que procuran asilo; talleres sobre naturalización y ciudadanía.
- Capacitación de trabajo y empleo.
- Clases de inglés y computación.

¿A quiénes ayudan? A todos. Deben ser inmigrantes legales para los servicios de empleo. **¿En qué idiomas ofrecen ayuda?** Español (P), albanés (P), ruso (P), francés, árabe, bosnio, creole haitiano. **¿Qué debo llevar?** Se necesitan documentos específicos para los servicios de empleo y servicios para refugiados. Llame para hacer una cita antes de venir. **¿En dónde tienen otros centros?** Hay 13 centros en Brooklyn. Llame para hacer una cita antes de venir. **Servicios legales:** 885 Flatbush Avenue, 2nd Floor, Brooklyn, N.Y. 11226, Teléfono: 1-718-287-0010. **Servicios de empleo y para refugiados:** 2211 Church Avenue, Room 202, Brooklyn, N.Y. 11226, Teléfono: 1-718-282-0108.

Citibank
Teléfono: 1-800-627-3999; Sitio Web: http://www.citibank.com

¿Qué tipo de ayuda ofrecen?
- Cuentas corrientes (de cheques) y de ahorro, seguro, inversiones, tarjetas de crédito, hipotecas y otros préstamos.

¿A quiénes ayudan? A todos. **¿En qué idiomas ofrecen ayuda?** Español (P). **¿Qué debo llevar?** Por lo menos dos formas de identificación: pasaporte de los EE.UU. o extranjero, tarjeta de registro de no residente con fotografía, certificado de naturalización con foto, documento de las Fuerzas Armadas, licencia de conducir y/o una tarjeta de crédito o de banco de una institución reconocida. **¿En dónde está ubicado?** Llame para averiguar cuál es la sucursal más cercana.

Citizens Advice Bureau (C.A.B.)
2054 Morris Avenue, Bronx, N.Y. 10453
Teléfono: 1-718-365-0910; Fax: 1-718-365-0697; Sitio Web: http://www.cabny.org

¿Qué tipo de ayuda ofrecen?
- Guarderías, programas para después de la escuela y durante el verano para niños y adolescentes y centros para jubilados (incluyendo comida, ejercicio y juegos).
- Asesoramiento sobre inmigración, ciudadanía y otros asuntos legales.
- Clases de E.S.O.L. y de educación cívica.
- Asistencia para empleo.
- Prevención de desalojo, asesoramiento para personas y familias desamparadas.
- Asesoramiento sobre seguro de salud.
- Orientación y manejo de casos para personas con SIDA.

¿A quiénes ayudan? A todos. **¿En qué idiomas ofrecen ayuda?** Español (P). **¿Qué debo llevar?** Nada. **¿En dónde tienen otros centros?** Más de 20 centros en el Bronx. Llame para hacer una cita antes de venir.

City Harvest Hunger Hot Line
575 Eighth Avenue, 4th Floor, New York, N.Y. 10018
Teléfono: 1-917-351-8700; Fax: 1-917- 351-8720; Sitio Web: http://www.cityharvest.org

¿Qué tipo de ayuda ofrecen?
- Programas de comida de emergencia.

¿A quiénes ayudan? A todas las personas necesitadas. **¿En qué idiomas ofrecen ayuda?** Español. **¿Qué debo llevar?** Documento de identidad y prueba de domicilio. Llame para hacer una cita antes de venir. **¿En dónde tienen otros centros?** Atiende a cientos de agencias en los cinco distritos.

City University of New York (CUNY)
1114 Avenue of the Americas, New York, N.Y. 10036
Teléfono: 1-212-997-CUNY (2869); Sitio Web: http://www.cuny.edu/

¿Qué tipo de ayuda ofrecen?
- Clases de inglés para prepararse para el ingreso a CUNY y para el examen T.O.E.F.L.
- Programas para estudiantes universitarios y de posgrado en todas las universidades

de humanidades y ciencias, gestión de empresas, ciencias de la salud, administración pública y servicios comunitarios y sociales, ingeniería, arquitectura y tecnologías relacionadas, derecho, bibliotecología, formación de docentes.

■ Asesoramiento para varios programas e instituciones.
■ Ayuda financiera.
■ Honores y programas los fines de semana.
■ Programas de ampliación de estudios y de desarrollo profesional con diploma.

¿A quiénes ayudan? A todos. **¿En qué idiomas ofrecen ayuda?** Varía según el recinto universitario. **¿Qué debo llevar?** Formulario de inscripción completado, cargo de $40, diploma de la escuela secundaria y/o copia del certificado académico traducidos. Estado de inmigración exacto o visa, actual o vencida. Calificación obtenida en el examen T.O.E.F.L. y SAT, si corresponde. El examen T.O.E.F.L. determina el nivel de capacidad en el idioma inglés necesario para estudiar en CUNY. **¿Dónde está ubicada?** Hay 20 recintos universitarios: 4 en Brooklyn, 3 en el Bronx, 7 en Manhattan, 5 en Queens, 1 en Staten Island.

Civilian Complaint Review Board (C.C.R.B.)
40 Rector Street, 2nd Floor, New York, N.Y. 10006
Teléfono: 1-212-442-8833 or 1-800-341-2272; Fax: 1-212-442-9109
Sitio Web: http://www.nyc.gov/ccrb

¿Qué tipo de ayuda ofrecen?
■ Quejas contra agentes del Departamento de Policía de la Ciudad de Nueva York por abuso o fuerza excesiva, abuso de autoridad, descortesía o lenguaje ofensivo.

¿A quiénes ayudan? A todos. **¿En qué idiomas ofrecen ayuda?** Chino (P) (cantonés, mandarín), español (P), árabe (P), fránces, ruso (P), polaco (P), coreano (P) e italiano. Para otros idiomas, indique el idioma que desea y su número de teléfono. El traductor le devolverá la llamada. **¿Qué debo llevar?** Toda la información que tenga sobre el incidente. La C.C.R.B. le pedirá la fecha, hora, ubicación y una descripción detallada del incidente y de los agentes de policía involucrados. Otra información útil incluye: números de la placa del automóvil, un número de arresto, número de registro del sumario de causa del tribunal y números de Teléfono. No es necesario que sepa el nombre y número de insignia del (de los) agente(s) que participaron en el incidente. **¿Tienen algún otro centro?** Sólo el centro que se menciona previamente.

Community Association of Progressive Dominicans
3940 Broadway, 2nd Floor, New York, N.Y. 10032
Teléfono: 1-212-781-5500; Fax: 1-212-927-6089
Sitio Web: http://home.att.net/~acdpinc/

¿Qué tipo de ayuda ofrecen?
- Representación legal y asesoramiento para casos de desalojo y temas relacionados con el dueño del edificio (landlord) y viviendas de bajos ingresos.
- Clases de inglés, de computación y de preparación para la ciudadanía y colonia de vacaciones.
- Asesoramiento y ayuda para completar formularios de solicitud para cupones de comida y asistencia pública.

¿A quiénes ayudan? A inmigrantes legales de bajos ingresos. **¿En qué idiomas ofrecen ayuda?** Español (P). **¿Qué debo llevar?** Tarjeta verde y/o permiso de trabajo/documentos que permiten trabajar; requisitos para el tamaño de la familia sólo para asuntos de vivienda. Llame para hacer una cita antes de venir. **¿En dónde tienen otros centros?** Hay un centro en el Bronx; 5 en el Alto Manhattan. Llame para hacer una cita antes de venir.

Community Healthcare Network, Bronx Center
975 Westchester Avenue, Bronx, N.Y. 10459
Teléfono: 1-718-991-9250/51; Fax: 1-212-991-3829; Sitio Web: http://www.chnnyc.org

¿Qué tipo de ayuda ofrecen?
- Atención de salud primaria para adultos, niños y aquellos con V.I.H.; planificación familiar y atención prenatal; exámenes de salud en la escuela; evaluación de asma; atención de salud mental; servicios de nutrición; servicios sociales.

¿A quiénes ayudan? A todos. **¿En qué idiomas ofrecen ayuda?** Español (P), chino (P) en el Bajo Manhattan, francés, creole haitiano en los centros de Brooklyn. **¿Qué debo llevar?** Talón del cheque de sueldo del empleador que indique cuánto gana y la necesidad de obtener un cargo reducido o tarjeta de seguro. Los adolescentes necesitan un documento de identidad. **¿En dónde tienen otros centros?** Hay 4 centros en Brooklyn; 3 en Manhattan; 1 en Queens. Llame para hacer una cita antes de venir.

CUNY Law School
Main Street Legal Services, Immigration and Refugee Rights Program
65-21 Main Street, Flushing, N.Y. 11367
Teléfono: 1-718-340-4300; Fax: 1-718-340-4478; Sitio Web: http://www.law.cuny.edu

¿Qué tipo de ayuda ofrecen?
■ Servicios legales para inmigrantes y asesoramiento de ciudadanía, incluyendo asilo y peticiones para traer a otros miembros de la familia; asuntos relacionados con la violencia doméstica; derechos de las personas de la tercera edad.
¿A quiénes ayudan? A todos. **¿En qué idiomas ofrecen ayuda?** Español, chino (cantonés) y bengali. Depende de los estudiantes que se inscriben cada semestre. Llame para hacer una cita antes de venir. **¿Qué debo llevar?** Llame antes y le informaremos. **¿Tienen algún otro centro?** Sólo la oficina que se menciona previamente.

Delgado Travel
7908 Roosevelt Avenue, Jackson Heights, N.Y. 11372
Teléfono: 1-718-426-0500; Fax: 1-718-397-0347

¿Qué tipo de ayuda ofrecen?
■ Transferencia de dinero; envío de paquetes; llamadas telefónicas internacionales; trámites de viaje.
¿A quiénes ayudan? A todos. **¿En qué idiomas ofrecen ayuda?** Español (P). **¿Qué debo llevar?** Depende de los servicios que procura. **¿En dónde tienen otros centros?** Hay 4 centros en el Bronx; 4 en Brooklyn; 5 en Manhattan; 12 en Queens. Llame para hacer una cita antes de venir.

The Door
121 Avenue of the Americas, New York, N.Y. 10013
Teléfono: 1-212-941-9090; Fax: 1-212-941-0714; Sitio Web: http://www.door.org

¿Qué tipo de ayuda ofrecen?
■ Servicios integrales para el desarrollo de la juventud, atención de salud, asesoramiento, educación, servicios legales, las artes y recreación.
¿A quiénes ayudan? A cualquier residente de Nueva York de 12 a 21 años. **¿En qué idiomas ofrecen ayuda?** Español y chino (cantonés y mandarín). El sitio Web está

disponible en inglés, español y chino. **¿Qué debo llevar?** Nada. **¿Tienen algún otro centro?** Sólo el centro que se menciona previamente.

Emerald Isle Immigration Center
59-26 Woodside Avenue, Woodside, N.Y. 11377
Teléfono: 1-718- 478-5502; Fax: 1-718-446-3727; Sitio Web: http://www.eiic.org

¿Qué tipo de ayuda ofrecen?
■ Inmigración y otros servicios legales, trámites, tarjeta verde, preparación para el examen de ciudadanía y referencias.
■ Búsqueda de trabajo y empleo.

¿A quiénes ayudan? A todos. **¿En qué idiomas ofrecen ayuda?** Español, francés. **¿Qué debo llevar?** Depende de los servicios que procura. **¿En dónde tienen otros centros?** Hay un centro en el Bronx. Llame para hacer una cita antes de venir.

Flatbush Development Corporations
1616 Newkirk Avenue, Brooklyn, N.Y. 11226
Teléfono: 1-718-859-3800; Fax: 1-718-859-4632

¿Qué tipo de ayuda ofrecen?
■ Para la vivienda, talleres para inquilinos y dueños de edificios (landlords), asociaciones de inquilinos.

¿A quiénes ayudan? Depende de los servicios que se procuren. Llame para hacer una cita antes de venir. **¿En qué idiomas ofrecen ayuda?** Español (P), chino (mandarín), cambodiano, francés y creole haitiano (P), tailandés. **¿Qué debo llevar?** Documento de identidad con foto, prueba de domicilio, tarjeta del Seguro Social si la tiene. **¿Tienen algún otro centro?** Sólo la oficina que se menciona previamente.

Forest Hills Community House
108-25 62nd Drive, Forest Hills, N.Y. 11375
Teléfono: 1-718-592-5757; Fax: 1-718-592-2933; Sitio Web: http://www.fhch.org

¿Qué tipo de ayuda ofrecen?
■ Clases de ciudadanía en inglés para jóvenes y adultos.
■ Clases de computación y capacitación laboral.

- Asesoramiento sobre beneficios, comida/nutrición y servicios de vivienda.
- Salud mental, programa para jubilados y cuidado de adultos.
- Programas de nivel preescolar.

¿A quiénes ayudan? A los residentes de Queens. **¿En qué idiomas ofrecen ayuda?** Español (P), árabe, idioma para sordomudos, francés, creole haitiano, hebreo, coreano y ruso. **¿Qué debo llevar?** Según los servicios que procura. Llame para hacer una cita antes de venir. **¿En dónde tienen otros centros?** Hay 15 centros en Queens. Llame para hacer una cita antes de venir.

Growing Up Healthy Hot Line
Teléfono: 1-800-522-5006

¿Qué tipo de ayuda ofrecen?
- Cupones de comida; cupones para tiendas de comestibles para padres con un hijo menor de 5 años a través del programa W.I.C. (mujeres, bebés y niños)
- Planificación familiar bajo Medicaid e información de salud.
- Mantenimiento de los ingresos.
- Servicios para jubilados.

¿A quiénes ayudan? Se ofrecen referencias solamente. **¿En qué idiomas ofrecen ayuda?** Intérpretes disponibles para varios idiomas.

HealthStat
Vea New York City Department of Health and Mental Hygiene (Departamento de Salud e Higiene Mental) (Página 268)

Hebrew Immigrant Aid Society (H.I.A.S.)
333 Seventh Avenue, New York, N.Y. 10001
Teléfono: 1-212-967-4100; Fax: 1-212-760-1833; Correo electrónico: info@hias.org
Sitio Web: http://www.hias.org

¿Qué tipo de ayuda ofrecen?
- Requisitos de inmigración y para la obtención de visas, solicitudes de documentos, respuestas a preguntas y representación legal; comida y vivienda para refugiados e inmigrantes; preparación para el examen de naturalización y la entrevista.

¿A quiénes ayudan? A todos. Es necesario hacer una cita; llame con anticipación. **¿En qué idiomas ofrecen ayuda?** Español, ruso (P), yiddish, y francés. **¿Qué debo llevar?** Nada. **¿Tienen algún otro centro?** Sólo el centro que se menciona previamente.

Hellenic American Neighborhood Action Committee (H.A.N.A.C.)
49 West 45th Street, 4th Floor, New York, N.Y. 10036
Teléfono: 1-212-840-8005 or 1-212-996-3949; Fax: 1-212- 840-8384
Correo electrónico: info@hanac.org; Sitio Web: http://www.hanac.org

¿Qué tipo de ayuda ofrecen?
- Representación legal, servicios de asesoramiento y apoyo.
- Talleres de empleo, preparación para trabajos, ubicación en empleos.
- Educación básica, instrucción para el G.E.D., pasantías.
- Clases de inglés y preparación para los exámenes de ciudadanía.
- Programas de extensión comunitarios, terapia para la familia, intervención en situaciones de crisis, terapia de parejas, cómo evitar que sus hijos sean colocados con una familia de crianza y servicios para jubilados.
- Clases de refuerzo y orientación, asesoramiento sobre finanzas
- Programas Beacon y para después de la escuela; colonias de vacaciones diurnas y programas de empleo para jóvenes.

¿A quiénes ayudan? A inmigrantes legales de bajos ingresos. **¿En qué idiomas ofrecen ayuda?** Español, griego e hindi. **¿Qué debo llevar?** Depende de los servicios que procura. **¿En dónde tienen otros centros?** Hay 2 centros en Manhattan; 2 en Queens. Llame para hacer una cita antes de venir.

Highbridge Community Life Center
979 Ogden Avenue, Bronx, N.Y. 10452
Teléfono: 1-718-681-2222; Fax: 1-718- 681-4137 or 1-718-992-3481

¿Qué tipo de ayuda ofrecen?
- Clases de inglés y clases de alfabetización en español; clases de educación básica y G.E.D.; programas para después de la escuela.
- Despensa de alimentos y servicios de comida al hogar.
- Servicios de empleo

¿A quiénes ayudan? A todos. **¿En qué idiomas ofrecen ayuda?** Español. **¿Qué debo llevar?** Nada. Debe inscribirse en enero, junio y/o septiembre. **¿Tienen algún otro centro?** Sólo la oficina que se menciona previamente.

HSBC Bank USA
Teléfono: 1-800-975-HSBC (1-800-975-4722)
Sitio Web: http://us.hsbc.com/

¿Qué tipo de ayuda ofrecen?
- Cuentas corrientes (de cheques) y de ahorro, seguro, inversiones; tarjetas de crédito, hipotecas y otros préstamos.

¿A quiénes ayudan? A los residentes con una dirección en los Estados Unidos y un número de Seguro Social válido o aquellos en el proceso de obtener uno; estudiantes de intercambio extranjeros. **¿En qué idiomas ofrecen ayuda?** ServiceLine (inglés) 1-800-975-HSBC (1-800-975-4722); ServiceLine (español) 1-888-433-4722; ServiceLine (la mayoría de los idiomas asiáticos, incluyendo cantonés y mandarín) 1-800-711-8001. **¿Qué debo llevar?** Número del Seguro Social o Número de Identificación de Contribuyente (los ciudadanos extranjeros necesitan una tarjeta verde o visa). Debe suministrar fecha de nacimiento, nombre de soltera de la madre, información de empleo, número de la licencia de conducir o número de identificación estatal; factura de servicios públicos o tarjeta de crédito de una institución de renombre como prueba de domiciliio. **¿En dónde tienen otros centros?** Llame a la sucursal más cercana, o visite el sitio Web y use el localizador de sucursales.

Human Resources Administration (H.R.A.)
Teléfono: 1-877-HRA-8411 (1-877-472-8411) (Línea de información)

¿Qué tipo de ayuda ofrecen?
- Cupones de comida y elegibilidad para Medicaid.
- Temas relacionados con guarderías infantiles y seguridad.

¿A quiénes ayudan? A todos. **¿En qué idiomas ofrecen ayuda?** Español, chino (cantonés, mandarín), ruso y vietnamita.

Human Resources Administration (H.R.A.), Refugee and Immigrant Center
2 Washington Street, New York, N.Y. 10004
Teléfono: 1-212-495-7050; Fax: 1-212- 495-7604

¿Qué tipo de ayuda ofrecen?
- Para solicitar asistencia pública, Medicaid y Medicare si tiene dificultad para hablar inglés.

¿A quiénes ayudan? Los requisitos de elegibilidad se basan en las necesidades. **¿En qué idiomas ofrecen ayuda?** Hay representantes que hablan español (P) en ambos centros; hay representantes que hablan chino (P) (cantonés y mandarín) sólo en el centro de Manhattan. Se ofrecen servicios de intérprete y material informativo en cambodiano, francés, ruso, creole haitiano, vietnamita, albanés y árabe. **¿Qué debo llevar?** Algún documento de identificación. **¿En dónde tienen otros centros?** Hay 1 centro en Brooklyn. Llame para hacer una cita antes de venir.

Immigration Advocacy Services
24-40 Steinway Street, Astoria, N.Y. 11103
Teléfono: 1-718- 956-8218; Fax: 1-718- 274-1615
Sitio Web: www.immigrationadvocacy.com

¿Qué tipo de ayuda ofrecen?
■ Para todo tipo de asunto relacionado con la inmigración, naturalización y ciudadanía.

¿A quiénes ayudan? A todos. **¿En qué idiomas ofrecen ayuda?** Español (P), chino (cantonés, mandarín), árabe (P), griego, italiano, portugués y urdu. **¿Qué debo llevar?** Nada. **¿En dónde tienen otros centros?** Sólo el centro que se menciona previamente.

Indochina Sino-American Community Center
170 Forsyth Street, New York, N.Y. 10002
Teléfono: 1-212- 226-0317; Fax: 1-212-925-0327
Correo electrónico: isacenter@zeronet.net
Sitio Web: http://www.asianweb.net/news/java/isasci.htm

¿Qué tipo de ayuda ofrecen?
■ Determinar su elegibilidad para recibir beneficios sociales y dónde solicitarlos.
■ Clases de inglés y de preparación para la ciudadanía.
■ Servicios de traducción.
■ Capacitación laboral y empleo.
■ Programas para jubilados.

¿A quiénes ayudan? A los residentes de Nueva York. **¿En qué idiomas ofrecen ayuda?** Chino (P) (cantonés, mandarín, fukinés) y vietnamita. **¿Qué debo llevar?** Cargo de inscripción y materiales para las clases. **¿Tienen algún otro centro?** Sólo el centro que se menciona previamente. Llame para hacer una cita antes de venir.

Jacob A. Riis Neighborhood Settlement House, Inc.
10-25 41st Avenue, Long Island City, N.Y. 11101
Teléfono: 1-718- 784-7447; Fax: 1-718- 784-1964
Correo electrónico: jriis@unhny.org; Sitio Web: http://www.riissettlement.org

¿Qué tipo de ayuda ofrecen?

■ Documentos de inmigración, servicios de empleo, asuntos relacionados con la vivienda y beneficios.

■ Programas para después de la escuela, programas para adolescentes, colonias de vacaciones.

■ Programas especiales para niñas y mujeres jóvenes.

■ Centro para jubilados con transporte disponible para aquellos de 60 años o más.

■ Clases de inglés y computación.

¿A quiénes ayudan? Depende de los servicios que se procuran. **¿En qué idiomas ofrecen ayuda?** Español (P). **¿Qué debo llevar?** Nada. **¿Tienen algún otro centro?** Sólo el centro que se menciona previamente.

Latino Workers Center
191 East Third Street, New York, N.Y. 10009
Teléfono: 1-212- 473-3936; Fax: 1-212- 473-6103

¿Qué tipo de ayuda ofrecen?

■ Derechos del empleado, salud y seguridad en el trabajo; cómo obtener indemnización por lesión y pérdida de sueldo.

¿A quiénes ayudan? A todos. **¿En qué idiomas ofrecen ayuda?** Español (P). **¿Qué debo llevar?** Nada. **¿Tienen algún otro centro?** Sólo el centro que se menciona previamente.

Legal Aid Society, Civil Division
199 Water Street, 3rd Floor, New York, N.Y. 10038
Teléfono: 1-212- 440-4300; Fax: 1-212- 509-8941; Sitio Web: http://www.legal-aid.org

¿Qué tipo de ayuda ofrecen?

■ Asistencia legal para asuntos relacionados con inmigración, vivienda, beneficios del gobierno, seguro social, consumidor, quiebra, empleo, desempleo, familia y salud.

¿A quiénes ayudan? A todos los inmigrantes. **¿En qué idiomas ofrecen ayuda?** En todos los idiomas. **¿Qué debo llevar?** Todos los documentos del tribunal y del gobierno que tenga. **¿En dónde tienen otros centros?** Centros en los cinco distritos y en los tribunales de vivienda. Para averiguar la dirección de los centros visite el sitio web que se menciona previamente.

Legal Services for New York City
350 Broadway, 6th Floor (Central Office), New York, N.Y. 10013
Teléfono: 1-212- 431-7200; Fax: 1-212-431-7232; Sitio Web: http://www.lsny.org/

¿Qué tipo de ayuda ofrecen?
■ Servicios legales gratis para asuntos relacionados con la familia, vivienda, beneficios, consumidor, salud, empleo, desarrollo económico y educación.
¿A quiénes ayudan? A los ciudadanos de los Estados Unidos e inmigrantes legales. No atiende a personas que están encarceladas. **¿En qué idiomas ofrecen ayuda?** Inglés solamente. **¿Qué debo llevar?** Las personas que no son ciudadanas deben traer su tarjeta verde, prueba de ingresos y cualquier documento pertinente al servicio que solicitan. **¿En dónde tienen otros centros?** Hay 3 centros en el Bronx; 8 en Brooklyn; 3 en Manhattan; 2 en Queens; y un proyecto de extensión en Staten Island. Llame para hacer una cita antes de venir.

Lower East Side People's Federal Credit Union
37 Avenue B, New York, N.Y. 10009-7441
Teléfono: 1-212-529-8197; Fax: 1-212-529-.8368
Correo electrónico: lespfcu@lespfcu.org; Sitio Web: http://www.lespfcu.org/index.html

¿Qué tipo de ayuda ofrecen?
■ Cuentas corrientes (de cheques) y de ahorro, depósito directo, acceso a cajeros automáticos (ATM) y préstamos.
¿A quiénes ayudan? A personas que trabajan o viven en el Lower East Side (de la calle 14 este hasta el puente de Brooklyn y desde la Tercera Avenida/Bowery hasta el East River), o que están afiliadas con una organización del Lower East Side; parientes de miembros actuales. **¿En qué idiomas ofrecen ayuda?** Español. **¿Qué debo llevar?** Dos documentos actuales de identidad, incluyendo uno con foto y firma; tarjeta del Seguro Social o prueba del número del Seguro Social; mínimo de $30; prueba de domicilio o trabajo en el Lower East Side, o una carta de una organización del Lower East Side con la que está afiliado. **¿En dónde tienen otros centros?** Cajeros automáticos gratis (ATMs) en todo Manhattan y Brooklyn.

Lutheran Medical Center
150 55th Street, Brooklyn, N.Y. 11220
Teléfono: 1-718- 630-7000/7210; Fax: 1-718- 492-5090
Sitio Web: http://www.lutheranmedicalcenter.com

¿Qué tipo de ayuda ofrecen?
- Médica, salud mental y atención primaria; V.I.H., SIDA y cáncer; centro para ataques apopléjicos.
- Servicios sociales y violencia doméstica.
- Beneficios del gobierno y asesoramiento sobre comida/nutrición.
- Información sobre inmigración y otros asuntos legales.

¿A quiénes ayudan? A todos. Servicios con descuento para los residentes de Brooklyn. **¿En qué idiomas ofrecen ayuda?** Español (P), chino (P) (cantonés, mandarín), ruso (P) y árabe (P). **¿Qué debo llevar?** Documento de identidad; prueba de domicilio; prueba de ingresos para recibir el descuento. **¿Tienen algún otro centro?** Hay 4 centros en Brooklyn. Llame para hacer una cita antes de venir.

Managed Care Consumers Assistance Program (M.C.C.A.P.)
Community Service Society of New York
105 East 22nd Street, New York, N.Y. 10010
Teléfono: 1-212- 614-5400 (Línea central de ayuda); Fax: 1-212- 614-5305
Sitio Web: http://www.mccapny.org

¿Qué tipo de ayuda ofrecen?
- Para elegir y usar un plan de atención de salud administrada, incluyendo información para personas con problemas de salud crónicos, tales como V.I.H. y SIDA, incapacidad física, de aprendizaje y desarrollo, y enfermedades mentales crónicas.
- Seguro de salud gratis o de bajo costo, incluyendo Medicaid, Medicare, Child Health Plus, Family Health Plus y seguro comercial.

¿A quiénes ayudan? A los residentes de Nueva York. **¿En qué idiomas ofrecen ayuda?** Inglés y español por intermedio de la línea central de ayuda. A través de agencias subcontratadas, chino (cantonés, mandarín), coreano, ruso, árabe, yiddish y creole haitiano. **¿Qué debo llevar?** Nada. **¿En dónde tienen otros centros?** Hay 5 agencias de referencia en el Bronx; 3 en Brooklyn; 14 en Manhattan; 3 en Queens; 1 en Staten Island.

Medical and Health Research Association of New York City, Inc. (M.H.R.A.)
Health Insurance Enrollment Project (H.I.E.P.)
40 Worth Street, Suite 720, New York, N.Y. 10013
Teléfono: 1-212-285-0220, ext. 130; Fax: 1-212-385-0565
Sitio Web: http://www.mhra.org

¿Qué tipo de ayuda ofrecen?
■ A elegir un plan de atención de salud administrada.
■ A obtener y recertificar seguro de salud de bajo costo o gratis, incluyendo
  Medicaid, Child Health Plus B, Family Health Plus y P.C.A.P.
¿A quiénes ayudan? A todos. **¿En qué idiomas ofrecen ayuda?** Español, chino (cantonés, mandarín), ruso, árabe, polaco, hebreo, italiano. **¿Qué debo llevar?** Prueba de ingresos (cuatro talones de cheque de sueldo recientes o una carta de su empleador; declaraciones de impuesto solamente si trabaja por cuenta propia); prueba de domicilio; documento de identidad: certificado de nacimiento o religioso, pasaporte o tarjeta verde; tarjeta del Seguro Social (para Medicaid y Family Health Plus solamente; no es necesario para Child Health Plus B). Prueba de su estado legal (tarjeta verde o solicitud para la tarjeta verde, carta de la U.S.C.I.S., visa, no es necesario para Child Health Plus B). **¿Tienen alguna otra oficina?** Hay 4 oficinas en Brooklyn y otra en Manhattan; 3 en Queens.

Medical and Health Research Association of New York City, Inc. (M.H.R.A.)
M.I.C.-Women's Health Services
225 Broadway, 17th Floor, New York, N.Y. 10007
Teléfono: 1-212- 267-0900; Fax: 1-212-571-5641
Sitio Web: http://www.mhra.org

¿Qué tipo de ayuda ofrecen?
■ Evaluación de cáncer, enfermedades por transmisión sexual, educación del
  V.I.H., asesoramiento y pruebas; planificación familiar; cuidado dental
  preventivo.
■ Atención prenatal; inscripción de mujeres que reúnen los requisitos en el
  Programa de Asistencia Prenatal (Prenatal Care Assistance Program — P.C.A.P.)
  y otros programas de Medicaid.
¿A quiénes ayudan? A todas las mujeres. Se acepta Medicaid, seguro comercial y dinero en efectivo. Los honorarios se basan en la capacidad de pago del cliente. **¿En qué idiomas ofrecen ayuda?** Español, francés y creole en todas las oficinas; chino

(cantonés, mandarín) en Fort Greene y Jamaica; punjabi, ruso y urdu en Astoria; árabe en Fort Greene; tagalog en Jamaica y Manhattan; guyanés y griego en Bushwick; rumano en Eastern Parkway. **¿Qué debo llevar?** Información de seguro, si está asegurada. De lo contrario, documento de identidad (pasaporte, certificado de nacimiento o tarjeta del Seguro Social); prueba de domicilio (factura de un servicio público en su nombre o carta del dueño del edificio (landlord) o de un amigo o familiar que viva con usted, indicando que usted vive allí), y prueba de ingresos. El personal podrá darle más información sobre la documentación necesaria si no está segura qué debe traer. **¿Tienen algún otro centro?** Hay 1 centro en el Bronx; 4 en Brooklyn; 1 centro en Manhattan; 2 en Queens.

Medical and Health Research Association of New York City, Inc. (M.H.R.A.)
New York City Neighborhood W.I.C. Program
40 Worth Street, Suite 720, New York, N.Y. 10013
Teléfono: 1-212- 766-4240; Fax:1-212-260-6200

¿Qué tipo de ayuda ofrecen?
- Educación y asesoramiento sobre nutrición; asesoramiento e instrucción sobre lactancia materna; referencias para otros proveedores de servicios humanos y de salud.
- Inscripción de votantes.

¿A quiénes ayudan? A mujeres embarazadas, mujeres que están amamantando o no después del parto, bebés y niños hasta los 5 años que residen en el estado de Nueva York. El límite de ingresos es de 185 por ciento del nivel federal de pobreza. **¿En qué idiomas ofrecen ayuda?** Español, chino (cantonés), creole-francés, ruso, italiano, polaco, bengali, yiddish, tagalog, árabe y urdu. **¿Qué debo llevar?** Referencia de un médico; prueba de domicilio; prueba de ingresos (salvo para los beneficiarios de Medicaid). **¿Tienen algún otro centro?** Hay 2 centros en el Bronx; 7 en Brooklyn; 2 en Manhattan; 7 en Queens.

MoneyGram
Teléfono: 1-800-926-9400
Sitio Web: http://www.moneygram.com

¿Qué tipo de ayuda ofrecen?
- Transferencia de dinero.

¿A quiénes ayudan? A todos. **¿En qué idiomas ofrecen ayuda?** Español (P). Otros idiomas varían según la localidad. **¿Qué debo llevar?** Dinero en efectivo que quiere enviar y la cantidad necesaria para pagar el cargo de envío; documento de identidad con foto si quiere enviar más de $900. **¿Tienen alguna otra oficina?** Tenemos oficinas en toda la ciudad de Nueva York. Llame al número de Teléfono central que se indica anteriormente y oprima su número de Teléfono de 10 dígitos para averiguar dónde queda la sucursal más cercana.

Morris Heights Health Center
85 West Burnside Avenue, Bronx, N.Y. 10453
Teléfono: 1-718- 716-4400; Fax: 1-718-294-6912
Sitio Web: http://www.morrisheights.org

¿Qué tipo de ayuda ofrecen?
- Atención de salud primaria; planificación familiar y atención de la salud reproductora para mujeres embarazadas, atención de salud para recién nacidos; exámenes físicos para la escuela; evaluación y cuidado del asma; atención de salud mental; servicios de nutrición; servicios sociales; y servicios especiales para adolescentes.

¿A quiénes ayudan? A todos. **¿En qué idiomas ofrecen ayuda?** Español (P), chino (cantonés — limitado), francés y ruso. Se proporcionarán intérpretes para los demás idiomas. **¿Qué debo llevar?** Certificado de nacimiento o licencia para conducir; prueba de bajos ingresos. Los honorarios se basan en la capacidad de pago del cliente. **¿En qué otro lugar están ubicados?** Otros 2 sitios en el Bronx. Llame para hacer una cita antes de venir.

New York Association for New Americans, Inc. (N.Y.A.N.A.)
17 Battery Place, New York, N.Y. 10004
Teléfono: 1-212- 425-2900/5051; Servicios Legales: 1-212-898-4180; Fax: 1-212- 425-7260
Sitio Web: http://www.nyana.org

¿Qué tipo de ayuda ofrecen?
- Documentos de la B.C.I.S., petición de familiares, visas de trabajo y solicitudes para residencia permanente; naturalización, preparación para el examen de ciudadanía.
- Orientación por abuso de drogas.
- Obtención de beneficios del gobierno.
- Búsqueda de empleo.
- Clases de inglés.

¿A quiénes ayudan? A los nuevos inmigrantes. **¿En qué idiomas ofrecen ayuda?** Español (P), chino (cantonés, mandarín, taiwanés) y ruso (P). En la oficina de Queens no se ofrece idioma chino. **¿Qué debo llevar?** Se requiere permiso de trabajo para ayuda en la búsqueda de empleo. Los honorarios varían según la dificultad del asunto. No se cobra por la consulta telefónica con un paraprofesional. **¿En dónde tienen otros centros?** Hay 1 centro en Brooklyn y otro en Queens. Llame para hacer una cita antes de venir.

New York City Administration for Children's Services
Division of Child Care and Head Start
66 John Street, New York, N.Y. 10038
Teléfono: 1-718-FOR-KIDS (1-718-367-5437)
Fax: 1-212-361-6023

¿Qué tipo de ayuda ofrecen?
■ Información sobre guarderías infantiles vecinales y programas para después de la escuela; ayuda financiera para el cuidado de niños; capacitación para agencias contratadas para el cuidado de niños.
¿A quiénes ayudan? A todas las personas que llaman. Los requisitos de elegibilidad para guarderías infantiles subsidiadas depende del ingreso y del motivo por el que necesita usar la guardería. **¿En qué idiomas ofrecen ayuda?** Español (P). **¿Qué debo llevar?** Tarjeta del Seguro Social o tarjeta verde, certificado de nacimiento, prueba de domicilio y de ingresos. **¿En dónde tienen otros centros?** Hay 1 centro en el Bronx, en Brooklyn, en Manhattan y en Queens. Llame para hacer una cita antes de venir.

New York City Child Care Resource and Referral Consortium
Teléfono: 1-888- 469-5999

¿Qué tipo de ayuda ofrecen?
■ Recursos y servicios de referencia para guarderías infantiles, programas para después de la escuela y ayuda financiera; capacitación para personas a cargo del cuidado de niños.
■ Información sobre salud y seguridad.
¿A quiénes ayudan? A todos. **¿En qué idiomas ofrecen ayuda?** Trataremos de ofrecer ayuda en todos los idiomas. **¿Qué debo llevar?** Prueba de ingresos. Llame para hacer una cita antes de venir.

New York City Commission on Human Rights
40 Rector Street, New York, N.Y. 10006
Teléfono: 1-212- 306-5070; Fax: 1-212-306-7474
Sitio Web: http://www.ci.nyc.ny.us/html/cchr/home.html

¿Qué tipo de ayuda ofrecen?
▪ Quejas por discriminación; vivienda justa, empleo y asuntos relacionados con el acoso basado en prejuicios.
¿A quiénes ayudan? A todos. ¿En qué idiomas ofrecen ayuda? Español (P), chino (cantonés, mandarín) (P) y francés (P). ¿Qué debo llevar? Tiene que tener una cita. Para hacer una cita llame al (212)1-212- 306-7450. ¿En dónde tienen otros centros? La comisión mantiene Centros de Servicios Comunitarios en toda la ciudad. Llame para hacer una cita antes de venir.

New York City Department of Education, Chancellor's Parent Hot Line
Teléfono: 1-178-482-3777; Sitio Web: http://www.nycenet.edu

¿Qué tipo de ayuda ofrecen?
▪ Toda la información necesaria relacionada con la educación de un niño en una escuela pública
▪ Referencias para centros comunitarios que ofrecen ayuda para cuestiones de aprendizaje no resueltas en la escuela o para atender asuntos administrativos relacionados con la escuela, incluyendo matriculación y transporte.
¿A quiénes ayudan? A todos. ¿En qué idiomas ofrecen ayuda? Español, chino (cantonés, mandarín) y otros idiomas con la ayuda de intérpretes. ¿Qué debo llevar? Llame antes de venir para que le informemos. ¿En dónde tienen otros centros? Centros de apoyo para el aprendizaje: 2 en el Bronx; 4 en Brooklyn; 2 en Manhattan; 4 en Queens; 1 en Staten Island.

New York City Department of Education, Office of Adult and Continuing Education
42-15 Crescent Street, Long Island City, N.Y. 11101
Teléfono: 1-718- 609-2770; Fax: 1-718-392-4768

¿Qué tipo de ayuda ofrecen?
▪ G.E.D., E.S.O.L., educación básica y capacitación en computación; capacitación

vocacional en electricidad, mecánica automotor, flebotomía (extracción de sangre); administración de un electrocardiograma (E.K.G.) y enfermería.

■ Ayuda para buscar trabajo, escribir el curriculum vitae y para entrevistas de trabajo para los estudiantes que han terminado un curso.

¿A quiénes ayudan? A personas mayores de 21 años que deben tomar un examen de evaluación. Se requiere G.E.D. o diploma de escuela secundaria para algunos cursos de capacitación. Guarderías infantiles disponibles en los centros de enseñanza de Brooklyn y Manhattan. Llame para hacer una cita antes de venir. **¿En qué idiomas ofrecen ayuda?** Todas las clases se dan en inglés. El G.E.D. es la única clase que se da en español. Llame para hacer una cita antes de venir. **¿Qué debo llevar?** Se requiere el pago de un honorario para el programa de enfermería y algunos cursos relacionados con la salud. **¿En dónde tienen otros centros?** Las clases de ofrecen en los cinco distritos. Llame para hacer una cita antes de venir.

New York City Department of Health and Mental Hygiene
125 Worth Street, New York, N.Y. 10013
Teléfono: 1-212-442-9666 (Menú de voz en inglés y español. La llamada puede ser transferida a un intérprete para la mayoría de los idiomas).
AIDS Hot Line (Línea informativa sobre el SIDA): 1-800-TALK-HIV (La llamada puede ser transferida a un intérprete para la mayoría de los idiomas).
Bureau of Day Care (Oficina de Guarderías Infantiles): 1-212-676-2444 (inglés y español).
Bureau of School Health (Oficina de Salud Escolar): 1-212-676-2500 (inglés solamente).
HealthStat: 1-888-692-6116 (español y mandarín).
Immunization Hot Line (Línea informativa sobre vacunas): 1-212-676-2273 (inglés y español).
Immunization Hot Line Referrals (Línea de referencia para vacunas): 1-800-325-CHILD (2445) (Si es necesario le devolverá la llamada una persona que habla su idioma).
Spanish Immunization Referrals (Línea de referencia para vacunas en español): 1-800-945-6466.
Women's Health Line (Línea informativa sobre la salud de la mujer): 1-212-230-1111 (Menú de voz en inglés y español. La llamada puede ser transferida a un intérprete para la mayoría de los idiomas).
Fax: 1-212- 442-5670; Sitio Web: http://www.nyc.gov/html/doh

¿Qué tipo de ayuda ofrecen?
■ Programa de maternidad, de salud reproductora y de bebés; programa de salud para mujeres; vacunas gratis contra la gripe y la neumonía; vacunas gratis si son un requisito para asistir a la escuela; certificados de nacimiento y de muerte.
■ Inscripción en seguros de salud pública gratis y de bajo costo.

■ Quejas sobre guarderías y programas relacionados.
■ Quejas sobre roedores y violaciones sanitarias.
¿A quiénes ayudan? A todos. **¿En qué idiomas ofrecen ayuda?** Todos los idiomas disponibles a través de intérpretes. **¿Qué debo llevar?** Prueba de domicilio para el programa de atención prenatal. **¿Tienen alguna otra oficina?** Sólo la oficina que se menciona previamente.

New York City Housing Authority (N.Y.C.H.A.)
250 Broadway, New York, N.Y. 10007
Teléfono: 1-212- 306-3000 (número de teléfono: central para todos los distritos);
1-212- 828-7100 (oficina de solicitud en Manhattan)
Sitio Web: http://www.nyc.gov/html/nycha

¿Qué tipo de ayuda ofrecen?
■ Cómo encontrar vivienda de bajo costo; programa de alquiler de vivienda sección 8.
■ Servicios sociales.
■ Programas educativos y recreativos.
■ Capacitación laboral.
¿A quiénes ayudan? A residentes de bajos ingresos de la ciudad de Nueva York. Se da prioridad a los residentes en refugios. **¿En qué idiomas ofrecen ayuda?** Español (P), chino (cantonés, mandarín, toisanés). Para más información llame al Language Bank at Equal Opportunity, 1-212-306-4443. **¿Qué debo llevar?** Cuando llame, tenga su número del Seguro Social a mano. **¿En dónde tienen otros centros?** Hay 1 centro en cada distrito. Llame para hacer una cita antes de venir.

New York City Workforce 1 Career Center
168-46 91st Avenue, 2nd Floor, Jamaica, N.Y. 11432
Teléfono: 1-718-557-6756
Sitio Web: http://www.nyc.gov/html/wia/html/career_centers.html

¿Qué tipo de ayuda ofrecen?
■ Evaluación de estudios y solicitud de ayuda financiera para estudiantes.
■ E.S.O.L., G.E.D. e información sobre alfabetización para adultos.
■ Búsqueda de trabajo, capacitación y empleo; curriculum vitae y preparación de carta de presentación; evaluación de destrezas de computación y talleres.
■ Beneficios del gobierno para personas que trabajan, tales como guarderías, Medicaid y otros seguros de salud gratis o de bajo costo.

¿A quiénes ayudan? A los residentes de Nueva York. **¿En qué idiomas ofrecen ayuda?** Español (P). Se ofrecen servicios de traducción. **¿Qué debo llevar?** Depende del servicio que procura. **¿En dónde tienen otros centros?** Hay 1 centro en el Bronx y otro en el Alto Manhattan

New York Immigration Hot Line
Teléfono: 1-800-566-7636

¿Qué tipo de ayuda ofrecen?
- Información y referencias sobre las leyes de inmigración, incluyendo petición de familiares, visas, ciudadanía, asilo político, estado de protección temporal, deportación y exclusión y exenciones especiales.
- Referencias para agencias municipales y estatales.
- Discriminación en el empleo y la vivienda.

¿A quiénes ayudan? A todos. **¿En qué idiomas ofrecen ayuda?** Español, chino (mandarín), francés, polaco, ruso, macedonio, indio, árabe, creole haitiano, hindi, albanés, turco, coreano y servocroata.

New York State Department of Labor, Division of Employment Services Office
138-60 Barclay Avenue, Flushing, N.Y. 11355
Teléfono: 1-718- 321-6307; 1-888-209-8124 (número de teléfono del estado de Nueva York para información general); Fax: 1-718-461-8572
Sitio Web: http://www.labor.state.ny.us/index.html

¿Qué tipo de ayuda ofrecen?
- Encontrar trabajo, conocer sus derechos como trabajador, cobrar seguro de desempleo si ha sido despedido.

¿A quiénes ayudan? A los residentes según su ubicación. **¿En qué idiomas ofrecen ayuda?** Español (P), chino (cantonés, mandarín) (P), creole. **¿Qué debo llevar?** Curriculum vitae, prueba de ciudadanía, tarjeta del Seguro Social si la tiene. Llame para hacer una cita antes de venir. **¿En dónde tienen otros centros?** Hay 3 centros en el Bronx; 3 en Brooklyn; 4 en Manhattan, 4 en Queens. Llame para hacer una cita antes de venir.

New York State Department of Labor, Division of Labor Standards
345 Hudson Street, New York, N.Y. 10014
Teléfono: 1-212-352-6700; Fax: 1-212-352-6593

¿Qué tipo de ayuda ofrecen?
- Leyes de trabajo estatales, trabajo de menores, salario mínimo, sueldo no pagado, pago de sueldo, suplementos al salario, horario de trabajo para las industrias de fabricación de ropa y agrícolas.

¿A quiénes ayudan? A víctimas de violaciones de la ley del trabajo en los cinco distritos. **¿En qué idiomas ofrecen ayuda?** Español (P). Para otros idiomas, traiga su propio intérprete. **¿Qué debo llevar?** Depende del servicio que procura. Llame antes de venir que le informaremos. **¿En dónde tienen otros centros?** Hay 1 centro en el Bajo Manhattan y otro en el Alto Manhattan. Llame para hacer una cita antes de venir.

New York State Division of Housing and Community Renewal (D.H.C.R.)
38-40 State Street, Albany, N.Y. 12207
Teléfono: 1-866-ASK-DHCR (1-866-275-3427); Fax: 1-518- 474-5752
Correo electrónico: DHCRInfo@dhcr.state.ny.us
Sitio Web: http://www.dhcr.state.ny.us

¿Qué tipo de ayuda ofrecen?
- Solicitudes de vivienda, antecedentes de alquiler, viviendas bajo la Sección 8, discriminación en la vivienda.

¿A quiénes ayudan? A todos. **¿En qué idiomas ofrecen ayuda?** Español. Se ofrecen servicios de traducción para otros idiomas. **¿Qué debo llevar?** Depende del servicio que se procura. **¿En dónde tienen otros centros?** Hay 1 centro en cada uno de estos distritos: Bronx, Brooklyn, Queens y Staten Island; 2 centros en Manhattan. Llame para hacer una cita antes de venir.

New York State Office of Temporary and Disability Assistance
Teléfono: 1-800-342-3009; Sitio Web: www.otda.state.ny.us

¿Qué tipo de ayuda ofrecen?
- Cupones de comida y Programa de Asistencia de Energía para el Hogar (Home Energy Assistance Program — HEAP).

■ Solicite una audiencia imparcial utilizando los servicios de Internet.
¿A quiénes ayudan? Llame para determinar su elegibilidad para los programas. Ofrece información a inmigrantes y refugiados, y referencias para obtener servicios de una red de agencias sin fines de lucro en todo el estado a través de la Oficina para Asuntos de Refugiados e Inmigración (Bureau of Refugee and Immigration Affairs — B.R.I.A.), 1-800-566-7636; 1-800-232-0212. **¿En qué idiomas ofrecen ayuda?** Español.

New York Urban League
204 West 136th Street, New York, N.Y. 10030
Teléfono: 1-212-926-8000, ext. 39; Fax: 1-212- 283-4948
Correo electrónico: nyulexec@aol.com; Sitio Web: http://www.nyul.org

¿Qué tipo de ayuda ofrecen?
■ Asesoramiento sobre desalojos, desamparo y viviendas subestándar e inadecuadas; cómo encontrar vivienda; mediación entre inquilinos y dueños de edificios (landlord), quejas de discriminación relacionadas con la vivienda; información y apoyo para comprar una vivienda.
■ Asesoramiento sobre beneficios de servicios sociales.
¿A quiénes ayudan? A todos. **¿En qué idiomas ofrecen ayuda?** Español. **¿Qué debo llevar?** Depende del servicio que procura. Llame para que le informen. **¿En dónde tienen otros centros?** Hay 1 centro en el Bronx; 2 centros en Brooklyn, en Manhattan, en Queens y en Staten Island. Llame para hacer una cita antes de venir.

Park Slope Safe Homes Project
P.O. Box 150429, Brooklyn, N.Y. 11215
Teléfono: 1-718- 499-2151; Fax: 1-718-369-6151

¿Qué tipo de ayuda ofrecen?
■ Servicios, refugio, asesoramiento y grupos de apoyo para mujeres abusadas y sus hijos.
■ Servicios para víctimas relacionados con la violencia entre mujeres.
¿A quiénes ayudan? A víctimas de la violencia doméstica y sus hijos. **¿En qué idiomas ofrecen ayuda?** Español (P) y árabe (P). **¿Qué debo llevar?** Nada. Llame para hacer una cita antes de venir. **¿Tienen alguna otra oficina?** Sólo la oficina que se menciona previamente.

People's Fire House
113 Berry Street, Brooklyn, N.Y. 11211
Teléfono: 1-718- 388-4696; Fax: 1-718-218-7367

¿Qué tipo de ayuda ofrecen?
- Asesoramiento para inquilinos y consejos para personas que buscan vivienda.
- Clases básicas de computación.

¿A quiénes ayudan? A todos. **¿En qué idiomas ofrecen ayuda?** Español (P); polaco (P).
¿Qué debo llevar? Cualquier tipo de documento de identidad y/o tarjeta del Seguro Social. Llame para hacer una cita antes de venir. **¿Tienen algún otro centro?** Sólo el centro que se menciona previamente.

Promesa, Inc.
1776 Clay Avenue, Bronx, N.Y. 10457
Teléfono: 1-718-960-7500; Fax: 1-718- 299-0463; Sitio Web: http://www.promesa.org

¿Qué tipo de ayuda ofrecen?
- Atención de salud primaria y para trastornos de conducta; rehabilitación por abuso de drogas y alcohol; servicios para el V.I.H. y SIDA, que incluyen atención primaria, orientación, pruebas, referencias y atención para personas adultas con SIDA.
- Viviendas de bajo costo; refugios para desamparados.
- Guarderías.
- Servicios para jóvenes que dejan sus hogares.

¿En qué idiomas ofrecen ayuda? Español (P). **¿A quiénes ayudan?** A todos. La ayuda para vivienda se basa en el nivel de los ingresos. **¿Qué debo llevar?** Tarjeta verde o prueba de ciudadanía y número del Seguro Social. **¿En dónde tienen otros centros?** Hay 15 centros de programas en el Bronx.

Queens Legal Services
8900 Sutphin Boulevard, Jamaica, N.Y. 11435
Teléfono: 1-718- 657-8611; Fax: 1-718- 526-5051
Sitio Web: http://www.queenslegalservices.org

¿Qué tipo de ayuda ofrecen?
- Ayuda legal gratis para vivienda, beneficios del gobierno, derechos del

consumidor, derechos de trabajo, educación en las escuelas públicas y problemas del derecho de familia.

■ Servicios legales para problemas especiales que confrontan las personas mayores, las víctimas de la violencia doméstica y aquellos con incapacidades, V.I.H. y SIDA.

¿A quiénes ayudan? A ciudadanos e inmigrantes legales que viven en Queens. Algunos servicios se basan en el nivel de ingresos. **¿En qué idiomas ofrecen ayuda?** Español. **¿Qué debo llevar?** Prueba de ingresos, tarjeta verde y cualquier documento relacionado con el caso, tales como documentos del tribunal. **¿En dónde tienen otros centros?** Hay otro centro en Queens. Llame para hacer una cita antes de venir.

Safe Horizon
2 Lafayette Street, New York, N.Y. 10007
Teléfono: 1-212-577-7700; 24-hour hot line: 1-800-621-HOPE (1-800-621-4673)
Fax: 1-212- 385-0331; Correo electrónico: feedback@safehorizon.org
Sitio Web: http://www.safehorizon.org

¿Qué tipo de ayuda ofrecen?
■ Ayuda financiera, asesoramiento en situaciones de crisis y referencias para víctimas de abuso y de delitos.
■ Línea de información general para víctimas, referencias y red de servicios.
■ Consejos, terapia de grupo, protección y ayuda para tratar con la policía.
■ Servicios para víctimas y asesoramiento para víctimas de la tortura en Jackson Heights.
■ Consejos y asesoramiento para casos de violación en Brooklyn.
■ Asesoramiento de emergencia y a corto plazo, protección y servicios para los supervivientes de un asalto sexual y víctimas por asociación.

¿A quiénes ayudan? A los residentes de Nueva York. A hombres y mujeres víctimas de asalto y violación de 13 años y mayores. **¿En qué idiomas ofrecen ayuda?** Español (P), chino (cantonés, mandarín), francés, creole haitiano, hindi, coreano, polaco, ruso y urdu. **¿Qué debo llevar?** Informes de la policía o cualquier documento relacionado con el caso. Se cobran honorarios por situaciones legales complejas sólo en base a la capacidad de pago. Llame para hacer una cita. **¿En dónde tienen otros centros?** 75 programas en los cinco distritos. Llame para hacer una cita antes de venir.

South Bronx Action Group
384 East 149th Street, Suite 220, Bronx, N.Y. 10455
Teléfono: 1-718-993-5869; Fax: 1-718- 993-7904
Correo electrónico: sbaginc@aol.com

¿Qué tipo de ayuda ofrecen?
■ Asesoramiento sobre las responsabilidades y los derechos básicos relacionados con la vivienda; servicios en el tribunal de vivienda, protección de sus derechos y talleres; referencias a agentes inmobiliarios para encontrar casa.
■ Clases de E.S.O.L. y de preparación para la ciudadanía.
¿A quiénes ayudan? A todos. **¿En qué idiomas ofrecen ayuda?** Español (P). **¿Qué debo llevar?** Nada. **¿Tienen alguna otra oficina?** Sólo la oficina que se menciona previamente.

Southeast Bronx Neighborhood Centers
955 Tinton Avenue, Bronx, N.Y. 10456
Teléfono: 1-718-542-2727; Fax: 1-718-589-2927
Correo electrónico: dymcenter@aol.com; Sitio Web: http://www.sebnc.org

¿Qué tipo de ayuda ofrecen?
■ Guarderías, cuidado de niños y programas para después de la escuela; servicios para adolescentes; centro para jubilados que incluye atención de salud en el hogar.
■ Referencia e inscripción para cupones de comida.
■ Cursos de tecnología de computación y servicios de asesoramiento en la elección de una carrera.
■ Ayuda para personas con incapacidades.
¿A quiénes ayudan? A los que tienen la tarjeta del Seguro Social. **¿En qué idiomas ofrecen ayuda?** Español. **¿Qué debo llevar?** Los servicios de guardería requieren la tarjeta del Seguro Social. Los cargos se basan en la capacidad de pago del cliente. **¿En dónde tienen otros centros?** Hay 3 centros en el Bronx. Llame para hacer una cita antes de venir.

Southside Community Mission, Immigration Program
250 Hooper Street, Brooklyn, N.Y. 11211
Teléfono: 1-718-387-3803; Fax: 1-718-387-3739

¿Qué tipo de ayuda ofrecen?
- Formularios de inmigración, peticiones de familia, cambios de estado, naturalización, permiso de trabajo, visas de residencia/residencia condicional.
- Solicitudes de ciudadanía y clases.
- Representación legal.

¿A quiénes ayudan? A todos. Cargo mínimo la primera visita. **¿En qué idiomas ofrecen ayuda?** Español. **¿Qué debo llevar?** El cargo mínimo depende del servicio. Llame para hacer una cita antes de venir. **¿Tienen algún otro centro?** Hay otro centro en el Bronx.

United Community Centers
613 New Lots Avenue, Brooklyn, N.Y. 11207
Teléfono: 1-718-649-7979; Fax: 1-718- 649-7256
Correo electrónico: uccinc@mindspring.com; Sitio Web: http://www.unhny.org

¿Qué tipo de ayuda ofrecen?
- Guarderías infantiles y programas para después de la escuela.
- Educación básica y clases de E.S.O.L.
- Programas para adultos de capacitación laboral en hardware de computadoras.
- Asuntos relacionados con la inmigración, deportación y ciudadanía.

¿A quiénes ayudan? A todos. **¿En qué idiomas ofrecen ayuda?** Español (P), creole haitiano. **¿Qué debo llevar?** Nada. Llame para hacer una cita para asuntos legales y de deportación. Programa de guardería para niños de 2 a 4 años basado principalmente en los ingresos y el lugar donde vive. **¿Tienen alguna otra oficina?** Sólo la oficina que se menciona previamente.

University Settlement Federal Credit Union
184 Eldridge Street, 4th Floor, New York, N.Y. 10002
Teléfono: 1-212- 674-9120; Fax: 1-212-254-5334
Sitio Web: http://www.universitysettlement.org

¿Qué tipo de ayuda ofrecen?
■ Cuenta de ahorro y préstamos con un interés bajo.
¿A quiénes ayudan? A residentes de bajos ingresos. **¿En qué idiomas ofrecen ayuda?**
Español. **¿Qué debo llevar?** Llame para que le informen. **¿En dónde están ubicados?**
Llame antes de venir para que le informemos.

University Settlement Society of New York
184 Eldridge Street, New York, N.Y. 10002
Teléfono: 1-212-674-9120; Fax: 1-212-475-3278
Correo electrónico: info@universitysettlement.org
Sitio Web: http://www.universitysettlement.org

¿Qué tipo de ayuda ofrecen?
■ Cuidado de bebés y niños de edad preescolar y guarderías infantiles, programas
  para después de la escuela, colonias de vacaciones de verano y diurnas.
■ Programas de alfabetización, servicio de empleo para jóvenes.
■ Servicios para adolescentes embarazadas, asesoramiento y servicios clínicos.
■ Servicios sociales, programas de nutrición, acompañamiento y de ayuda
  telefónica para los ancianos.
■ Servicios para familias que estuvieron sin hogar.
¿A quiénes ayudan? A inmigrantes y neoyorquinos de bajos ingresos. **¿En qué idiomas
ofrecen ayuda?** Chino (P) (cantonés, mandarín), español (P), ruso y bengali. **¿Qué
debo llevar?** Los honorarios de algunos de los programas se basan en una escala móvil
según los ingresos de la familia. Llame para informarse. **¿En dónde están ubicados?**
Llame antes de venir para que le informemos.

Western Union
Teléfono: 1-800-325-6000; 1-800-325-4045 (español)
Sitio Web: http://www.westernunion.com

¿Qué tipo de ayuda ofrecen?
■ Transferencia de dinero.
¿A quiénes ayudan? A todos. **¿En qué idiomas ofrecen ayuda?** Varía según la localidad, pero la línea de información cuenta en todo momento con operadores que hablan español. **¿Qué debo llevar?** El dinero en efectivo que desea enviar y el cargo de envío; documento de identidad con foto si quiere enviar más de $1,000. **¿En dónde tienen otros centros?** Llame o visite nuestro sitio web.

Y.M.C.A. of Greater New York
333 Seventh Avenue, 15th Floor, New York, N.Y. 10001
Teléfono: 1-212-630-9600

100 Hester Street (Sucursal de Chinatown), New York, N.Y. 10002
Teléfono: 1-212- 219-8393; Fax: 1-212- 941-9046; Sitio Web: http://www.ymcanyc.org

¿Qué tipo de ayuda ofrecen?
■ Talleres para padres, asesoramiento
para la familia (sucursal de Chinatown solamente), programas para después de la escuela y programas para adolescentes.
¿A quiénes ayudan? La sucursal de Chinatown ofrece asesoramiento para familias que tienen un hijo de 4 a 18 años. La sucursal principal ofrece otros programas y referencias para los Y.M.C.A. vecinales. **¿En qué idiomas ofrecen ayuda?** Chino (P) (cantonés, mandarín) y español (P). **¿Qué debo llevar?** Llame para que le informen. **¿En dónde tienen otros centros?** Hay 2 centros en el Bronx; 9 en Brooklyn; 4 en Manhattan; 7 en Queens; 4 en Staten Island.

ÍNDICE

NOTAS

[1] Ewen, Elizabeth, *Immigrant Women in the Land of Dollars,* New York: Monthly Review Press, 1985, p. 61. [2] Historia oral con Rafael Guzman, Colección del Lower East Side Tenement Museum. [3] Charles T. Anderson entrevistado por Dana Gumb, Entrevista #005. Voices from Ellis Island: An Oral History of American Immigrants, A Project of the Statue of Liberty-Ellis Island Foundation. [4] Entrevista con Irma Olivo por Lisa Chice, 2002. [5] *The Italian-American Catalog.* Joseph Giordano (editor). Garden City, NY: Doubleday, 1986. [6] Khandelwal, Madhulika S., *Becoming American, Being Indian: An Immigrant Community in New York City,* Ithaca, NY: Cornell University Press, 2002, p. 130. [7] Historia oral con Max Mason, Colección del Lower East Side Tenement Museum. [8] Ling Leung, informe no publicado, 1999. [9] Inmigrante llamado Padrone, de Italia, en *America, the Dream of my Life: Selections from the Federal Writers' Project's New Jersey Ethnic Survey.* David Steven Cohen (editor). New Brunswick : Rutgers University Press, 1990. [10] Historia oral con Jose Zambrano, Colección del Lower East Side Tenement Museum. [11] Kisseloff, Jeff, *You Must Remember This: An Oral History of Manhattan from the 1890s to World War II.* New York: Harcourt Brace Jovanovich, 1989. p. 562. [12] Maricela Gonzalez, informe no publicado, 1999. [13] Hardayal Singh, "Being Indian in New Jersey," en *Asian American Experiences in the United States.* Joann Faung Jean Lee (editor), Jefferson, NC: McFarland and Company, 1991. [14] Pak Ping, informe no publicado, 1999. [15] Historia oral con Josephine Esposito, Colección del Lower East Side Tenement Museum. [16] Entrevista con Georgina Acevedo por Lisa Chice, 2002. [17] *Autobiografías Espirituales.* Louis Finkelstein (editor), New York, NY: Harper and Brothers, 1952. [18] Entrevista con Kaynam Hedayat por Lisa Chice, 2002.

《紐約時報》
紐約市移民指南

Joan P. Nassivera

Lower East Side Tenement Museum
（下東城廉租公寓博物館）
合作編寫

目錄

前言和致謝

"多年來，有很多人關心我們的需要和問題，並努力去解決問題。現在我們想根據自己的經歷，告訴你一些實實在在的東西。

"大多數新移民在剛到這裡時都很難得到需要的資訊。這裡的一切對他們來說都是陌生的。他們不知道怎樣上學、找工作、醫院在哪裡、如何得到有保險的醫療保健等等。我們自己就曾經花錢買過本來可以免費得到的東西，也曾被老闆剝削，因為我們不知道自己的權利。

"我們全心全意地幫助新移民。想講講自己的故事，以便今天剛剛到來的人們有我們不曾得到的介紹說明，不會再犯同樣的錯誤。"

這裡都是新近到紐約市的移民的講述，他們來自中國大陸、墨西哥、多米尼加共和國、香港、厄瓜多爾、馬達加斯加和薩爾瓦多。

他們可能和你的處境相似，或者和十年前你母親的處境相似，或者和更上一輩你的祖父的處境相似。他們遠離祖國，在一個充滿無限希望的城市追求更美好的生活。有些人在這裡有家人或朋友，其他人則舉目無親。

有些人從小生活在警察和政府官員令人懼怕的城市裡，因此沒有向本來可以指點迷津的紐約市有關機構和官員求助。還有一些人雖然求助了，但卻碰了壁，或從一個錯誤的機構介紹到錯誤的人那裡，毫無所得而倍感挫折。但儘管遇到重重困難，他們仍然堅信自己的紐約生活歷程會取得成功。本書的每一頁處處可見這種堅定的決心。

這些移民與你有同樣的夢想－每一個紐約人的夢想：有一份工資不錯的工作、一個安全的住所、政府官員不腐敗或濫用權力、享受多樣化教育機會、由訓練有素的醫生和護士提供醫療照顧。

紐約能提供所有這一切，而且更多。但對大多數移民來說，實現更美好的生活意味著在一座複雜的、令人迷惑的城市中摸索前進。每天都會帶來更多的問題：怎樣才能找到可以一個住得起的地方？有沒有人可以照顧孩子，以便我可以上夜班？如果我很窮，生了病，醫生會替我看病嗎？哪裡可以學英語？如果我不說英語，在緊急情況下我能得到幫助嗎？怎樣才能成為美國公民？

在這本書中，《紐約時報》和下東城廉租公寓博物館將回答這些問題和移民每天要問的幾百個其他問題。

一百五十多年來，《紐約時報》一直是紐約不斷變化的移民構圖中充滿活力的重要部分。在20世紀早期來的歐洲移民組成的社區，和今天拉丁美洲、亞洲與其他地區移民組成的社區中，《紐約時報》都是重要的、受尊敬的成員。

在1863年到1935年之間，曾經有來自20多個國家的約7,000名移民居住過下東城廉租公寓博物館所在的下東城廉租公寓樓。博物館為本地區廣泛的移民經驗提供了豐富的歷史視野，而這個地區目前仍然是數千名來美國的新移民的第一個家園。博物館還以許多不同的方式服務於當代移民，包括提供免費英語課程，在課程中向新移民介紹老移民的故事。

《紐約時報》的特色是獨創、機智、有益的報導。當移民們在博物館的課堂裡和紐約其他地方講述他們建設和改善生活有什麼需要時，我們仔細聆聽。

有一次在課上，學生們瞭解到19世紀到達艾麗斯島的移民如何遇到了會說他們自己的語言、幫助他們解決基本需要的慈善工作者。這段歷史讓一名學生喊道："我們到甘乃迪機場時沒有人來幫忙。一個人都沒有！" 現在，《紐約時報》和博物館已經協力為今天的移民編寫了第一本綜合、易用的指南。

新到本市者可利用的另一個資源是市長移民事務辦公室，其宗旨是通過建立市政府機構和移民社區之間的溝通和聯繫，促進移民來紐約的人參加本市生活的各個方面。請訪問該辦公室的網頁www.nyc.gov/immigrants。

指南的每一章都經過參加廉租公寓博物館課程的移民和移民權利團體和服務提供機構（包括紐約新美國人聯合會、紐約移民聯盟和大學服務中心）的專家的審閱。他們的工作不僅是核對事實，而且要保證指南完全和準確地回答讀者的需要：當代移民、他們的雇主和幫助他們在這座世界上最偉大的城市奮鬥的人們。

很多人為這項工作貢獻甚多。首先是時報的Alyse Myers和廉租公寓博物館的Ruth J. Abram,他們的遠見和對紐約移民社區的理解是這一項目獲得成功的前提。

《紐約時報》的Meighan Meeker和Tessa Rosario以及廉租公寓博物館的Liz Ševčenko是計畫主任，他們對每一個階段進行了監督，他們最重要並且令人煩惱的任務是不斷地提醒我，"最後期限"這個詞在新聞編輯部以外的地方也是有意義的。

廉租公寓博物館的Alison Bowles, Lisa Chice和Michael Sant' Ambrogio監督管理移民專家的研究和審核工作，這一重任則是由Bowles女士，Chice女士，Geovanny Fernandez, Jana Hasprunova, Sushma Joshi, Stephen Morton, Marilyn Ordoñez, Elizabeth Rivera 和 Rosten Woo承擔的。

慷慨地為本書花費時間，提出建議的移民服務提供者及其所在機構有：John Albert, Safe Horizon（安全地平線）; Asian Americans for Equality（亞洲人平等會）; Emily Blank, Cypress Hills Advocates for Education（塞浦路斯山爭取教育協會）; Sister Mary Burns, Maura Clarke/Ita Ford中心; Maria Contreras-Collier, Ethel Cordova and Idalia Garcia, Cypress Hills Family Day Care Program/Cypress Hills Child Care

Network（塞浦路斯山家庭托兒計劃/塞浦路斯山兒童照顧網）；Ellen Davidow, Administrative Services Unit, New York State Department of Labor, Division of Labor Standards（紐約州勞工廳勞工標準處行政服務組）；Sara Dunne, Hard Work Disabilities Project of St. Barbara's Church（聖芭芭拉教堂艱苦工作殘障項目）；Andrew Friedman, Make the Road by Walking（闊步開路）；Roberta Herche, New York Association for New Americans（紐約新美國人聯合會，簡稱N.Y.A.N.A.）；Steve Jenkins, Make the Road by Walking and Workplace Justice Project（闊步開路和工作場所公平項目）；Wasim Lone, Good Old Lower East Side（昔日美好的下東城，簡稱G.O.L.E.S.）；Jacqueline Lugo, La Providencia；David Morales, Banco Popular；Melissa Mowery, Church Avenue Merchants Block Association（教堂大道商人區協會，簡稱C.A.M.B.A）；Jimmy Yan, Advocates for Children（兒童支持會）；Margie McHugh and Dan Smulian, the New York Immigration Coalition（紐約移民聯盟）。

《紐約時報》紐約市移民指南 得以面世是得到以下團體的大力支持：Louis and Anne Abrons Foundation, Altman Foundation, Carnegie Corporation of New York（紐約卡內基公司）, Nathan Cummings Foundation, J.M. Kaplan Fund, 以及 Wolfensohn Family Foundation。

特別鳴謝：Susan Chira, Deborah Hartnett, Nancy Lee, Diane McNulty, Jennifer Pauley, Lee Riffaterre, Susan Rose, Arlene Schneider, Katherine Snider, Gabrielle Stoller 和 Fran Straus.

最後但並非最不重要的是，一些移民的熱情、建議和毅力一直指導著這個項目，他們是：阿根廷：Julia Justo, Fernando Salamone；巴西：Marli Silva；中國大陸：May Chen, Pak Ping Ng；多米尼加共和國：Nayib Ega, Andrea Hernandez, Rosalba Jimenez, Paulenia Ortiz, Yleana Paulino, Esther Pestituyo, Rosalina Rodriguez, Victoria Rosario；厄瓜多爾：Laura Pilozo, Judith Tagle；薩爾瓦多：Ernesto Ibañez；幾內亞：Aminato Conde Diallo；香港：Ling Leung；伊朗：Doran Gowhari；立陶宛：Zoya Shterenberg；馬達加斯加：Sophie Herivelomalala；墨西哥：Gilela Bello, Maricela Gonzalez, Alicia Julian, Enriqueta Ramirez, Anselmo Zanes；波蘭：Karolina Gorak, Ilya Seldinas；波多黎各：Mercy Alves, Carmen Diaz, Judith Marinez, Placida Rodriguez；俄羅斯：Inna Kaminskaya, Marina Lebedeva, Olga Seldina；和烏克蘭：Marik Davydov.

他們為本指南提供了關於他們的夢想的最動人的描述："我們希望這個計畫不是結束，而是新移民的美好開始，因為有其他人關心並幫助那些來紐約追求更美好的生活的人們。"

Joan P. Nassivera
紐約市, 2003年12月

如何使用本指南

本指南最主要的目的是對你（移民）、你的僱主和許多政府工作人員、社會公益服務提供者有用，他們的任務就是幫助你在新的家園－紐約市取得成功。以下是幫助你最充分地利本指南的一些提示。

尋找專題

本指南分為幾章。目錄中每一章的標題和簡介反映了你在定居時要處理的一大課題。例如，"住房"一章講的是找住處；"勞動和就業"一章中包括關於找工作的建議和根據法律你必須得到多少收入的資料。在"教育"一章中，你可以知道如何帶你的孩子到公立學校註冊，到哪裡學習英語。

尋找答案

各章都由問題組成，這些問題是我們的移民/審核人員認為初到紐約頭幾個星期或頭幾個月中最重要和最難回答的問題。每一個回答都提供基本資訊，並經常包括機構名稱和電話號碼，以便進一步瞭解詳情。許多答案中也包括有用的網站網址。

獲得更多的幫助

各章中都有灰色的專欄，其中包括能提供更多資訊和幫助的社區團體和社會公益服務機構的名稱。當一個團體或機構名稱的後面跟著一個頁碼時，意思是我們的移民/審核人員認為這個團體或機構非常有幫助和可靠，因此可以在本指南後面的資料名錄中找到關於它的更詳細的資料。

　　在名錄中，每一篇簡介上方出現的圖標表示該資源機構、團體或服務提供者的業務範圍，例如，居住或兒童保育。

　　只要有可能，每一處資料機構、團體或服務提供者的名稱後面都會標有其最常用的簡稱。

　　每一篇機構簡介會詳細說明機構、團體或服務提供者的地點、電話和傳真號碼、電子郵件地址和網站地址、所提供的服務、使用的語言、需要的文件或其他要求。

多語言格式

指南全書依次以英文、西班牙文和中文印刷。

　　我們的審核人員（包括移民和服務提供者）向我們強調：有些資訊非常重要，應該在本指南中多次提及。例如辦理永久居留卡（也叫外國人登記卡，通常稱為"綠卡"）的基本步驟。綠卡是對居住、就業等移民生活的很多方面至關重要的文件。因此，你會發現這些步驟在"合法身份"一章中有說明，並在"住房"、"勞動和就業"、"文件證件"幾個章節裡都有提及。

　　由於每一個答案都力圖足夠全面以自成一體，特殊重要的資訊，例如新成立的聯邦Department of Homeland Security（國土安全部）的兩個主要部門－the Bureau of Immigration and Customs Enforcement（美國移民和海關執法局，簡稱B.I.C.E.）及the United States Citizenship and Immigration Services（美國公民和移民服務局，簡稱U.S.C.I.S.）在不同的地方多次加以介紹和說明。

　　我們盡一切努力保證本指南中的所有資料在付印時都是準確和最新的。但請務必記住，移民法和影響移民的政策是經常修訂的，尤其是2001年9月11日以後。另外，其他政府機構，以及社會公益服務團體和移民服務提供者也會改變政策和計劃。因此，最好與本指南後面資源名錄中列出的一個團體或機構聯繫，或諮詢有聲譽的移民事務律師，以查明本指南所涉及事項的最新資料。

　　我們希望足夠的興趣和資金能使我們更新這本指南，並能以其他語言印刷。歡迎你向 immigrantguide@nytimes.com 發送電子郵件，就如何改進和其他語言版本表達你的意見、批評和建議。我們無法答覆你的電子郵件，但是在編輯下一版時，將會參考你的意見。

住房

"**我**們那陽光燦爛、空氣新鮮的山居被四堵牆和四面八方擠在一起的人所取代。寂靜和陽光,過去的情景現在被新都市蒙太奇所取代。鋪著鵝卵石的街道,一排排沒有盡頭的、單調的廉價公寓遮去了天空。貨車、大車和馬車混合的交通,馬蹄聲在夜晚嚓出了火花。不知附近哪裡失了火,頓時聽到一陣叮噹的鈴聲和警報的呼嘯聲。潮濕的門廳,長長的木樓梯和走廊的廁所"

Leonard Covello,意大利人,1910年代 [1]

■

紐約市住宅短缺,尤其是缺少中低收入居民能負擔得起的住宅。這意味著對大多數移民來說,找房子可能是漫長而困難的過程,但當然並非不可能。儘管可負擔得起的住宅經常供不應求,移民們總是能成功地找到房子。幾個世紀以來他們都在紐約安家,塑造、再塑造著這座城市。

我怎樣才能在紐約找到公寓?

■ 與幫助移民找房子的社區團體取得聯繫。
■ 問你去的宗教場所或你要去居住的地區宗教場所的牧師和人員。
■ 尋找張貼在公共場所(比如酒店、洗衣店或教堂)的房屋出租廣告。
■ 在公共場所張貼你自己的啟示("找房子。願付500美元/每月")。
■ 在日報和社區報紙中尋找想合租房間或公寓的人刊登的廣告,或出租公寓一覽表。到Village Voice或LOOT等免費報紙裡去找。這種廣告可能會讓你去找經紀人或代理人，他們是做什麼的以及收費標準將在後文說明。

如果我看到了一則我負擔得起的公寓出租廣告，我該怎麼辦？

迅速行動。打上面登出的電話號碼，立即預約看房時間。

房東、房地產經紀人和租房代理人可以合法地收取哪些費用？

房東可以向你收取保證金，通常相等於一個月的租金。房地產經紀人為了幫助你找到你租的房子可以向你收取傭金，通常為第一年租金的12%－15%。只有在得到由房東簽字的租屋合同後才應該付傭金。住宅仲介機構可以為向你提供可租房屋一覽表而向你收取一筆費用。但如果你沒有租一覽表中的房屋，仲介機構應該只留下15美元，退還你其他所有費用。

房東、房地產經紀人和租房代理人收取哪些費用是非法的？

除法定租金和保證金以外，任何人要求你支付額外的獎金都是非法的。這種非法的額外獎金經常被稱為開門費（key money）。

報紙廣告或租房啟示中的"no fee"是什麼意思？

意思是除了保證金之外你不必付額外的費用。

我給房東的保證金是如何使用的？

只有在當你未付清房租就搬走時，或當房間損毀過於嚴重，你搬出後房東不得不進行修繕時，房東才可以扣留保證金。如果你付清了全部房租，而且房間沒有受到損害，房東必須在你搬走時退還保證金。

需要更多幫忙嗎？

這些團體提供找房子的諮詢：

- Asian Americans for Equality（亞洲人平等會，簡稱A.A.F.E.）（382頁）
- Chinese-American Planning Council（華人策劃協會）（389頁）
- Flatbush Development Corporation（Flatbush開發公司）（394頁）
- Hellenic American Neighborhood Action Committee（美國希臘裔社區行動委員會，簡稱H.A.N.A.C.）（396頁）
- People's Fire House（人民消防站）（411頁）

> **不要相信房東承諾的任何事，除非這些內容寫進了你們雙方簽字的租屋合同中。 只要合同生效，你的房東不能改變合同中的內容。**

房屋租賃合同中都有什麼內容？

- 你每月必須支付多少房租。
- 你可以在房屋中居住多久。
- 誰支付公用事業費，比如電費、煤氣費、暖氣費和電話費。

我必須要簽房屋租賃合同嗎？

不，這並不是強制性的，但是如果沒有房屋租賃合同，你所擁有的權利會很少，並很難在法庭上證明。

我必須支付公用事業費嗎？

是的，房客幾乎總是要負責安裝大多數公用事業設備並為之支付錢，如電和暖氣。這意味著你必須打電話給公用事業公司，告訴他們你將於某日期搬入房屋，從該日起公用事業費的賬單應該寄給你。大多數的房屋是通電話的，但房客通常必須自備電話機，並選擇本地電話營運商，長途電話營運商和付費計劃。

所有的長途電話付費計劃似乎都太貴了。往家裡和其他地方打電話，怎樣才能負擔得起？

許多移民買電話卡打電話。電話卡的種類和價格決定你可以打到哪裡，打多長時間。許多人推薦用電話卡打國際長途電話，因為這種辦法比使用國際長途付費計劃更省錢。

哪裡能買到電話卡？

酒店、報攤、電話卡專賣店和一些支票－現金兌換處。

房東可以拒絕租給我房子嗎？

可以。房東可以決定把房子租給什麼人。例如，如果房東認為你付不起房租，你可能被拒絕。但是房東不能以你的年齡、種族、宗教、國籍、工作、性取向、婚姻狀況、懷孕情況、殘疾或有多少子女為由拒絕把房子租給你。

我的房東想知道我的收入水平。我必須告訴他嗎？

是的。而且他也有權看工資存根或其他收入證明，以保證你能賺到足夠的錢支付房租。

我的房東什麼時候可以漲我的房租，可以漲多少？

當你的租屋合同到期時，房東可以漲房租。漲房租是以Rent Guidelines Board（房租指導委員會）的規定為根據的。欲瞭解更多資訊，請給委員會打電話1-212-385-2934（僅限英語）或訪問網站www.housingnyc.com。

我認為我的房東收我的房租太多了。我該怎麼辦？

打電話給Office of Rent Administration（房租管理局辦事處）1-718-739-6400（英語和西班牙語），並索要一份你的房屋的出租史。在談判第一份租屋合同時，或面臨第一次房屋漲租時，你可以這樣做。

我以現金支付房租。我怎樣才能證明自己已經支付了每月的房租呢？

你務必要從房東那裡取得收據，收據上應該寫有日期、你支付的數額、你的姓名以及房間號和地址。收取房租的人必須在收據上簽字，並寫明他的名稱。

誰可以和我在我的房間裡同住，我的房東有權知道什麼人和我同住嗎？

你的直系親屬可以和你同住，也可以有一位室友及室友的未成年子女。但是衛生局規定不得人口過密。你可以在以下網址找到相關規定www.housingnyc.com/index.html。房東可以詢問是否有人和你同住，但是不能問那個人同你的關係。

與我同居的人簽署的租屋合同。我可以在房間裡住嗎？

可以，但簽署租屋合同的人必須仍然住在那裡。如果簽署租屋合同的人不住在房間裡，房東可以驅逐居住者。只有原始的房客可以續簽租屋合同。

我房間裡的東西壞了。我該怎麼辦？

如果不是你弄壞的，你沒有責任去修理它或支付修理費用。可以要求房東或管理員去修理。如果是你弄壞的，你有責任將物品修理好或支付修理費用。

根據法律，房東必須為我做什麼？

- 不論什麼時候都要供應熱水（至少要達到華氏120度）。
- 自10月1日起至5月31日止供應暖氣。如果從早上6時到晚上10時，室外溫度低於華氏55度，必須有足夠的暖氣，使你的房間裡達到至少華氏68度。如果從晚上10時到早上6時，室外溫度低於華氏40度，你的房間的溫度至少要達到華氏55度。

■ 在住宅單元內的任何一間用於睡覺的房間的15英尺以內安裝煙感警報器。

■ 為任何有10歲以下（含10歲）兒童居住的住宅單位安裝窗鐵柵。

■ 在有6歲以下（含6歲）兒童居住的住宅單位中，拆除或完全遮蓋任何牆皮剝落或表面塗以含鉛油漆的牆。含鉛油漆主要見於1960年以前建造或刷油漆的住宅單位中。

■ 盡一切力量保證你的住宅單位中沒有蟑螂、老鼠或其他害蟲。

如果我無法按期支付租金會怎樣？

立刻告訴房東。如果他知道你有財務上的困難，他可能會同意延期收房租或堅持讓你只付部分房租。有了錢以後要立即向房東付錢，並取得收據。

我的房東不同意延期交房租。我該怎麼辦？

把錢放在安全的地方。不要花掉。如果房東想驅逐你，你在法庭上反對驅逐，你會需要拖欠的房租。

如果我沒有按期支付房租，或者如果我做了租房屋合同不允許做的事，會怎麼樣？

你的房東可以到法庭請求法官命令你搬走。房東不能讓你搬走，或者拿走你的傢具和衣物不歸還，或把它們扔到大街上。

需要更多幫忙嗎？

如果我的房東不供應暖氣或提供熱水，或者我認為我成為住房歧視的受害者，或者我作為房客的權利被侵犯了，我該怎麼辦？

欲就供應暖氣或熱水進行投訴，可打電話:

■ 公民服務中心的電話，311

欲就房屋歧視和房客權利投訴，可打電話：

■ Asian Americans for Equality（亞洲人平等會）（382頁）

■ Chinese-American Planning Council（華人策進協會）（389頁）

■ Flatbush Development Corporation（Flatbush 開發公司）（394頁）

■ Jacob A. Riis Neighborhood Settlement House（Jacob A. Riis街坊文教館）（399頁）

■ New York City Commission on Human Rights（紐約市人權委員會）（405頁）

■ New York State Division of Housing and Community Renewal（紐約州住房和社區翻新處，簡稱D.H.C.R.）（409頁）

■ Promesa（411頁）

■ Queens Legal Services（皇后區法律服務）（412頁）

房東要讓我搬出去，必須出示什麼？

房東不能驅逐你。只有縣治安官或市執法官才能執行法庭的驅逐令，並且必須向你出示驅逐令。欲瞭解詳情，請訪問www.housingnyc.com/resources/attygenguide.html。

驅逐令必須使用我自己的語言嗎？

驅逐通知使用英語和西班牙語。法庭公文只使用英語，但法庭有翻譯可供利用。

如果我收到了驅逐令或搬出通知，我該怎麼辦？

立即打電話給房產律師。如果驅逐通知上指定了出庭日期，一定要按時出庭。如果你不出庭，可能會早於驅逐日就被驅逐。

如果我沒有合法身份，我的房東可以在沒有法庭命令時驅逐我嗎？

不管你的移民身份如何，如果房東或管理人沒有驅逐令就把你鎖在房間外，你應該報警。但是你需注意，房東可能會告訴Bureau of Immigration and Customs Enforcement（移民海關執法局，簡稱B.I.C.E.）你沒有合法身份。隸屬於United States Department of Homeland Security（美國國土安全部的）B.I.C.E.承擔著一些多年來由 Immigration and Naturalization Services（移民歸化局，簡稱I.N.S.）承擔的責任。

我連找到的便宜房子都無法負擔。 還有別的辦法嗎？

New York City Housing Authority (紐約市住房管理局，簡稱N.Y.C.H.A.)（407頁）為低收入居民提供相當好的住房，但需等待相當的長的時間。

我該怎樣申請低收入住房？

填寫好申請表，申請表可在五個行政區申請辦事處得到。欲知道它們的地址，請

需要更多幫忙嗎？

以下這些組織可以幫助房客反對驅逐：

- Eviction Intervention Services（驅逐調解服務），1-212-308-2210（英語和西班牙語）
- Church Avenue Merchants Block Association（教堂大道商人區協會，簡稱C.A.M.B.A.）（389頁）
- Citizens Advice Bureau（公民顧問局，簡稱C.A.B.）（390頁）
- New York Urban League（紐約城市聯盟）（410頁）
- South Bronx Action Group（南布朗士行動團體）（413頁）

打電話給紐約市住房管理局（N.Y.C.H.A.）1-212-306-3000（407頁）或者拜訪他們的網站www.nyc.gov/html/nycha/html/ boroughoffices.html.

我沒有合法身份，這會有麻煩嗎？

當本書付印時，只要求廉租房申請家庭中的一個人必須是合法移民。這就是說，入住者中必須有一個人有永久居留卡（也叫外國人登記卡，俗稱"綠卡"），表示他或她在美國合法居住，或者必須是公民。根據家庭中居住的無正式文件的移民的人數，市政府補貼房租的金額也將減少。然而，移民政策經常變化，所以最好向本指南後面資源名錄中列出的移民支持團體查詢，或者如果你花得起費用，向聲譽較好的移民事務律師查詢。

我怎樣才能獲得綠卡？

獲得綠卡經常是漫長而複雜的過程，而且影響移民的政策經常變化。"合法身份"一章從第364頁起對基本步驟進行了說明。你應該總是向本指南後面的資源名錄中列出的移民服務提供者求助，或者如果你花得起費用，向聲譽較好的移事事務律師求助。

我的收入高於低收入者廉租房的資格要求，但我還是租不起私人住宅。有什麼辦法嗎？

紐約市有約125,000套供中等收入人員居住的由市補貼或州補貼的出租房和合作式公寓。被稱為米切爾-拉馬斯。要取得租住的資格，對你的家庭收入會有限制，對在單位中居住的人口數量多少也有限制。

如果我找了又找，但還是找不到在我的預算之內的公寓怎麼辦？有沒有應急住房，或者有什麼其他地方可以讓我去住？

紐約市Department of Homeless Services（無家可歸者服務局）為男女和家庭提供無家可歸者庇護所，而不追究其移民身份，並設有活動中心，為無家可歸者提供熱食、衣物、醫療護理、淋浴和洗衣處，還提供咨詢、職業介紹及其他社會服務。它的總部地址位於曼哈頓下城的33 Beaver Street，電話是1-212-361-8000（英語和西班牙語）。欲尋找附近的活動中心，可給總部打電話，或訪問該局的網站www.nyc.gov/html/dhs/html/ di-directions.html。

　　如果你無法到這些地方，也不要絕望。全市的許多社區宗教場所、診所和社會公益服務機構都為處境困難的人提供庇護所、備餐室、危機干預及其他服務。本指南提到的團體及結尾處資源名錄中列出的團體將可以幫助你，或把你介紹給可以提供幫助的人。

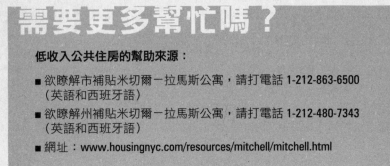

需要更多幫忙嗎？

低收入公共住房的幫助來源：

- 欲瞭解市補貼米切爾－拉馬斯公寓，請打電話 **1-212-863-6500**
  （英語和西班牙語）
- 欲瞭解州補貼米切爾－拉馬斯公寓，請打電話 **1-212-480-7343**
  （英語和西班牙語）
- 網址：www.housingnyc.com/resources/mitchell/mitchell.html

■

"當我初到這個國家時，我到了位於Ludlow街38號的一處廉租公寓樓。等我到了公寓時，我問，廁所在哪兒？我以為只要按一下按鈕，廁所就會自動出現。再按下另一個按鈕，浴缸就會自動出現，但那天晚上我猛然醒悟情況並非如此。我的叔叔、嬸子，還有五個孩子住在一個公寓裡。過了幾年我才真正明白這就是其他國家的人所稱的黃金鋪地的'美妙城市'。"

Rafael Guzman, 多米尼加人, 1966年 [2]

勞動和就業

"**我** 走街串巷地找工作，看到了這座龐大的建築，上面有一個大牌子寫著"職業介紹所"。於是我走進去，請求介紹一份工作。當然，他一點兒瑞典語也不會說，我也不會說英語，但我還是能讓他明白，我需要一份工作。他說，'等一下，我去找一位你的同胞來。'他找到了一位鐵匠工頭，是瑞典人。他說，'噢，我可以僱用你這樣的小夥子。'"

Charles T. Anderson, 瑞典人, 1925年 [3]

■

在一個新的國家裡找工作，乍想之下可能就讓人感到忐忑不安，但紐約市有許多找工作的地方，有許多資源可以利用，以幫助你找到一份工作。

怎樣才能找到工作？
■ 向親友打聽哪裡有工作或者誰可能會僱人。
■ 在有工廠、商店或者餐館的地方多走走，看看哪裡的窗戶上貼有"招工"的啟示。走進貼有招工啟示的商家，找負責人或者瞭解招工情況的人聊一聊。
■ 翻閱以你的母語出版的報紙。他們會有專版刊登招工廣告。
■ 和幫助找工作和安排工作的組織聯繫。

我可以按日工作嗎？
想打散工的人經常在街頭聚在一起，等待需要服務的人開車過來，提供清潔、園

> **需要務必記住的是，如果你沒有正式身份並在美國工作，你仍然受到適用於有正式身份人的同樣勞動法律的保護。 但如果美國政府得知你沒有正式身份，你可能會被起訴和驅逐出境。**

藝或者澆注混凝土之類的工作。散工通常會為小時工資或者日工資討價還價。警告：有時僱用散工的人會在一天或一個星期結束時拒絕支付工資。如果發生這種情況，應該聯繫警方，告訴他們你對僱主所瞭解的全部情況。

根據法律，僱主可以問哪些問題？
僱主可以問你有什麼技能、以及為什麼想為他們工作。如果僱主打聽你的年齡、種族、宗教、國籍、性取向、懷孕與否或者殘障情況則是非法的。

必須進行體檢嗎？
不一定要進行體檢，除非所有僱員都被要求進行體檢。檢查的結果是保密的，不得用於歧視殘障人士。

我在得到工作之前要接受藥物檢查嗎？
許多僱主會檢查有沒有使用大麻和古柯鹼等非法藥物，如果在血檢或尿檢中發現這些藥物，就不會僱用你。如果你沒有通過檢查，但只使用過醫生開的藥或者在藥店買的藥，比如止咳藥，可以要求重新進行檢查。

找工作需要哪些文件？
找工作需要兩份文件，一份用來表明你是誰，另一份用來表明你有資格工作。所有的僱主必須為每一名員工填寫I-9表格。

I-9表是什麼？
I-9表是所有的僱主必須為每一名僱員填寫和簽字的文件。僱主必須檢查每一名僱員的就業資格和身份證件。在工作的第一天，你必須填寫好表格的第一部分。

我的I-9表會被交給美國移民當局嗎？
不會，I-9表格不會交給聯邦政府備案。

我需要什麼文件才能證明我可以合法地工作？

永久居留卡，也叫外國人登記卡，俗稱的綠卡，或者就業授權書，也叫E.A.D.，兩者都能表明你有合法的資格工作。

我怎樣才能獲得綠卡？

獲得綠卡的過程經常是漫長而複雜的，而且影響移民的政策經常變化。"合法身份"一章自第364頁起介紹了基本步驟。你應該總是向本指南後面的資源名錄中列出的移民服務提供者求助，或者如果你花得起費用，向聲譽較好的移民事務律師求助。

獲得綠卡需要多久？我能一直工作到獲得綠卡的時候嗎？

如果你的護照蓋了說明你的申請尚待處理的章，你可以工作。美國法律對每一年的移民簽證號的數量有限制，這意味著即使United States Citizenship and Immigration Services (美國公民和移民服務局，簡稱U.S.C.I.S.，也是隸屬於國土安全部的一個部門)批准了你的移民簽證申請，你可能也無法立即得到移民簽證號。從U.S.C.I.S.批准你的移民簽證申請到得到移民簽證號，你可能要等2到10年，或者更久。美國法律還按照國別限制移民簽證的數量。你將收到以郵件寄來的批准通知書，然後應該去位於曼哈頓下城的聯邦廣場26號美國公民和移民服務局紐約市地區辦事處（U.S.C.I.S. New York City District Office, 26 Federal Plaza）領取卡片。當它過期時，你必須再填寫一份申請並支付費用。如果你不這樣做，就是非法工作。

我需要就業授權書(E.A.D.)嗎？

如果你不是美國公民或合法的永久居民，你可能需要申請一份就業授權書（E.A.D.），以證明你可以在美國工作。如果U.S.C.I.S.在90天內既未批准也沒拒絕你的E.A.D.申請，你可以申請臨時E.A.D.（庇難申請人可以申請30天以內的臨時E.A.D.，但是他們必須自提交了填寫完整的原始庇難申請之日起150天後才能申請E.A.D.。）

怎樣才能獲得就業授權書，或者E.A.D.？

填寫U.S.C.I.S.的I-765表。仔細閱讀全文，提交正確的文件、照片和費用。你應該在原始E.A.D.到期前6個月，申請續期E.A.D.。

如果我被拒絕了會怎樣？我可以申訴嗎？

如果你的E.A.D.申請被拒絕了，你會收到一封信，告知你拒絕的原因。你不能向

需要更多幫忙嗎？

許多團體幫助找工作和安排工作。以下是其中的幾家：

- Chinese-American Planning Council（華人策劃協會）（第389頁）
- Church Avenue Merchants Block Association（教堂大道商人區協會，簡稱 C.A.M.B.A.）（第389頁）
- Citizens Advice Bureau（公民顧問局）（第390頁）
- Hellenic American Neighborhood Action Committee（美國希臘裔社區行動委員會，簡稱H.A.N.A.C.）（第396頁）
- Jacob A. Riis Neighborhood Settlement House（Jacob A. Riis 街坊文教館）（第399頁）
- New York Association for New Americans（紐約新美國人聯合會，簡稱N.Y.A.N.A.）（第404頁）
- New York City Department of Education, Office of Adult and Continuing Education（紐約市教育局，成人和繼續教育辦公室）（第406頁）
- New York City Workforce 1 Career Center（紐約市勞工第一職業中心）（第408頁）
- University Settlement Society of New York（紐約大學街坊文教協會）（第415頁）

更高層的權力機關申訴，但是可以向拒絕申請的U.S.C.I.S.辦事處提出重新申請或復議的請求。重新申請請求必須說明在重新申請過程中將會提供新的事實，並必須附以正式書面陳述或其他證據。復議請求必須表明拒絕的裁決是根據做出裁決時檔案中的證據對法律或U.S.C.I.S.政策的錯誤執行。

如果我沒有合法身份，可以工作嗎？

可以，儘管你的移民身份有問題，你仍可以被僱用，但是雇用你的人或公司屬於違法。如果你憑偽造的文件獲得工作，你也屬於違法。美國有嚴格的法律要求僱主檢查所有新員工的移民身份，包括1986年以前，即該法律生效以前就來到美國的人。然而，影響移民的政策經常變化，所以最好向本指南後面資源名錄中列出的移民支援團體查詢，或者如果你負擔得起費用，向聲譽好的移民事務律師查詢。

作為勞工，我享有哪些權利？

不論你是否有合法身份，都享有幾項基本權利：

- 政府規定的法定最低工資的權利。截止到2003年12月，最低工資標準是每小時5.15美元。

- 定期休息的權利。如果公司簽訂的合同規定有帶薪假期，則假期期間必須仍然支付工資。
- 讓你的僱主支付傷殘保險和社會安全保險等的權利。
- 基本的健康和安全防護的權利，本章後文將予以說明。

每一名勞工必須得到法定最低工資嗎？

不，有些勞工不受最低工資法保護，包括兼職的在僱主家裡臨時照看兒童者，住在所要照顧的病人或老人家裡但不做家務的家庭護理員，計程車司機和其他幾種人。想瞭解哪些人不受最低工資法保護，請撥打United States Department of Labor, Wage and Hour Division（美國勞工部工資和工時處）的免費電話1-866-487-9243（英語和西班牙語），或者訪問其網站 http://www.dol.gov/。

我賺的錢可以超過法定最低工資嗎？

可以。你的僱主支付你的工資不能低於法定最低工資，但是他或她有向你支付更多工資的自由。

我必須工作多少小時才能得到加班費？

如果你不是住在僱主家的傭工，你有權得到一個付薪星期內40個工時以外的工時的加班費。（一個付薪周是指一個七天的星期，但不一定是從星期日到星期六的日曆周。一個付薪周可能從星期一算起直到星期日，或者從星期三算起直到下星期二，等等。）如果你是住在僱主家的傭工，你有權得到一個付薪周內超出44個工時以外的加班費。

工間休息和週末班會計入付薪周內的總工時數嗎？

很多用餐休息時間及其他休息時間，不論是帶薪的還是不帶薪的，都不計入付薪周的總工時數。還要記住，加班費是以40工時的付薪周為基礎的。你不能只因為在某一天工作超過8小時或在星期六或星期日工作就有權得到加班費。

加班費的標準是什麼？

一星期中超出40小時或一天中超出10小時的每1小時加班工資率應是正常工作每小時費率的一倍半。因此如果你正常的小時費率是6美元，一星期工作45小時，你將得到40工時的工資240美元（6美元×40小時）外加5小時加班所得的45美元（9美元×5小時），一星期共得285美元。

我在一家按件計酬的成衣廠工作。我仍然有權得到法定最低工資和加班費嗎？

你仍然必須至少得到法定最低工資，並且如果你在必要的工時以外加班，必須得到加班費。

如果我做保姆或者女僕，我所服務的家庭知道我有權得到加班費和其他福利嗎？
在紐約市，如果你是通過職業介紹所被僱用的，這家介紹所必須給你和你的僱主一張列出你的權利的表格，上面包括加班費及其他福利。僱主必須在表格上簽字，表示他或她瞭解到你有什麼權利。

我可以收現金工資嗎？
盡可能不要收現金，因為它通常意味著你的僱主不會支付稅、社會安全保險和勞工傷害保險等等。收現金也難以證明你曾經工作過，從而難以享受社會安全福利金和工人撫恤金等福利。

什麼是社會安全保險？
是由僱主和工人支付保險費的一種保險計劃，當工人達到退休年齡或者因生病、殘疾而無法再工作時，這項保險計劃將支付保險金。

沒有合法身份的勞工能得到社會保險嗎？
不能。

什麼是勞工傷害保險？
是一種由僱主支付保險費的保險，當全職或兼職的員工受工傷，或者因工作受傷或得病而無法工作並需要照顧時，這種保險將為大部分人提供福利和支付醫療護理費用。

沒有合法身份的勞工能得到勞工傷害保險嗎？
可以。在紐約州，沒有合法身份的勞工受到勞工傷害保險法律的完全保護。

僱主能從我的工資裡扣除其他項目的金額嗎？
除法律或政府規定的專案（比如所得稅、法庭命令的兒童撫養費、債務人工資扣押）和經過你允許並增加你的福利的項目（例如保險費、工會會費、購買美國儲蓄債券的費用）以外，僱主不得從你的工資扣除任何費用。

什麼是所得稅？
在美國，如果你的收入超過一定水平，就必須納稅。聯邦政府和紐約州均要求你每年遞交被稱為"所得稅申報表"的表格。這些以每年4月15日為截止日期的表格會

需要更多幫忙嗎？

填寫納稅申報表格非常複雜。如果你負擔得起費用，可以僱一名專攻稅法的
會計。如果你沒有錢僱用會計，可以聯繫以下這些機構，它們可以提供免費
的報稅幫助。它們可能做不了所有的申報，有些機構為接受其服務的人規定
了收入指標。大多數機構只在納稅季節開業，即從1月中旬到4月中旬：

- Internal Revenue Service Taxpayer Assistance Unit（國稅局納稅人援助組），可在 www.irs.gov 查詢其辦事處地址。每一家辦事處均提供多語種幫助。
- Community Tax Aid（社區稅務援助），電話：1-212-788-7552（僅限英語）
- Community Food Resource Center（社區食品資源中心），電話：1-866-WAGE-PLUS （1-866-924-3758）（英語）或 1-866-DOLARES（1-866-365-2737）（西班牙語）
- Volunteer Income Tax Assistance（義務所得稅援助，簡稱VITA），電話：1-718-488-3655（僅限英語）

向政府報告在過去的日曆年度中你賺了多少錢，又是如何花掉的。當你遞交這些
表格時，同時也要支付所欠的所得稅款。

我怎樣才能知道我是否欠稅？

如果你的移民身份要求你繳納所得稅，並且如果根據你的年齡、婚姻狀況及你是
否是一家之主，你的總收入超過一定的最低額，就必須為在美國所賺得的收入繳
納所得稅。

我在工作時會得到小費。僱主能拿走我的小費嗎？

除非你是在衣帽間工作，否則僱主不可以要求得到或者接受任何你得到的小費。
如果你是一名侍者或者餐飲業服務工作人員，並且你的小費收入達到每小時1.85
美元，你的僱主可以從你的法定最低工資裡扣除最多每小時1.85美元。如果你在
宴會、聚會或其他特殊場合工作，客人支付的帳單包括一定百分比的小費，你的
僱主可以將小費分給所有為聚會服務的僱員。

如果我在工作中能得到小費，我的僱主必須支付我其他報酬嗎？

是的。如果你是一名侍者或者餐飲服務工作人員，你的報酬必須至少要相當於法
定最低工資減去你得到的小費的金額。

如果我是看門人或者樓房管理員，我的僱主可以從我的工資中扣除小費嗎？

你的僱主（房東或物業經理）不能從你的工資中扣除小費。看門人的法定最低工
資是根據建築物中住宅單元或辦公室的數目計算的，而不是按小時費率計算的。

我必須在工作時穿制服嗎？如果必須穿，誰支付制服的費用？

你的僱主可以要求你穿制服。如果你必須從僱主那裡買制服，僱主必須在你購買制服不久後報銷你為此支出的全部費用。如果你從另一家公司購買制服，你的僱主必須報銷一部分費用。你的僱主還必須清洗或乾洗制服，或者為此而出資。

我的僱主應該多久付我一次工資？

對於體力勞工，例如技工、女僕和園丁，必須每週支付全額工資，並應在他們工作的那一周結束後七天之內支付。辦公室及其他工作人員（週薪超過600美元者外）每月必須至少支付兩次工資。

如果我沒有去上班，我能領到工資嗎？

不能。但是僱主只能扣除你缺席期間的工資數額。例如，如果你少工作四小時，你的僱主不能扣除八小時的工資。

對工作的小時數有什麼限制嗎？我可以休息嗎？

對每天的工時數沒有限制。在許多工作場所，例如工廠、商店、餐館和全年開業的旅館，工人在一個日曆周內必須至少休息一天（連續24小時）。還要記住，如果你不是入住僱員，在一個付薪周內工作超過40小時，憩必須得到加班費。如果你是入住僱員，在一個付薪周內工作超過44小時或一天工作超過10小時，必須得到加班費。

我能有用餐休息時間嗎，我的僱主必須為休息期間支付工資嗎？

你有權擁有用餐休息時間。一次值班超過6小時的員工必須有至少半小時的不間斷的用餐時間。你的僱主不是必須要為用餐休息時間支付工資，除非公司簽署了有這種規定的合同。

我可以不帶薪休假嗎？

根據Family and Medical Leave Act of 1993（1993年聯邦探親假和病假法），僱員人數超過50人以上的僱主必須允許他們在一定條件下不帶薪休假最長達12周。欲瞭解詳情，可以訪問勞工部的網站 **www.dol.gov/esa/regs/statutes/whd/fmla.**

我的僱主為我支付健康保險。 如果我丟了工作會怎樣？

如果你辭職或者失去工作，並已經由僱主提供的健康保險承保了至少3個月，根據一個叫做Cobra的計劃（儘管Cobra保險要貴得多），你必須被允許再支付最多18個月的保險費。

　　如果你因為堅持這些權利而受到歧視，你可以採取法律行動，比如提出正式的投訴或訴訟，但要等到政府或法院出面糾正針對你的違法行為，可能需要幾年

需要更多幫忙嗎？

很多團體可以向你說明你作為工人的權利，如果你的權利受到侵犯，還可以提供幫助。以下是其中幾家團體：

- Asian American Legal Defense and Education Fund（亞美法律援助處）（第381頁）
- Chinese Staff and Workers' Association（華人職工會）（第388頁）
- Latino Workers Center（拉美裔員工中心）（第399頁）
- Legal Aid Society（法律援助協會）（第400頁）
- New York City Commission on Human Rights（紐約市人權委員會）（第405頁）
- New York State Department of Labor, Division of Employment Services Office（紐約州勞工廳就業服務處）（第409頁）
- Queens Legal Services（皇后區法律服務）（第412頁）

的時間。

我會因為移民身份而受到不同的對待嗎？

根據聯邦法律，僱主因為原國籍而歧視僱員或求職人員是非法的。不能因為出生地、祖先或者英語說得不好而否定一個人在工作上的平等機會。

我必須在工作場所說英語嗎？

只有當你的僱主表明英語對工作來說是必要的時候，你才必須說英語。

我必須達到多大年齡才能工作？

14歲的學生就可以獲得僱用證書，通常叫做工卡，但是他們不能在工廠裡工作。學生普通僱用證書可以發給16或17歲的學生，全職工作證書可以發給不上學或者為參加全職工作而退學的16歲和17歲的人。 未成年人可以工作的小時數根據其年齡和是否上學而定。

■

"**我** 的表弟有會計學的碩士學位，並在多明尼加共和國有一份很棒的工作，但是他寧可在這裡的超級市場工作，可以賺到更多的錢。我的父母也是。...他們兩個在多明尼加都是專業人員，但是由於某種原因他們覺得這裡生活更好，他們也在超級市場裡工作多年了。"

Irma Olivo, 多米尼加人, 2003年 [4]

兒童保育

多數人不知道街坊文教館其實是結合社會公益服務的俱樂部。The Hudson Guild (哈得孫協會) 是一座有五層樓的貧民窟兒童遊樂場，裡面設有乒乓室和彈子房，一間製造燈具的商店，一家上演業餘愛好者演出劇目的戲院，一處可以進行拳擊和打籃球的體育館。裡面有為我們介紹情況的顧問，時至今日想起這位小夥子來，還覺得很親切。與其說他們是被派來監督我們的，不如說他們更像是朋友。我還記得其中一位幫助我們吃一盒偷來的巧克力，而沒有責怪我們。他做得很對；我們後來都信任他。由於哈得孫協會的工作而避免入獄的青少年的數量遠超過一千名警察的作用。"

Mario Puzo, 意大利移民的兒子, 回憶1930年代 [5]

任何一位父母或者照顧孩子的人都知道，撫養孩子是可怕而艱難的事，但也讓人受用無窮。在一座不熟悉的城市裡養育小孩更讓人尤其緊張。本章將幫助你瞭解可以得到哪些兒童保育，如何找到適合你和你的家人的生活和工作方式及地點的保育。

紐約市有哪些類型的有組織的兒童保育？

對於幼兒來說，主要有三種類型：

■ 家庭日托，由在市衛生局註冊或領取執照的人在家裡照看六個星期到四、五歲大的兒童。這些家庭最多可以照看12名兒童。

- 日托中心，場所通常大於大多數家庭日托的場所。照看的兒童人數則不一定。
- 保育園，為四歲兒童設立的。向孩子們教授基本的學習和社會技能，為他們上幼稚園打下基礎。

什麼是Head Start（提前教育計劃）？

提前教育計劃是一項聯邦計劃，通過向低收入家庭的幼兒教授數學、顏色和基本的閱讀技巧等來為他們上學打下基礎。每一個地區中心都規定有自己的兒童年齡限制。

什麼是Early Head Start（早期提前教育計劃）？

早期提前教育計劃是一項聯邦計劃，它為從新生直至三歲的嬰兒提供日托，也為低收入家庭的少女媽媽提供產前護理。

我怎樣才能查到我的住處或工作地點附近有沒有提前教育計劃或者早期提前教育計劃中心？

有幾種辦法：

- 給Head Start Information and Publication Center（提前教育計劃資訊和出版物中心）打免費電話 1-866-763-6481（僅限英語），告訴他們你所在的州和郵遞區號。他們會為你找到最方便的中心。

需要更多幫忙嗎？

聯繫以下兩個介紹紐約市兒童保育資訊的主要來源：

- New York City Administration for Children's Services Division of Child Care and Head Start（紐約市兒童服務局兒童照顧和提前教育計劃處）（第405頁）
- New York City Child Care Resource and Referral Consortium（紐約市兒童保育資源和介紹協會）（第405頁）

你還可以聯繫以下團體：

- Brooklyn Chinese-American Association（布祿崙華人協會）（第384頁）
- Chinese-American Planning Council（華人策劃協會）（第389頁）
- Citizens Advice Bureau（公民顧問局，簡稱C.A.B.）（第390頁）
- Forest Hills Community House（Forest Hills 社區會所）（第395頁）
- Promesa（第411頁）
- Southeast Bronx Neighborhood Centers（東南布朗士社區中心）（第413頁）
- United Community Centers（聯合社區中心）（第414頁）
- University Settlement Society of New York（紐約大學街坊文教協會）（第415頁）

- 給New York City Administration for Children's Services Division of Child Care and Head Start（紐約市兒童服務局兒童照顧和提前教育計劃處）打電話1-718-FOR-KIDS（第405頁）。
- 在以下網址使用全國提前教育計劃的搜索www.acf.hhs.gov/programs/hsb/hsweb/index.jsp.

和我一樣，我的孩子沒有合法身份。我還能為孩子爭取到兒童保育嗎？

接受政府資金的計劃，包括市計劃和提前教育計劃，需要父母提供社會安全卡，因此你的孩子不太可能從他們那裡得到保育。獲得社會安全卡的事項將在"文件證件"一章中說明。如果你沒有合法身份，可以向家庭照顧者支付現金讓她照顧你的兒童。

我要上夜班，有時週末也上班。有什麼辦法可以找到人照顧我的孩子嗎？

由於大多數中心和計劃只在星期一至星期五早晨到傍晚的時間工作，改變工作時間，工作時間特殊都會使找兒童保育非常困難。另外，只有當父母可以提供證據（例如，僱主的信）來證明他們必須在其他時間工作時，才能得到為保育財務協助。

一些其他建議：

- 付錢給你認識和信任的人（或許是親友）到你家裡來照顧孩子。不論你是在白天、夜晚或者週末工作，這樣做都可以解決問題。
- 尋找願意在他們自己家裡照顧你的孩子的其他人。紐約市兒童服務局兒童照顧

需要更多幫忙嗎？

可向以下組織諮詢課後計劃的情況：

- Alianza Dominicana（多米尼加聯盟）（第381頁）
- Brooklyn Chinese-American Association（布祿崙華人協會）（第384頁）
- Citizens Advice Bureau（公民顧問局，簡稱C.A.B.）（第390頁）
- The Door（門）（第394頁）
- Hellenic American Neighborhood Action Committee（美國希臘裔社區行動委員會，簡稱H.A.N.A.C.）（第396頁）
- Jacob A. Riis Neighborhood Settlement House（Jacob A. Riis 街坊文教館）（第399頁）
- New York City Administration for Children's Services Division of Child Care and Head Start（紐約市兒童服務局兒童照顧和提前教育計劃處）（第405頁）
- New York City Child Care Resource and Referral Consortium（紐約市兒童保育資源和介紹協會）（第405頁）
- Y.M.C.A. of Greater New York（大紐約地區基督教青年會）（第416頁）

需要更多幫忙嗎？

可向以下組織諮詢暑假計劃的情況：

- Alianza Dominicana（多米尼加聯盟）（第381頁）
- Brooklyn Chinese-American Association（布祿崙華人協會）（第384頁）
- Citizens Advice Bureau（公民顧問局，簡稱C.A.B.）（第390頁）
- Community Association of Progressive Dominicana（進步多米尼加人僑界聯合會）（第392頁）
- Hellenic American Neighborhood Action Committee（美國希臘裔社區行動委員會，簡稱H.A.N.A.C.）（第396頁）

和提前教育計劃處（第405頁）可以提供名單及電話號碼。

- 與你的夥伴或其他可以照顧你的孩子的人輪流錯開工作時間。
- 使用幾種不同的兒童照顧方式，例如，當你傍晚上班時使用日托中心，當你在更晚的時間工作時找親屬幫忙。
- 和另一個家庭合作輪流照顧兩家的孩子。另外一家每照顧你的孩子一小時，你就照顧他們的孩子一小時。

我聽説找人照顧很小的嬰兒更難。是真的嗎？

是的，許多兒童保育中心要求孩子要學會大小便，但通常只有兩歲或更大的孩子才能學會大小便。另外，由政府頒發執照的家庭保育供應者只能照顧兩名不足兩歲的嬰兒。

有什麼辦法能找到人照顧六歲以下幼兒嗎？

與本章前文介紹過的機構聯繫，紐約市兒童服務局兒童照顧和提前教育計劃處，電話1-718-FOR-KIDS（第405頁），或者New York City Child Care Resource and Referral Consortium（紐約市兒童保育資源和介紹協會），電話1-888-469-5999（第405頁）。

我的孩子白天大多數時間都要上學。有什麼地方可以讓他們放學以後去嗎？

Partnership for After-School Education（課後教育夥伴組織）在其網站上有課後計劃線上名錄，地址是http://www.pasesetter.com//#asp_directory。你也可以給該組織打電話1-212-571-2664（英語和西班牙語）。

New York City Department of Youth and Community Development（紐約市青少年和社區發展局）開辦有Beacon Schools（燈塔學校），這種學校每週必須至少開放六天。它們通常開放到晚上10點，在週末、假日和其他學校的假期期間也開

> **尋找價格低廉的兒童保育可能會很困難。**
> **應該經常致電和訪問兒童保育中心，**
> **這樣一旦有機會，所有人都會知道你有興趣。**

放。它們提供輔導並幫助做家庭作業，還為成年人提供英語和電腦課程，也組織娛樂和文化活動。欲知附近地區有沒有燈塔學校，請打電話 1-212-676-8255（英語和西班牙語），或訪問網站www.nyc.gov/html/dycd/pdf/beacondirectory.pdf。

夏天學校放假時，我的孩子能去哪裡呢？

燈塔學校在夏天也為父母要工作的兒童開放。

當我打電話詢問多數兒童保育專案的情況時，他們會問我哪些問題？

他們問的問題可能涉及到你的家庭、你和家人的收入、你是否接受政府救濟或福利，在你家或工作地點附近照顧你的孩子是否更方便等。

如果我已被列入低收入家庭兒童保育排隊名單，我該做什麼？

經常打電話過去，讓主管的人知道你真的很需要尋找兒童保育，以便去工作。經常去兒童保育中心查看排隊進展情況。如果每個人都知道你有意找人照顧孩子，可能會有機會。

要為我的孩子辦理兒童保育手續，需要哪些文件？

需要有病歷表，上面要有每一個孩子的醫療和牙科資料，包括疫苗接種紀錄。可以從兒童保育計劃經營者那裡索要病歷表，它必須由醫生填寫。

可能還需要孩子的出生證明（出生證、洗禮檔案或護照）；家庭成員的社會安全卡；以及你的護照、出生證、綠卡或其他證明你有合法身份的證件。

我要交給孩子的照顧者或保育中心哪些物品？

一定要問一下。一些服務提供者要求你帶尿片或食物，因為由照顧孩子的家庭或中心購買這些東西會開支太大。

在尋找兒童保育提供者時還應該注意什麼？

你應該瞭解：

■ 在家或保育中心工作的人是否已經接受過無犯罪記錄檢查。
■ 如果他們為外出實地考察而離開中心，或如果有事發生而你無法及時趕來接孩子，誰來照顧孩子。
■ 如果孩子在保育中心生病了，中心會怎麼做。
■ 孩子會因為哪些過錯受罰，如何受罰。

我的收入還不足以支付兒童保育。能尋求到一些幫助嗎？

在紐約市，政府救濟機構會努力為你尋找你負擔得起的兒童保育。聯邦政府可以資助低收入工作家庭，從社會救濟轉向工作的家庭，父母一方正參加職業或教育專案、或正在積極找工作、或因病或其他原因無法照顧小孩的家庭獲得領有執照的兒童保育。請打電話給紐約市兒童服務局兒童照顧和提前教育計劃處，電話1-718-FOR-KIDS（第405頁），或者紐約市兒童保育資源和介紹協會，電話1-888-469-5999（第405頁），本章前文均已列出了這兩個機構的情況。欲在填表、辦手續或費用等方面尋求幫助，可打Human Resources Administration Info Line（人力資源管理局資訊專線）1-877-472-8411（第397頁）。

我可以收回支付兒童保育的費用嗎？

如果你繳納所得稅，可以通過稅額減免收回部分但非全部的兒童保育費用。

可以聯繫以下地方查詢最新的關於兒童保育稅額減免的資訊：

■ Internal Revenue Service（美國國稅局），1-800-TAX-1040（英語和西班牙語）。
■ New York State Department of Taxation（紐約州稅務廳），1-800-225-5829（僅限英語）。

我被告知我沒有資格享受由政府補貼的兒童保育。我該怎麼辦？

你可以申訴。親自去Office of Administrative Hearings（行政聽證辦公室）請求舉行公正的聽證會。你可以去位在紐約市的兩個辦公室中的任何一個，位址分別是：位於曼哈頓中城的330 West 34th Street三樓，或者位於布祿崙下城的14 Boerum Place一樓。

我覺得我的孩子在我現在使用的保育提供者那裡沒有得到好的照顧。我可以向哪裡投訴？

New York City Department of Health and Mental Hygiene（紐約市健康與心理衛生局）的日托計劃，電話為1-212-676-2444（第407頁），監督兒童保育計劃，並就所有針對提供兒童保育的家庭、中心和計劃的投訴進行調查。可打電話提出投訴。

■

"**每**天工作了幾小時後，我回到家裡迎接我的孩子放學回家。這比朝九晚五期間離開家時好多了。雖然我有正式的工作，但微薄的薪水都花在了孩子的日托上。誰能每天接送我的孩子上日托呢?"

住在皇后區的年輕母親，印度人，1990年代 [6]

教育

"**我**"上的第一所學校位於Orchard街97號的拐角處。帶我們去學校的是住在90號的表兄弟，他們已經是很美國化的孩子了。他們帶我們進去，然後就讓我們自己待在那裡了。首先看到的是一間教室裡的一班少年很順從地坐著，老師在教室前面。她站在黑板前，正在寫著我從沒見過的英語字母。我得到了一個筆記本和一支鉛筆，按我的理解，我應該努力模仿著寫下這些字母的形狀。我不知道自己在做什麼，一輩子也沒見過多少這樣的形狀。這像是不會游泳的人在大海中游泳，實在是令人不知所措。"

Max Mason, 俄羅斯人, 1921年 [7]

■

紐約市為兒童和成年人提供多種教育方式。本章將說明本市公立學校體系的基本情況，還將介紹成年人可以到哪裡學英語。

我沒有合法身份，我的孩子能在紐約上學嗎？
可以。移民身份無關緊要。所有居住在美國的5－21歲的青少年都有權享受免費公共教育。6－17歲的孩子必須上學。

我怎樣給我的孩子註冊上學？
5－13歲的孩子按居住地點分配到小學和中學，在分配的學校進行登記。欲瞭解有關你的街坊的小學和初中情況，請打Chancellor's Parent Hot Line（校長的家長熱線）1-718-482-3777（英語和西班牙語；配有廣東話、普通話和其他語言的翻

譯）（第406頁），或者查看教育局的網站**www.nycenet.edu**尋找Learning Support
Center（助學中心）的地點，助學中心提供各類資料和在你家附近的服務。

教育局的接線員只説英語嗎？

對於大多數的語言來說，你的電話將被接到一位翻譯那裡。

我的孩子的年齡超過13歲了。我該怎樣為她註冊入學？

要上中學的學生的父母可以聯繫 New York City Department of Education,
Chancellor's Parent Hot Line（紐約市教育局校長的家長熱線）1-718-482-3777（英
語和西班牙語；配有廣東話、普通話和其他語言的翻譯）（第406頁）。

我怎樣才能知道我的孩子被派到哪個區或者哪所學校？

請打校長的家長熱線1-718-482-3777（英語和西班牙語；配有廣東話、普通話和
其他語言的翻譯）（第406頁）。

所有的小學和中學都講授同樣的課程嗎？

不，有許多種不同的課程。例如，不是所有的學校都有幼稚園學齡前計劃。

我的孩子必須達到多大年齡才能上學？

- 幼稚園學齡前計劃 孩子必須在當學年的12月31日前滿4歲。
- 幼稚園 孩子必須在當學年的12月31日前滿5歲。
- 一年級 孩子必須在當學年的12月31日前滿6歲。

給孩子註冊入學要準備哪些文件？

註冊入學的孩子必須由父母或者法定監護人陪伴，並帶以下文件：

- 地址證明。如果父母或者監護人是主要房屋承租人，請帶上租屋合同或者Con
  Edison公司、電話公司或者其他公用事業公司開的帳單。如果父母或法定監護
  人不是房屋主要承租人，請帶去以下文件中的兩件：
- 租屋合同和主要房屋承租人的證明信，說明要註冊入學的孩子的住址和全名。
- 僱主或者社會服務機構的聲明，說明父母的地址。
- 駕駛執照。
- 醫療保險卡。
- 出生證、護照或者洗禮證明（蓋印並有授權簽字）。
- 最後的成績單（如果孩子曾經上過學）。
- 疫苗接種紀錄。

如果我沒有孩子註冊入學所需要的文件該怎麼辦？

你通常可以使用其他文件。例如，保險卡可以代替住址證明。欲知哪些文件可以被接受，請打校長的家長熱線1-718-482-3777（英語和西班牙語；配有廣東話、普通話和其他語言的翻譯）（第406頁）。

怎樣才能查到孩子入學前需要接種哪些疫苗？

根據孩子的年齡而不同。請打校長的家長熱線1-718-482-3777（英語和西班牙語；配有廣東話、普通話和其他語言的翻譯）詢問（第406頁）。

如果我的孩子沒有接種入學要求的疫苗該怎麼辦？

如果你答應在一定時期內接種疫苗，你的孩子仍然可以上學。你必須證明你已經約了醫生進行接種。如果你不能讓孩子得到疫苗接種，孩子可能無法上學。

需要更多幫忙嗎？

欲在附近尋找免費的高品質英語課程，可撥打Literacy Assistance Center（識字援助中心）的介紹熱線1-212-803-3333（只有語音資訊存貯系統，限英語和西班牙語），或訪問中心的網站 www.lacnyc.org/hotline/nycalidirectory.htm.

以下社區組織也開設課程：

- Alianza Dominicana（多米尼加聯盟）（第381頁）
- Brooklyn Chinese-American Association（布祿崙華人協會）（第384頁）
- Cabrini Immigrant Services（卡布里尼移民服務）（第385頁）
- Catholic Migration Services（天主教移民服務）（第386頁）
- Chinatown Manpower Project（華埠人力中心）（第388頁）
- Chinese Immigrant Services（華人移民服務）（第388頁）
- Church Avenue Merchants Block Association（教堂大道商人區協會，簡稱 C.A.M.B.A.）（第389頁）
- Community Association of Progressive Dominicans（進步多米尼加人僑界聯合會）（第392頁）
- Indochina Sino-American Community Center（美東越棉寮華僑社區中心）（第398頁）
- Jacob A. Riis Neighborhood Settlement House（Jacob A. Riis街坊文教館）（第399頁）
- New York Association for New Americans（紐約新美國人聯合會，簡稱 N.Y.A.N.A.）（第404頁）
- South Bronx Action Group（南布朗士行動團體）（第413頁）
- United Community Centers（聯合社區中心）（第414頁）
- University Settlement Society of New York（紐約大學街坊文教協會）（第415頁）

我付不起孩子為了上學而接種疫苗的費用。我該怎麼辦？

要得到免費的疫苗接種，可以到New York City Department of Health and Mental Hygiene（紐約市健康與心理衛生局）（第407頁）辦的七處免預約疫苗接種門診之一。欲知這些診所的詳情，請打電話1-212-676-2273或訪問該局網站www.nyc.gov/html/doh/html/imm/imm.html。

我的國家的學校和美國不同。這裡的教師怎樣確定我的孩子上哪一年級？

小學生是按照年齡分年級的，除非其他因素表明需要分到其他年級。中學生在本國上過的課程可以算一些學分。

我的孩子只懂一點兒英語。她能上學嗎？

當你為孩子註冊時，會得到一份家庭語言調查，以查明在家裡說哪種語言。根據這項調查，學校將決定你的孩子是否要接受語言評定測試，也叫L.A.B.測試。學生的L.A.B.成績不到40分的必須參加說其他語言者的英語課程(E.S.O.L.)或雙語課程。

誰來決定我的孩子上哪種英語課程？

由你決定。

公立學校的兩種英語課程，E.S.O.L.和雙語教育有什麼不同？

雙語課程的目的是讓學生在學英語的同時仍然保持其母語流利。在雙語教育課程中，數學、科學和社會學科都是以學生的母語講授的。使用和教授的另一種語言是英語。

E.S.O.L.計劃的目的是讓學生的英語變得流利起來。所有的課程均用英語教授。

所有的學校都有針對我的語言的雙語課程和E.S.O.L.課程嗎？

每一所學校都必須提供E.S.O.L.課程，但所針對的語言各有不同。

我想讓我的孩子上雙語課程，但是她的學校沒有針對我們的母語的雙語課程。我該怎麼做？

你有權把你的孩子送到本學區另一家有這種課程的學校去。請打校長的家長熱線1-718-482-3777（英語和西班牙語；配有中文廣東話、普通話和其他語言的翻譯）(第406頁)。

"" 如果你申請讓你的孩子轉到你所在街坊
以外的公立學校上學，不會問你有關你
或你孩子的移民身分的問題。""

我的孩子無學習能力，需要特殊的幫助。她還能上公立學校嗎？

可以。聯邦法要求無學習能力的孩子必須在限制最少的環境裡得到學業成功的機會。你的孩子將接受一次評估，以便讓學校的官員確定什麼最適合她的需要。她可以在適當的輔助服務之下在普通教育教室裡上一些課程，或者在特殊教育教室裡上課。*沒有父母的同意，任何孩子都不能進特殊教育的課堂上課。*

我住家附近的公立學校不是很好。我的孩子能去遠一些的好學校嗎？

理論上是可以的，但經常很難做到。你的孩子想轉入的學校必須還有位置，因此先要聯繫那所學校問一下。然後再填寫一份特許申請，叫做variance。

為了讓我的孩子能不去最近的公立學校，而去其他學校，我應該到哪裡去拿特許申請表？

到你的孩子註冊的學區督學辦公室去申請特許。欲尋找辦公室的地點，請打校長的家長熱線1-718-482-3777（英語和西班牙語；配有廣東話、普通話和其他語言的翻譯）（第406頁）。或者訪問**Department of Education's Division of Food Services and Transportation**（教育局食品服務和交通處）的網址**www.opt-osfns.org/schoolinfo/Superintendents.cfm**。

想為我的孩子申請進入最近的公立學校以外的其他學校，有年度申請最後期限嗎？

沒有。你可以在任何時候要求轉學。*不會被問起孩子或父母的移民身份。*

我想回到學校學英語。有什麼適合我去的學校嗎？

有許多計劃的英語課程是收費的，有時費用還很高。但是本市各地都有高質量的免費英語課程。

我可以上學學習除英語之外的其他科目嗎？

紐約市提供課程幫助你取得普通教育文憑，也叫G.E.D.，G.E.D.相當於中學畢業文憑。上大學和申請許多工作時都要求有這個文憑。本市除提供E.S.O.L.課程外，還以英語、西班牙語和法語提供G.E.D.課程。

我想獲得G.E.D.，但是我認為自己還沒準備好。有什麼課程或者計劃可以幫助我進行準備嗎？

City University of New York（紐約市立大學，即CUNY）在其13個學院中提供免費的成人基本技能課。欲瞭解詳情，可打電話1-212-541-0390（僅限英語）。

我真的很想回到中學上學，但是我有工作及其他職責，而且我的英語説得不好。會有哪所學校接受我嗎？

Manhattan Comprehensive Night and Day High School（曼哈頓日夜中學，位於240 Second Avenue，電話1-212-353-2010，英語、西班牙語和普通話）是為有以下情況的學生開辦的：年齡為17－21歲，上學曾遇到問題，只懂很少一點兒英文，或者有其他問題，使其不太可能通過必要的標準化考試和在合理時間內畢業。白天、晚上和週末都可以上課。教師、律師、義工及其他人員可以幫助學生解決任何需要，例如配眼鏡或者找住處。

有什麼入學條件嗎？

有。學校的校舍僅能容下800名學生，所以要求申請人必須已經取得了15個中學學分。外國學生必須能以某種語言閱讀和寫字，要高於小學水平，會進行一次入學考試。

需要更多幫忙嗎？

欲瞭解其他的教育計劃和機會，可打電話給以下機構：

- Archdiocese of New York, Superintendent of Schools（紐約大主教管區，督學）（第381頁）
- Chinese-American Planning Council（華人策劃協會）（第389頁）
- The Door（門）（第394頁）
- Forest Hills Community House（Forest Hills社區會所）（第395頁）
- Hellenic American Neighborhood Action Committee（美國希臘裔社區行動委員會，簡稱H.A.N.A.C.）（第396頁）
- Highbridge Community Life Center（Highbridge社區生活中心）（第397頁）
- New York City Department of Education, Office of Adult and Continuing Education（紐約市教育局，成人和繼續教育辦公室）（第406頁）
- New York City Workforce 1 Career Center（紐約市勞工第一職業中心）（第408頁）
- People's Fire House（人民消防站）（第411頁）

我能在紐約市立大學（CUNY）上大學課程嗎？

可以。許多移民到紐約市立大學上課並獲得學位，因為入學容易，學費很低。它有數千種課程，白天晚上在本市許多地方都可以上課。CUNY有一本名為 "Opportunities for Adults"（《成年人的機會》）的指南，是專門為幫助你這樣的人編寫的。內有課程、服務、學費等方面的資訊和電話號碼表。還有將工作、家庭責任和學習結合起來的成年人的成功故事。欲獲此指南，請給CUNY的Office of Admission Services（CUNY的招生服務辦公室）打電話1-212-997-2869（第391頁），或訪問CUNY的招生網站 www.cuny.edu。

我想在紐約市立大學的學院讀一個學位，但是我的英文不好，有什麼辦法嗎？

有。CUNY有語言沉浸計劃，可以幫助移民在開始上大學課程之前提高英語水平。白天晚上均可上課。欲瞭解詳情，可聯繫 CUNY的招生服務辦公室，電話1-212-997-2869（第391頁）。

■

"我 去的第一所學校是個成人E.S.L.[英語作為第二語言]學校。老師不允許學生在課堂上使用辭典，我們只能聽他解釋單字。為了讓我們理解 'sleeping' 這個詞，他躺到了地上。為了教我們怎樣報時，他帶來了一個鬧鐘。我仍然記得他講的一切，因為他的講述給我留下了深刻的印象，這種印象至今不忘。"

Ling Leung, 中國人, 1999年 [8]

理財

"在那種情況下，大多數同胞很快就把他們所有的積蓄委託給我管理，並且不要任何利息。我則把他們的和自己的儲蓄投資於房地產，並存入各家銀行。"

不知名的意大利移民, 1887年 [9]

■

只有懂得如何存錢、如何明智地購買你需要和想要的東西，才能在紐約（或者其他大多數地方）生活得長久。本章將帶你認知紐約市不同的銀行系統，向你解釋自動櫃員機，即A.T.M.是如何工作的，並且探討從哪些便宜的地方給你的國家匯款。

在紐約把錢存哪裡比較安全？

銀行和信用合作社是安全地存放你帶到美國的錢、你的工資或者政府救助金的地方。把錢存到銀行必須先開立一個帳戶，把錢存到信用合作社則必須先加入合作社。

如何在銀行或信用合作社開戶？

每家銀行和信用合作社對開戶都有不同的要求，所以需要諮詢銀行的工作人員或客戶代表。通常需要提供郵寄地址證明，例如水電費帳單，以及社會安全卡或號碼。（"文件證件"一章有關於獲得社會安全號和卡的資訊。）有時還需要出示兩種身份證件，通常是帶照片的證件，例如護照或者簽證、駕駛執照、工作證、非居民登記卡、入籍證、軍人證或者主要的信用卡。

我沒有駕駛執照，也沒有工作。到哪裡才能得到其他身份證明，以便用於開戶和其他事情？

你可以從Department of Motor Vehicles（機動車管理局）取得帶照片的非司機州身份證。具體說明請見網站www.nydmv.state.ny.us。因為911之後對安全的重視程度提高，這個局經常在其網站上更新可接受的身份證明和出生日期的列表。你也可以給該局打電話1-212-645-5550或1-718-966-6155（英語和西班牙語）。

銀行和信用合作社之間有什麼區別？

銀行是由一家公司所有，而信用合作社是由所有把錢投放到這家機構的人擁有，他們被稱為會員。要成為信用合作社的會員，你通常必須住在某個地區、或為某家公司工作、或是某個工會或社會組織的成員。由於銀行的營業點比信用合作社多得多，所以在這方面它可能比信用合作社更方便些。但是信用合作社只要求有很少的錢就可以加入，通常是10－20美元。儘管信用合作社通常提供較銀行略低的貸款利率和稍高的存款利息，但二者都提供類似的基本服務。

選擇銀行或信用合作社時，我應注意什麼？

問自己以下問題：
- 這家銀行或者信用合作社是否是由Federal Deposit Insurance Corporation（聯邦存款保險公司，簡稱F.D.I.C.）或National Credit Union Administration（國家信用合作社管理局,簡稱N.C.U.A.）保險的？
- 我必須要出示什麼身份證明才可以開戶？
- 月費的情況如何？
- 我必須在帳戶中保留最低存款額嗎？
- 我在開立帳戶或存錢（支票）後，要等多久才能取款？
- 外州的支票是否會受到不同的處理？
- 存錢、取錢或每月開支票是否有次數限制？
- 如果我不去營業點而使用自動櫃員機，銀行是否要收取額外的費用？
- 我能否得到信用卡？如果可以，年費和利率是多少？

選擇了銀行或者信用合作社以後，我該做什麼？

確定你想開哪種帳戶。最主要的兩種類型是支票帳戶和儲蓄帳戶。

需要更多幫忙嗎？

以下是在全市都有營業點的幾家大型銀行：

- Banco Popular（大眾銀行）（第382頁）
- Cathay Bank（國泰銀行）（第385頁）
- Chase（大通銀行）（第387頁）
- Citibank（花旗銀行）（第390頁）
- HSBC（匯豐銀行）（第397頁）

以下是全市的一些信用合作社：

- Bethex Federal Credit Union（Bethex聯邦信用合作社）（第383頁）
- Bushwick Cooperative Federal Credit Union（Bushwick聯邦信用合作社）（第384頁）
- Lower East Side People's Federal Credit Union（下東城人民聯邦信用合作社）（第400頁）
- University Settlement Federal Credit Union（大學街坊文教協會聯邦信用合作社）（第414頁）

銀行或信用合作社的帳戶是如何運作的？

你存入支票或儲蓄帳戶裡的錢叫做存款。你取出來的錢叫做取款。支票帳戶還允許你為帳戶裡的錢開支票。儲蓄帳戶會根據你的存款向你支付一個小百分比的錢，叫做利息。

支票帳戶付利息嗎？

有的時候付利息，但通常必須要在帳戶裡存到幾千美元才可以得到利息。

支票對我有什麼用？

可以用來支付帳單和其他開支，方式是或者通過郵寄支票的方式，或者把支票直接拿到給你寄帳單的地方。使用支票付款很方便，也便於掌握租金、食品雜貨、電話、汽油和電等費用的支出情況。

我開出的支票會被如何處理？

作為開支票對象的個人或企業會簽字並將其兌現。這就意味著，你開支票的金額會從你的帳戶提走，被作為開支票對象的人或企業得到，或者存入他們的銀行帳戶。

我能拿回我開的支票嗎？

有些銀行會把已經兌現的支票退回給開支票的人。已經被兌現的支票叫做註銷支票。還有一些銀行不退還支票，但會寄給你一張由你開出的已兌現支票清單，這個清單叫做對帳單。如果有人懷疑你是否已經付了賬，你的註銷支票或列出已兌現支票的對帳單就是你已經付過賬的證明。

關於銀行帳戶還有什麼重要的事項要瞭解？

■ 一定要仔細地對你開過的每一張支票保存記錄。

■ 仔細地為每一次存款和取款保存記錄。

■ 仔細檢查每一份對帳單，並和你自己的記錄進行對比，確保一切吻合。一定要扣除任何服務費或支票費，並加上你賺得的利息。

■ 如果你有疑問或對某些事不清楚，可以帶上你的支票簿和對帳單去銀行找客戶服務代表詢問。

■ 當你訂支票時，別忘了在上面印上你的地址號碼。

我見到的支票上的左下角有"MEMO"的字樣。這是什麼意思？

這裡是你為了付賬而寫下帳號的地方，或者寫下附注，以提醒你這張支票是做什麼用的。

如果有人付我支票，我該怎麼做？

你必須在支票背面簽名，這叫做背書。然後到銀行或支票兌現處兌換成現金，或者存入你的銀行帳戶，或者用自動櫃員機存錢，本章後文還將進行介紹。

在支票上簽名有什麼規則嗎？

沒有什麼規則，但是要注意一些事項。一定要用墨水筆簽字，並且一定要在你背書並打算存入你的銀行帳戶的支票背面寫上"for deposit only"（僅用於存款）的字樣和你的銀行帳號。這樣，如果你丟了這張支票，其他人也不能拿來兌現。如果你想去銀行而不是用自動櫃員機存款，最好等進了銀行再為支票背書。這樣，如果你丟了這張支票，其他人也不能冒充你來兌現。

如果我開的支票金額超過了我帳戶中的金額會怎麼樣？

如果你開的支票金額大於帳戶中的金額，你的支票會跳票，也就是會被拒付，並退回到你的銀行。不要這樣做。你可能會被銀行或收到被拒支票的公司罰款。此外你還將得到不良的信用評級，使你難以得到信用卡或進行分期付款購物等等。

什麼是儲蓄帳戶？它是如何運作的？

儲蓄帳戶適合於你短期內不需要的錢。銀行會為你存在儲蓄帳戶中的錢支付利息。不同銀行和不同類型的帳戶利息也不同。你可以以現金或銀行支票的形式從儲蓄帳戶中提取款項。存款既可以存現金，也可以存支票，但是你可能必須等5-20天才能取出你以支票存入的款項。

如果我沒有銀行或信用合作社的帳戶，怎樣才能兌現支票和支付帳單？

支票兌現服務機構可以讓你將支票兌現，並支付某些帳單，但要收取費用。記住，這裡收的費用通常比銀行和信用合作社為同樣服務收取的費用高得多。

支票兌現服務機構是如何運作的？

支票兌現服務機構可兌現工資支票及其他支票，但要收取費用。有些服務機構可以兌現私人支票；另一些服務機構則不兌現私人支票，或者要為此收取更高的費用。你還可以在某些支票兌現服務機構支付帳單，也要收費。

如果我沒有銀行或信用合作社的帳戶，怎樣才能給我家寄錢？

Western Union, 1-800-325-6000（或西班牙語幫助電話 1-800-325-4045）（第415頁）和MoneyGram, 1-800-926-9400（第403頁）等電匯服務機構可以以電匯方式向世界各地匯款或接收來自世界各地的匯款，但要收取費用。你還可以買匯票，匯票可以用於支付費用和寄錢。根據支票清算或到期日及其他規則，它們都有不同的價格和不同的身份要求和時間要求，因此要多看看，貨比三家。

電匯服務是如何運作的？

你要去電匯機構填表，只能用英語和西班牙語填寫。要告訴機構的職員想匯多少錢，以及收款人的姓名和地址，接受款項的人被稱為收款人。你還應該把要寄的錢和該機構收取的服務費交給機構的職員。職員會給你一個號碼，通常叫做控制號，你必須把這個號碼告訴收款人。在一天之內，寄出的錢就可以以收款人的本國貨幣或者美元領取了。要領取匯來的錢，收款人必須去電匯機構的營業點，把控制號告訴辦事員。

警告！

千萬不要從任何國家把現金裝在美國或者國際郵件裡寄。在美國，通過郵件和DHL（敦豪速遞公司）、Federal Express（聯邦快遞公司）等國際郵遞公司寄錢是非法的。

> **使用A.T.M.的費用加起來也會不少，**
> **所以要儘量只使用屬於你的銀行或**
> **信用合作社的A.T.M.。**

我可以把錢匯到銀行帳戶裡嗎？

可以。如果你或者收款人在銀行有帳戶，而且你知道帳戶號碼，可以利用匯款服務把錢匯到這個帳戶裡。

我怎麼能知道哪些匯款機構可以信任？

向曾經成功地往家裡匯過款的同胞打聽一下。他們可能知道可以幫助你的聲譽較好的代理人或者服務代表。如果Western Union, 1-800-325-6000（西班牙語幫助電話為1-800-325-4045）（第415頁）在你的國家有分支機構，它可能是最經濟、最有效的匯款方式。如果收款人在你的國家有銀行帳戶，通過銀行電匯是很保險的。

我需要把錢匯到沒有銀行或Western Union分支幾構的地方。能做到嗎？

通常會有小的私營機構處理這種業務，例如Delgado Travel（Delgado旅行社）（第393頁）。向熟人打聽一下他們通過哪些聲譽好的機構匯款。第一次最好少匯一些錢作為試驗。一旦你確認收款人收到了錢，就可以匯較大的金額。

匯票是如何運作的？

你在銀行、支票兌現處或者郵局買一張匯票，上面的面額正是你要給別人匯款的數額或你想付的帳單的數額。匯票通常在郵局買最便宜，一旦在兌現前丟失或者被盜，也可以追蹤得到。不是所有的企業都接受匯票。

什麼是自動櫃員機，它是如何運作的？

自動櫃員機通常稱為A.T.M，屬於銀行或信用合作社，可以允許你每天24小時使用大多數銀行功能。你的銀行或者信用合作社會發給你一張A.T.M.卡，並讓你選擇個人識別號，或者叫PIN，作為口令。每一台A.T.M.都會一步一步地告訴你如何使用，但所有的A.T.M.基本上都以同樣的方式工作：

1. 把你的卡插入或者刷過A.T.M的狹槽。
2. 在鍵區輸入你的PIN號。
3. 完成交易。你可以取現金、存款、轉賬和查看餘額。

4. 每次使用A.T.M.時,一定要取得收據,也就是表明你處理賬目情況的一張紙。
   把交易情況記入你的支票簿或者儲蓄帳戶記錄。

我只會很少一點兒英文。A.T.M.機上的指令會用我的母語嗎?

紐約市大多數A.T.M.都使用英語和西班牙語指令。在有大量說其他語言的移民的
地區,機器上也會有相關語言的指令。

A.T.M.機是免費使用的嗎?

不是。通常你開有帳戶的銀行或信用合作社會允許你每月免費使用它的A.T.M.機
進行一定次數的存款和取款交易。但是屬於其他銀行的機器會自動扣除費用,通
常是在每次使用時從你的帳戶中扣除75美分到1.5美元不等。這些費用加起來也會
不少,所以要儘量少用不屬於你的銀行或信用合作社的A.T.M.。

我能用我的A.T.M.卡買東西嗎?

只有當你的銀行或者信用合作社允許,並且你的收入足夠多,或者已經存入足夠
多的錢從而有資格時。如果你這樣使用你的卡,它就被叫做簽帳卡。

簽帳卡是如何運作的?

你在商店結賬櫃檯的一台小機器上刷你的卡,然後輸入PIN碼。這就授權銀行或
者信用合作社從你的帳戶中扣除你購買的物品的花費,就象開支票一樣。有些銀
行可能會收費,就象它們對使用A.T.M機收費一樣。

警告!

A.T.M.使用很方便,但要注意以下事項:

■ 得到A.T.M.卡後一定要立即在背面簽名,這樣一旦卡片丟失或者被盜,別人
也難以使用。

■ 不要在卡片上或者與卡片放在一起的紙上寫下你的PIN號碼。

■ 不要讓任何人看到你鍵入PIN號,或者在你取款後跟著你一起離開機器。

■ 不要在夜晚一個人使用A.T.M.。

■ 儘量在封閉的、光照充足的地方使用A.T.M.機,少用街上的A.T.M.機。

■ 千萬不要讓任何人,尤其是陌生人使用你的A.T.M.卡,即使是在你不知道如
何使用機器時別人主動提出要幫助你。

■ 在使用A.T.M.機取出現金後,一定要在離開門廳或機器前把卡、錢和收據放
進口袋或錢包裡。

什麼是信用卡？

信用卡讓你先買商品和服務，以後再付賬。有時可以用信用卡借款，叫做現金預付。

怎樣才能得到一張信用卡？

首先，你必須有一個社會安全號和很多其他證件文件。你還必須填寫一份申請。銀行、商店、支票兌現服務處和許多其他地方都可以找到申請表。銀行將研究你的全部申請資料，以決定你是否有能力使用這種卡。如果被批准，你將可以用這張卡買一定金額的商品。這個金額就是你的信貸限額。在每月底時，銀行或信用卡公司會寄來一份對帳單，上面列出你買的所有東西，並通知這個月的最低還款額。

信用卡是免費使用的嗎？

有些是，但是許多信用卡要收取年費。如果在任何一個月你不全額支付所購商品的費用或歸還你在該月所借的現金，你會為未歸還的餘額被收取一筆費用。這筆費用被稱為利息或信貸費用，大約是餘額的5%－21%，或者更高。

我有一張本國的信用卡。可以在這裡使用嗎？

如果是American Express卡（美國運通卡）、Visa卡（維薩卡）或者MasterCard（萬事達卡）等主要信用卡，通常可以使用。只要保證帳單能寄給你或轉到你在紐約的地址。

我有工作，但是我需要更多的錢。我的老家不能給我寄錢，我也用不起信用卡。我該怎麼辦？

如果你合格的話，銀行或信用合作社可能會借給你錢，你要為此支付利息。每一家銀行或信用合作社都有不同的規定和條件，所以最好詢問它們的出納員或者信

警告！

總會有人會為很高的利息借給你錢。他們被稱為放高利貸者，經常對急需錢的貧窮移民進行掠奪。他們時常在移民工作的工廠和居住的地區附近逗留。儘量不要向這些人借錢，因為你可能無法還清他們的利息和費用，然後他們會命令你為他們做越來越多的事。這些事通常是非法的或令人生厭的，你是不會想去做的。如果你不照高貸款者說的做，他們可能會威脅要傷害你或你的家庭。

關於信用卡的要和不要

- 如果你不想支付利息或信貸費用，只有在購買你每月有能力支付的商品時才使用信用卡。
- 不要忘記付款，否則你的卡可能會被註銷。
- 保存好所有的信用卡收據，這樣才會知道你用信用卡買了什麼，花費是多少。
- 檢查每月的信用卡對帳單，如果你為沒買過的東西被收了費，應立即告知銀行或信用卡公司。

貸員。

■

"**我**的第一份工作是掃地。我的第一張支票是那個星期掙到的125美元。我想起厄瓜多爾的貨幣，在那裡月薪80美元就不錯了。所以當我得到五天工作賺到的支票時，我說,'哦，上帝，我發財了。' 但過了三、四個星期我就沒那麼興奮了，因為我要付房租、買公車的票、買食物。我意識到自己並不像開始時想像得那麼富有。"

Jose Zambrano, 厄瓜多爾人, 2001年 [10]

醫療保健和保險

"**我**們從來沒看過醫生。如果溜冰扭傷了手腕,我們總是去找祖母。她會拿出一根繩子,把它拉開、浸在蛋清裡,然後用繃帶把它綁在我們的手腕上,它會變得像上石膏一樣堅硬,這樣手腕就會好轉一些。她就像脊椎按摩師。祖母是一個地道的意大利式祖母。她還用某種油來給我們按摩。治療發燒,她就會揉搓我們手上所有的肌肉然後拉動一個手指。如果嗓子疼,她會揉搓我們的淋巴結然後拔一根頭髮。確實有效。"

Marie Cutaia,意大利移民的孫女,回憶1920年代 [11]

■

二十一世紀的美國醫療系統已經從家庭醫護發展到以基因為基礎的疾病檢查、顯微外科、末期病人收容。不論是自費還是通過保險或政府救濟,你能為上述服務及許多其他服務付得起多少錢將在很大程度上決定你能得到哪種醫療保健。紐約市有很多不同的公立和私立醫院和診所,包括低收費的和向無合法身份的移民提供治療的。紐約市還有很多不同種類的私營的和受政府資助的保險計劃。

　　本章將介紹本市的幾種基本的醫療保健服務情況,同時推薦你到一些機構瞭解關於服務的更多訊息,以及你有資格享受哪些服務,怎樣才能得到你需要的照顧和保險。

如果我傷、病得很重,需要立即治療,我該怎麼辦?
盡快去附近最近的醫院。

如果我傷、病得太重，無法自己去醫院或看醫生，怎麼辦？

打911緊急電話。告訴接線員你的困難以及所在位置。救護車會把你接送到附近醫院的急診室。

911緊急電話的接線員會講我的母語嗎？

很快就可以找到會講很多種語言的接線員。

如果出現緊急情況，但我被送到我負擔不起費用或沒有保險的醫院怎麼辦？

醫院如果拒絕為你進行急診治療就是違法的。可以向醫院詢問你是否有資格根據收入和支付能力享受費用減免，或者如果你沒有合法身份，是否能夠享受緊急Medicaid。如果你收到了賬單，也不必一次付清，可以和醫院商量一個付款時間表。

我只會講很少的英語。醫院裡的人能理解我的意思嗎？

Patients' bill of rights（病人權利法案）要求醫院提供一名口譯或翻譯。即使你帶了親友為你進行翻譯，但仍應該堅持讓醫院給你找一名翻譯。

如果不屬於緊急情況卻需要住院，而我又沒有保險，怎麼辦？

你所前往的醫院必須替你找一家不需要保險就可以接收你的醫院。所有公立醫院必須為你提供照顧，不論你有無保險、移民身份和支付能力如何。

我沒有保險，也付不起太多的費用。如果生病了，但又不屬於緊急情況，我該怎麼辦？

如果你有輕微的不適或糖尿病、哮喘或愛滋病等慢性病，你仍然可以在醫院急診室裡接受治療，但是可能要等很長時間才可以看醫生。儘量不要在星期六晚上去急診室，對於大多數急診室來說那是最忙的時候。

如果沒有危及生命的不適，應該去免費或費用較低的診所。你有時可以在診所約診，這樣就不用等太久。紐約的公立醫院和診所可以為沒有保險而且無法承

獲得治療

當本書付印時，紐約市的醫院如果拒絕為沒有合法身份的移民治療是違法的。紐約市的公立醫院的官方政策是不得報告移民身份。私立醫院或診所也沒有被要求或鼓勵報告你的移民身份。

需要更多幫忙嗎？

以下醫院和健康保健機構提供免費的或低費用的服務：

- Bellevue Hospital Center（Bellevue 醫院中心）（第383頁）
- Charles B. Wang Community Health Center（王嘉廉社區醫療中心）（第387頁）
- Community Healthcare Network（社區保健網）（第393頁）
- Lutheran Medical Center（路德教會醫療中心）（第401頁）
- Morris Heights Health Center（Morris Heights 健康中心）（第404頁）
- Promesa（第411頁）

擔保健費用的病人看病。公立醫院的列表可以在以下網址找到：**www.nyc.gov/html/hhc.home/html**。他們提供多種一般性的和專科醫療保健，像牙科問題、糖尿病和藥物濫用的治療。你將被要求分享你的收入情況，並和醫院或診所討論付費方案。如果你打電話的醫院或親自去的醫院不提供你需要的服務，可以要求那裡的工作人員送你去提供你需要的服務的醫院。

治療常見傷、輕微不適或慢性病的醫院和診所有哪些？

- 所有紐約市所屬的公立醫院、診所或護理計劃。
- 有些小學、中學的學校保健診所。其規模很不相同，小的只是一個護士每星期去一次學校，提供視力和聽力檢查，大的則是服務項目齊全、滿足學生身心健康需求的診所。
- 衛生局的診所診斷並治療性病和肺結核；打各種免疫針；檢查乳腺癌；照顧孕婦、新生兒的母親和新生兒；同時為愛滋病病毒感染提供匿名的咨詢和測試。

如果沒有保險，我需要為醫院或診所的非急診治療付多少費用？

通常取決於你的收入。詢問醫院或診所是否浮動計費，也就是收費的數額與收入相對應，這樣收入少的人只需付很少的費用或不付費。如果你一定要付費，通常可以分期支付。

我必須向醫院或診所出示收入證明嗎？

是的。你通常會被要求提供最近的工資單或僱主的信，儘管有些醫院和診所接受自己申報收入的自我聲明表。

因此我是否真的需要健康保險？

是的。你不能預測你的醫療費用會是多少。如果你和你的家人很少生病，醫療保健支出可能會很低。但是，如果你或者你的家人生病或受傷，你的支出就會很高－甚至高得讓你自己無法負擔。如果你符合條件，應該儘量參加健康保險。

每份工作都有健康保險嗎？

不，但大多數全職工作會提供某種健康保險，大多數半職工作則不提供。如果你能通過工作得到保險，通常全部或大部分支出將從你的工資中扣除。

如果我有健康保險，每次看醫生或按處方買藥時，我都必須支付全部費用嗎？

不一定。看醫生或處方藥等一些服務可能會向你收取費用，通常為5至20美元，這叫做co-payment（共付額）。有些保險計劃沒有共付額，而是要求你支付看醫生或處方等費用的若干百分點。

我丟了工作，我的健康保險怎麼辦？

一種叫做Cobra的聯邦法允許你自己支付最多18個月的集體健康保險，儘管Cobra要貴得多。保費標準與你的雇主為你支付的集體保費的標準相同。Medicaid向低收入、無法負擔健康保險的人提供保險，它也許可以為你的配偶及子女支付家庭保險。

我的配偶的工作保險計劃也為我提供保險，如果我們離婚了或者我的配偶去世了，該怎麼辦？

根據Cobra，你自己可以支付保險費用，同時你家裡的其他成員也可能有資格享受Medicaid提供的保險。

如果我的僱主不支付健康保險，或者我不工作而且無法承擔保險怎麼辦？

你可以自己購買健康保險，但是私營保險非常貴，一個月要繳300到500美元，甚至更多。如果你能承擔就去買。另外，許多低收入的個人和家庭符合免費或低費用的健康保險計劃，如Medicaid、Family Health Plus、Child Health Plus或者Healthy NY，本章後文將加以具體介紹。

怎樣才能知道紐約的免費或低費用健康保險計劃的內容，以及我是否符合要求，如何申請？

以下幾個問題的回答將說明這些計劃。欲進一步瞭解關於它們的基本情況，請打本市Human Resources Administration（人力資源管理局，簡稱H.R.A.）的Info Line

需要更多幫忙嗎？

以下機構提供如何獲得健康保險的資訊：

- Asian Americans for Equality（亞洲人平等會，簡稱A.A.F.E.）（第382頁）
- Citizens Advice Bureau（公民顧問局，簡稱C.A.B.）（第390頁）
- The Door（門）（第394頁）
- Managed Care Consumer Assistance Program（管理保健消費者援助計劃，簡稱 M.C.C.A.P.），Community Service Society of New York（紐約社區服務協會）（第401頁）

（資訊專線）1-877-472-8411（第397頁）。

欲查詢你及你的家人是否符合這些計劃的要求，請打Department of Health and Mental Hygiene（健康與心理衛生局）的自動按鍵式電話熱線HealthStat, 1-888-692-6116（第395頁）。你會被問到一些問題，以確定你和你的家人符合哪種計劃的要求，以及最方便你們去註冊的地點。

另外，你還可以去社區組織的辦公室、社會服務組織、健康計劃及參加這些健康計劃的醫生和醫院、以及城市健康診所。欲得到這些地方和團體的地址以及聯繫資料，請打HealthStat line（HealthStat專線）（第395頁）的電話或訪問由Mayor's Office of Health Insurance Access（市長健康保險辦公室）辦的網站，www.nyc.gov/html/hia/ html/places.html。

什麼是Medicaid？

Medicaid 是向部分低收入並且無法承擔健康保險的人群提供的保險。

沒有合法身份的移民能否得到Medicaid？

只有當他們懷孕或需要急診醫療並且符合其他資格要求條件時才可以。但其他移民都可以。在紐約，合法移民和被United States Citizenship and Immigration Services（美國公民和移民服務局，簡稱U.S.C.I.S.）稱為Prucol的沒有合法身份的移民可能符合Medicaid的條件，無論他們是什麼時候到的美國。Prucol分為幾種，包括被批准居留或暫停驅逐，並允許無限期留在美國的移民。這些移民必須符合其他資格條件（如收入水平）才能註冊參加Medicaid。

Medicaid申請表上沒有要求填寫其他家庭成員的移民情況，紐約州不與聯邦政府分享表上的這些資料。作為United States Department of Homeland Security（美國國土安全部）的一個機構的U.S.C.I.S.已經決定，參加Medicaid不會影響家裡任何成員申請綠卡、成為美國公民、贊助家庭成員做保人或進入、離開美國旅行。

如何才能知道我是否符合Medicaid的要求，如果符合，到哪裡去申請？

接受政府救濟或福利救濟的人自動符合要求。殘障人士也符合要求。欲查詢你是否符合條件以及到哪裡申請，請打HealthStat line（HealthStat專線）1-888-692-6116（第395頁），或H.R.A. Info Line（人力資源管理局資訊專線）1-877-472-8411（第397頁），或者訪問網站www.nyc.gov/html/hra/html/serv_medicaid.html。

申請Medicaid應該帶些什麼？

儘量將以下文件都帶上：年齡證明（例如出生證明）；國籍或移民身份證明；你的住址證明，例如房租收據或房東聲明；如果有工作，現在的工資支票的票根；其他收入的證明，比如社會安全支票票根或銀行存摺。

申請的過程是否很困難？

是的。在登記註冊以前，所有Medicaid申請者都面臨許多官僚政治的挑戰，而且移民必須證明他們的合法身份。由於Prucol種類繁多以及所有需要的表格和信件，他們面臨的困難尤其大。但一定要記住，不要在得到你有權得到的福利之前就放棄。

如果我符合Medicaid的參加條件，我拿什麼向醫生或診所證明呢？

你會收到一張保險身份證明卡，以便在需要醫療服務時使用。

Medicaid會為我和我的家人需要的醫療保健負擔全部費用嗎？

不會。有些服務是不在承保範圍內的，而且在得到某些其他服務之前，你必須先核對它們是否在承保範圍之內。這叫做prior approval（預先核准）。

我需要為Medicaid付費嗎？在看接受Medicaid病人的醫生時，需要付費嗎？

不需要。保險是免費的，而且服務也不收其他費用，即co-payments（共付額）。

什麼是Family Health Plus？

Family Health Plus是面向19歲到64歲、沒有以個人名義或通過工作購買健康保

需要更多幫忙嗎？

你可以在以下地方得到有關Medicaid的更多資訊：

- 紐約州的 Medicaid 幫助專線：1-800-541-2831（英語、西班牙語、廣東話、普通話）
- Medical and Health Research Association of New York City（紐約市醫療和健康研究協會，簡稱M.H.R.A.）（第402頁）
- New York City Workforce 1 Career Center（紐約市勞工第一職業中心）（第408頁）

需要更多幫忙嗎？

以下團體可以幫助你申請Family Health Plus：

- Alianza Dominicana（多米尼加聯盟）（第381頁）
- Caribbean Women's Health Association（加勒比婦女健康協會）（第385頁）
- Chinese-American Planning Council（華人策劃協會）（第389頁）
- Medical and Health Research Association of New York City（紐約市醫療和健康研究協會）（第402頁）

險，而收入又超出了Medicaid標準的人群設立的公共健康保險計劃。它提供免費的綜合保險，包括預防、主要保健、住院、處方和其他服務。

沒有合法身份的移民是否符合Family Health Plus的條件？
不符合。沒有合法身份的移民不能享受Family Health Plus。

如何才能知道自己是否符合Family Health Plus的條件？如果我符合條件，去哪裡申請？
19歲到64歲，沒有以個人名義或通過工作享受健康保險，同時也不符合其他公共健康保險計劃（例如Medicare或Medicaid）的參加要求的紐約居民可以申請Family Health Plus。欲瞭解地點和聯繫資訊，可打HealthStat line（HealthStat專線）1-888-692-6116（第395頁），或者造訪網站www.nyc.gov/html/hia/html/places.html。

Family Health Plus的資格要求中有沒有收入限制？
你和你的家人收入是否符合Family Health Plus的要求取決於家庭人口的多少。

我家裡有銀行帳戶，是否仍可以申請Family Health Plus？
是的。對其他財產和資源沒有限制。

我懷孕了，是否可以參加Family Health Plus？
可以，如果你符合收入條件，但這個條件比Medicaid的條件要高一些。

什麼是Child Health Plus？
Child Health Plus是由紐約州資助的保險計劃，其面向對象是沒有保險的19歲以下青少年。

我的孩子沒有合法身份，他們可以得到Child Health Plus嗎？

無論移民身份如何，19歲以下的青少年都符合Child Health Plus的要求。

　　Child Health Plus的申請表上沒有詢問其他家庭成員的移民情況，同時紐約州也不與聯邦政府分享表格上的資料。U.S.C.I.S.已經決定，使用Child Health Plus不會影響家裡其他成員申請綠卡、成為公民、贊助家庭成員做保人或在美國國內和國外旅行。

我需要為Child Health Plus付費嗎？

你可能需要付一筆數額很小的月費才能參加這個計劃，但是當你的孩子看醫生時，你不需要付任何費用。

Child Health Plus的承保範圍是什麼？

如果你的孩子符合Child Health Plus的要求，你要選擇一個本地提供者，他/她會決定根據計劃你可以享受哪些服務，看哪些醫生。

我怎樣才能知道我的孩子是否符合要求？如果符合要求，如何申請？

打HealthStat line（HealthStat專線）1-888-692-6116（第395頁），或者訪問網站www.nyc.gov/html/hia/html/places.html。欲瞭解可以註冊登記的地點以及關於Child Health Plus 的更多資訊，可打電話1-800-698-4543（英語和西班牙語）。

什麼是Healthy NY？

Healthy NY是一個面向符合某些資格要求條件的在職人員的低費用健康保險。

如何才能知道我是否符合Healthy NY的資格要求？如果符合要求，如何申請？

可打HealthStat line（HealthStat專線）1-888-692-6116（第395頁），或者訪問網站www.nyc.gov/ html/hia/html/places.html。

什麼是Medicare？

Medicare是一種為65歲以上老人以及不滿65歲、接受社會安全殘障補助超過24個月的殘障人士設立的聯邦健康保險計劃。它可以支付部分醫院費用和醫療保健費用。它分為Medicare A部分和Medicare B部分。

我的移民身份是否會影響我能否享受Medicare？

要享受Medicare，你必須是具有合法身份的移民，但不一定是公民。總括來說，如果你超過65歲、是美國公民或永久居民，而且你或你的配偶已經在享受Medicare的崗位上工作超過了10年，你就符合參加要求。

對於任何一部分Medicare，是否有標準的費用？

每一部分都有一定的月費，又稱"保費"，並且在某個時期內你必須為治療支付一定數額的費用，由Medicare支付其餘部分。你支付的那部分被稱為deductibles（自付額）。Medicare的兩部分還有專項資金供你每次看醫生或使用病房時支付費用，它們叫做co-payment（共付額）。

Medicare A部分支付哪些費用？

當你在留院三天後被收治在醫院的私人半專用病房或被送到專業的療養院時，Medicare A部分（醫院保險）將幫助支付護理費用。當你在醫院或專業療養院時，它還將為幾品脫的血液支付費用。它還為末期患者支付經Medicare批准的收容所照顧，並為某些家庭健康保健服務付費。它不支付個人用房、私人護士或房間裡的電話或電視的費用。

Medicare B部分支付哪些費用？

Medicare B部分（醫療保險）幫助支付以下費用：除常規體檢之外的醫生服務；門診病人醫療和手術服務及用品；在門診病人手術中心進行的診斷試驗和得到許可的手術；作為門診病人時得到的血液；輪椅、病床和助步車等耐用醫療器械。它還為Medicare A部分所列的某些家庭健康保健服務承保。

Medicare還為以下項目支付費用：

- 救護車服務（當其他形式的運輸會威脅到你的健康時）
- 人造眼和人造肢體及其備用部件
- 手臂、腿部、背部和頸的支架
- 脊柱按摩療法服務，僅限於對脊柱的操作
- 急診醫療
- 白內障手術後一副標準眼鏡框和適當鏡片
- 由Medicare承保的移植手術的藥物療法
- 有斑點的眼睛退化治療
- 糖尿病或腎病患者的醫學營養療法
- 某些醫藥用品
- 個別的門診病人處方藥物
- 某些預防性服務
- 假肢器官，包括胸部修補物
- 某些醫生第二意見
- 專業人員（包括診所的社工、醫生助手和執業護士）的服務
- 糖尿病患者的治療鞋

- 在某些條件下在Medicare許可的中心進行的移植手術
- X光、核磁共振、CAT掃描、心電圖和其它診斷檢查。

Medicare A部分（醫院保險）的費用是多少？

大多數人不需要為A部分支付保險費，因為他們或他們的配偶在工作時已經繳過Medicare稅了。但是他們可能要支付其他自付額和共付額，這兩項的數額是不確定的。

我沒有繳過Medicare稅，是否依然可以享受Medicare A部分的服務（醫院保險）？

如果你或你的配偶在工作時沒有繳過Medicare稅，而你的年齡已經超過65歲，你可能依然可以購買A計劃。打電話1-800-633-4227（英語和西班牙語）或者訪問網址www.medicare.gov。

Medicare B部分（醫療保險）的費用是多少？

2003年初的月保費是58.70美元。這個費率每年都會調整；你可以打電話1-800-633-4227（英語和西班牙語）或訪問網址www.medicare.gov瞭解最新資訊。

我無法承擔Medicare B部分（醫療保險），該怎麼辦？

有四種計劃是面向需要幫助支付Medicare保費的低收入人群的。可以打人力資源管理局的資訊專線1-877-472-8411（第397頁）。

做好準備！

早在緊急情況發生以前，就要準備一個清單，列出你要告訴醫生和護士的事情，這樣你就可以帶著它去醫院。清單內容應該包括：

- 得過的嚴重疾病
- 曾做過的手術
- 過敏情況
- 慢性病
- 服過的藥（如果有時間，把它們一起帶上）
- 症狀，像疼痛、赤紅、噁心、麻木、腫脹等等，以及這些症狀是何時開始的
- 家族病史
- 生日
- 社會安全號（如果有的話）
- 姓名、地址和僱主的電話號碼（如果你有工作）

我如何才能參加Medicare？

本市Department for the Aging（老人局）有一個叫做UNIForm的篩選工具，它可以幫助查明你是否符合聯邦、州以及市一級的主要福利計劃。全市所有的老年人中心都有這個工具。欲查詢離你最近的老年人中心，可以打電話給New York City Department for the Aging Senior Call Center（紐約市老人局老年電話中心），1-212-442-1000（英語、西班牙語、廣東話、普通話以及其他語言）。你也可以訪問網址home.nyc.gov/html/dfta。你也可以通過Social Security Administration（社會安全局）或打電話1-800-772-1213（英語和西班牙語）進行註冊。

我必須用無法承擔的藥物治療，我該怎麼辦？

很多健康保險計劃不承擔處方藥物的費用。還有一些計劃對其承擔費用的藥物的支出或品牌有限制。以下這些計劃也許會對你支付處方藥有幫助：

- AIDS Drug Assistance Program（愛滋病藥物援助計劃，簡稱A.D.A.P.）為感染愛滋病病毒以及有相關病症的低收入人群支付藥費。電話1-800-542-2437（英語和西班牙語）。
- Elder Pharmaceutical Insurance Coverage（老人藥物保險，簡稱EPIC）是面向65歲以上低收入人群的處方藥物計劃。欲瞭解更多資訊以及申請，可打EPIC的免費服務電話1-800-332-3742（英語和西班牙語）。

我沒有合法身份，是否還有資格參加低價處方藥物計劃？

有。不管你的移民身份如何，你都有可能符合A.D.A.P.和EPIC的參加要求。

低價處方藥物計劃是否有收入限制和共付額？

是的，但有關規定會有調整，所以最好打上面提供的電話瞭解最新的收入限制以及共付額標準。

■

"我 八年前來到這個國家時，對於生病、急診或簡單體檢的去處，簡直是一無所知。跟許多其他人一樣，我們來到這個國家沒有合法的證件，所以都很害怕。其實真不該那樣，因為我們把健康甚至生命都置於危險中了。幸運的是，美國許多城市的健康保險系統都很有效率，而且一般來說也很公平。最值得稱道的是，有一些服務是免費的，而且歧視是違法的。"

Maricela Gonzalez，墨西哥人，1999年[12]

安全

"**我**把社區的人召集到一起，成立了美國印度人團結會。我們組織了五次示威活動。自從我們採取了行動以後，形勢有了好轉。以前，他們每天都攻擊印度人。攻擊過20多個不同的家庭。他們衝進住家、印度人開的商店。攻擊去購物的印度婦女。他們在街上對印度人指指點點，並毆打他們。但現在情況得到了控制。我們在街上走時，沒有那麼害怕了。"

Hardayal Singh, 印度人, 1977年 [13]

∎

紐約的治安狀況可能處於過去二十年來最好的時期。自1990年代中期以來，犯罪率穩定下降，911事件以後，犯罪率甚至下降得更快。

但911事件本身證明，這座城市正面臨越來越大的恐怖主義威脅。這一威脅已經對許多移民的生活產生了重大影響。

911襲擊事件導致了United States Department of Homeland Security（美國國土安全部）的成立，以前由Immigration and Naturalization Service（移民歸化局）或I.N.S.執行的很多職能都由這個新部門接管了。該部的Bureau of Immigration and Customs Enforcement（美國移民和海關執法局，簡稱B.I.C.E.）主動搜尋簽證已經過期的人、沒有執行驅逐出境令的人、或者沒有合法身份的人。有合法身份但是已經被宣判有罪的人很可能被驅逐出境。

本章將重點講述居住在美國和紐約市的移民的權利和安全問題。安全涉及許多事項，其中包括如何保護你自己免遭強姦、搶劫等罪行，以及如果你成了犯罪受害人、或者是警方、B.I.C.E.不當行為的受害人，你該怎麼辦。

警方可以在任何時候進入我家進行搜查嗎？
不能。除非警官帶有必須由法官簽字的有效命令，否則你有權拒絕警察進入你家。這個命令被稱為許可令。

有時警方可以在沒有許可令的時候搜查我家嗎？
是的。在緊急情況下，警官可以不持許可令就進入你家搜查，緊急情況的例子比如有人在你家尖叫著求助，或者警方正在追捕某人。

United States Department of Justice（美國司法部）有可能會允許利用911事件以後制定的聯邦條例讓地方警察局在無許可令的情況下就逮捕被懷疑違反移民法的移民。但是還不清楚地方警察局（包括紐約警察局）會如何解讀和利用這些條例。此外，影響移民的政策經常發生變化，所以最好向本指南後面的資源名錄中列出的移民支持組織瞭解一下，或者，如果你付得起費用，最好向聲譽良好的移民律師瞭解一下。

如果警方有許可令，但是我不想讓他們搜查我家，應該怎麼辦？
一定要告訴警察你不同意進行搜查。這將使搜查的範圍僅限於許可令中指定的部分。問一下你是否可以監視搜查過程。如果可以，你應該作筆記，記下警官的姓名、警徽號碼和所屬機構等內容。儘快給律師或移民支持者打電話。

如果警方強行進入我家搜查該怎麼辦？
按以上的方法做。

如果警察在街上讓我站住該怎麼辦？
你有權問警察你是否可以走。要有禮貌，把手放在警察看得見的地方。不要跑開

必須帶上以下物品才能出門

除了簽證、工作許可證、出入境卡（I-94卡）等移民文件或綠卡外，還要隨身攜帶可以接你電話、聲譽良好的移民律師的姓名和電話號碼。移民法很難掌握，而且自911事件以來進行了許多修改，還可能要做更多的修改。移民和海關執法局不會向你說明你的權利或選擇。一旦遇到B.I.C.E.的探員，馬上給你的律師打電話。如果無法打電話或電話打不通，要一直設法聯繫到律師。

需要更多幫忙嗎？

以下機構和團體可以提供法律咨詢和介紹服務：

- Asian American Legal Defense and Education Fund（亞美法律援助處）（第381頁）
- The Bronx Defenders（布朗士辯護人）（第384頁）
- Caribbean Women's Health Association（加勒比婦女健康協會，簡稱C.W.H.A.）（第385頁）
- CUNY Law School－Main Street Legal Services, Immigration and Refugee Rights（紐約市立大學法學院－緬因街法律服務，移民和難民權利）（第393頁）
- Legal Aid Society（法律援助協會）（第400頁）
- New York Association for New Americans（紐約新美國人聯合會，簡稱N.Y.A.N.A.）（第404頁）
- New York City Commission on Human Rights（紐約市人權委員會）（第405頁）
- Queens Legal Services（皇后區法律服務）（第412頁）
- Safe Horizon（安全地平線）（第412頁）

或想拒捕。不要做任何聲明。不要在任何你不理解的文件上簽字。要求見律師。聯繫下一頁框中列出的團體。

如果警方讓我站住，並決定對我進行搜身，我該怎麼辦？

你不一定要同意接受搜查。如果你不同意，就清楚地說：＂我不同意搜查,＂並按前面答問中說明的作法做。

如果警察傷害我或者侵犯我的權利，我該怎麼辦？

你有權要求那名警官告訴你他的名字和警徽號碼。如果他拒絕，要設法從制服上記下號碼。儘快記錄下發生過的一切，並給你受的傷（如傷口或瘀血）拍照。儘量設法找到目擊事件過程的人。

欲尋求法律咨詢，請聯繫一家以上列出的組織，並撥打Civilian Complaint Review Board hot line（民眾投訴審查委員會熱線）1-800-341-CCRB（2272）（第392頁）。

什麼是Civilian Complaint Review Board（民眾投訴審查委員會）？

這個委員會簡稱C.C.R.B.，是一家獨立的市政府機構，與警察局沒有關聯，有權調查關於警察過失行為的報告。投訴可以由受害者或目擊者提出。你不必一定是美國公民或紐約市居民才能提出投訴。一定要儘快提出投訴，因為委員會只有18個月的時間調查投訴。

我應該帶哪些文件證明我的移民身份？

如果你是永久居民，帶上你的永久居留卡（也叫外國人登記卡，通常叫做綠卡）或護照。如果你是以非移民身份入境的外國人，帶上你的出入境卡（I-94卡），即護照中的標記，和/或由國土安全部的另一個部門United States Citizenship and Immigration Services（美國公民和移民服務局，簡稱U.S.C.I.S）頒發的其他身份證明。

如果警察要求我出示移民證件，我該怎麼辦？

向警察詢問你是否可以走。如果你被告知可以，就走開。如果你被告知不能走，你就是被扣押了。這不一定意味著你要被逮捕。警方可以對你進行"搜身"，這就是說他們可以隔著衣服從上到下輕拍你的身體。不要允許警方進一步搜查。告訴警察："我不同意。我想同我的律師講話。"

在我告訴警察我不同意搜查，我想聯繫我的律師以後，如果他們繼續對我進行搜查，該怎麼辦？

保持冷靜。不要同警察或B.I.C.E.的探員打架。你可能會受傷或被捕。你應不斷地

需要更多幫忙嗎？

如果你或者你認識的人成為家庭暴力的受害者，可以打以下這些熱線和組織的電話：

- New York State Domestic Violence Hot Line（紐約州家庭暴力熱線），1-800-942-6906（僅限英語）
- New York State Domestic Violence Hot Line（紐約州家庭暴力熱線），1-800-942-6908（僅限西班牙語）
- New York City Domestic Violence Hot Line（紐約市家庭暴力熱線），1-800-621-4673（英語、西班牙語、廣東話、普通話）
- CUNY Law School－Main Street Legal Services, Immigration and Refugee Rights（紐約市立大學法學院－緬因街法律服務，移民和難民權利）（第393頁）
- Park Slope Safe Homes Project（Park Slope安全家庭計劃）（第410頁）
- Queens Legal Services（皇后區法律服務）（第412頁）

> **如果你在街上被警察叫住，
> 要有禮貌，把手放在警察看得見的地方。
> 不要跑開或想拒捕。**

說："我不同意。我想同我的律師講話。"記下警官的姓名、徽章號碼和所屬機構。如果你被扣押，甚至被逮捕，你不需要回答問題或做出聲明。

如果我被扣留或逮捕，我必須告訴我的姓名嗎？
從法律上講，你不必說出你的姓名，除非他們懷疑你犯了罪。但是拒絕透露姓名可能會引起懷疑。要知道，警方或者B.I.C.E.探員可能隨身帶著應驅逐的外國人名單。告訴一個假名可能本身算不上可以提起訴訟的犯罪，但是這樣做是非法的，而且如果你這樣做，警方或B.I.C.E.可能會拘押你。

如果我正在開車時，被警察攔下該怎麼辦？
你必須出示你的駕駛執照、車輛登記證和保險證明，儘管警方也許還是能合法地搜查你的汽車，但是你不必同意接受搜查。

我沒有合法身份。B.I.C.E.探員能在沒有許可令的情況下逮捕我嗎？
能。如果B.I.C.E.探員認為你非法居留美國，並且在得到逮捕令之前你可能逃走，他可以在沒有逮捕令的情況下逮捕你。

如果我被B.I.C.E.的探員逮捕會怎樣？我會簡單地只是被送上飛機回到我的國家嗎？
在大多數情況下，你必須在移民法庭進行一場由移民法官主持的聽證會。但是法律沒有規定法院要等多久才為你舉行聽證會。

有什麼辦法可以不經過移民法官舉行的聽證會就把我驅逐出境？
如果你屬於下列幾種情況就可以：放棄聽證會的權利、同意不舉行聽證會就離境、已經被判犯有某些罪行、在邊境被捕或過去曾經被驅逐出境過。

如果我有綠卡及其他文件，我也可能被驅逐出境嗎？
被判犯有移民法定義為"重罪"的移民可能會被驅逐出境。重罪一覽表可以到以下網址查詢www.newamericans.com/citizen/articles/felonieslist.html。最好就有關定罪會對移民身份產生什麼影響的問題進行法律咨詢。

911之後的移民法

911恐怖襲擊以後通過的法律允許移民和海關執法局（B.I.C.E.）將移民監禁在監獄裡幾週、幾個月或更長時間。法律沒有規定移民法官必須在什麼時候審理你的案子。如果法官認定你對社會有威脅，或者想逃走，他或她可以下令讓你留在監獄裡。此外，有些法律規定，如果你被控告有恐怖主義行為，或者已經被判有某些罪行，你就不能獲釋。

我被判有罪，但不必坐牢。我仍然會被驅逐出境嗎？

是的。如果你已經在美國被判有罪－即使你只支付罰金而不必去坐牢－在出國旅行前有必要咨詢一下移民律師（提供法律咨詢的團體的名單見第348頁）。如果你出境後又想入境，並且/或者如果你在申請公民身份，你通常會有被驅逐出境的危險。

B.I.C.E.真的會為輕罪而追捕我嗎？

總是有這種風險。即使B.I.C.E.探員沒有在追蹤你，在你服完刑後申請公民身份或者其他移民福利時，或者在出國度假或商務旅行後返回美國時，你可能會和B.I.C.E.發生接觸。

當我被B.I.C.E.探員攔住或收押時，我應該簽署什麼文件嗎？

不要在任何你不理解的文件上簽字。在由B.I.C.E.探員提供的文件上簽字，可能會表示你放棄某些權利或同意回到你自己的國家。應該聯繫移民律師或移民支持者。

如果B.I.C.E.的探員到我工作的地方來了怎麼辦？

自911以來，警方和B.I.C.E.探員更頻繁地在沒有許可令的情況下到工作場所尋找沒有合法身份的勞工，或者被懷疑有恐怖主義行為或與恐怖分子有牽連的勞工。在這種情況下，只需說你想見律師或者移民支持者。在見到律師以前，你告訴B.I.C.E.探員的任何資訊都可能會對你的案子不利。

如果發生緊急情況我該怎麼辦？

用最近的電話撥打911，這是警方的應急電話號碼。打這個電話是免費的。警方會自動查到你打電話的方位，除非你使用的是移動電話。你不必說出自己的姓名。總會有接線員或翻譯人員可以說紐約市的幾種主要外語。

緊急情況要到什麼時候才算嚴重到應該打911的程度？
- 當發生犯罪行為時。
- 當有生命危險時。
- 當有人受了重傷、或者很需要醫治時。

對於鄰居吵鬧或有人販賣毒品等不太緊急的事，我應該怎樣投訴？
對於非緊急情況，可打Citizen Service Center（公民服務中心）電話311。這個於2003年3月啟動的電話轉接中心使你只要撥一個容易記的號碼－311－就可以聯繫到本市的大多數非緊急政府服務部門，可以做的事情包括報告公寓裡沒有供應暖氣或熱水，或查明你住的地區什麼時候收垃圾等等。311公民服務中心全天24小時開通，並有170種語言的幫助。

如果我不會說英語，我能去警察局報告輕罪或投訴嗎？
轄區內有很多非英語人口的警察局會設有雙語接待員，他們就住在轄區內。他們將幫助你或找人幫助你處理任何同警察局的工作和人員有關的事務。如果你的問題不屬於警方處理的範圍，雙語接待員會設法（也許通過打311電話）找到相關的機構幫助你。

如果我被強姦了該怎麼辦？
- 強姦是一種犯罪行為，施暴者可能是朋友、配偶、同居夥伴或親屬。立即撥打911向警方報案。*即使進行強姦的人是你認識或你愛的人，強姦也不是你的錯。不要感到害羞。*
- 告訴警方強姦的詳細過程（不論如何隱秘）以及你記得的任何關於強姦者的事。
- 不要進行清洗或者沖洗。儘快進行醫療檢查和婦科檢查。儘量帶上警官和你一起去。
- 做愛滋病病毒和愛滋病檢查，立即向醫生索取抗愛滋病的藥物。
- 聯繫為性攻擊受害者提供服務的組織。

需要更多幫忙嗎？

以下這些組織為性虐待受害者提供治療和諮詢：

- Bellevue Hospital Center（Bellevue醫療中心）（第383頁）
- Safe Horizon（安全地平線）（第412頁）

有時我的配偶或我的同居夥伴掌摑我或打我。有什麼辦法嗎？

有。在美國，對配偶、同居夥伴和兒童進行身體虐待是非法的，會被逮捕。你應該報警，還應該打移民服務機構或家庭暴力熱線。

■

"新 移民由於人生地不熟，很容易成為犯罪行為的受害者。我在來紐約的頭兩年被搶劫了四次，這讓我覺得紐約並不是一個可以安居的地方。我想必須找個辦法解決這個問題。一名警官告訴我一系列安全生活的須知，比如要時刻注意周圍的情況，不要在沒有人的地方行走。這樣我遇到的犯罪現象就少了很多。我希望這可以給新移民一些幫助。"

Pak Ping, 中國人, 1999年 [14]

政府救濟

"那 時叫家庭救濟。現在叫福利救濟了；那時是家庭救濟。你知道，他們會給你馬鈴薯和奶油一類的東西。我記得有一次和鄰居一起去取馬鈴薯和奶酪。我想奶酪盒都是從那裡來的吧。"

Josephine Esposito，意大利移民的女兒，回憶 1930年代 [15]

•

如果你不能工作，如果你找不到工作或者如果你的工作工資不夠，政府救濟和食物券也許能幫助你支付食品、衣物、租金、燃氣、電和其他公用事業和家庭開支。

什麼是政府救濟？
政府救濟常被稱為福利救濟，指向家庭收入低於政府確定的聯邦貧困線或紐約貧困標準的人提供錢和其他救濟的許多不同的政府計劃。

什麼是"family assistance"（家庭補助）？哪些人符合條件？可以得到多少補助？補助多長時間？
家庭補助是一種向貧困家庭提供現金的福利救濟或政府救濟。1996年8月以後來美國，並且在美國居住不滿五年的人不符合條件。符合條件的成年人可以接受共60個月的家庭補助，這個時期不一定是連續計算的。

補助金取決於家庭人口和收入多少。家庭收入是指家庭中所有成年人賺的錢。例如，如果你獨自生活，每月收入是400美元，而紐約貧困線是每月500美元，你就有資格獲得政府救濟。但是如果還有其他人生活在家庭裡，大家共賺800美元，你的收入水平就高於聯邦貧困線，不符合條件。

家庭補助的補助金每月支付兩次，用於衣、食、住的支出。達到了60個月的期限以後，受益的成年人及其家人將不再有資格享受更多的家庭補助。

什麼是"safety net assistance"（安全網補助）？什麼人符合條件？可以得到多少補助？補助多長時間？

安全網補助也是一種福利救濟或政府救濟。它也提供補助，但是是為了那些沒有資格享受家庭補助的人：來美國不到五年的單身成年人、無子女夫婦和新移民，而不論其家庭人口多少。已經使用完五年家庭補助資格的人也能享受到補助。其補助金也是每月支付兩次，用於衣、食、住的支出。

我可以得到政府救濟嗎？

也許可以。不同的計劃有不同的資格要求和貧困標準。是否符合條件取決於你的移民身份、何時來美國、年齡、健康狀況和家庭收入。

申請政府救濟

分步指南

1. 去說你母語的社區組織或當地的Human Resources Administration（人力資源管理局，簡稱H.R.A.）收入資助中心/就業中心拿資料頁和 申請表。H.R.A.必須給你一份申請表。欲知中心地址，可打H.R.A. Infoline（H.R.A.資訊專線）1- 877-HRA-8411(1-877-472-8411)（第397頁）。

2. 如果可以的話，應該當場填寫好申請並提交。如果你需要幫助，就要提出來，不要因為出錯而延誤得到補助的時間。如果你把申請帶回去填寫，也要儘快填寫好並提交給當地的H.R.A.中心。

3. 在七個工作日內，你必須進行一次面試。進行面試的人會詢問你的教育、培訓和工作經歷；能做什麼類型的工作；你對未來就業的打算和你的兒童保育需要。

4. H.R.A.的社會福利工作者將登門訪問，以確認你住在所說的住址，而且你的生活水平看起來沒有高於聯邦貧困線。如果你的生活水平看起來高於貧困線，社會福利工作者會認為你在家庭收入方面沒有說實話。

5. 一般來說，H.R.A.會在30到45天內通知你是否有資格領取政府救濟，但是有時可能會需要更長時間，你必須經常詢問。如果你在這段時間裡還沒有得到答覆，也不要放棄。繼續去辦事處詢問你的申請的處理結果。

我怎樣才能瞭解所有不同的政府救濟？

網址為www.govbenefits.gov/GovBenefits/jsp/GovBenefits.jsp的GovBenefits Web site（政府救濟網）是個既方便又有效的工具。你只要回答一些關於你自身情況的問題，就會得到你可能符合條件的政府計劃清單及申請資訊。

我沒有合法身份。如果我造訪關於政府救濟的網站，政府會得到我的居住地址及其他資料嗎？

不會。這些網站是完全保密的。你不必說出自己的姓名、電話號碼、社會安全號或者任何其他可用於識別你的資訊。

如果我不能肯定自己是否符合某項政府救濟計劃的條件，我該怎麼辦？

如果你認為需要某種救濟，例如食物券，但是不能確定你是否符合條件，就應該去申請。法律和要求的條件總是在變，所以如果你不得不多次申請並申請多項計劃，請不要氣餒。

我能一邊工作一邊得到政府救濟嗎？

可以，只要你的家庭收入不超過州和聯邦的資格標準。

我沒有合法身份。我能得到政府救濟嗎？

資格要求取決於你需要的服務種類。許多政府救濟只提供給合法居住在美國的移民。但有些救濟，如緊急Medicaid、產前保健、食品室和施粥所的食品則面向所有紐約市居民，而不論其移民身份如何。紐約市的機構有時必須詢問身份，以便確定某人是否符合某一計劃的條件。在本指南付印時，他們還沒有義務將你的非法身份報告給美國國土安全部的Bureau of Immigration and Customs Enforcement（美國移民和海關執法局），或稱為B.I.C.E.（這個部已經接管了許多多年來由移民歸化局執行的職能）。然而，影響移民的政策經常變化，最好向本指南後面的資源名錄中列出的移民支持團體詢問一下，或者如果你負擔得起費用，向聲譽良好的移民律師咨詢。

如何申請政府救濟？

在紐約市，大多數政府救濟計劃要通過Human Resources Administration（人力資源管理局，簡稱H.R.A.）申請。去該局的Refugee and Immigrant Center（難民和移民中心）（第398頁）。如果你說英語有困難，可以在申請政府救濟、Medicaid和Medicare時尋求幫助。工作人員可以說幾種語言，包括西班牙語、廣東話、俄語、阿爾巴尼亞語、越南語、日語、阿拉伯語和幾種非洲方言。

我可以通過電話申請政府救濟嗎？

由於電話總是佔線，非常困難。去H.R.A. Income Support Center（H.R.A.的收入資助中心）申請會更容易、更可靠。

我到申請政府救濟的中心以後要做哪些事情？

你會得到一頁關於得到福利救濟及其他政府救濟的權利的資料，並需要填寫一份申請。

在申請政府救濟的中心，一切都以英語進行嗎？

不。資料會有五種語言的版本：英語、西班牙語、華語、俄語和阿拉伯語。

怎樣才能知道我的政府救濟申請已經被批准了還是被拒絕了？

你會得到一份書面通知。如果申請沒得到批准，通知書必須說明原因。如果對決定不滿，你有權要求進行公平聽證，以反駁不批准的決定。通過公平聽證你可以向行政法法官闡述你的情況和為什麼你認為拒絕決定是錯誤。

如果我申請政府救濟被拒絕，怎樣才能得到聽證的機會，以對拒絕決定進行申訴？

去Office of Administrative Hearings（行政聽證辦公室）要求舉行公平聽證。它們的地址是位於曼哈頓中城的330 West 34th Street 三樓，和位於下城布碌崙的14 Boerum Place 一樓。

如果我一直在領取補助，但卻被告知我不再符合條件，該怎麼辦？ 補助會一直發放到我舉行聽證嗎？

在通知你的補助要減少或停止的那封信的右上角有一個日期，如果從這個日期起10天內你要求舉行公平聽證，你有權享受補助、食物券和Medicaid，直到舉行公平聽證。

記下來

在申請政府救濟時，一定要記錄下你與人力資源管理局的任何一次聯繫。記下你提交補助申請的日期。如果H.R.A.沒有立即從你應得補助的日期起發放補助，記下申請日期可能有助於你獲得補發的補助。還要記下每一名與你打過交道的H.R.A.官員和職員的姓名。

> **一定要申請你需要的任何一種政府救濟,即使你認為自己不符合條件。法律不斷變化。如果你不得不申請多次,或者申請多個救濟計劃,也不要氣餒。**

如果我舉行了公平聽證,並被告知我有權享受補助,他們會立即開始或者恢復補助嗎?
不一定。有時補助需要過幾個月才能到來。

如果我領取政府救濟,我必須為政府工作作為回報嗎?
某些工作要求,又稱工作福利,可以以教育的方式得到滿足。此外,如果你符合以下某一種情況,可以免除工作福利:
- 殘障人士
- 殘障人士的照顧者
- 60歲以上老人
- 年齡不滿16歲者,或者年齡不滿19歲的全日制學生
- 處於懷孕的最後一個月
- 照顧新生兒的母親

我照顧小孩多久以後就必須加入工作福利,以便我能繼續領取政府救濟?
領取政府救濟的母親一生中可以有12個月來照顧新生兒,但是照顧每一個孩子不得超過3個月。你可以就3個月的規定申請延期,但不得根據12個月的規定申請延期。

什麼是食物券?什麼人符合領取食物券的條件?
食物券是在加盟食品店和超級市場購買食物和相關商品的代金券。不是只有貧困的人才有資格領取食物券,許多移民都符合領取條件。欲瞭解你是否有資格領取食物券,或者想知道全市20處食物券辦公室的地點,可以給H.R.A.打電話1-877-472-8411(第397頁),或者訪問人力資源管理局網站www.nyc.gov/html/hra/html/serv_foodstamps.html。

如果我沒有合法身份,可以領取食物券嗎?
沒有合法身份的移民有多種,其中很多種移民現在是符合領取條件的。最好到人力資源管理局就業中心或者食物券辦公室提出申請。

需要更多幫忙嗎？

欲知最新的政府救濟法規，可以聯繫你的市議會議員。如果不知道你的市議會議員是誰，可以打League of Women Voters Telephone Information Service（**女性選民聯盟電話資訊服務**）1-212-213-5286（**僅限英語**），並告訴他們你的地址。可聯繫以下團體就政府救濟進行咨詢：

- Asian American Legal Defense and Education Fund（亞美法律援助處，簡稱A.A.L.D.E.F.）（第381頁）
- Asian Americans for Equality（亞洲人平等會，簡稱A.A.F.E.）（第382頁）
- Brooklyn Chinese-American Association（布碌崙華人協會）（第384頁）
- Charles B. Wang Community Health Center（王嘉廉社區醫療中心）（第387頁）
- Chinatown Manpower Project（華埠人力中心）（第388頁）
- Chinese-American Planning Council（華人策劃協會）（第389頁）
- Church Avenue Merchants Block Association（教堂大道商人區協會，簡稱C.A.M.B.A.）（第389頁）
- City Harvest Hunger Hot Line（城市豐收饑餓熱線）（第391頁）
- Community Association of Progressive Dominicans（進步多米尼加人僑區聯合會）（第392頁）
- Forest Hills Community House（Forest Hills社區會所）（第395頁）
- Indochina Sino-American Community Center（美東越棉寮華僑社區中心）（第398頁）
- Jacob A. Riis Neighborhood Settlement House（Jacob A. Riis街坊文教館）（第399頁）
- Legal Aid Society, Civil Division（法律援助協會，民事部）（第400頁）
- Legal Services for New York City（紐約市法律服務）（第400頁）
- Lutheran Medical Center（路德教會醫療中心）（第401頁）
- Medical and Health Research Association of New York City（紐約市醫療和保健研究協會，簡稱M.H.R.A.）（第403頁）
- New York Association for New Americans（紐約新美國人聯合會，簡稱N.Y.A.N.A.）（第404頁）
- New York City Neighborhood W.I.C. Program（紐約市社區W.I.C.計劃）（第403頁）
- New York State Office of Temporary and Disability Assistance（紐約州臨時和殘障援助辦公室）（第410頁）
- Queens Legal Services（皇后區法律服務）（第412頁）
- Southeast Bronx Neighborhood Centers（東南布朗士社區中心）（第413頁）

食物券辦公室的工作人員會説我的母語嗎？

市政府必須提供免費的西班牙語、廣東話、普通話、阿拉伯語、俄語的譯本和翻譯人員，如果需要，還要提供其它語種的譯本和翻譯。

我要真的拿著食物券在商店裡使用嗎？

不用。你會得到一張電子補助金轉賬（E.B.T.）卡，在紐約市，你可以憑這張塑料簽帳卡領取政府救濟（福利救濟）金以及使用食物券。

在哪裡可以領取E.B.T.卡？我必須使用這張卡嗎？

這張卡將通過郵件郵寄給你。如果你領取福利補助和/或食物券，就必須使用它。沒有免除或者特准例外。

我的E.B.T.卡上會有我的照片嗎？

有些卡上面印有照片，還有一些卡沒有照片。你的卡無論有沒有照片都是有效的。

E.B.T.卡可以在哪里使用？

可以在商店和有Quest®標誌的自動櫃員機（A.T.M.）上使用。

E.B.T.卡能用來做什麼？

■ 使用食物券或現金補助購買食物及其他物品。
■ 從現金帳戶提取現金。
■ 在允許前去購物的E.B.T.使用者從賬戶中提取現金回饋的商店裡提取現金回饋。

我用E.B.T.卡購買食物時必須付費嗎？

不。食物購買決不會收費。只要你的帳戶中還有足夠的食物券，你買多少次食物都不用付費。

我用E.B.T.卡從自己的帳戶取現金時必須付費嗎？

不一定。任何收費的商店、支票兌現處或者A.T.M.必須貼出佈告告知收費事項，你應該避免使用他們的服務。

我怎樣才能知道哪裡可以使用E.B.T.卡，哪裡會收費呢？

只要打電話給1-800-289-6739（英語和西班牙語），就可以有人告訴你不收費的A.T.M.的位置。

我最多可以用E.B.T.卡提取現金多少次而不用付費呢？

如果使用不收費場所，一個月可以提取四次現金。四次機會用完後，當月每次提取現金將收費85美分。

記下這些電話號碼

撥打花旗銀行客戶服務電話1-888-328-6399（英語和西班牙語）做以下事情：

- 掛失和更換丟失的、被竊的或損毀的E.B.T.卡。
- 更改E.B.T.卡的密碼，也叫PIN。
- 報告現金補助額有誤。
- 報告A.T.M.或商店存在的問題。
- 查詢目前帳戶餘額和最近10筆交易。
- 報告帳戶中的錯誤。
- 打電話給1-800-289-6739（英語和西班牙語）查詢不收費的A.T.M.的位置。
- 打電話給New York City Message Center（紐約市訊息中心）1-877-879-4194（英語和西班牙語），收聽有關於你的政府救濟專業的語音留言。

怎樣才能知道我的E.B.T.賬戶中還有多少現金補助和食物券？

可以打Citibank Customer Service（花旗銀行客戶服務）免費電話1-888-328-6399（英語和西班牙語）查詢食物券和現金補助的餘額以及最近10筆交易的記錄。有些A.T.M.和商店的收款機會在收據上打印出你的餘額。即使機器不能用於提取現金或者以食物券支付，也要保存好收據。

如果我的E.B.T.卡丟失或被盜，該怎麼辦？

立即 撥打花旗銀行客戶服務電話1-888-328-6399。如果你使用按鍵式電話，錄音應答系統會應答並要求你按數字1選擇英語，或按2選擇西班牙語。指示你的帳戶"停止支付"。如果有人在你指示停止支付之前就使用了你的卡，你就會丟失這些補助並無法挽回。

當我就E.B.T.卡問題撥打花旗銀行客戶服務電話時，可以同真人講話嗎？

可以。當你撥打電話1-888-328-6399時，錄音應答系統會應答並要求你按數字1選擇英語，或按2選擇西班牙語。不要按任何按鍵，不理所有錄音指令。等一會兒你就能接通可以解答你問題的人。

除食物券以外，還有什麼其他的計劃能幫助我養家糊口嗎？

Special Supplemental Nutrition Program for Women, Infants and Children（婦女、嬰兒和兒童特別補充營養計劃），又稱W.I.C.，為懷孕或哺乳的低收入女性或撫養有"營養風險"（即有某些內科或飲食疾病）的5歲以下兒童的低收入女性提供免費的補充食物、營養教育和醫療保健介紹。W.I.C.不論移民身份如何均可提供。

怎樣才能知道我的孩子或我本人是否有資格享受W.I.C.?

撥打紐約州衛生廳的免費幫助電話:Child and Adult Care Food Program(兒童和成人照顧食品計劃)1-800-942-3858(僅限英語);Growing Up Healthy hot line(健康成長熱線)1-800-522-5006(第395頁)。

■

"我仍然記得和母親去福利補助辦公室的情形一排很長的隊,長久的等待和母親受到的對待。我感覺到母親臉上的屈辱感。但沒有別的辦法。我父親是一名洗碗工,母親要照顧我們七個孩子。我記得每月的1日和16日,母親都會早起等待郵差的到來。當支票送來以後,我們總能得到一頓盛宴。哈哈,但是如果那天支票沒有送到,我們就有麻煩了。我們靠食物券買吃的,靠救濟款支付水電費。我的姐姐埃娃已經當了多年的社會福利工作者,情況發生了很大的變化,謝天謝地,我不需要靠救濟過日子了。"

Georgina Acevedo,波多黎各移民的女兒,回憶60年代 [16]

合法身份

當我成為美國公民的那一刻、當我第一次投票選舉美國總統時、當我看著我的長子註冊去公立學校上學時，我激動得無法自持。那是漫長暗夜後的黎明。'美國'這個詞的韻律都會讓我感到平靜、安慰和希望"。

Simon Finkelstein，俄羅斯人，1890年代 [17]

■

當你希望在美國永久居住（又叫做尋求合法永久居留或綠卡身份），或者從國外到美國作短暫或為特定目的居留（例如，作為旅遊者或勞工），美國政府會以各種簽證承認你合法的意圖或身份。

正如本指南已經幾次提到的，911事件發生以後，United States Department of Homeland Security（美國國土安全部）接管了很多 Immigration and Naturalization Service（移民歸化局，簡稱I.N.S.）的職能。國土安全部所屬的處理移民權益的部門 United States Citizenship and Immigration Services（美國公民和移民服務局，簡稱 U.S.C.I.S.）將審查簽證和永久居留卡（也叫外國人登記卡，也通常叫"綠卡"）申請。U.S.C.I.S.也處理移民的入籍申請。

這一章將介紹允許人們從其他國家合法進入美國的最常見的簽證種類，同時介紹一下永久居留卡（通常被稱為"綠卡"）及其重要性，以及獲得綠卡的複雜而長達數年的過程。最後將介紹申請成為公民（也叫做"歸化"）所要經歷的漫長過程、公民所享受的權益以及想成為公民的人可能要參加的考試的部分樣題。

911事件以後，國土安全部的另一個部門Bureau of Immigration and Customs

Enforcement（美國移民和海關執法局，簡稱B.I.C.E.）更嚴密地追蹤有合法身份和沒有合法身份的移民。移民政策經常更換而且通常變得更加嚴格。因此，請務必隨時注意你自己是否有合法身份，以及這一點對你在美國正在從事的或將從事的事有何影響。

本指南後面的資源名錄裡列出的圖書館以及移民支援團體都有人員或參考資料可以說明有關合法身份的更多細節和重要性，以及獲得綠卡或成為公民的手續。鑑於影響移民的政策時常改變，最好去諮詢一家上述組織或聲譽良好的移民律師。

什麼是簽證？

簽證是一種需要進行申請的進入美國的許可證。如果需要，簽證通常可在美國駐在國外的領事館獲得。簽證說明訪問的目的，比如商務、旅遊等等，有時在一個特定時期內幾次往返美國有效。

所有的簽證都一樣嗎？

不，不是所有的簽證都一樣。非移民簽證是簽發給生活在另一個國家為了特定的目的希望暫時來美國的人。非移民簽證簽發給旅遊者、商人、學生、短期工人和外交人員等人。

移民簽證簽發給想在美國永久生活和工作的人。在大多數情況下，你的親屬或僱主為你（受益人）向U.S.C.I.S.提出移民申請，以獲得成為移民的機會。（一些申請者，包括具有特殊才能的工人、投資者以及某些特殊的移民可以以自己的名義提出申請。）一旦獲得資格，你就需要申請成為合法永久居民。

獲得移民簽證總是一個非常複雜的過程，一般至少需要2年，多則10年，甚至更久。在這期間，你務必以合法的身份居留，因為你必須以合法的身份改變身份，例如從非移民簽證轉換為移民簽證和永久居民身份。

對於很多種類的非移民簽證，你需要向美國駐在國外的領事館直接申請。除了通過Diversity Visa Lottery（移民大抽獎計劃）贏得的簽證以外（在本章的後面予以解釋），所有的移民簽證必須先向U.S.C.I.S.申請。

United States Department of State（美國國務院）負責向希望移民美國的外國公民發放簽證號碼。欲進一步瞭解美國國務院發放簽證的過程，可訪問網站 **http://travel.state.gov/visa_services.html**。

什麼是綠卡？

綠卡，又稱永久居留卡或外國人登記卡，是證明一名移民可以在美國合法工作、同時可以在美國永久居留的文件。如果你有綠卡，你就是合法的永久居民，具有合法身份。

如何才能得到綠卡？

要成為永久居民，有兩種基本程式，即家庭關係程式和工作需要程式。不論你走哪種程式，如果你身在美國，必須有合法身份才能調整身份。

如果我沒有合法身份會怎樣？

如果你非法進入美國，或者經許可進入美國後非法居留或未經許可打工，你就無法調整身份，除非你符合某些免除或赦免的條件。通常，你必須先離開美國，再申請移民簽證。注意，你可能會被禁止重返美國3至10年。所以，在離開美國前向本指南後面資源名錄裡列出的聲譽良好的移民律師或移民服務提供者尋求幫助是極為重要的。

他們也可以幫助確定你是否符合允許你在申請移民簽證期間留在美國的免除或赦免的條件。

需要更多幫忙嗎？

以下機構提供在移民問題方面聲譽良好的法律咨詢：

- Asian American Legal Defense and Education Fund（亞美法律援助處）（第381頁）
- Caribbean Women's Health Association（加勒比婦女健康協會）（第385頁）
- Catholic Charities Office for Immigrant Services（天主教慈善機構移民服務辦公室）（第386頁）
- Catholic Migration Services（天主教移民服務）（第386頁）
- Citizens Advice Bureau（公民顧問局，簡稱C.A.B.）（第390頁）
- CUNY Law School－Main Street Legal Services, Immigration and Refugee Rights Program（紐約市立大學法學院－緬因街法律服務，移民和難民權計劃）（第393頁）
- Emerald Isle Immigration Center（Emerald Isle移民中心）（第394頁）
- Hebrew Immigrant Aid Society（希伯來移民援助協會，簡稱H.I.A.S.）（第396頁）
- Hellenic American Neighborhood Action Committee（美國希臘裔社區行動委員會，簡稱H.A.N.A.C.）（第396頁）
- Legal Aid Society, Civil Division（法律援助協會，民事部）（第400頁）

> **綠卡證明一位移民
> 可以在美國合法工作
> 和永久居住。**

家庭關係程式是怎樣進行的？

這個程式分兩步走：

1. 由一名美國公民或合法永久居民提出U.S.C.I.S.的I-130表，即 Petition for Alien Relative（外國親屬申請表），將你列為有資格申請移民簽證者。
2. 申請獲得批准後，一旦有了簽證號碼，你就可以申請成為合法永久居民。

這個程式看起來很簡單，為什麼需要那麼長時間？

簽證號碼數量有限，可能要等上幾年才能獲得。因此，雖然你的第一項申請可能會很快得到批准，但要等到有簽證號並獲得合法永久居民身份，可能要2至10年，甚至更久。

對於這一漫長的程式來説，有什麼速度更快的例外情況嗎？

有，但只有在有現成簽證的情況下才行，而且例外只適用於直系親屬，即美國公民的父母、配偶和21歲以下未婚子女。

對於直系親屬來説，程式是怎樣的？

如果這些親屬能得到現成的簽證號，並且他們身在美國，兩項申請幾乎可以同時進行。如果希望移民的親屬在國外，在美國的家人可以提出申請，申請材料將被轉到美國駐未來移民所在的國家的領事館，他們可以在那裡申請移民簽證來美國。最好能諮詢本指南後面資源名錄裡列出的聲譽較好的移民律師或移民服務提供者。

工作需要程式是怎樣進行的？

在多數情況下，這個程式分三步走，也需要幾年的時間。

1. 由僱主申請工作證明，這可能需要2－4年時間。
2. 得到證明後，必須提出U.S.C.I.S. I-140表，即Petition for Alien Worker Status（外國勞工申請表）。
3. 在外國勞工申請得到批准後，必須申請將你的身份調整為永久居民。只有具備合法身份時才能調整身份。

需要更多幫忙嗎？

這些機構和組織提供公民申請和入籍過程方面的幫助：

- Brooklyn Chinese-American Association（布碌崙華人協會）（第384頁）
- Caribbean Women's Health Association（加勒比婦女健康協會，簡稱C.W.H.A.）（第385頁）
- Catholic Charities Office for Immigration Services（天主教慈善機構移民服務辦公室）（第386頁）
- Catholic Migration Services（天主教移民服務）（第386頁）
- Chinese Immigrant Services（華人移民服務）（第388頁）
- Church Avenue Merchants Block Association（教堂大道商人區中心，簡稱C.A.M.B.A.）（第389頁）
- Emerald Isle Immigration Center（Emerald Isle移民中心）（第394頁）
- Hebrew Immigrant Aid Society（希伯來移民援助協會，簡稱H.I.A.S.）（第396頁）
- Immigration Advocacy Services（移民支持服務）（第398頁）
- New York Immigration Hot Line（紐約移民熱線）1-800-566-7636（第408頁）
- South Bronx Action Group（南布朗士行動團體）（第413頁）
- Southside Community Mission, Immigration Program（南部社區慈善會，移民計劃）（第413頁）
- United Community Centers（聯合社區中心）（第414頁）

欲瞭解更多關於入籍資格條件、要求及考試的情況，請訪問U.S.C.I.S.的網站：http://uscis.gov。

對於這一漫長的程式來說，有什麼速度更快的例外情況嗎？

有，如果你與美國公民結婚，或者如果你是美國公民的直系親屬，或者如果你符合245(i)法的規定（不是普遍性赦免，只是有限的減免，適用於2000年12月31日以前來到美國，並在2001年4月30日或者以前就提出申請合法永久居民身份的人）。

沒有人保證我，有什麼辦法可以得到移民簽證嗎？

Diversity Visa Lottery（移民大抽獎）計劃每年向美國移民率低的國家發放55,000個移民簽證。有關這個大抽獎如何運作的具體情況，請造訪網址www.immigration.gov/graphics/services/residency/divvisa.htm。

如果我抽中移民大抽獎，意味著什麼？

意味著你也許可以申請永久居留身份。

如何才能得到入籍申請用的U.S.C.I.S.的N-400表？

打U.S.C.I.S.表格熱線1-800-870-3676（英語和西班牙語）。你也可以通過網站索取http://uscis.gov。

如果申請成為公民，我是否要接受面試或詢問？

是的。所有的申請者都必須經過面試，通常被稱為入籍面試。

我什麼時候可以進行公民申請面試？

在紐約，面試通常會安排在U.S.C.I.S.接到你的N-400申請表後的一年到18個月之間。

怎樣才能知道公民面試的時間和地點？

你會收到郵件通知，告訴你時間、地點以及必須要帶的材料。

如果我錯過了公民面試怎麼辦？

不要錯過面試。你的申請可能會被推遲一年或更久，甚至被拒絕。請向本指南最後資源名錄中列出的移民服務提供者尋求幫助。

面試是怎樣進行的？

U.S.C.I.S.的代表會：

- 更新和審查N-400入籍申請表上的內容。
- 審查你的證明文件，包括過去5年的報稅表、綠卡、出生證明、護照，等等。
- 測試你對美國歷史和政府的知識，以及你讀、寫、說英語的能力，除非你符合殘疾人免試或其他免試條件。

我想成為美國公民的理由是什麼？

有很多理由。以下是一些移民告訴我們的重要理由：

- 公民有權選舉聯邦、州以及地方官員。他們是制定政府政策的人，而這些政策會影響你在紐約的日常生活。
- 只有公民才有資格擔任市、州或聯邦政府的大多數公職以及聯邦、州和市政府的某些工作。
- 公民可以離開美國在其他國家居住任意長的時間，同時美國公民在某些國家旅行會更方便一些。

- 公民可以請求許可更多種類的家庭成員來美國。
- 公民不會被阻止再次進入美國。
- 公民不能被驅逐出境。
- 公民不用操心每10年續期一次綠卡。
- 退休後遷往其他國家的公民可以從由政府管理的社會安全計劃，退休計劃和殘障計劃領到全部福利金。而大多數合法永久居民在回到美國住滿一個月之前只能領到六個月的福利金。有一些例外，還有幾個國家不允許美國將社會安全福利金寄到他們那裡去。欲查詢有哪些例外和國家，以及有關移民對社會安全福利金的影響，請瀏覽以下網址，**www.ssa.gov.immigration**。這個網站有多種語言的入口和翻譯。
- 有些國家承認"雙重國籍"。這就允許加入美國國籍的公民依然可以保留其出生國家的國籍。
- 公民可以享有更多的公共福利以及更多的教育獎學金和補助金。
- 在某些情況下，與身為美國公民的父母同住的未滿18歲的合法永久居民可以自動成為公民。這意味著他們以後不必再經歷漫長而複雜的入籍過程了。

誰符合成為美國公民的標準？

有一些基本要求：

- 你的年齡至少要達到18歲。
- 你必須成為合法永久居民（綠卡持有者）至少已滿5年，或者是成為合法永久居民至少已滿3年，並且在此期間與一名美國公民保持婚姻關係，而且在申請入籍時依然與該名美國公民保持婚姻關係。
- 你必須在提出公民入籍申請的那個州至少已經住滿三個月。
- 你必須在過去的5年裡一直納稅。
- 如果你是18歲至26歲之間的男子，你必須已經登記註冊義務兵役。
- 你必須道德良好，這可以通過繳稅、登記義務兵役和無犯罪判決記錄得到體現。
- 你必須能說、讀、寫和聽懂基本的英語，同時表明你瞭解美國歷史和政府的基本常識。老年人和殘疾人在這方面可以有例外。你應該向本指南後面資源名錄中列出的移民服務提供者諮詢。
- 必須在過去5年裡或最近的3個月裡，至少有一半時間裡居住在美國。
- 除非得到U.S.C.I.S重新入境的許可證，否則你不能離開美國進行6個月以上的旅行。
- 儘管你可以和其他美國公民一樣旅行，但你必須有永久生活在美國的意圖。

- 你必須說明你是否因過錯（包括違反交通規則）而被捕或罰款。再次建議你向本指南後面資源名錄中列出的有聲譽的移民律師或移民服務提供者進行諮詢。

我需要什麼才可以成為美國公民？

- 很多表格，包括N-400表，入籍申請表。
- 兩張2英寸乘2英寸的彩色照片（露出右耳的四分之三正面照）。
- 綠卡的影印件，正面和反面。
- 申請費和手印費。可以用匯票或個人支票向U.S.C.I.S.支付。在支票的正面寫上你的姓名、地址和外國人登記號。*這些費用會定期發生變化，所以應該詢問U.S.C.I.S.或者移民律師或者支持者團體你需要支付多少費用。*
- 結婚證影印件（如果有結婚證的話）。*如果你作為美國公民的配偶申請，你的配偶的美國護照。*
- U.S.C.I.S. N-648表，即醫學免試表。*如果你有精神或生理殘障而造成你難以學習英語和/或參加入籍考試，則需上繳由心理學家或內科醫師填寫的這種表格。*

入籍考試是怎麼進行的？

面試官可能從100個問題中選擇10到15個問題口頭問你。

我必需全部答對入籍考試的問題嗎？

不用，但你必須至少答對10道題中的6道題。

我已經在美國生活和努力工作了很長時間了，但卻沒有時間或教育機會來學好英語或瞭解政府。這意味著我不能成為公民嗎？

不一定。65歲以上並已經在美國獲得合法身份超過20年的申請者可能得到特殊的照顧。如果你年齡達到50歲以上並已經在美國獲得合法身份超過20年，或者你年齡達到55歲以上並已經在美國獲得合法身份超過15年，可以選擇用你的母語進行關於歷史和政府方面的考試。

入籍考試中有可能被問到的問題有哪些？

這有五個樣題：

1. 美國國旗上的條紋代表什麼？
   他們代表最早的13個州，或殖民地。
2. 憲法是什麼？
   這個國家的最高法律。

需要更多幫忙嗎？

這些機構和組織提供公民申請和入籍過程方面的幫助：

- Asian Americans for Equality（亞洲人平等會，簡稱A.A.F.E.）（第382頁）
- Catholic Migration Services（天主教移民服務）（第386頁）
- Community Association of Progressive Dominicans（進步多米尼加人僑界聯合會）（第392頁）
- Forest Hills Community House（Forest Hills社區會所）（第395頁）
- Hellenic American Neighborhood Action Committee（美國希臘裔社區行動委員會，簡稱H.A.N.A.C.）（第396頁）
- Indochina Sino-American Community Center（美東越棉寮華僑社區中心）（第398頁）
- New York Association for New Americans（紐約新美國人聯合會，簡稱N.Y.A.N.A.）（第404頁）
- South Bronx Action Group（南布朗士行動團體）（第413頁）
- Southside Community Mission, Immigration Program（南部社區慈善團，移民計劃）（第413頁）

3. 國會是什麼？

是參議院和眾議院。

4. 1620年移居美國的清教徒為什麼來美國？

為了宗教自由。

5. 誰是Martin Luther King Jr.（小馬丁・路德・金）？

一位民權領袖。

怎樣準備入籍考試呢？

許多圖書館、社區以及移民支援團體都提供輔導和其他幫助。

如果我沒能表明我能夠讀、寫和聽懂基本的英語，或者如果我沒有通過入籍考試怎麼辦？

如果你一項或兩項都沒有通過，U.S.C.I.S.會為你約定下一次面試。到時你會再次接受考試，如果仍不能通過考試，你的入籍申請就會被拒絕。

如果因為英語讀寫能力不足或沒有通過考試，我的入籍申請被拒絕，我是否可以再次申請？如果可以，在什麼時候申請？

可以在你選擇的任何時間再次申請。當你學到的英語或歷史和政府知識足以通過考試時，應馬上再次提出申請。

如果我認為我的入籍申請被拒絕是不公平的，我可以做些什麼呢？

可以。如果你的申請被拒絕了，你會得到一封信告訴你原因，同時說明如何要求聽證。信裡附有N-336表。你必須在接到拒絕信後30天內，把填好的表以及相應的費用一同寄回U.S.C.I.S.。在本指南付印時，費用標準是195美元。如金額不正確，請求信會被退回。建議到U.S.C.I.S.網址核對一下正確的費用金額，http://uscis.gov。

通過了考試以後會怎樣？

U.S.C.I.S.有120天的時間決定批准或拒絕你的入籍申請。如果你的申請被批准了，你會收到郵件通知宣誓入籍的時間和地點。

我搬家了。我應該如何通知U.S.C.I.S.？

你必須在搬家後10天內把新住址通知U.S.C.I.S.。你可以透過電話通知他們，但只能就入籍申請一事。電話號碼是1-800-375-5283（英語和西班牙語）。涉及合法永久居留以及其他方面的申請，你必須填寫AR-11表，即地址變更表，並將其寄到你提出申請的移民辦事處。表格應以保證郵件的方式寄出，並要求回執。你自己一定要留一份副本。

有什麼辦法可以瞭解我入籍申請的情況呢？

有。打電話給U.S.C.I.S. National Customer Service Center（全國顧客服務中心），1-800-375-5283（英語和西班牙語）。如果有申請收據號碼或從U.S.C.I.S.服務中心申請地點得到的號碼，你就可以在U.S.C.I.S.的網址查看你申請的情況。http://uscis.gov。

我的孩子不是在美國出生的，他們怎樣才能成為公民呢？

不在美國出生的未滿18歲的子女，如果和身為美國公民的父親或母親生活在一起，並且是合法的永久居民，通常符合成為公民的條件。欲瞭解關於18歲以上子女以及子女入籍的其他更多具體問題的資訊，請向本指南後面資源名錄中列出的有聲譽的移民律師或移民服務提供者尋求幫助。

我應該取得什麼文件來證明我的孩子是美國公民呢？

入籍證書或美國護照。

∎

"**我** 來美國是因為伊朗的新宗教和獨裁政權。那段經歷是令人興奮的、艱難的，有時也讓人不愉快。在溶入了美國的新文化和享受了美國的那種生活方式以後，我認識到自己已經成了美國人。我已經習慣了其自由、禮儀、多元化文化和人們。成為美國公民對於我來說是邁出很大的一步。我捫心自問為什麼要成為公民。第一個答案就是方便－持有美國護照、就業機會等等。但是我認識到還有意義更深遠的好處。這就是成為民主的、可以發揮作用的一員。我可以為保存美國文化和意識形態做貢獻，以保證我的孩子有幸福的一生。"

Kaynam Hedayat，伊朗人， 2002年 [18]

文件證件

本指南總是提到劃分申請簽證資格的文件證件（簽證對每一名來美國的移民都是必不可少的），以及電話卡等其他使生活更方便和減少購買商品及服務支出的文件。

本章將介紹幾種你應該隨時帶在身上的重要文件證件。

簽證
簽證是需要申請的進入美國的許可。

非移民簽證發給生活在其他國家並希望為特定目的臨時到美國來的人。非移民簽證發給旅遊者、商人、學生、臨時工人和外交官等人。

移民簽證發給想在美國永久地生活和工作的人。這通常是獲得永久居留卡或外國人登記卡（通常叫做"綠卡"）的過渡性步驟。多數人是通過其親屬或未來雇主提出申請獲得移民簽證的。這一過程可能要2到10年，甚至更久，詳情請見"合法身份"一章的第364頁。

有些人可能被允許以自己的名義提出申請，包括受到虐待的美國公民的配偶、受虐待或被遺棄的青少年，或有超常才能的外國人。

就業授權書（E.A.D.）
這種文件表明你獲准在美國工作，即使你不是美國公民或者合法的永久性居民（已經獲得永久居留卡，也叫外國人登記卡，通常稱為綠卡）。

綠卡
證明你是合法的美國永久居民，有權在美國居住和工作。要獲得綠卡，必須經歷

2至10年，甚至更久的很漫長、很複雜的過程，這一過程在下文和"合法身分"這一章有介紹。由於這一過程太複雜，你應該向一位聲譽良好的移民事務律師尋求幫助，或向本書後面資源名錄中列出的許多移民支持團體尋求幫助。

以下是獲得綠卡的基本步驟：

1. 由一名親屬（使用U.S.C.I.S. I-130表，即Petition for Alien Relative外國親屬申請表）或僱主（使用U.S.C.I.S. I-140表，即Petition for Alien Worker外國勞工申請表）為你向U.S.C.I.S.提出移民申請，將你劃入可以申請移民簽證的分類。一旦有移民簽證，而你又身在美國，並有合法身份，你可以申請將身份調整為合法永久居民。如果你不在美國，被批准的申請將被轉到美國駐外領事館，以便你完成獲得移民簽證的過程。

2. 你將得到一個移民簽證號碼，即使你已經身在美國。

3. 如果你已經身在美國，你可以利用U.S.C.I.S. I-485表，即Application to Register Permanent Residence or to Adjust Status（永久居留權申請表或調整身份申請表）將身份調整為合法永久居民。如果你不在美國，請到當地的美國領事館完成辦理移民簽證的程序。

網址：www.immigration.gov/graphics/howdoi/LPReligibility.htm

電話：National Customer Service Center（全國顧客服務中心），1-800-375-5283（英語和西班牙語）

駕駛執照

在大多數情況下，如果你持有其他國家的有效駕駛執照，你就可以在紐約開車。事實上，只要你還是向你發放駕駛執照的國家的合法居民，New York State Department of Motor Vehicles（紐約州機動車管理局，簡稱D.M.V.）建議你不要申領紐約州的駕駛執照。

如果你有其他國家頒發的駕駛執照，並申領紐約州的駕駛執照，你必須做以下這些事：

1. 通過筆試。

2. 上一個五小時的課程。

3. 通過路考。

4. 出示綠卡。

5. 出示社會安全卡或者社會安全管理局的信，說明你不能得到社會安全卡的理由。

6. 交出你的外國駕駛執照。除非你要求保留，否則這個執照將在60天內被

> ## 在通常情況下，
> ## 持其他國家有效駕駛執照的人
> ## 可以在紐約合法駕駛車輛。 ""

D.M.V.銷毀。如果你需要拿回你的外國駕駛執照，可向D.M.V.在當地的辦事處（你申領駕駛執照的地點）提出來。

如果是第一次申領駕駛執照，你必須至少年滿16歲，並做以下幾件事：
1. 申請學習許可證。
2. 繳納申請費和駕駛執照費。
3. 通過視力檢查和筆試。
4. 練習，準備路考。
5. 通過電話或互聯網預約路考時間。
6. 通過路試。

網址： www.nydmv.state.ny.us/license.htm

電話： 曼哈頓區、布朗士區，1-212-645-5550（英語和西班牙語）；布碌崙區、皇后區、斯坦頓島，1-718-966-6155（英語和西班牙語）

非司機照片身份證

如果你沒有駕駛執照，你可以向D.M.V.申領非司機照片身份證。這種證件同駕駛執照一樣包含個人資料、照片、簽字和防止塗改和欺詐的保護措施。要取得這種身份證，你必須提供身份和出生日期的證明。

網址： www.nydmv.state.ny.us/license.htm

電話： 曼哈頓區、布朗士區，1-212-645-5550（英語和西班牙語）；布碌崙區、皇后區、斯坦頓島，1-718-966-6155（英語和西班牙語）

社會安全卡

社會安全卡申請表被稱為SS-5表。任何從來沒有社會安全卡、需要更換社會安全卡或者已經更改姓名的人都要用這張表。欲索取這種表格，可以打電話給Social Security Administration（社會安全局）或造訪其網站。

表格上的說明會解釋如何填寫表格以及需要哪些證明文件。填寫好申請材料後，請將它與證明文件的原始件或複印件一起交到或者郵寄到最近的社會安全辦事處。原始文件將很快歸還。社會安全辦事處在收到所有需要的材料後，將在大約兩星期後把卡片寄給你。

網址：www.ssa.gov
電話：1-800-772-1213（英語和西班牙語）

電子補助金轉帳（E.B.T.）卡

E.B.T.卡是一張塑膠簽帳卡，你可以持卡在紐約市領取政府救濟金（福利救濟）和使用食物券。你可以在市人力資源管理局的任何一處就業中心或食物券辦事處申請這種卡。它將以郵件方式寄給你，你必須使用它領取救濟和/或食物券。
網址：www.nyc.gov/html/hra/html/serv_foodstamps.html
電話：1-877-472-8411（英語、西班牙語、廣東話和普通話）(第397頁)

自動櫃員機（A.T.M.）卡

當你在銀行或信用合作社開立支票帳戶或儲蓄帳戶時，就會得到一張A.T.M.卡。持這種卡可以在A.T.M.上享受存款和提取現金等銀行服務，而不用去銀行了。

申請卡片時，你會被要求選擇一個密碼或者PIN。此後，每當你把卡放入A.T.M.時，你將被要求輸入你的密碼，然後才能提取現金或享受其他銀行服務。

不要讓別人使用你的A.T.M.卡，也不要把你的密碼告訴別人。

欲知如何獲得A.T.M.卡，可打電話給你的銀行或信用合作社，或者造訪其網站。

MetroCard（捷運卡）

要乘坐地鐵，必須使用捷運卡，而不能用現金。乘坐New York City Transit（紐約市捷運局）經營的公共汽車則既可以使用捷運卡，也可以使用現金。使用捷運卡乘坐地鐵或本地公共汽車時，支出費用會低於現行的資費標準。你還可以在地鐵和公共汽車之間和不同線路的公共汽車之間進行一次免費換乘。如果你年齡在65歲以上，或者有身體或精神殘障，還可以申請優惠捷運卡，持這種卡可以半價乘車。

捷運卡的運作是這樣的：你付一定金額的費用，這筆費用被輸入卡片，然後每次你在地鐵旋轉式柵門或公共汽車讀卡器上刷卡時，就會從卡內金額中扣除車費。當卡內的全部金額用盡時，就該為卡充值或者購買一張新卡了。

你可以在地鐵車站的售票處、捷運卡自動販賣機、捷運卡售卡和有捷運卡標記的商店買到捷運卡。

按次計價（或者普通型）捷運卡面值有很多種。如果你的消費超過一定金額，就會被多贈送一次乘坐機會。

還有幾種不限乘坐次數的捷運卡，它們面值不等，在一定時期內不限乘坐次數。

網址： www.mta.nyc.us/metrocard
電話： 1-212-638-7622（英語、西班牙語、廣東話和普通話）

電話卡

如果在你住的地方沒有電話或長途電話公司，或者如果你使用收費公用電話，購買電話卡是個好辦法。買這種卡就是為向許多地方打長途電話預付費用。

電話卡可以在酒店、超級市場和便利店等許多地方買到。注意，你買的電話卡一定要有有效的客戶服務電話號碼。

通常來說，你支付一定數額的費用買卡，或者購買一定長度的通話時間。

大多數預付電話卡都有免費的接入電話號碼和一個密碼（PIN）。打電話時，撥通接入號碼，再輸入密碼。電話語音系統會提示你輸入欲撥打對方的電話號碼。

電話費會從電話卡內的餘額扣除。你會被告知卡上還有多少分鐘，或者多少金額。

如果你已經打光了卡上的所有時間，而且不能充值，就必須購買新卡。

由於某些公司的電話卡定價過高，一定要多看看，貨比三家，確保你得到的通話時間與花費相比是公平的。

Federal Trade Commission（聯邦貿易委員會）建議你在購買電話卡之前要問四個問題：

1. 每次打電話的*接通費*是多少？
2. 有*服務費*嗎？
3. 有*維護費*嗎？
4. 有*失效日期*嗎？不要購買沒等你用完所有通話時間就可能失效的電話卡。

資源名錄

大多數紐約人會告訴你，重要的是你認識什麼人，而不是你知道什麼。實際上對新來的人來說，兩者都很重要。

關於這座城市本身就已經有很多事要瞭解：它的各種族的聚居區、公共汽車和地鐵線路、公立學校體系等等不一而足。你需要瞭解的和你想瞭解的事經常看起來似乎是太多太多。但並非如此。

在指南的正文中，許多機構、團體和服務提供者的後面都有頁碼，指引你參閱這裡的資源名錄部分的某一頁。資源名錄提供了這些機構、團體和服務提供者的詳細情況，它們經過了移民的審核，被認為是非常有幫助的和可靠的。

每一則介紹上面的圖標表示該資源機構、團體或者服務提供者處理的事項，例如，住房或者兒童保育。

每一家資源機構、團體或者服務提供者的名稱後面都有其最常見的簡稱。

然後每一則介紹會詳細列出資源機構、團體或者服務提供者的地點、電話號碼和傳真號碼、電子郵件地址和網站地址、提供的服務內容、使用的語言，以及要求遞交的文件或其他必要條件（如果有的話）。列出的語種如果後面跟有（P）字樣，表示該機構、團體或服務提供者提供這種語言的印刷材料。

資源名錄是非常便利的參考材料，因此當你在紐約市四處闖蕩時可能想隨身攜帶本指南。

資源介紹圖標說明：

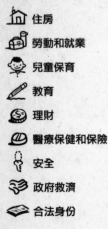

住房

勞動和就業

兒童保育

教育

理財

醫療保健和保險

安全

政府救濟

合法身份

Alianza Dominicana, Inc.（多米尼加聯盟）
地址：**2410 Amsterdam Avenue, 4th Floor, New York, N.Y. 10033**
電話：**1-212-740-1960; 傳真：1-212-740-1967**
網址：**http://www.alianzadom.org/index.html**

我能得到哪些幫助？
■ 英語班、G.E.D.和電腦基礎知識（西班牙語）。
■ 課後輔導和暑期青少年計劃。
■ 移民家庭援助。
■ 社區保健服務；獲得健康保險。
■ 為受H.I.V.或愛滋病影響或感染的人提供雙語/跨文化服務。
你們為哪些人提供幫助？所有人。**你們提供哪種語言的幫助？**西班牙語（P）。
我必須帶什麼東西去嗎？帶身份證會有幫助，但並不要求一定要帶身份證。**你們
還在其他地方設有辦事處嗎？**在布朗士設有1個辦事處；在曼哈頓設有10個。請
提前打電話。

Archdiocese of New York, Superintendent of Schools（紐約大主教管區，督學）
地址：**1011 First Avenue, New York, N.Y. 10022**
電話：**1-212-371-1000**

我能得到哪些幫助？
■ 得到曼哈頓、布朗士和史坦頓島的公立學校名錄。
■ 瞭解如何與學校預約時間面談，開放參觀日是怎麼回事。
你們為哪些人提供幫助？所有人。**你們提供哪種語言的幫助？**西班牙語（P）。
我必須帶什麼東西去嗎？不要求帶什麼。**你們還在其他地方設有辦事處嗎？**
只在以上地點設有唯一一家機構。

**Asian American Legal Defense and Education Fund（亞美法律援助處，簡稱
A.A.L.D.E.F.）**
地址：**99 Hudson Street, New York, N.Y. 10013**
電話：**1-212-966-5932, 1-212-966-6030; 傳真：1-212-966-4303**
網址：**http://www.aaldef.org**

我能得到哪些幫助？
■ 提供移民法和家庭法方面的免費咨詢。
■ 協助入籍申請。

■ 政府救濟。
■ 就業歧視和勞工權利。
■ 警察行為不當。
你們為哪些人提供幫助？ 所有人。法律服務必須預約。**你們提供哪種語言的幫助？** 說中文（P）（廣東話、普通話、臺山話）、孟加拉語、印地語、韓國語、他加祿語和烏爾都語的人請打電話1-212-966-5932或1-212-966-6030。**我必須帶什麼東西去嗎？** 請提前打電話預約，並瞭解帶哪些資料、文件和法律文書。**你們還在其他地方設有辦事處嗎？** 只在以上地點設有唯一一家機構。

Asian Americans for Equality（亞洲人平等會，簡稱A.A.F.E.）
地址：277 Grand Street, 3rd Floor, New York, N.Y. 10002
電話：1-212-680-1374; 傳真：1-212-680-1815; 電子郵件：info@aafe.org
網址：http://www.aafe.org

我能得到哪些幫助？
■ 基本的居住權利和職責；居住法律援助和代理；購房咨詢，可負擔的抵押貸款的取得。
■ 政府救濟和保健咨詢。
■ 入籍咨詢和公民課程。
■ 小企業咨詢和可承受的融資。
■ 電腦基礎知識。設備齊全的電腦中心提供多種課程。
你們為哪些人提供幫助？ 所有人。**你們提供哪種語言的幫助？** 西班牙語（P）、中文（P）（廣東話、普通話）、孟加拉語、韓國語。 **我必須帶什麼東西去嗎？** 根據需要的服務而定。**你們還在其他地方設有辦事處嗎？** 在曼哈頓下城設有5個辦事處；在皇后區設有1個辦事處。請提前打電話。

Banco Popular（大眾銀行）
電話：1-800-377-0800; 網址：http://www.bancopopular.com

我能得到哪些幫助？
■ 儲蓄賬戶和支票賬戶、信用、保險、投資、貸款和抵押貸款。
你們為哪些人提供幫助？ 所有人。**你們提供哪種語言的幫助？** 西班牙語（P）。**我必須帶什麼東西去嗎？** 欲辦理普通個人銀行業務，至少要帶兩種身份證明：美國或非美國護照、帶照片的非永久居民登記卡、帶照片的入籍證書、軍人身份證、駕駛執照和/或主要的銀行卡或信用卡。**你們還在其他地方設有辦事處嗎？** 在布朗士設有5處；在布碌崙設有9處；在曼哈頓設有10處；在皇后區設有3處。請提前打電話。

Bellevue Hospital Center（Bellevue醫院中心）
地址：462 First Avenue, New York, N.Y. 10016
電話：1-212-562-4141; 網址：http://www.nyc.gov/bellevue

我能得到哪些幫助？
■ 哮喘、糖尿病、營養、戒煙、壓力管理和體重管理。
■ 健康普查、課程和支持團體。
■ 強姦醫務所。
■ 為需要不間斷的醫療照顧的人提供長期照顧。
■ 為家庭的所有成員提供預防保健和主要保健。
■ 常規牙科檢查和牙科照顧；口腔和齒齦疾病治療。
你們為哪些人提供幫助？所有人。**你們提供哪種語言的幫助？**最常用的是西班牙語（P）、中文（廣東話、普通話）、孟加拉語、波蘭語、法語和俄語；可提供135種語言的服務；現場有翻譯人員。**我必須帶什麼東西去嗎？**如果有的話，帶保險卡。**你們還在其他地方設有辦事處嗎？**在布朗士設有5處；在布碌崙有6處；在曼哈頓有5處；在皇后區有2處；在史坦頓島有1處。請提前打電話。

Bethex Federal Credit Union（Bethex聯邦信用合作社）
地址：20 East 179th Street, Bronx, N.Y. 10453
電話：1-718-299-9100; 傳真：1-718-294-4950
網址：http://www.bethexfcu.org

我能得到哪些幫助？
■ 支票和儲蓄賬戶；貸款。
你們為哪些人提供幫助？所有人。**你們提供哪種語言的幫助？**每個營業網點都有說西班牙語（P）的人員。**我必須帶什麼東西去嗎？**20美元（10美元會費，10美元存入新開立的儲蓄賬戶）。住址證明（電話或公用事業賬單）、帶照片的身份證和社會安全片或綠卡。**你們還在其他地方設有辦事處嗎？**在布朗士設有3個辦事處；在曼哈頓設有1個辦事處。請提前打電話。

The Bronx Defenders （布朗士辯護人）
地址：860 Courtlandt Avenue, Bronx, N.Y. 10451
電話：1-718-838-7878; 傳真：1-718-665-0100
電子郵件：shaynak@bronxdefenders.org; 網址：http://www.bronxdefenders.org

我能得到哪些幫助？
- 為受到罪行指控的人提供法律咨詢；民事法律服務。
- 殘障和停職問題。
- 藥物成癮。
- 社會福利事業介紹。

你們為哪些人提供幫助？布朗士區因犯罪被逮捕的人或害怕被捕的人。（不要求一定是布朗士的居民。）**你們提供哪種語言的幫助？**西班牙語（P）。**我必須帶什麼東西去嗎？**根據需要的服務而定。**你們還在其他地方設有辦事處嗎？**只在以上地點設有唯一一家機構。

Brooklyn Chinese-American Association（布碌崙華人協會）
地址：5002 Eighth Avenue, 2nd Floor, Brooklyn, N.Y. 11220
電話：1-718-438-9312; 傳真：1-718-438-8303

我能得到哪些幫助？
- 入籍咨詢。
- Medicaid和食物券。
- 翻譯服務。
- 幼兒園學齡前計劃、日托、課後和暑期計劃；老年人中心。
- 英語、商務和電腦班；兒童中文班。
- 健康教育。

你們為哪些人提供幫助？只為布碌崙的合法居民提供幫助。**你們提供哪種語言的幫助？**中文（P）（廣東話、普通話）。**我必須帶什麼東西去嗎？**不要求帶什麼。**你們還在其他地方設有辦事處嗎？**在布碌崙設有4個辦事處。請提前打電話。

Bushwick Cooperative Federal Credit Union（Bushwick聯邦信用合作社）
地址：1475 Myrtle Avenue, Brooklyn, N.Y. 11237
電話：1-718-418-8232; 傳真：1-718-418-8252; 電子郵件：bushwickfcu@rbscc.org

我能得到哪些幫助？
- 支票和儲蓄賬戶；貸款；理財基礎知識。

你們為哪些人提供幫助？所有人。**你們提供哪種語言的幫助？**西班牙語。**我必須帶什麼東西去嗎？**二種身份證明，至少要有一種帶照片；住址證明；社會安全卡；保險對帳單或者工資存根。**你們還在其他地方設有辦事處嗎？** 只在以上地點設有唯一一家機構。

✎

Cabrini Immigrant Services（卡布里尼移民服務）
地址：139 Henry Street, New York, N.Y. 10002
電話：1-212-791-4590; 傳真：1-212-791-4592

我能得到哪些幫助？
■ 填寫表格和申請；獲得必要的介紹。
■ 英語課（要求承諾每週至少上一天課）。
■ 免費食物。
你們為哪些人提供幫助？所有人。**你們提供哪種語言的幫助？**西班牙語（P）、中文（P）（普通話）。**我必須帶什麼東西去嗎？**不要求帶什麼。所有的服務都是免費的。註冊八月和/或十二月的課程。**你們還在其他地方設有辦事處嗎？**只在以上地點設有唯一一家機構。

✒ 🖱 🔑

Caribbean Women's Health Association （加勒比婦女健康協會，簡稱C.W.H.A.）
地址：123 Linden Boulevard, Brooklyn, N.Y. 11226
電話：1-718-826-2942; 傳真：1-718-826-2948; 網址：http://www.cwha.org

我能得到哪些幫助？
■ 在移民法院及家庭團聚和驅逐出境聽證會上進行法律代理。
■ 入籍申請和考試準備。
■ 公共衛生；H.I.V.和愛滋病服務；母嬰保健和W.I.C.。
你們為哪些人提供幫助？所有人。**你們提供哪種語言的幫助？**西班牙語、海地語（P）、克裡奧爾語（P）、法語（P）。也備有其他的語言的翻譯人員。請提前打電話。**我必須帶什麼東西去嗎？**為法律援助支付的少量費用。請提前打電話。**你們還在其他地方設有辦事處嗎？**在布碌崙設有2個辦事處；在皇后區設有2個辦事處。請提前打電話。

💲

Cathay Bank（國泰銀行）
電話：1-800-9CATHAY (1-800-922-8429)

我能得到哪些幫助？
■ 支票和儲蓄賬戶；個人退休賬戶和定期存款；汽車、家庭資產淨值和抵押貸款；外幣兌換。**你們為哪些人提供幫助？**所有人。**你們提供哪種語言的幫助？**中文（廣東話、普通話）（P）**我必須帶什麼東西去嗎？**至少要帶兩種身份證明：美國或非美國護照、帶照片的非永久居民登記卡、帶照片的入籍證書、軍人身份證、駕駛執照和/或主要的銀行卡或信用卡。**你們還在其他地方設有辦事處嗎？**在布碌崙區設有1個分支機搆；在曼哈頓有1個分支機構；在皇后區有1個分支機構。請提前打電話。

Catholic Charities Office for Immigrant Services（天主教慈善機構移民服務辦公室）
地址：**1011 First Avenue, 12th Floor; New York, N.Y. 10022**
電話：**1-212-419-3700, 1-800-566-7636**（欲取得下列語言的幫助）
傳真：**1-212-751-3197; 網址：http://www.catholiccharities.org**

我能得到哪些幫助？
■ 提供移民和難民重新安置方面的法律援助；為被拘捕的尋求庇護者提供法律代理。
■ 歸化和入籍文件。
你們提供哪種語言的幫助？西班牙語（P）、中文（普通話）（P）、阿拉伯語、法語、海地克裡奧爾語、意大利語、日語、韓國語、波蘭語、旁遮普語、俄語、塞爾維亞克羅地亞語、土耳其語和烏爾都語。**你們為哪些人提供幫助？**所有人。**我必須帶什麼東西去嗎？**雖然經濟困難的人不會被拒絕，但要準備50美元服務費。請提前打電話。**你們還在其他地方設有辦事處嗎？**擴大範圍服務地點（每月）：布朗士和史坦頓島。請提前打電話。

Catholic Migration Services（天主教移民服務）
地址：**1258 65th Street, Brooklyn, N.Y. 11219**
電話：**1-718-236-3000; 傳真：1-718-256-9707; 電子郵件：migration@aol.com**
網址：**www.catholicimmigration.org**

我能得到哪些幫助？
■ 提供移民方面的法律幫助。
■ 英語夜校（各種水平的）；入籍班。
■ 電腦基本技能、烹調技術、住宅和工作地點清潔方面的課程。
你們為哪些人提供幫助？所有人。**你們提供哪種語言的幫助？**西班牙語（P）、阿爾巴尼亞語、希臘語、意大利語、海地克裡奧爾語和波蘭語。請提前打電話。**我必須帶什麼東西去嗎？**少量服務費。請提前打電話。**你們還在其他地方設有辦事處嗎？**在皇后區設有1處。

Charles B. Wang Community Health Center（王嘉廉社區醫療中心）
地址：**268 Canal Street, New York, N.Y. 10013**
電話：**1-212-379-6998; 傳真：1-212-379-6930**

我能得到哪些幫助？
■ 主要保健、婦女保健、產科、婦科、癌症檢查、內科、兒科、兒科心臟病學、青少年保健、過敏、牙齒保健、眼科保健、泌尿科、針灸、專科照顧、心理健康、健康教育、疾病預防。
■ Child Health Plus和Family Health Plus的註冊。
■ 社會福利、W.I.C.。
你們為哪些人提供幫助？所有人。**你們提供哪種語言的幫助？**中文（廣東話、普通話、臺山話、上海話和臺灣話）。請提前打電話。**我必須帶什麼東西去嗎？**Medicaid和第三方保險證明；支付能力證明，例如工資存根和納稅證明；你有的任何證明文件。根據支付能力，收費20－60美元不等。**你們還在其他地方設有辦事處嗎？**在曼哈頓下城設有1處；在皇后區設有1處。

Chase（大通銀行）
電話：**1-800-CHASE24 (1-800-242-7324); 網址：http://www.chase.com**

我能得到哪些幫助？
■ 支票和儲蓄賬戶、信用卡、投資、保險、抵押貸款及其他貸款。
你們為哪些人提供幫助？有美國通訊地址和有效的社會安全號碼的美國公民。**你們提供哪種語言的幫助？**服務熱線（英語、西班牙語；僅限區號為212、516、585、914、718的人打入）935-9999。服務熱線（英語、中文）1-212-809-6464。服務熱線（韓國語雙語）1-212-809-3737。**我必須帶什麼東西去嗎？**出生日期證明、母親的娘家姓、就業資料、駕駛執照或者州身份證。**你們還在其他地方設有辦事處嗎？**請打電話詢問最近的分行地點。

Chinatown Manpower Project, Inc.（華埠人力中心）
地址：70 Mulberry Street, New York, N.Y. 10003
電話：1-212-571-1690; 傳真：1-212-571-1686; 網址：www.cmpny.org

我能得到哪些幫助？
■ 英語、入籍和工作技能發展方面的課程。
■ 電算化會計記帳和會計、基本的辦公室技能和電腦操作等方面的職業訓練。
■ 為個人和小企業提供企業培訓、財務計劃、商業咨詢和技術援助。
■ 入籍咨詢。
你們為哪些人提供幫助？紐約市居民。**你們提供哪種語言的幫助？**中文（廣東話、普通話）。**我必須帶什麼東西去嗎？**綠卡或社會安全卡；地址證明。請提前打電話。**你們還在其他地方設有辦事處嗎？**在布碌崙設有1處；在曼哈頓下城設有1處。請提前打電話。

Chinese Immigrant Services（華人移民服務）
地址：133-54 41st Avenue, 4th Floor, Flushing, N.Y. 11355
電話：1-718-353-0195; 傳真：1-718-359-5065

我能得到哪些幫助？
■ 華人移民支持團體和青少年團體。
■ 家庭衝突的咨詢和調解。
■ 就多種社會和法律問題提供資料、介紹和咨詢。
■ 英語班和關於美國文化和制度的課程。
你們為哪些人提供幫助？紐約市居民。**你們提供哪種語言的幫助？**中文（P）（廣東話、普通話）。**我必須帶什麼東西去嗎？**不要求帶什麼。**你們還在其他地方設有辦事處嗎？**只在以上地點設有唯一一家機構。

Chinese Staff and Workers' Association （華人職工會）
地址：15 Catherine Street, 2nd Floor, New York, N.Y. 10038
電話：1-212-619-7979; 傳真：1-212-374-1506

我能得到哪些幫助？
■ 就餐館、成衣和服務業的規章制度和勞動標準提供法律咨詢；職工教育和領導能力發展。
你們為哪些人提供幫助？所有人。**你們提供哪種語言的幫助？**中文（P）（廣東話、普通話、福建話）。**我必須帶什麼東西去嗎？**不要求帶什麼。**你們還在其他地方設有辦事處嗎？**在布碌崙設有1處。請提前打電話。

Chinese-American Planning Council （華人策劃協會，簡稱C.P.C.）
地址：150 Elizabeth Street, New York, N.Y. 10012
電話：1-212-941-0920; 傳真：1-212-966-8581; 網址：http://www.cpc-nyc.org

我能得到哪些幫助？
- 服裝、旅館、文書和多媒體行業的就業培訓。
- 為成人員工提供成人掃盲班和過渡就業。
- 為受911事件影響的人提供專案管理和咨詢服務。
- Child Health Plus、Family Health Plus、食物券及其他福利。
- 公平住房。
- 亞裔兒童保育資源和介紹，以及家庭服務。
- 為發育性殘障兒童的父母提供保健服務。
- 幫助預防H.I.V.、愛滋病和吸毒。

你們為哪些人提供幫助？所有人，但主要是居住在華埠、下東城、法拉盛和Sunset Park的亞洲移民和亞裔美國人。**你們提供哪種語言的幫助？**中文（P）（廣東話、普通話）。**我必須帶什麼東西去嗎？**帶上身份證明會有幫助。**你們還在其他地方設有辦事處嗎？**在曼哈頓設有11個日托中心、2個老年人中心、2個專案管理所、1個就業和培訓站和1個青年就業計劃站；在布碌崙設有分支機構、1個就業和培訓站及3個青年服務站；在皇后區設有分支機構、1個日托中心和1個老年人中心。請提前打電話。

Church Avenue Merchants Block Association, Inc. （教堂大道商人區協會，簡稱C.A.M.B.A.）
地址：1720 Church Avenue, 2nd Floor, Brooklyn, N.Y. 11226
電話：1-718-287-2600; 傳真：1-718-287-0857; 網址：http://www.camba.org

我能得到哪些幫助？
- 為面臨驅逐和申請福利被拒絕的人提供顧問、代理和緊急援助。
- 移民法律服務；針對難民和庇護尋求者的服務；入籍和公民研討班。
- 職業培訓和安置工作。
- 英語和電腦班。

你們為哪些人提供幫助？所有人。如需要職業介紹服務，必須有合法身份。**你們提供哪種語言的幫助？**西班牙語（P）、阿爾巴尼亞語（P）、俄語（P）、法語、阿拉伯語、波斯尼亞語、海地克裡奧爾語。**我必須帶什麼東西去嗎？**需要就業和難民服務的人應該帶有關文件。請提前打電話。**你們還在其他地方設有辦事處嗎？** 在布碌崙設有13處。請提前打電話。**法律服務地址**：885 Flatbush Avenue, 2nd Floor, Brooklyn, N.Y. 11226, 電話：1-718-287-0010。**就業和難民服務地址**：2211 Church Avenue, Room 202, Brooklyn, N.Y. 11226, 電話：1-718-282-0108。

Citibank（花旗銀行）
電話：**1-800-627-3999;** 網址：**http://www.citibank.com**

我能得到哪些幫助？
■ 支票和儲蓄賬戶、保險、投資、信用卡、抵押貸款及其他貸款。
你們為哪些人提供幫助？ 所有人。**你們提供哪種語言的幫助？** 西班牙語（P）。**我必須帶什麼東西去嗎？** 至少二種身份證：美國或非美國護照、帶照片的非居民登記卡、帶照片的入籍證明、軍人身份證、駕駛執照和/或主要的銀行卡或信用卡。**你們還在其他地方設有辦事處嗎？** 請打電話詢問最近的分行地點。

Citizens Advice Bureau（公民顧問局，C.A.B.）
地址：**2054 Morris Avenue, Bronx, N.Y. 10453**
電話：**1-718-365-0910;** 傳真：**1-718-365-0697;** 網址：**http://www.cabny.org**

我能得到哪些幫助？
■ 面向兒童和青少年的日托、課後計劃和夏令營計劃，以及老年人中心（包括食物、身體鍛煉和遊戲）。
■ 就移民、入籍及其他法律問題進行咨詢。
■ E.S.O.L.和公民課程。
■ 就業幫助。
■ 防止驅逐，為無家可歸者和家庭提供咨詢。
■ 健康保險咨詢。
■ 為愛滋病患者提供咨詢和病症管理。
你們為哪些人提供幫助？ 所有人。**你們提供哪種語言的幫助？** 西班牙語（P）。**我必須帶什麼東西去嗎？** 不要求帶什麼。**你們還在其他地方設有辦事處嗎？** 在布朗士設有20餘處站點。請提前打電話。

City Harvest Hunger Hot Line（城市豐收饑餓熱線）
地址：**575 Eighth Avenue, 4th Floor, New York, N.Y. 10018**
電話：**1-917-351-8700; 傳真：1-917-351-8720**
網址：**http://www.cityharvest.org**

我能得到哪些幫助？
■ 應急食品計劃。
你們為哪些人提供幫助？所有有需要的人。**你們提供哪種語言的幫助？**西班牙語。**我必須帶什麼東西去嗎？**身份證和住址證明。請提前打電話。**你們還在其他地方設有辦事處嗎？**在五個區設有數百處機構。

City University of New York（紐約市立大學，CUNY）
地址：**1114 Avenue of the Americas, New York, N.Y. 10036**
電話：**1-212-997-CUNY (2869); 網址：http://www.cuny.edu/**

我能得到哪些幫助？
■ 為CUNY入學和T.O.E.F.L.（託福）考試輔導英語班。
■ 各學院提供文科和理科、商務、保健學、公共事務和社區、社會福利事業、工程、建築和有關技術、法律、圖書館學、師範教育等科目的本科和研究生課程。
■ 提供關於各種課程和機構的咨詢。
■ 經濟資助。
■ 榮譽課程和週末課程。
■ 繼續教育和專業訓練證書課程。
你們為哪些人提供幫助？所有人。**你們提供哪種語言的幫助？**各分校各有不同。**我必須帶什麼東西去嗎？**填寫完整的申請表格、40美元費用、翻譯好的中等學校文憑/證書和/或成績單。確切的移民身份和簽證，不論是有效的還是過期的。如果需要，託福成績和SAT成績。託福可以確定在CUNY學習的語言能力。**你們還在其他地方設有辦事處嗎？**設有20處分校：布碌崙4處、布朗士3處、曼哈頓7處、皇后區5處、史坦頓島1處。

Civilian Complaint Review Board（民眾投訴審查委員會，簡稱C.C.R.B.）
地址：**40 Rector Street, 2nd Floor, New York, N.Y. 10006**
電話：**1-212-442-8833** 或 **1-800-341-2272; 傳真：1-212-442-9109;**
網址：**http://www.nyc.gov/ccrb**

我能得到哪些幫助？
■ 就過度或不必要使用武力、濫用職權、行為魯莽或語言無禮投訴紐約市警察局的警官。
你們為哪些人提供幫助？所有人。**你們提供哪種語言的幫助？**中文（P）（廣東話、普通話）、西班牙語（P）、阿拉伯語（P）、法語、俄語（P）、波蘭語（P）、韓國語（P）和意大利語。欲獲得其他語種的幫助，請說明要求的語種和你的電話號碼。翻譯人員會回電。**我必須帶什麼東西去嗎？**你所掌握的關於事件的全部資料。C.C.R.B.會詢問事件發生的日期、時間、場所和事件經過的詳細說明及涉及的警官。其他有用的資料包括：車輛牌照號碼、逮捕號碼、法庭備審案件目錄號碼和電話號碼。你不必一定要知道當事警官的姓名或警徽號碼。**你們還在其他地方設有辦事處嗎？**只在以上地點設有唯一一家機構。

Community Association of Progressive Dominicans（進步多米尼加人僑界聯合會）
地址：**3940 Broadway, 2nd Floor, New York, N.Y. 10032**
電話：**1-212-781-5500; 傳真：1-212-927-6089; 網址：http://home.att.net/~acdpinc/**

我能得到哪些幫助？
■ 就驅逐進行法律代理和咨詢，房東問題和低收入住房。
■ 英語、電腦和入籍班以及夏令營。
■ 為申請食物券和政府救濟提供咨詢和幫助。
你們為哪些人提供幫助？必須有合法身份並收入較低。**你們提供哪種語言的幫助？**西班牙語（P）。**我必須帶什麼東西去嗎？**綠卡和/或就業許可證/工卡；在住房方面對家庭規模的要求。請提前打電話。**你們還在其他地方設有辦事處嗎？**在布朗士有1處；在曼哈頓上城有5處。請提前打電話。

Community Healthcare Network, Bronx Center（社區保健網，布朗士中心）
地址：975 Westchester Avenue, Bronx, N.Y. 10459
電話：1-718-991-9250/51; 傳真：1-212-991-3829
網址：http://www.chnnyc.org

我能得到哪些幫助？
■ 為成年人、兒童和H.I.V.感染者提供主要醫療保健；家庭計劃和產前護理；學校
 體檢；哮喘檢查；心理健康照顧；營養服務；社會福利事業。
你們為哪些人提供幫助？所有人。**你們提供哪種語言的幫助？**在曼哈頓下城辦事
處有西班牙語（P）、中文（P）；在布碌崙辦事處有法語、海地克裡奧爾語。**我
必須帶什麼東西去嗎？**工資存根或寫明工資標準並要求減免費用的僱主信，或者
保險卡。青少年要帶身份證。**你們還在其他地方設有辦事處嗎？**在布碌崙設有4
個辦事處；在曼哈頓設有1個；在皇后區設有1個。請提前打電話。

CUNY Law School
Main Street Legal Services, Immigration and Refugee Rights Program（紐約市立大學
法學院－緬因街法律服務，移民和難民權利計劃）
地址：65-21 Main Street, Flushing, N.Y. 11367
電話：1-718-340-4300; 傳真：1-718-340-4478
網址：http://www.law.cuny.edu

我能得到哪些幫助？
■ 入籍和移民法律服務，包括庇護和家庭申請；家庭暴力問題；老年人法律。
你們為哪些人提供幫助？所有人。**你們提供哪種語言的幫助？**西班牙語、中文
（廣東話）和孟加拉語。取決於每學期註冊的學生。請提前打電話。**我必須帶什
麼東西去嗎？**請提前打電話。**你們還在其他地方設有辦事處嗎？**只在以上地點設
有唯一一家機構。

Delgado Travel （Delgado旅行社）
地址：7908 Roosevelt Avenue, Jackson Heights, N.Y. 11372
電話：1-718-426-0500; 傳真：1-718-397-0347

我能得到哪些幫助？
■ 電匯；運輸包裝；國際長話；旅行安排。

你們為哪些人提供幫助？所有人。**你們提供哪種語言的幫助？**西班牙語（P）。**我必須帶什麼東西去嗎？**取決於尋求的服務。**你們還在其他地方設有辦事處嗎？**在布朗士設有4處；在布碌崙設有4處；在曼哈頓設有5處；在皇后區設有12處。請提前打電話。

The Door（門）
地址：121 Avenue of the Americas, New York, N.Y. 10013
電話：1-212-941-9090; 傳真：1-212-941-0714; 網址：http://www.door.org

我能得到哪些幫助？
■ 綜合性青少年成長服務、保健、咨詢、教育、法律服務、藝術、以及娛樂。
你們為哪些人提供幫助？任何12到21歲的紐約市居民。**你們提供哪種語言的幫助？**西班牙語和中文（廣東話和普通話）。我們有英語、西班牙語和中文網站。**我必須帶什麼東西去嗎？**不要求帶什麼。**你們還在其他地方設有辦事處嗎？**只在以上地點設有唯一一家機構。

Emerald Isle Immigration Center（Emerald Isle移民中心）
地址：59-26 Woodside Avenue, Woodside, N.Y. 11377
電話：1-718-478-5502; 傳真：1-718-446-3727; 網址：http://www.eiic.org

我能得到哪些幫助？
■ 移民及其他法律服務、文書工作、綠卡、入籍考試準備和介紹。
■ 找工作和安置工作。
你們為哪些人提供幫助？所有人。**你們提供哪種語言的幫助？**西班牙語、法語。**我必須帶什麼東西去嗎？**取決於尋求的服務。**你們還在其他地方設有辦事處嗎？**在布朗士設有1處。請提前打電話。

Flatbush Development Corporation（Flatbush開發公司）
地址：1616 Newkirk Avenue, Brooklyn, N.Y. 11226
電話：1-718-859-3800; 傳真：1-718-859-4632

我能得到哪些幫助？
■ 住房、房客和房東研討班、房客協會。
你們為哪些人提供幫助？取決於尋求的服務。請提前打電話。**你們提供哪種語言的幫助？**西班牙語（P）、中文（普通話）、柬埔寨語、法語和海地克裡奧爾語

（P）、泰語。**我必須帶什麼東西去嗎？**帶照片的身份證、住址證明、社會安全卡（如果有的話）。**你們還在其他地方設有辦事處嗎？**只在以上地點設有唯一一家機構。

Forest Hills Community House（Forest Hills社區會所）
地址：108-25 62nd Drive, Forest Hills, N.Y. 11375
電話：1-718-592-5757; 傳真：1-718-592-2933; 網址：http://www.fhch.org

我能得到哪些幫助？
■ 為青少年和成年人開設的英語入籍班。
■ 電腦班和職業培訓。
■ 福利咨詢、食物/營養和住房服務。
■ 心理健康、老年人計劃和成人日托。
■ 幼兒計劃。
你們為哪些人提供幫助？皇后區居民。**你們提供哪種語言的幫助？**西班牙語（P）、阿拉伯語、北美手語、法語、海地克裡奧爾語、希伯來語、韓國語和俄語。**我必須帶什麼東西去嗎？**取決於尋求的服務。請提前打電話。**你們還在其他地方設有辦事處嗎？**在皇后區設有15處站點。請提前打電話。

Growing Up Healthy Hot Line（健康成長熱線）
電話：1-800-522-5006

我能得到哪些幫助？
■ 食物券；通過W.I.C.向有5歲以下小孩的父母發放副食券。
■ Medicaid家庭計劃和健康資料。
■ 生活費用。
■ 老年人服務。
你們為哪些人提供幫助？只限被介紹來的人。**你們提供哪種語言的幫助？**有多種語言的翻譯人員。

HealthStat
見New York City Department of Health and Mental Hygiene（紐約市健康與心理衛生局）（第407頁）

Hebrew Immigrant Aid Society（希伯來移民援助協會，簡稱H.I.A.S.）
地址：333 Seventh Avenue, New York, N.Y. 10001
電話：1-212-967-4100; 傳真：1-212-760-1833; 電子郵件：info@hias.org
網址：http://www.hias.org

我能得到哪些幫助？
■ 簽證和移民資格、文件申請、解答問題和法律代理；難民和移民的食物和住
  房；準備入籍考試和面試。
你們為哪些人提供幫助？ 所有人。要求預約；請事先打電話。**你們提供哪種語言
的幫助？** 西班牙語、俄語（P）、意第緒語和法語。**我必須帶什麼東西去嗎？**
不要求帶什麼。**你們還在其他地方設有辦事處嗎？** 只在以上地點設有唯一一家
機構。

**Hellenic American Neighborhood Action Committee（美國希臘裔社區行動委員會，
簡稱H.A.N.A.C.）**
地址：49 West 45th Street, 4th Floor, New York, N.Y. 10036
電話：1-212-840-8005 或1-212-996-3949; 傳真：1-212-840-8384;
電子郵件：info@hanac.org; 網址：http://www.hanac.org

我能得到哪些幫助？
■ 法律代理、咨詢服務和辯護。
■ 就業研討會、工作準備、工作安置。
■ 基礎教育、G.E.D.指導、見習安排。
■ 英語課和入籍考試輔導。
■ 社區擴大服務、家庭療法、危機干預、夫妻咨詢、防止寄養和老年人服務。
■ 個別指導、顧問和理財咨詢
■ 課後和燈塔計劃；日間夏令營和青年就業計劃。
你們為哪些人提供幫助？ 有正式身份的低收入移民。**你們提供哪種語言的幫助？**
西班牙語、希臘語和印地語。**我必須帶什麼東西去嗎？** 取決於需要的服務。**你們
還在其他地方設有辦事處嗎？** 在曼哈頓設有2個辦事處；在皇后區設有2個辦事
處。請提前打電話。

Highbridge Community Life Center（Highbridge 社區生活中心）
地址：979 Ogden Avenue, Bronx, N.Y. 10452
電話：1-718-681-2222; 傳真：1-718-681-4137或1-718-992-3481

我能得到哪些幫助？
■ 英語課和西班牙語掃盲班；基礎教育和G.E.D.課；課後計劃。
■ 食品室和流動餐飲。
■ 就業服務。
你們為哪些人提供幫助？所有人。**你們提供哪種語言的幫助？**西班牙語。**我必須帶什麼東西去嗎？**不要求帶什麼。必須在一月、六月和/或九月註冊。**你們還在其他地方設有辦事處嗎？**只在以上地點設有唯一一家機構。

HSBC Bank USA（美國匯豐銀行）
電話：1-800-975-HSBC (1-800-975-4722)
網址：http://us.hsbc.com/

我能得到哪些幫助？
■ 支票和儲蓄賬戶，保險，投資，信用卡，抵押貸款及其他貸款。
你們為哪些人提供幫助？已經有或者正在申請有效的社會安全號的並在美國有地址的美國居民，外國交換學生。**你們提供哪種語言的幫助？**服務熱線（英語）1-800-975-HSBC（1-800-975-4722）。服務熱線（西班牙語）1-888-433-4722 。服務熱線（多數亞洲語言，包括廣東話和普通話）1-800-711-8001。**我必須帶什麼東西去嗎？**社會安全號或報稅號（非美國公民需要綠卡或者簽證）。必須提供出生日期、母親的娘家姓、就業資料、駕駛執照或者州身份證號；作為住址證明的公用事業帳單或者主要信用卡。**你們還在其他地方設有辦事處嗎？**請打電話查詢最近的分行，或者訪問網站，使用分行地址查詢功能。

Human Resources Administration（人力資源管理局，H.R.A.）
電話：1-877-HRA-8411（1-877-472-8411）

我能得到哪些幫助？
■ 食物券和Medicaid資格。
■ 兒童保育和安全問題。
你們為哪些人提供幫助？所有人。**你們提供哪種語言的幫助？**西班牙語、中文（廣東話、普通話）、俄語和越南語。

Human Resources Administration (H.R.A.), Refugee and Immigrant Center（人力資源管理局，難民和移民中心）
地址：2 Washington Street, New York, N.Y. 10004
電話：1-212-495-7050; 傳真：1-212-495-7604

我能得到哪些幫助？
■ 如果你說英語有困難，可以協助申請政府救濟、Medicaid和Medicare。
你們為哪些人提供幫助？根據貧困程度確定資格。**你們提供哪種語言的幫助？**兩個辦事均有說西班牙語（P）的工作人員；只有曼哈頓辦事處才有說中文（P）（廣東話、普通話）的工作人員。有柬埔寨語、法語、俄語、海地克裡奧爾語、越南語、阿爾巴尼亞語和阿拉伯語翻譯人員及印刷材料。**我必須帶什麼東西去嗎？**某種身份證明。**你們還在其他地方設有辦事處嗎？**在布碌崙設有1處。請提前打電話。

Immigration Advocacy Services（移民支持服務）
地址：24-40 Steinway Street, Astoria, N.Y. 11103
電話：1-718-956-8218; 傳真：1-718-274-1615
網址：www.immigrationadvocacy.com

我能得到哪些幫助？
■ 任何移民、入籍和公民身份事務。
你們為哪些人提供幫助？所有人。**你們提供哪種語言的幫助？**西班牙語（P）、中文（廣東話、普通話）、阿拉伯語（P）、希臘語、意大利語、葡萄牙語和烏爾都語。**我必須帶什麼東西去嗎？**不用帶什麼。**你們還在其他地方設有辦事處嗎？**只在以上地點設有唯一一家機構。

Indochina Sino-American Community Center（美東越棉寮華僑社區中心）
地址：170 Forsyth Street, New York, N.Y. 10002
電話：1-212-226-0317; 傳真：1-212-925-0327
電子郵件：isacenter@zeronet.net
網址：http://www.asianweb.net/news/java/isasci.htm

我能得到哪些幫助？
■ 確定享受社會福利的資格，提供申請地點的資料。
■ 英語和入籍班。

■ 翻譯服務。
■ 職業培訓和就業。
■ 老年人計劃。
你們為哪些人提供幫助? 紐約市居民。**你們提供哪種語言的幫助?** 中文(P)
(廣東話、普通話、福建話)和越南語。**我必須帶什麼東西去嗎?** 課程的登記和
材料費。**你們還在其他地方設有辦事處嗎?** 只在以上地點設有唯一一家機構。請
提前打電話。

Jacob A. Riis Neighborhood Settlement House, Inc. (Jacob A. Riis街坊文教館)
地址:**10-25 41st Avenue, Long Island City, N.Y. 11101**
電話:**1-718-784-7447; 傳真:1-718-784-1964; 電子郵件:jriis@unhny.org**
網址:**http://www.riissettlement.org**

我能得到哪些幫助?
■ 移民證件、就業服務、住房問題和社會福利。
■ 課後計劃、青少年計劃、青少年夏令營。
■ 面向少女和年輕婦女的特別計劃。
■ 老年人中心,可為60歲以上老人提供交通工具。
■ 電腦基礎班和英語班。
你們為哪些人提供幫助? 取決於需要的服務。**你們提供哪種語言的幫助?** 西班牙
語(P)。**我必須帶什麼東西去嗎?** 不用帶什麼。**你們還在其他地方設有辦事處
嗎?** 只在以上地點設有唯一一家機構。

Latino Workers Center (拉美裔員工中心)
地址:**191 East Third Street, New York, N.Y. 10009**
電話:**1-212-473-3936; 傳真:1-212-473-6103**

我能得到哪些幫助?
■ 僱員權利、職業保健和安全;為受傷和失去工資獲得補償。
你們為哪些人提供幫助? 所有人。**你們提供哪種語言的幫助?** 西班牙語(P)。
我必須帶什麼東西去嗎? 不用帶什麼。**你們還在其他地方設有辦事處嗎?** 只在以
上地點設有唯一一家機構。

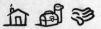

Legal Aid Society, Civil Division（法律援助協會，民事部）
地址：199 Water Street, 3rd Floor, New York, N.Y. 10038
電話：1-212-440-4300; 傳真：1-212-509-8941; 網址：http://www.legal-aid.org

我能得到哪些幫助？
■ 提供移民、住房、政府福利、社會保障、消費、破產、就業、失業、家庭和健康問題方面的法律援助。
你們為哪些人提供幫助？所有的移民。**你們提供哪種語言的幫助？**所有語言。**我必須帶什麼東西去嗎？**你所有的法院和政府文件。**你們還在其他地方設有辦事處嗎？**在五個區和住房法院中均設有地區辦事處。欲查詢辦事處地點，請訪問上面列出的網站。

Legal Services for New York City（紐約市法律服務）
地址：350 Broadway, 6th Floor（中心辦事處）, New York, N.Y. 10013
電話：1-212-431-7200; 傳真：1-212-431-7232; 網址：http://www.lsny.org/

我能得到哪些幫助？
■ 免費提供家庭、居住、福利、消費、健康、就業、經濟發展和教育等方面的法律服務。
你們為哪些人提供幫助？美國公民和有合法身份的移民。不為囚犯提供服務。
你們提供哪種語言的幫助？只提供英語的。**我必須帶什麼東西去嗎？**非公民必須帶綠卡、收入證明和任何與所需要的服務有關的文件。**你們還在其他地方設有辦事處嗎？**在布朗士有3處；在布碌崙有8處；在曼哈頓有3處；在皇后區有2處；在史坦頓島有擴展服務計劃。請提前打電話。

Lower East Side People's Federal Credit Union（下東城人民聯邦信用合作社）
地址：37 Avenue B, New York, N.Y. 10009-7441
電話：1-212-529-8197; 傳真：1-212-529-8368; 電子郵件：lespfcu@lespfcu.org
網址：http://www.lespfcu.org/index.html

我能得到哪些幫助？
■ 儲蓄和支票存款，直接存款，A.T.M.和貸款。
你們為哪些人提供幫助？在下東城生活或工作的人（從東14街到布碌崙大橋之間，和三大道/Bowery街到東河之間），或者屬於下東城的組織的人；現成員的親屬。**你們提供哪種語言的幫助？**西班牙語。**我必須帶什麼東西去嗎？**兩種有效身份證,其中一種要帶有照片和簽字的;社會安全卡或者社會安全號證明;至少30美元;在下東城的住處或就業證明,或者你參加的下東城的組織出具的信函。**你們還在其他地方設有辦事處嗎?**遍佈曼哈頓和布碌崙的免費A.T.M.機。

Lutheran Medical Center(路德教會醫療中心)
地址:**150 55th Street, Brooklyn, N.Y. 11220**
電話:**1-718-630-7000/7210; 傳真:1-718-492-5090**
網址:**http://www.lutheranmedicalcenter.com**

我能得到哪些幫助?
■ 醫療、心理健康、主要保健、H.I.V.和愛滋病、癌症;中風中心。
■ 社會福利和家庭暴力。
■ 政府福利和食品/營養咨詢。
■ 關於移民及其他事務的資訊。
你們為哪些人提供幫助?所有人。布碌崙居民獲得服務時可以享受價格折扣。**你們提供哪種語言的幫助?**西班牙語(P)、中文(P)(廣東話、普通話)、俄語(P)和阿拉伯語(P)。**我必須帶什麼東西去嗎?**身份證;住址證明;獲得價格折扣需要收入證明。**你們還在其他地方設有辦事處嗎?**在布魯克林設有4個辦事處。請提前打電話。

Managed Care Consumer Assistance Program(管理保健消費者援助計劃,簡稱M.C.C.A.P.),Community Service Society of New York(紐約社區服務協會)
地址:**105 East 22nd Street, New York, N.Y. 10010**
電話:**1-212-614-5400(中央幫助熱線);傳真:1-212-614-5305**
網址:**http://www.mccapny.org**

我能得到哪些幫助?
■ 選擇和使用一種管理保健計劃,包括對患有H.I.V.和愛滋病,身體、認識和發育性殘障,以及慢性精神病等慢性病的人提供資訊。
■ 免費或低價健康保險,包括Medicaid、Medicare、Child Health Plus、Family Health Plus和商業保險。
你們為哪些人提供幫助?紐約市居民。**你們提供哪種語言的幫助?**中央幫助熱線有英語和西班牙語服務。分包機構有中文(廣東話、普通話)、韓國語、俄語、阿拉伯語、意第緒語和海地克裡奧爾語服務。**我必須帶什麼東西去嗎?**不用帶什麼。**你們還在其他地方設有辦事處嗎?**在布朗士有5處介紹機構;在布碌崙有3處;在曼哈頓有14處;在皇后區有3處;在史坦頓島有1處。

@

Medical and Health Research Association of New York City, Inc.（紐約市醫療和保健研究協會，簡稱M.H.R.A.）
Health Insurance Enrollment Project（健康保險註冊項目，簡稱H.I.E.P.）
地址：40 Worth Street, Suite 720, New York, N.Y. 10013
電話：1-212-285-0220, ext. 130; 傳真：1-212-385-0565; 網址：http://www.mhra.org

我能得到哪些幫助？
■ 選擇管理保健計劃。
■ 免費或低價健康保險的獲得和續期，包括Medicaid、Medicare、Child Health Plus B、Family Health Plus和P.C.A.P.。
你們為哪些人提供幫助？ 所有人。**你們提供哪種語言的幫助？** 西班牙語、中文（廣東話、普通話）、俄語、阿拉伯語、波蘭語的、希伯來語、意大利語。**我必須帶什麼東西去嗎？** 收入證明（四張最近的工資存根或者你的僱主出具的證明信；如果是自僱人員，要求所得稅申報表）；住址證明；身份證：出生證或宗教證明、護照或綠卡；社會安全卡（Medicaid和Family Health Plus要求；Child Health Plus B則不需要）。國籍情況證明（綠卡或綠卡申請、U.S.C.I.S.的信、簽證；Child Health Plus B不需要）。**你們在哪裡辦公？** 在布碌崙設有4個辦事處；在曼哈頓設有1個；在皇后區設有3個。

@

Medical and Health Research Association of New York City, Inc.（紐約市醫療和健康研究協會，簡稱M.H.R.A.）
M.I.C.-Women's Health Services（M.I.C.－婦女健康服務）
地址：225 Broadway, 17th Floor, New York, N.Y. 10007
電話：1-212-267-0900; 傳真：1-212-571-5641; 網址：http://www.mhra.org

我能得到哪些幫助？
■ 癌症檢查；性病和愛滋病感染教育、咨詢和檢查；家庭計劃；預防性牙科保健。
■ 產前護理；符合條件的婦女註冊產前護理幫助計劃（P.C.A.P.）及其他Medicaid計劃。
你們為哪些人提供幫助？ 所有婦女。接受Medicaid、商業保險和現金。根據病人的支付能力收費。**你們提供哪種語言的幫助？** 所有的中心均有西班牙語、法語和克裡奧爾語服務；Fort Greene和Jamaica中心有中文（廣東話、普通話）服務；Astoria中心有旁遮普語、俄語和烏爾都語服務；Fort Greene中心有阿拉伯語服務；Jamaica和曼哈頓中心有他加祿語服務；Bushwick中心有圭亞那語和希臘語服務；Eastern Parkway中心有羅馬尼亞語服務。**我必須帶什麼東西去嗎？** 如果你有保險，請帶上保險資料。如果沒有保險，請帶身份證（護照、出生證或者社會安全卡）；住址證明（以你的名義的公用事業帳單，或者你的房東或與你同住的朋友、親戚的信，說明你住在該地址），以及收入證明。如果你不能確定帶哪些文件，工作人員可以提供幫助。**你們還在其他地方設有辦事處嗎？**在布朗士有1處；在布碌崙有4處；在曼哈頓還有1處；在皇后區有2處。

Medical and Health Research Association of New York City, Inc.（紐約市醫療和健康研究協會，簡稱M.H.R.A.）
New York City Neighborhood W.I.C. Program（紐約市社區W.I.C.計劃）
地址：40 Worth Street, Suite 720, New York, N.Y. 10013
電話：1-212-766-4240; 傳真：1-212-260-6200

我能得到哪些幫助？
■ 營養教育和咨詢；母乳餵養的咨詢和指導；介紹其他健康和人力服務供應者。
■ 選民登記。
你們為哪些人提供幫助？孕婦、進行母乳餵養和不進行母乳餵養的產後婦女、5歲以下並是紐約州居民的嬰幼兒。收入限制標準相當於聯邦貧困線的185%。**你們提供哪種語言的幫助？**西班牙語、中文（廣東話）、法語－克裡奧爾語、俄語、意大利語、波蘭語、孟加拉語、意第緒語、他加祿語、阿拉伯語和烏爾都語。**我必須帶什麼東西去嗎？**醫生介紹；住址證明；收入證明（享受Medicaid者除外）。**你們還在其他地方設有辦事處嗎？**在布朗士有2處；在布碌崙有7處；在曼哈頓有2處；在皇后區有7處。

MoneyGram
電話：1-800-926-9400
網址：http://www.moneygram.com

你們提供哪些服務？
■ 匯款。
你們為哪些人提供幫助？所有人。**你們提供哪種語言的幫助？**西班牙語（P）。各機構提供不同語言的服務。**我必須帶什麼東西去嗎？**要電匯的現金和費用；如果匯款超過900美元，要帶有照片的身份證。**你們還在其他地方設有辦事處嗎？**紐約市各處都有。打上面提供的電話，再輸入你的10位電話號碼，就可以找到最近的分支機構。

Morris Heights Health Center（Morris Heights保健中心）
地址：85 West Burnside Avenue, Bronx, N.Y. 10453
電話：1-718-716-4400; 傳真：1-718-294-6912; 網址：http://www.morrisheights.org

我能得到哪些幫助？
■ 主要保健；家庭計劃和孕婦生育保健，新生兒保健；學校體檢；哮喘檢查和照
顧；心理健康照顧；營養服務；社會福利；以及特別青少年服務。

你們為哪些人提供幫助？ 所有人。**你們提供哪種語言的幫助？** 西班牙語（P）、
中文（有限的廣東話）、法語和俄語。其他語種可找到翻譯人員。**我必須帶什麼
東西去嗎？** 出生證或駕駛執照；低收入證明。根據支付能力收費。**你們還在其他
地方設有辦事處嗎？** 在布朗士還設有2個分支機搆。請提前打電話。

**New York Association for New Americans, Inc.（紐約新美國人聯合會，簡稱
N.Y.A.N.A.）**
地址：17 Battery Place, New York, N.Y. 10004
電話：1-212-425-2900/5051; 法律服務 1-212-898-4180; 傳真：1-212-425-7260
網址：http://www.nyana.org

我能得到哪些幫助？
■ U.S.C.I.S.文件、親屬申請、工作簽證和永久居留權申請；入籍、公民和考試
輔導。
■ 藥物濫用咨詢。
■ 獲得政府福利。
■ 找工作和工作安置。
■ 英語班。

你們為哪些人提供幫助？ 新移民。**你們提供哪種語言的幫助？** 西班牙語（P）、
中文（廣東話、普通話、臺灣話）、俄語（P）。皇后區辦事處沒有中文服務。
我必須帶什麼東西去嗎？ 安置工作要求有工作許可。費用根據問題的複雜性而
定。通過電話向專業人員助手咨詢不收費。**你們還在其他地方設有辦事處嗎？** 在
布碌崙設有1處；在皇后設有1處。請提前打電話。

New York City Administration for Children's Services
Division of Child Care and Head Start（紐約市兒童服務局兒童照顧和提前教育計劃處）
地址：66 John Street, New York, N.Y. 10038
電話：1-718-FOR-KIDS (1-718-367-5437); 傳真：1-212-361-6023

我能得到哪些幫助？
■ 關於附近地區日托和課後照顧的資料；兒童保育資助；承包提供者機構的
　培訓。
你們為哪些人提供幫助？所有打電話的人。兒童保育資助的資格取決於收入和保
育原因。**你們提供哪種語言的幫助？**西班牙語（P）。**我必須帶什麼東西去嗎？**
社會安全卡或者綠卡、出生證、住址證明和收入證明。**你們還在其他地方設有辦
事處嗎？**在布朗士、布碌崙、曼哈頓和皇后區各有1處。請提前打電話。

New York City Child Care Resource and Referral Consortium（紐約市兒童保育資源和
介紹協會）
電話：1-888-469-5999

我能得到哪些幫助？
■ 日托、課後照顧和財政資助的資源和介紹服務；兒童保育供應者的培訓。
■ 健康和安全資料。
你們為哪些人提供幫助？所有人。**你們提供哪種語言的幫助？**我們將盡力以任何
語言提供幫助。**我必須帶什麼東西去嗎？**收入證明。請提前打電話。

New York City Commission on Human Rights（紐約市人權委員會）
地址：40 Rector Street, New York, N.Y. 10006
電話：1-212-306-5070
傳真：1-212-306-7474
網址：http://www.ci.nyc.ny.us/html/cchr/home.html

我能得到哪些幫助？
■ 歧視投訴；公平住房，就業和與偏見有關的騷擾問題。
你們為哪些人提供幫助？所有人。**你們提供哪種語言的幫助？**西班牙語（P）、
中文（廣東話、普通話）（P）和法語（P）。**我必須帶什麼東西去嗎？**必須進行
面談預約。預約請打電話1-212-306-7450。**你們還在其他地方設有辦事處嗎？**委
員會在全市各處均設有社區服務中心。請提前打電話。

New York City Department of Education, Chancellor's Parent Hot Line
（紐約市教育局，校長的家長熱線）
電話：1-718-482-3777; 網址：http://www.nycenet.edu

我能得到哪些幫助？

■ 所有關於子女接受公立學校教育的資訊

■ 為在學校不能解決的問題介紹至學區學習支持中心，或處理學校校務，包括註
　冊和交通。

你們為哪些人提供幫助？ 所有人。**你們提供哪種語言的幫助？** 西班牙語、中文
（廣東話、普通話），並有其他語種的翻譯。**我必須帶什麼東西去嗎？** 請提前打
電話。**你們還在其他地方設有辦事處嗎？** 學習支持中心：在布朗士有2處；在布
碌崙有4處；在曼哈頓有2處；在皇后區有4處；在史坦頓島有1處。

New York City Department of Education, Office of Adult and Continuing Education
（紐約市教育局，成人和繼續教育辦公室）
地址：42-15 Crescent Street, Long Island City, N.Y. 11101
電話：1-718-609-2770; 傳真：1-718-392-4768

我能得到哪些幫助？

■ G.E.D.、E.S.O.L.、基礎教育和電腦培訓；電器修理、汽車技工、靜脈放血（抽
　血）、做心電圖和護理等職業訓練。

■ 幫助完成學業的學生找工作、寫簡歷和面試技巧。

你們為哪些人提供幫助？ 年齡必須在21歲以上，並參加工作安置考試。一些培訓
課程要求G.E.D.或者中學畢業文憑。布碌崙和曼哈頓學習中心有兒童保育服務。
請提前打電話。**你們提供哪種語言的幫助？** 所有課程均使用英語。G.E.D. 是唯一
用西班牙語講課的課程。請提前打電話。**我必須帶什麼東西去嗎？** 護理課程和某
些有關保健的課程需要收費。**你們還在其他地方設有辦事處嗎？** 在所有五個區均
開設課程。請提前打電話。

New York City Department of Health and Mental Hygiene（紐約市健康與心理衛生局）
地址：**125 Worth Street, New York, N.Y. 10013**
電話：**1-212-442-9666**（英語和西班牙語語音選項。大多數語言的電話將被接通到
　一位翻譯人員那裡）
愛滋病熱線：**1-800-TALK-HIV**（大多數語言的電話將被接通到一位翻譯人員那裡）
日托處：**1-212-676-2444**（英語和西班牙語）
學校健康處：**1-212-676-2500**（僅限英語）
HealthStat：1-888-692-6116（西班牙語和普通話）
免疫熱線：**1-212-676-2273**（英語和西班牙語）
免疫熱線介紹：**1-800-325-CHILD (2445)**（必要時，你將接到說你的語言的人回電）
西班牙語免疫介紹：**1-800-945-6466**
婦女健康熱線：**1-212-230-1111**（英語和西班牙語語音選項。對大多數語言來說，
　電話可以轉接到翻譯人員那裡）
傳真：**1-212-442-5670; 網址：http://www.nyc.gov/html/doh**

我能得到哪些幫助？
■ 母親、生育和嬰兒健康計劃；婦女健康計劃；免費的流感和肺炎疫苗注射；如
　果因上學需要，免費的免疫接種；出生和死亡證明。
■ 加入免費和低價的公共健康保險。
■ 關於日托家庭、中心和計劃的投訴。
■ 醫齒動物和健康侵害投訴。
你們為哪些人提供幫助？所有人。**你們提供哪種語言的幫助？**通過翻譯可提供任
何語言的服務。**我必須帶什麼東西去嗎？**產前護理計劃需要住址證明。**你們還在
其他地方設有辦事處嗎？**只在以上地點設有唯一一家機構。

New York City Housing Authority（紐約市住房管理局，簡稱**N.Y.C.H.A.**）
地址：**250 Broadway, New York, N.Y. 10007**
電話：**1-212-306-3000**（各區的中心號）；**1-212-828-7100**（曼哈頓申請辦事處）；
網址：**http://www.nyc.gov/html/nycha**

我能得到哪些幫助？
■ 尋找價格可承受的住房；Section 8出租房屋計劃。
■ 社會服務。
■ 教育和娛樂計劃。
■ 職業培訓。
你們為哪些人提供幫助？紐約市低收入居民。優先為收容所的居民提供服務。**你
們提供哪種語言的幫助？**西班牙語（P）、中文（廣東話、普通話、臺山話）。

欲知詳情，請打電話給Language Bank at Equal Opportunity（機會均等語言庫）1-212-306-4443。**我必須帶什麼東西去嗎？**打電話時要準備好你的社會安全號碼。**你們還在其他地方設有辦事處嗎？**在每一區設有1處。 請提前打電話。

New York City Workforce 1 Career Center （紐約市勞工第一職業中心）
地址：**168-46 91st Avenue, 2nd Floor, Jamaica, N.Y. 11432**
電話：**1-718-557-6756**
網址：**http://www.nyc.gov/html/wia/html/career_centers.html**

我能得到哪些幫助？
■ 教育評定和學生資助申請。
■ E.S.O.L.、G.E.D.和成人掃盲資訊。
■ 找工作、培訓和工作安置；簡歷和附信的寫作；電腦技能評定和研討。
■ 政府工作支持福利，例如兒童保育、Medicaid及其他免費或低價健康保險。
你們為哪些人提供幫助？紐約市居民。**你們提供哪種語言的幫助？**西班牙語（P）。備有翻譯服務。**我必須帶什麼東西去嗎？**取決於需要的服務。**你們還在其他地方設有辦事處嗎？**在布朗士有1處，在曼哈頓上城有1處。

New York Immigration Hot Line（紐約移民熱線）
電話：**1-800-566-7636**

我能得到哪些幫助？
■ 關於移民法的資訊和介紹，包括親屬申請、簽證、公民身份、政治避難、臨時保護身份、驅逐出境和特准例外。
■ 介紹市、州的服務。
■ 就業和住房歧視。
你們為哪些人提供幫助？所有人。**你們提供哪種語言的幫助？**西班牙語、中文（普通話）、法語、波蘭語、俄語、馬其頓語、印第安語、阿拉伯語、海地克裡奧爾語、印地語、阿爾巴尼亞語、土耳其語、韓國語和塞爾維亞-克羅地亞語。

New York State Department of Labor, Division of Employment Services Office（紐約州勞工廳，就業服務處）
地址：**138-60 Barclay Avenue, Flushing, N.Y. 11355**
電話：**1-718-321-6307, 1-888-209-8124**（紐約州一般資訊電話號碼）；
傳真：**1-718-461-8572; 網址：http://www.labor.state.ny.us/index.html**

我能得到哪些幫助？
■ 找工作、瞭解作為工人的權利、如果你被解僱，獲得失業保險。
你們為哪些人提供幫助？當地居民。**你們提供哪種語言的幫助？**西班牙語（P）、中文（廣東話、普通話）（P）、克裡奧爾語。**我必須帶什麼東西去嗎？**簡歷、國籍證明、社會安全卡（如果有的話）。請提前打電話。**你們還在其他地方設有辦事處嗎？**在布朗士設有3處；在布碌崙設有3處；在曼哈頓設有4處；在皇后區設有4處。請提前打電話。

New York State Department of Labor, Division of Labor Standards（紐約州勞工廳勞工標準處）
地址：**345 Hudson Street, New York, N.Y. 10014**
電話：**1-212-352-6700; 傳真：1-212-352-6593**

我能得到哪些幫助？
■ 州勞動法、童工、法定最低工資、未付工資、工資支付、工資追加、成衣業和農業的工時規定。
你們為哪些人提供幫助？所有五個區內違反勞動法的受害者。**你們提供哪種語言的幫助？**西班牙語（P）。其他語言請自帶翻譯。**我必須帶什麼東西去嗎？**根據需要的服務而定。請提前打電話。**你們還在其他地方設有辦事處嗎？**在曼哈頓下城設有1個辦事處，在曼哈頓上城設有1個辦事處。請提前打電話。

New York State Division of Housing and Community Renewal（紐約州住宅和社區翻新處，簡稱D.H.C.R.）
地址：**38-40 State Street, Albany, N.Y. 12207**
電話：**1-866-ASK-DHCR (1-866-275-3427); 傳真：1-518-474-5752**
電子郵件：**DHCRInfo@dhcr.state.ny.us; 網址：http://www.dhcr.state.ny.us**

我能得到哪些幫助？
■ 住房申請、房屋出租史、Section 8房屋、住房岐視。

你們為哪些人提供幫助？所有人。**你們提供哪種語言的幫助？**西班牙語。提供其他語言的翻譯服務。**我必須帶什麼東西去嗎？**根據需要的服務而定。**你們還在其他地方設有辦事處嗎？**在布朗士、布碌崙、皇后區和史坦頓島各有1處辦事處；在曼哈頓有2處辦事處。請提前打電話。

New York State Office of Temporary and Disability Assistance（紐約州臨時和殘障援助辦公室）
電話：**1-800-342-3009; 網址：www.otda.state.ny.us**

我能得到哪些幫助？
■ 食物券和家庭能源援助計劃（HEAP）。
■ 通過網上服務要求舉行公平聽證。
你們為哪些人提供幫助？請打電話確定計劃的資格要求。通過難民和移民事務處（B.R.I.A.）向紐約州各地的非盈利機構提供難民和移民資料及服務介紹，電話1-800-566-7636；1-800-232-0212。**你們提供哪種語言的幫助？**西班牙語。

New York Urban League（紐約城市聯盟）
地址：**204 West 136th Street, New York, N.Y. 10030**
電話：**1-212-926-8000, 內線39; 傳真：1-212-283-4948; 電子郵件：nyulexec@aol.com**
網址：**http://www.nyul.org**

我能得到哪些幫助？
■ 提供驅逐、無家可歸、住房不達標等問題的咨詢；找住處；房客/房東調解；住房歧視投訴；購房資料和支持。
■ 社會服務福利的咨詢。
你們為哪些人提供幫助？所有人。**你們提供哪種語言的幫助？**西班牙語。 **我必須帶什麼東西去嗎？**根據需要的服務而定。請提前打電話。**你們還在其他地方設有辦事處嗎？**在布朗士有1處辦事處；在布碌崙、曼哈頓、皇后區和史坦頓島各有2處辦事處。請提前打電話。

Park Slope Safe Homes Project（Park Slope安全家庭計劃）
地址：**P.O. Box 150429, Brooklyn, N.Y. 11215**
電話：**1-718-499-2151; 傳真：1-718-369-6151**
我能得到哪些幫助？
■ 向被毆打的婦女及其子女提供服務、收容、咨詢及支持團體。

■ 為婦女間暴力的受害者提供服務。
你們為哪些人提供幫助？家庭暴力受害者及其子女。**你們提供哪種語言的幫助？**西班牙語（P）和阿拉伯語（P）。**我必須帶什麼東西去嗎？**不要求帶什麼。請提前打電話。**你們還在其他地方設有辦事處嗎？**只在以上地點設有唯一一家機構。

People's Fire House（人民消防站）
地址：**113 Berry Street, Brooklyn, N.Y. 11211**
電話：**1-718-388-4696; 傳真：1-718-218-7367**

我能得到哪些幫助？
■ 為找住房的人提供房客咨詢和顧問。
■ 電腦基礎知識。
你們為哪些人提供幫助？所有人。**你們提供哪種語言的幫助？**西班牙語（P）；波蘭語（P）。**我必須帶什麼東西去嗎？**任何身份證和/與社會安全卡。請提前打電話。**你們還在其他地方設有辦事處嗎？**只在以上地點設有唯一一家機構。

Promesa, Inc.
地址：**1776 Clay Avenue, Bronx, N.Y. 10457**
電話：**1-718-960-7500; 傳真：1-718-299-0463**
網址：**http://www.promesa.org**

我能得到哪些幫助？
■ 主要和行為保健；毒品濫用康復；愛滋病病毒感染和愛滋病服務，包括為愛滋病患者提供主要保健、咨詢、檢查、介紹和成人日托。
■ 可負擔得起的住房；無家可歸者的收容中心。
■ 日托。
■ 離家出走的青少年服務。
你們提供哪種語言的幫助？西班牙語（P）。**你們為哪些人提供幫助？**所有人。住房援助有收入限制要求。**我必須帶什麼東西去嗎？**綠卡或國籍證明，以及社會安全號。**你們還在其他地方設有辦事處嗎？**在布朗士有15個計劃服務辦事處。

Queens Legal Services（皇后區法律服務）
地址：8900 Sutphin Boulevard, Jamaica, N.Y. 11435
電話：1-718-657-8611; 傳真：1-718-526-5051
網址：http://www.queenslegalservices.org

我能得到哪些幫助？
- 免費提供住房、政府救濟、消費者權利、勞工權利、公立中小學教育和家庭法等問題的法律援助。
- 就老年人、家庭暴力受害者和殘障人士、愛滋病病毒感染或愛滋病患者面臨的特殊問題提供法律服務。

你們為哪些人提供幫助？居住在皇后區的公民和有合法身份的移民。有些服務根據收入提供。**你們提供哪種語言的幫助？**西班牙語。**我必須帶什麼東西去嗎？**收入證明、綠卡和任何與案件有關的文件，例如法庭文件。**你們還在其他地方設有辦事處嗎？**在皇后區另設有1處辦事處。請提前打電話。

Safe Horizon（安全地平線）
地址：2 Lafayette Street, New York, N.Y. 10007
電話：1-212-577-7700; 24小時熱線：1-800-621-HOPE (1-800-621-4673)
傳真：1-212-385-0331; 電子郵件：feedback@safehorizon.org
網址：http://www.safehorizon.org

我能得到哪些幫助？
- 為犯罪和虐待受害者提供財政幫助、危機咨詢和介紹。
- 一般受害者的服務熱線、介紹和服務網絡。
- 提供與警方打交道的咨詢、團體咨詢、辯護和幫助。
- 在Jackson Heights為酷刑受害者提供服務和咨詢。
- 在布碌崙提供強姦意識咨詢。
- 為性攻擊倖存者和間接受害者提供緊急和短期咨詢、辯護和服務。

你們為哪些人提供幫助？紐約市居民。男女強姦和攻擊受害者年齡要求在13歲以上。**你們提供哪種語言的幫助？**西班牙語（P）、中文（廣東話、普通話）、法語、海地克裡奧爾語、印地語、韓國語、波蘭語、俄語和烏爾都語。**我必須帶什麼東西去嗎？**警方報告或任何與案件有關的物件。只有複雜的法律問題才收費，收費標準根據支付能力而定。請打電話預約。**你們還在其他地方設有辦事處嗎？**在五個區有75項計劃。請提前打電話。

South Bronx Action Group（南布朗士行動團體）
地址：384 East 149th Street, Suite 220, Bronx, N.Y. 10455
電話：1-718-993-5869; 傳真：1-718-993-7904; 電子郵件：sbaginc@aol.com

我能得到哪些幫助？
■ 關於基本的住房權利和責任的咨詢；住房法院服務，辯護和研討班；介紹房地
　產經紀人找房子。
■ 入籍課和E.S.O.L.班。
■ 移民和歸化服務。
你們為哪些人提供幫助？所有人。**你們提供哪種語言的幫助？**西班牙語（P）。
我必須帶什麼東西去嗎？不要求帶什麼。**你們還在其他地方設有辦事處嗎？**只在
以上地點設有唯一一家機構。

Southeast Bronx Neighborhood Centers（東南布朗士社區中心）
地址：955 Tinton Avenue, Bronx, N.Y. 10456
電話：1-718-542-2727; 傳真：1-718-589-2927; 電子郵件：dymcenter@aol.com
網址：http://www.sebnc.org

我能得到哪些幫助？
■ 兒童保育、日托和課後計劃；青少年服務；老年人中心，包括家庭照顧。
■ 食品券介紹和登記。
■ 電腦技術課程和職業輔導服務。
■ 殘障人士幫助。
你們為哪些人提供幫助？必須有社會安全卡。**你們提供哪種語言的幫助？**西班牙
語。**我必須帶什麼東西去嗎？**兒童保育服務要求有社會安全卡。根據支付能力付
費。**你們還在其他地方設有辦事處嗎？**在布朗士設有3處。請提前打電話。

Southside Community Mission, Immigration Program（南部社區慈善團，移民計劃）
地址：250 Hooper Street, Brooklyn, N.Y. 11211
電話：1-718-387-3803; 傳真：1-718-387-3739

我能得到哪些幫助？
■ 移民表格、家庭申請、身份調整、入籍、職業許可、居留簽證/有條件居留。
■ 入籍申請和課程。
■ 法律代理。

你們為哪些人提供幫助？所有人。第一次要交少量費用。**你們提供哪種語言的幫助？**西班牙語。**我必須帶什麼東西去嗎？**少量費用的標準按服務有所不同。請提前打電話。**你們還在其他地方設有辦事處嗎？**在布朗士還設有一處。

United Community Centers（聯合社區中心）
地址：**613 New Lots Avenue, Brooklyn, N.Y. 11207**
電話：**1-718-649-7979; 傳真：1-718-649-7256; 電子郵件：uccinc@mindspring.com**
網址：**http://www.unhny.org**

我能得到哪些幫助？
■ 日托和課後計劃。
■ 基礎教育和E.S.O.L.班。
■ 面向成年人的電腦硬件職業培訓計劃。
■ 移民、驅逐和入籍問題。
你們為哪些人提供幫助？所有人。**你們提供哪種語言的幫助？**西班牙語（P）、海地克裡奧爾語。**我必須帶什麼東西去嗎？**不要求帶什麼。法律問題和驅逐問題請打電話預約。2－4歲兒童日托計劃主要根據收入和住處。**你們還在其他地方設有辦事處嗎？**只在以上地點設有唯一一家機構。

University Settlement Federal Credit Union（大學街坊文教協會聯邦信用合作社）
地址：**184 Eldridge Street, 4th Floor, New York, N.Y. 10002**
電話：**1-212-674-9120; 傳真：1-212-254-5334**
網址：**http://www.universitysettlement.org**

我能得到哪些幫助？
■ 儲蓄和低息貸款。
你們為哪些人提供幫助？低收入居民。**你們提供哪種語言的幫助？**西班牙語。**我必須帶什麼東西去嗎？**請提前打電話。**你們還在其他地方設有辦事處嗎？**請提前打電話。

University Settlement Society of New York（紐約大學街坊文教協會）
地址：**184 Eldridge Street, New York, N.Y. 10002**
電話：**1-212-674-9120; 傳真：1-212-475-3278**
電子郵件：**info@universitysettlement.org**
網址：**http://www.universitysettlement.org**

我能得到哪些幫助？
■ 嬰幼兒日托服務，課後計劃，日營和夏令營。
■ 掃盲計劃，青年就業服務。
■ 少女懷孕服務、咨詢和臨床服務。
■ 老年人社會福利、營養、護送和電話慰問計劃。
■ 面向曾經無家可歸的家庭的服務。
你們為哪些人提供幫助？移民和低收入紐約市居民。**你們提供哪種語言的幫助？**中文（P）（廣東話、普通話）、西班牙語（P）、俄語和孟加拉語。**我必須帶什麼東西去嗎？**有幾項計劃根據家庭收入多少收費。請提前打電話。**你們還在其他地方設有辦事處嗎？**請提前打電話。

Western Union
電話：**1-800-325-6000, 1-800-325-4045**（西班牙語）
網址：**http://www.westernunion.com**

我能得到哪些幫助？
■ 匯款。
你們為哪些人提供幫助？所有人。**你們提供哪種語言的幫助？**各分支機搆提供不同的語言幫助，但熱線會一直有西班牙語接線員。**我必須帶什麼東西去嗎？**要匯的現金和費用；如果匯款超過1,000美元，要帶有照片的身份證。**你們還在其他地方設有辦事處嗎？**請打電話或到我們的網站查詢。

Y.M.C.A. of Greater New York（大紐約地區基督教青年會）
地址：**333 Seventh Avenue, 15th Floor, New York, N.Y. 10001**
電話：**1-212-630-9600**

地址：**100 Hester Street（華埠分會）, New York, N.Y. 10002**
電話：**1-212-219-8393; 傳真：1-212-941-9046**
網址：**http://www.ymcanyc.org**

我能得到哪些幫助？
■ 家長研討會、家庭咨詢服務（僅在華埠分會）、課後計劃和青少年計劃。
你們為哪些人提供幫助？ 華埠分會為有4至18歲子女的家庭提供咨詢。主分會提供其他計劃，並介紹其他地區的基督教青年會。**你們提供哪種語言的幫助？** 中文（P）（廣東話、普通話）和西班牙語（P）。**我必須帶什麼東西去嗎？** 請提前打電話。**你們還在其他地方設有辦事處嗎？** 在布朗士有2處；在布祿崙有9處；在曼哈頓有4處；在皇后區有7處；在史坦頓島有4處。

索引

附註

[1] Ewen, Elizabeth，《*Immigrant Women in the Land of Dollars*》，紐約：Monthly Review Press，1985年，第61頁。 [2] Rafael Guzman口述史，下東城廉租公寓博物館搜集。 [3] Charles T. Anderson，由 Dana Gumb採訪，第005號採訪。《Voices from Ellis Island: An Oral History of American Immigration》，Statue of Liberty / Ellis Island Foundation專案。 [4] 摘自Lisa Chice對 Irma Olivo的採訪錄，2002年。 [5]《*The Italian-American Catalog*》，Joseph Giordano（編輯）。紐約州Garden City市: Doubleday，1986年。 [6] Khandelwal, Madhulika S.，從《*Becoming American, Being Indian: An Immigrant Community in New York City*》，紐約州Ithaca市: Cornell University Press，2002年，第130頁。 [7] Max Mason口述史，下東城廉租公寓博物館搜集。 [8] 摘自Ling Leung的未出版的論文，1999年。 [9] 摘自《*America, the Dream of My Life: Selections from the Federal Writers' Project's New Jersey Ethnic Survey*》中 Padrone（意大利男性移民）的話。 David Steven Cohen（編輯）。新澤西州New Brunswick市: Rutgers University Press，1990年。 [10] Jose Zambrano口述史，下東城廉租公寓博物館搜集。 [11] Kisseloff, Jeff，《*You Must Remember This: An Oral History of Manhattan from the 1890s to World War II*》。紐約：Harcourt Brace Jovanovich，1989年，第562頁。 [12] Maricela Gonzalez，未出版論文，1999年。 [13] Hardayal Singh，摘自《*Asian American Experiences in the United States*》一書中《Being Indian in New Jersey》一文。 Joann Faung Jean Lee（編輯），北卡羅來納州Jefferson市: McFarland and Company，1991年。 [14] 摘自Pak Ping的未出版的論文，1999年。 [15] Josephine Esposito口述史，下東城廉租公寓博物館搜集。 [16] 摘自Lisa Chice對Georgina Acevedo 的採訪錄，2002年。 [17]《*Spiritual Autobiographies*》，Louis Finkelstein（編輯），紐約州紐約市: Harper and Brothers，1952年。 [18] 摘自Lisa Chice對Kaynam Hedayat的採訪錄，2002年。